VALUES-DRIVEN

ENTREPRENEURSHIP

AND SOCIETAL

IMPACT

Setting the Agenda
for Entrepreneuring
Across (Southern) Africa

First published in 2021.

ISBN: 978-1-86922-897-2 (Printed)
eISBN: 978-1-86922-898-9 (PDF ebook)

Published by KR Publishing
P O Box 3954
Randburg
2125
Republic of South Africa

Tel: (011) 706-6009
Fax: (011) 706-1127
E-mail: orders@knowres.co.za
Website: www.kr.co.za

Typesetting, layout and design: Cia Joubert, cia@knowres.co.za
Cover design: Marlene De Lorme, marlene@knowres.co.za
Editing and Proofreading: Valda Strauss, valda@global.co.za
Project management: Cia Joubert, cia@knowres.co.za

VALUES-DRIVEN **ENTREPRENEURSHIP** AND SOCIETAL IMPACT

Setting the Agenda for Entrepreneuring
Across (Southern) Africa

Edited by

Prof. Kurt April

Dr. Badri Zolfaghari

kr
publishing

2021

Acknowledgements

We are grateful that KR Publishing chose to take on this book project with us, and we felt completely supported by their professional team, specifically Wilhelm Crous, Cia Joubert and Tina van der Westhuizen. Thank you, Wilhelm, for your decades of ongoing work to humanize organizational life on our African continent, and your passion for bringing rigour to its practices. We would like to make a special mention of Cia Joubert, who has been a tremendous partner for us during the completion of this book – putting in long hours with us (mostly outside of normal work hours) to bring this book to fruition.

The initial idea for the book was borne out of the insights of many of the panelists and specialists, which were initially shared and developed at the Allan Gray International Conference for academics and practitioners from around the globe. The Conference was the fruition of the collaboration between ourselves and colleagues at the University of Cape Town: Prof. Ralph Hamman and Vedantha Singh from the Research Office, as well as the Allan Gray Centre's Logistics Manager, Ms. Glenda Weber. We are indeed grateful to all of our contributing authors, who are colleagues and fellow researchers, and have a particular interest in shifting the narratives about the continent of Africa – while being realistic about its challenges and successes in providing positive societal value for more citizens on the continent. Thank you for taking the time to provide your valuable contributions, while working through the balancing act of work, family, and societal responsibilities during the Covid-19 pandemic.

My life-long partner and, often, co-researcher, Amanda, who is the best writer and editor I know, and with whom I have interrogated a multitude of ideas, constructs and perspectives, across many disciplines, throughout most of my life – she has literally made me a better researcher, provided ongoing support and, as in all things to do with my son and I, generously shares her incredible heart and person. I am forever indebted! My teenage son Jordan has pushed me, and continues to push me to the periphery of my understanding of the modern world and, regularly, introduces me to new concepts, innovative techniques and problem-solving ideas – an engineering mind with a caring heart, his balanced spirit and orientation towards humanity are all that I could have hoped for in a child of mine.

Prof. Kurt April
March 2021

I would like to sincerely thank Kurt, for not only supporting our Conference, but also driving the publishing of this book. Through this journey, I have had the privilege of witnessing the entrepreneurial spirit of Africa and Africans, and have developed a deep sense of gratitude – which I will always carry with me. I want to thank all of our contributors for being the change they want to see in the world and for sharing their journeys with us, such that we are inspired to follow suit. I would also like to thank my husband, Farsan, for always encouraging me to follow my curiosity and for being the thoughtful soundboard that I need.

Dr. Badri Zolfaghari
March 2021

Kurt (Allan Gray Chair) and Badri (Allan Gray Associate) are both associated with the Allan Gray Centre for Values-Based Leadership at the Graduate School of Business of the University of Cape Town, and remain deeply thankful for Allan and Gill Gray's generous endowment which ensures that we can continue the privilege of being able to research and publish, as well as teach and supervise emerging and established leaders within the disciplines of entrepreneurship and organizational sustainability in, and about, sub-Saharan Africa. We remain committed to this work and the vision of Allan Gray for the Centre to practically translate values-based principles and responsible practices into business and society.

Table of Contents

About the Editors

Prof. Kurt A. April, a Fellow of the Royal Society for Arts, Manufactures and Commerce (United Kingdom), is currently the Allan Gray Chair specialising in Leadership, Diversity & Inclusion and Director of the Allan Gray Centre for Values-Based Leadership at the Graduate School of Business, University of Cape Town (1998-present), is Adjunct Faculty of Saïd Business School (University of Oxford, UK, 2000-present), and is an Orchestrator & Faculty Member of DukeCE (Duke University, USA, 2008-present). Previously, he was a Research Fellow of Ashridge-Hult (UK, 2004-2016), Visiting Professor at London Metropolitan University (UK, 2014-2017), Visiting Professor at Rotterdam School of Management (Erasmus University, Netherlands, 2001-2013), and Visiting Professor in the Faculty of Economics & Econometrics (University of Amsterdam UvA, Netherlands, 2004-2007). Outside of academia, Kurt is the Managing Partner of LICM Consulting (SA, 2001-present), Managing Director: Leadership, Diversity & Inclusion Practice at Oxford Acuity (Singapore, 2019-present), Shareholder and Executive Director of the Achievement Awards Group (SA, 2007-present), Shareholder of bountiXP (Pty) Ltd (SA, 2019-present), as well as Ambassador of the global Unashamedly Ethical movement (2016-present). He plays a range of roles and consults to many companies and organizations around the globe, having worked in 24 countries. In 2018, Kurt was the Winner of the Black Management Forum's 'Thought Leader of the Year 2017' Category, won the 2010-2011 Global Honors Award (New York): "For demonstrating exemplary achievement and distinguished contributions to the business community", in 2011 was inducted into lifetime membership of the New York-based Madison Who's Who (USA), and in 2009 was recognized as one of the world's 'Top 100 Educators' for 2009 in additional to the International Plato Award for Educational Achievement also awarded later in the year by the International Biographical Centre in Cambridge (UK). He was also awarded the Teacher of the Year Award on the Associate in Management (AIM) Programme at the Graduate School of Business (UCT) and, in 2008, was formally inducted (lifelong membership) into the New York-based Continental Who's Who (USA). Kurt is an Advisory Board Member to a number of international academic journals, and holds a PhD in Economics & IT Strategy, Certificate in Japanese Production, an MBA, MSc(ElecEng) in Electronic Engineering, Higher Diploma in Education (HDE), BSc(ElecEng) in Electrical Engineering, National Diploma in Electronic Engineering (NDip EE), National Diploma in Logic Systems (NDip LS) completed at the University of Cape Town (SA), University of Oxford (UK), Wingfield College (SA) and AOTS Nagoya (Japan). He has published 193 peer-reviewed academic articles, book chapters, conference papers, dissertations and op-eds, and written 9 books previously. Author email: kurt.april@uct.ac.za

Dr. Badri Zolfaghari is currently a Lecturer in Strategy and International Business, and an Associate of the Allan Gray Centre for Values-Based Leadership at the University of Cape Town's Graduate School of Business, South Africa. Her research interests lie within the field of organizational behaviour and entrepreneurship, with a focus on multi-level trust development across cultures, trust development in culturally diverse start-up teams, cultural diversity and integration, and the strategic management of culturally diverse workforces. Her work has been published in the form of articles and book chapters in outlets such as European Management Journal and Field Guide to Intercultural Research. Badri received her PhD from Durham University Business School, UK, focusing on the topic of interpersonal trust development in multinational organizations. Author email: badri.zolfaghari@uct.ac.za

About the Contributors

Sarah-Anne Alman has over a decade of experience in Entrepreneurship and a track record of successful Leadership of Entrepreneurial Ventures within organizations. Her experience spans entrepreneurship, strategy, corporate innovation, education, management and business development. Originally trained as a designer, Sarah-Anne's experience was in the media and publishing industry within research and development and new product planning for the Penguin Group. She subsequently founded the Solution Space at the University of Cape Town's Graduate School of Business, through a partnership with industry, as a living laboratory for the development and testing of real solutions, to real problems. Sarah-Anne has also consulted and provided strategic advice to a variety of clients, from private investors to corporate innovation teams. She is currently the Director of Product Innovation for GVI and Director of the Impact Academy, a pioneering provider of experiential education for students looking to build a career in sustainable development. She has previously published a book chapter with the British Council on the Third Mission of Universities and has spoken at numerous events, including the World Economic Forum Young Global Shapers and at the Singularity University. Sarah-Anne holds an MBA from UCT Graduate School of Business, and a BA (Hons) from Central Saint Martins, University of London. Author email: sarahannealman@gmail.com

Dr. Ann Armstrong has an eclectic set of interests. She has published on greening business school curricula, on mapping the social economy, and on the role of stokvels in South Africa, to name a few. Ann has recently co-authored a book that examines B Corps in the historical and current context of capitalism. She has also co-authored two books on the social economy – one which focusses on Canada and a companion volume that focusses on the United States. Similarly, Ann teaches a variety of courses in the Organizational Behaviour field; for example, Change Management and Organization Design (she has also co-authored the most popular Canadian textbook on Organization Theory and Design.) She teaches at the undergraduate, graduate, and executive levels. Ann serves as the Academic Director for the Business Edge program of the Intercultural Skills Lab at the Rotman School of Management, University of Toronto, Canada. The program works with talented, internationally educated professionals, to smooth their transition into Canadian workplaces. She also co-designed a program for MBA and JD students which places them on Non-Profit Boards to work collaboratively on governance projects. Ann received her PhD in Organizational Behaviour from the University of Toronto, Canada. Author email: ann.armstrong@utoronto.ca

Dr. Wanda Chunnett, based in Cape Town, is a Director for a multinational organization specializing in the commercial management of large infrastructure, mining, oil & gas and real estate projects. She has more than 40 years of experience working with large private and public sector entities, delivering value from project concept to execution. Part of her portfolio of responsibilities includes the sustainable development of emerging and small businesses. Thanks to her efforts, her organization has been recognized by the South African Top Empowerment Awards as the winner of the 2019 Enterprise & Supplier Development Award, and was a finalist in the Standard Bank Top Women Awards Top Gender Empowered Organization: Skills Development in 2019. Wanda has a BSc from Rhodes University, as well as an Executive MBA and PhD from the University of Cape Town. Author email: wanda.chunnett@outlook.com

Dr. Babar Dharani, based in Cape Town, is a Senior Lecturer in the Allan Gray Centre for Values-Based Leadership at the Graduate School of Business of the University of Cape Town (South Africa) specialising in leadership and happiness. He is a Business Finance Professional and a Fellow of the Institute of Chartered Accountancy in England and Wales, and has lived and worked in a number of countries, including: Dubai UAE, Mauritius, England, Kenya, among others. Having held executive leadership positions in finance in the Diamond industry, his prime area of interest in academia is leadership development, focusing on happiness and well-being in organizations, and he regards matters of diversity and inclusion as one of the fundamental pillars for it. Babar, who regularly appears as an expert on radio shows, is the co-author of two books coming out in 2021: *Lived Experiences of Exclusion: The Psychological & Behavioural Effects* (Emerald Publishing) and *The Poetic Journey of Leadership*, as well as several book chapters, peer-reviewed academic papers and newspaper-op eds. Author email: babar.dharani@uct.ac.za

Assoc. Prof. Michel Ehrenhard is an Associate Professor of Strategic Entrepreneurship in the Department of High-Tech Business & Entrepreneurship of the University of Twente, Netherlands, and the Programme Director responsible for the BSc and MSc in International Business Administration. His research is at the intersection of entrepreneurship, organization theory, and organizational behaviour, and focuses on why and how managers and entrepreneurs create, sustain and resist disruptive social and organizational change – as well as the impact of such change. Michel has published in journals such as the *Journal* of *Business Venturing, Technological Forecasting & Social Change, Social Science & Medicine*, and the *Government Information Quarterly*. He holds a MSc in Public Administration and a PhD in Business Administration, both from the University of Twente. His PhD thesis was awarded the 2010 Best Dissertation Award of the Public and Non-Profit Division of the Academy of Management. Furthermore, he was part of a team that received one of six Twitter #datagrants, and in another team that won the Best Developmental Paper in Leadership Award at the British Academy of Management. Author email: m.l.ehrenhard@utwente.nl

Prof. André Habisch is a Professor of Social Ethics and Social Policy at the Faculty of Economics, Catholic University of Eichstätt-Ingolstadt, where he is responsible for the Master's program 'Entrepreneurship and Innovation.' He teaches Sustainable Entrepreneurship, Social Innovation and Applied Business Ethics. André studied Theology at the Universities of Münster and Tübingen and Economics at the Free University of Berlin, earning professional degrees in both subjects. A doctorate at the University of Tübingen and a habilitation at the University of Würzburg completed his academic qualifications in 1998, the same year he received the call to the Catholic University. Parallel to his academic work, he developed an extensive commitment in politics, business and civil society, for example, as a Scientific Member of two Commissions of Enquiry of the German Bundestag, as a Scientific Advisor to the Association of Catholic Entrepreneurs, and as Chairman of the Board of Trustees of the Bayer Cares Foundation. Guest Professorships have taken him to the Universities of Milan, Nottingham, Bangkok, Chongqing (China) and Beersheva (Israel). Author email: andre.habisch@ku.de

Prof. Martin Hall is currently an Emeritus Professor and Associate of the Allan Gray Centre for Values-Based Leadership at the University of Cape Town's Graduate School of Business, and a learning architect specializing in the conceptualization, design and production of digitally-enhanced learning across all modalities. He was previously Vice-Chancellor of the University of Salford in Manchester (UK), and Deputy Vice-Chancellor at the University of Cape Town. Trained as an archaeologist, he has published extensively on pre-colonial African history, the materiality of colonialism, and the ways in which the past is appropriated in contemporary politics and culture. He is a Fellow of the Royal Society of South Africa, a Life Fellow of the University of Cape Town, and a Principal Fellow of the Higher Education Institute (United Kingdom). Martin holds a PhD from the University of Cambridge (UK), and an Honorary Doctorate from the University of Salford (UK). Author email: martin.hall@uct.ac.za

Rajesh Jock is a Consultant who specialises in leadership development, emotional intelligence, executive coaching, goal-setting and personal motivation, culture improvement, team development, strategic influence, diversity management, workplace justice, and change management. As a Coach and Facilitator, Rajesh has facilitated breakthroughs in interpersonal behaviours and relationships for employees in government, state-owned entities and companies in the private sector. He has also done mentoring in Technical, Vocational Education and Training Colleges. He has 26 years' working experience, of which 16 years was spent as a Senior Manager in the government, and has also worked in the manufacturing industry sector and trade union. Rajesh holds a Diploma in Technology, Bachelor of Commerce Hons, Postgraduate Diploma in Marketing, Postgraduate Higher Diploma in Company Law, and Masters of Philosophy: Management Coaching. Author email: rajesh@futureview.co.za

Robin Koopman has significant and diverse experience in Strategic Planning and Project Management, with experience in both public and private sector planning and infrastructure and housing implementation projects. His entrepreneurial spirit and desire to explore the implementation of technology in the built environment led to his establishment of a niche-built environment consulting practice in 2016, further leading to his involvement with Cognitive Systems, a South African software engineering company driven by biologically-inspired computing, as Managing Director in 2017. Robin's focus is on the business applications of Cognitive Systems' Artificial Mind Engine (AME), a biologically inspired architecture for in-stream cognitive computing, which allows the delivery of real-time predictive analytics on constantly changing data in motion. He is responsible for Cognitive Systems, and their subsidiaries, commercialisation of the AME, driving business development, and the application and delivery of their technology in client environments. Author email: robin@cognitivesystems.ai

Dr. Raymond Loohuis gained professional experience as Strategic Marketing and Business Development Manager at various corporations active in the European automotive industry. He holds a PhD in Social Sciences and currently is a senior staff member of the Entrepreneurship & Technology Management Group (Behavioral, Management and Social Science Faculty – BMS) at the University of Twente, Netherlands. In this role, he is able to fruitfully combine prior business experience with his academic career as Senior Lecturer in the areas Strategic Marketing Management and Business Innovation. Raymond is also strongly committed to innovate the educational system, by implementing challenge-based learning frameworks to enhance the development of enterprise skills competences through a stronger engagement with practice. He recently received the BMS faculty's External Affairs Award for his achievements. Raymond has published in the *Journal of Supply Chain Management, Journal of Service Theory and Practice*, as well as book chapters in volumes on the sociology of organizations and strategic alliance management. Author email: r.p.a.loohuis@utwente.nl

Vincent Meurens is a Strategic Technology Entrepreneur, driven by innovations that create impact, generate value, and bring change for the good. Throughout his career, Vincent has held various senior management positions for large and international companies in both the banking and ICT industry, where he was responsible for launching new products, the definition of go-to-market strategies, and geographic expansions. His all-inclusive approach and network are built on the bases of trust, integrity, and mutually beneficial relationships. In 2018, Vincent was a Founding Member of EPCON, a South African-Belgian company, specialized in the use of real-world data and evidence to quantify health risks of the population, at community- and individual levels. Under his leadership, the company realized operations in South- and

Western Africa, the Middle East and Europe, where it supports public health partners and the government in the definition of tailored interventions for active case finding, monitoring and evaluation of TB programs. Author email: vincent@epcon.ai

Prof. Carla Millar is an international academic with solid business and consultancy experience. As Unilever's first female graduate Line Manager, renowned for her 'clinical eye', she helped turn its research laboratory discoveries into new marketing concepts, launching innovative brands. She was co-opted on MNC Boards, the EU's ESC, was on the Board of the Dutch Network of Female Professors, the Advisory Board, Dutch Knowledge Centre for Non-Executive Directors, and held several Visiting Professorships. Carla holds a BSc and MA (Tilburg), MPhil (Turin) and PhD in "Culture vs. Globalisation" (City University London), and currently is an Emeritus Professor, University of Twente, and elected Fellow, Academy of Marketing, having been Dean/CEO of TSM Business School in the Netherlands, CEO of City University's Management Development Centre, and Fellow of Ashridge in the United Kingdom. Carla inspires people, is a mentor to colleagues, and remains an active Ambassador for the advancement of women. Her research focuses on leadership, strategy and CG, knowledge-intensive institutions, culture, global branding, business ethics, innovation and resilience. She has published over 100 papers in, for example, JMS, BJM, MIR, JBE, JOCM, CG, SIJ, B&S, IJHRM, TFSC, and CMR, guest edited 14 Special Issues, and co-authored books on 'Emergent Globalisation' and 'Knowledge Entanglements' with Prof. Chong Choi and 'Leadership and Global Ethics' with Dr. Eve Poole. Author email: c.millar@utwente.nl

Dr. Lidewij Niezink, based in France, has been working on the development of empathy theory and practice for nearly 20 years. She writes, consults, trains and speaks on empathy for scientific, professional and lay publics. She teaches Applied Psychology at the Hanze University of Applied Sciences in the Netherlands and works as an independent empathy scholar focusing on integrating practice-based experiential methods with fundamental and applied research. She holds a PhD from the University of Groningen, The Netherlands, and publishes in national and international (academic) books and journals. She also authored a book on Critical Information Literacy. Lidewij was a Fellow of the Mind and Life Summer Research Institute in 2007 and was elected a Fellow of the ICCO in 2013 before joining the International Center as the Director of Research. Her work now focuses on empathy praxis. Together with Dr Katherine Train, she founded Empathic Intervision (www.empathicintervision.com). They develop evidence-based empathy interventions and education for diverse organizations, to identify opportunities and co-create solutions to challenges. They are also writing a book on Integrative Empathy, combining research from science in psychology, philosophy, social neuroscience, the arts and anthropology. Author email: lidewij@empathicintervision.com

Ndidi Nwuneli, a social entrepreneur based in Nigeria, is the Co-Founder and Managing Partner of Sahel Consulting Agriculture & Nutrition Ltd., as well as the co-founder of AACE Foods, the Founder and Chair of Nourishing Africa, and the Founder of LEAP Africa. She started her career as a management consultant with McKinsey & Company (Chicago, New York, and Johannesburg offices), and holds an MBA from Harvard Business School, and undergraduate degree with honours from the Wharton School of the University of Pennsylvania. She was a Senior Fellow at the Mossavar-Rahmani Center for Business & Government at the Harvard Kennedy School and an Aspen Institute New Voices Fellow. Ndidi was recognized as a Young Global Leader and Schwab Social Innovator by the World Economic Forum and received a National Honor from the Nigerian Government. Ndidi serves on boards of the Rockefeller Foundation, AGRA, Global Alliance for Improved Nutrition (GAIN), Nigerian Breweries Plc. (Heineken), Godrej Consumer Products Ltd. India, Fairfax Africa Holdings Canada, Royal DSM Sustainability Board, Netherlands, and the African Philanthropy Forum. Ndidi is the author of Social Innovation in Africa: A Practical Guide for Scaling Impact and Food Entrepreneurs in Africa: Scaling Resilient Agriculture Businesses, both published by Routledge. Author email: nnwuneli@sahelcp.com

Assoc. Prof. Hamieda Parker completed her Chemical Engineering degree, an MBA, and her PhD at the University of Cape Town. After graduating from Chemical Engineering, she worked as a Product Development Engineer on a fibre manufacturing plant for four years. On completing her MBA at UCT she was selected to go to the Wharton Business School, University of Pennsylvania, USA. While working as a Consultant at the Wharton Entrepreneurship Centre, she lectured on the basic Business Planning Course and she provided strategic, operational and marketing consulting services to a portfolio of companies, ranging from start-up to $10 million USD in sales. She completed her PhD on the Sainsbury split site doctoral scholarship based at the University of Oxford's Saïd Business School, England. She was awarded the Harvard-Mandela Fellowship and presented her research on entrepreneurship amongst disadvantaged communities at Harvard University, USA. She has served on the faculty of the Graduate School of Business, UCT, teaching the Operations, Innovation and the Supply Chain Management courses for the last twenty years. She was the Founder Chairperson and is the current Chairperson of the Business School's Transformation Forum. She has published widely on the topics of business collaboration, innovation and social entrepreneurship, resilience, sustainability, supply chain management, psychological safety, and team learning. Author email: hamieda.parker@uct.ac.za

Assoc. Prof. Camaren Peter is based in the Allan Gray Centre for Values-Based Leadership at the Graduate School of Business. His academic research and practice leverages complexity theory to help leaders and decision-makers tackle the grand challenges of the 21st Century. These range from political, technological and socio-cultural transitions and their implications, to powerful global change phenomena such as the fourth industrial revolution, urbanization, resource scarcity, ecosystems degradation and climate change. He has worked with a variety of global institutions and organizations, most prominently with the United Nations. Camaren holds a cum laude BSc (Hons) degree in Theoretical Physics, an MSc in Astrophysics, and a PhD in Business Administration. He is also the Director and Executive Head of the Centre for Analytics and Behavioural Change (CABC NPC). He was awarded a National Research Fellowship Postdoctoral Fund (2010-2012) and received three research and performance excellence awards while employed at the Council for Scientific and Industrial Research (CSIR) between 2001 and 2008. He is an author and has published widely in both scholarly and praxis-oriented discursive streams. Author email: camaren.peter@uct.ac.za

Dr. Anet Potgieter is the Co-Founder and Technical Director at Cognitive Systems, a South African software engineering company, as well as Co-Founder of EPCON, a European-South African joint venture. These companies focus on the integration of intelligent software agents into communities – enabling collaboration between humans, processes and Things. With her team of scientists, Anet created the Artificial Mind Engine (AME), a data-agnostic real-time analytics platform for the mining of 'perishable' or 'actionable' insights in the growing Internet of Things (IOT) and Big Data environments, solving the challenges of volume, velocity and variety. She has published extensively in academic journals and scientific encyclopaedias around the world. Topics include: how adaptive Bayesian agents enable distributed intelligence; automatic detection of anomalies in real-time data; understanding distributed knowledge networks; segmenting and tracking individuals through artificial intelligent video surveillance; the usefulness of Bayesian agencies on the internet; and the engineering of emergence. She holds a PhD in Computer Science and was a Senior Lecturer at the University of Cape Town (UCT). The main focus areas of her teaching and research included Agent-based systems, robotics, distributed AI, and computational intelligence. Author email: anet@cognitivesystems.ai

Matthys Potgieter is a South African Medical Doctor turned Bioinformatician, working in molecular epidemiology, medical image processing, human machine interfaces and the Internet of Things (IOT). Matthys obtained a MBChB from the University of Cape Town in 2012, and is currently pursuing a PhD in Pathogen Virulence focusing on Mycobacterium Tuberculosis Virulence and Metaproteomic Analysis of the human microbiome. He is the Co-Founder and Director at Cognitive Health Solutions, a subsidiary of Cognitive Systems, as well as the Co-Founder of EPCON, a South African-Belgian company. Matthys is the Science Lead and Data Engineer in these companies, coaching the technical teams in AI technologies in the emerging Internet of Things (IOT). In 2019, Matthys received a Human Proteome Organisation (HUPO) 2019 Student/ECR Travel Award. His international publications include a paper on proteogenomic analysis of mycobacterium smegmatis using high resolution mass spectrometry and MetaNovo: A probabilistic approach to peptide and polymorphism discovery in complex metaproteomic datasets. Author email: thys@cognitivesystems.ai

Dana Rissley is a socially conscious entrepreneur with interests in the social impact space, social entrepreneurship and business development & finance consulting. She works closely with large corporates and SMEs to understand and measure their social impact and Corporate Social Responsibility initiatives. She also enjoys working with social entrepreneurs to bring their socially conscious startups to life. Formerly, she worked as the Financial Director & South African General Manager of a multi-billion dollar American engineering & manufacturing company. Dana leverages knowledge and insights gained in her corporate role to help organizations improve their operations and financial reporting to grow and improve their businesses. She earned an MBA (with distinction) from the University of Cape Town. Her final dissertation was on the subject of income inequality and its economic impact, which she presented at an international Business & Economics Conference in Vienna, Austria. In addition, Dana has an undergraduate degree in Business with Finance, Accounting, & International Business specializations from Indiana University Bloomington, USA and holds the Certified Public Accountant (CPA) designation in the United States. Originally from the USA, she has been calling South Africa home for the past 5 years. Author email: dana@utandoimpact.com

Assoc. Prof. Mikael Samuelsson has been involved in award-winning research, consultancy work and training of entrepreneurs and managers since 1998. His research is used in both education and in governmental programs for entrepreneurs. He is involved in international and national development programs in, the USA, Europe, Sweden, Uganda, Kenya, Zambia, Mozambique Namibia and Botswana. Mikael is the founder of three business incubators/accelerators and has extensive experience from technology transfer and tech start-up sectors, as a Founder, CEO and Investor. Between 1997 and 2014 he served as the CEO for SSE Business Labs, with prominent start-ups such as Klarna and Quiniyx, both so-called Unicorn, valued at over $1 billion USD. His start-up experience ranges from life science companies, such as Spatial Transcriptomics, to fast-moving consumer goods. Mikael holds a Bachelor of Business Administration degree, a Master of Science in Marketing degree, and a PhD in Entrepreneurship from Jönköping International Business School, Jönköping University in Sweden. Author email: mikael.samuelsson@uct.co.za

Gary Smith is a Social Entrepreneur, Business Coach and Management Consultant. He has more than 20 years' experience as an Entrepreneur and 10 years as an Entrepreneurship Support Practitioner, with a particular focus on recruiting, training, and coaching high-potential entrepreneurs along their journey to becoming preferred suppliers. He designs and implements structured programmes that address the learning and development requirements of entrepreneurs in a practical way. Gary has personally trained hundreds of aspiring entrepreneurs in townships and rural communities throughout South Africa, and prides himself on making a positive impact on job creation through entrepreneurship development. His holistic approach provides entrepreneurs with all the skills, knowledge, tools and support they need to build and grow a profitable and sustainable business. Gary holds an MBA specializing in Strategic Planning, and is currently completing a Doctorate of Business Leadership with the University of South Africa (UNISA), School of Business Leadership, focusing on the development of an Entrepreneurship Propensity Index as a measure of new venture creation potential. Author email: gary@ubuntubusiness.co.za

Dr. Christina Swart-Opperman was a Senior Lecturer in the Allan Gray Centre for Values-Based Leadership at the Graduate School of Business, University of Cape Town up until early 2021, focusing on human resources management, emotions management, women empowerment and personal development. Her qualifications include a PhD in Business Administration from the University of Cape Town, a DPhil from North-West University, as well as an MA in Industrial Psychology, BA Honours and BA from North-West University. She is a registered Industrial Psychologist (Heath Professionals Council of SA) and works as a Consultant to many corporate organizations and government institutions. Christina gained a wide range of experience as the Namibian Director of the People Consulting Practice of PwC, and is the Owner of CO Holdings cc (focusing on human capital consulting) and former business, KnowledgeWorkx Namibia (specializing in intercultural intelligence). She is also a serial entrepreneur, continuously on the lookout for new challenges. Overall, she is passionate about Africa and the empowerment of her people, especially women and children. As Namibian Economist Business Woman of the Year in 2002, she founded the Christina Swart-Opperman Aids Orphan Foundation Trust in February 2003 and continued this service for 10 years, contributing towards social reform in Namibia. Currently she serves on a number of Boards in Namibia, as a Council Member for the University of Namibia, and as Member of the Namibia National Governing Board of the African Peer Review Mechanism. Author email: cso@mweb.com.na

Dr. Nicky Terblanche is a Senior Lecturer and Research Supervisor on the MBA, MPhil Coaching and PhD programmes at the University of Stellenbosch Business School (USB), South Africa. His academic interests include both leadership coaching and information system. He also runs an executive and leadership coaching practice.

He has an MPhil in Management Coaching, an MScEng in Electronic Engineering, and a PhD in Business Management. His research interests include transition coaching, transformative learning, social network analysis, complexity theory and the use of artificial intelligence and machine learning in coaching and management. He has published in a number of international academic journals, and regularly presents at international conferences. Author email: nicktyt@usb.ac.za

Dr. Katherine Train is an independent practitioner and researcher. Since 2005, she has been researching, developing learning material and presenting training on professional development, well-being, presence, empathy, compassion fatigue and burnout in various sectors. When training as a pharmacist, she realised that she had technical expertise, but lacked skills to adequately understand her patients. This led to a directed exploration of these capacities, as coaching training and as research towards a Masters and PhD degree. Her research interest has been in the application of empathy in organizations in South Africa whilst the country is emerging as a new democracy with its cultural and resource diversity and history of social upheaval. She holds a PhD from the Graduate School of Business, University of Cape Town. Together with Dr Lidewij Niezink she founded Empathic Intervision (www.empathicintervision. com). They develop evidence-based empathy interventions and education for diverse organizations to identify opportunities and co-create solutions to challenges. They are also writing a book on Integrative Empathy, combining research from science in psychology, philosophy, social neuroscience, the arts and anthropology. She has published in international academic journals, and has a chapter in a book on Dynamic Presencing. Author email: kath@empathicintervision.com

Henri Tshiamala is a streetwise Entrepreneur, an Entreprenelogist, an Entrepreneurial Leadership Trainer, an Educator, a Business Coach and Mentor, a small business Turnaround Strategist, a freelance Real Estate Practitioner, a Public Speaker and a Church Pastor. He has more than 30 years' experience in entrepreneurship and entrepreneurial leadership development – starting as a refugee hustler on the streets of Johannesburg and Cape Town, after leaving the Democratic Republic of the Congo, to being the Co-Owner, with his wife Christina, of the companies: Our Heritage Home and Craft, Imani African Gemstones Jewelry, Aemathyst Store, Mbinguni Kwema Store, among others. Henri is the creator of the luxury brand, Samuel Henri. He also founded a philanthropic training and upskilling project called: 'The Entreprisor', to upskill, train and support the deserving underprivileged. Prior to, and during his entrepreneurial journey, he held roles at Truworths, Metrorail, Tellumat, and as procurement professional at the head-office of the largest retailer in Africa, Shoprite-Checkers. Henri is a holder of an Electrical Engineering National Diploma (NDip from the Cape Peninsula University of Technology), an MBA from the University of Cape Town's (UCT) Graduate School of Business (GSB), a Certificate in Real Estate and currently is a PhD candidate at UCT's GSB. Author email: tshhen001@gmail.com

Prof. Marius Ungerer is currently a Professor and a core faculty member at the University of Stellenbosch Business School (USB), where he teaches strategic management, leadership and change management on programs such as the MBA, MPhil in Management Coaching and the Post-Graduate Diploma in Leadership. He has successfully supervised seven completed PhDs and more than 150 masters' degrees. His publications include 11 books with co-authors, 25 peer-reviewed journal publications and 23 publications in popular business magazines. He received three Rector's awards from Stellenbosch University for outstanding performance and the USB recognised him in 2017 with the "Most inspirational lecturer on the MBA" award. In 2018, he received a Research Excellence award in the category 'research outputs' awarded by the Vice-Rector of Research, University of Stellenbosch. He regularly consults to industry in his specialization areas. Author email: mariusu@usb.ac.za.

Shiela Yabo is currently a Business Strategist, Venture Builder & Project Manager with an interest in how human behavioural science impacts the world of business. She has a Bachelor of Social Science in Social Anthropology & Gender Studies, completed the Associate in Management Programme, and hold a Postgraduate Diploma in Management Practice (specializing in Business Administration), both awarded with distinction, from the Graduate School of Business, University of Cape Town. With experience in entrepreneurship on the continent of Africa and recently from Silicon Valley in the USA, she has a wealth of praxis knowledge in new venture launch & support, business acceleration, systems thinking, and leadership through mentorship. Shiela has designed and executed multiple entrepreneurship and innovation support programmes at the University of Cape Town, as well as for external partners. She is currently Programme Manager for the Solution Space, an ecosystem for early-stage ventures at the Graduate School of Business, UCT. She is responsible for Strategic and Operational Management, Planning, Programme Design & Delivery of Entrepreneurship programmes. She is also an experienced Ideation Bootcamp Facilitator and Angel Investor. Author email: shiela.yabo@gsb.uct.ac.za

Ndileka Zantsi is experienced in the areas of management consulting, project management; defining, leading and implementing projects of a national scale. Expertise include Economic and Small Medium Enterprise Development , academic programme facilitation, curriculum design, corporate stakeholder relationship management in Academic Institutions, entrepreneurial ecosystem and management. She has consulted to a range of organisations such as; public & private sector, non-profit organisations on projects related to skills development, capacity building, entrepreneurship and social innovation. Ndileka holds a Post Graduate Diploma in Management from Graduate School of Business. She Manages the Solution Space an eco-system for early ventures based in Philippi Township, Cape Town. Author email: ndileka.zantsi@gsb.uct.ac.za

Introduction

Entrepreneurship research and practice has received a great deal of attention in the past decade. Due to the role that entrepreneurial activities can play in tackling grand challenges, the predominant focus of such studies has been on the entrepreneurial journey, the network, the impact, the process, as well as the cultivation of 'the entrepreneur'. However, as studies in entrepreneurship have grown, maintaining the balance between objective and subjective implications have proven to be challenging. To this end, there has been an increase in calls for 'contextualizing' entrepreneurship research, cutting across levels of analysis in order to be able to provide relevant suggestions for research and practice. In an attempt to address this call, this book provides the first theoretical and empirical collection of studies that are embedded in and borne out of the context of (southern) Africa. The continent is home to seven out of ten fastest growing economies in the world, and from a business perspective, it is considered by Alex Liu, chairman of A.T Kearney "a large-scale start-up".[1] Yet, little is known about the state of entrepreneurial activities that aim to shape the continent's future. This book delves into the micro- and macro-level foundations of entrepreneurial activities across southern Africa, providing theoretical frameworks that take into consideration the entrepreneurial ecosystem in the continent, as well as the formal and informal economy that contribute to the growth and development of its countries.

This book is divided into three sections. The first section sets the context for entrepreneurship, with considerations given to its embeddedness in the broader environment. Examining entrepreneurship and entrepreneuring on a systems-level, this section begins with a chapter that discusses the role of the fourth industrial revolution and its influence on the entrepreneurial state in Africa, and given that, offers an 'ecosystem' perspective for the examination of entrepreneurship. Having set the scene for the complexities that 4IR impart, Chapter two offers a path towards managing complex systems through the use of networks consisting of simple software agents, which uses probabilistic reasoning to adapt to their environments. Chapter three examines the contextual challenges facing social enterprises in Africa, such as the lack of data, cultural heterogeneity, fragmented ecosystems, infrastructure and financing, and offers recommendations to various stakeholders for overcoming these challenges in order to scale social impact. The fourth chapter in this section provides a model for the utilization of networks, and in doing so, it sheds light on the economic benefits of migration capital and how development programmes such as the Caravan Programme can leverage such capital to provide economic growth for migrants' host countries. Undertaking a multi-case approach, Chapter five encourages reframing strategies in order to mobilize values and action for the creation of a 'regional bio-

---

1   WEF, 2019.

energy niche.' This chapter calls for attention to the taken-for-granted socio-cognitive frames related to traditional uses of energy. It provides framing strategies for actors operating in this field. Within the education sphere, Chapter six explores how innovative and context-appropriate, video-led case studies can widen and strengthen the impact of curriculum design and delivery across education by restoring the agency of voice. It argues that in order for educational institutions to widen the impact of values-led enterprises, they need to democratise their curriculum by allowing all voices to come through. This chapter offers innovative practices that facilitate this process.

The second section is dedicated to the role of organizational-level activities in entrepreneurial developments. Chapter seven examines the role of B-Corporations on the African continent and discusses the activities that these organizations engage in, in order to provide impact for the environment they are operating in. Notwithstanding their limitations, recommendations are made for the development of B-Corporations on the continent. Chapter eight explores the ways in which we can undertake collaborative methods to grow a venture, particularly under resource-constrained environments. It argues that it is, in fact, collaboration and partnering, and not competition that fosters growth, and provides a step-by-step description of how this process can be implemented. Continuing on the path of new venture support, Chapter nine illustrates the 'lessons learnt' in the process of supporting early-stage entrepreneurs during their incubation journey. This study is built on primary findings triangulated from founders, funders, industry experts and incubation programme partners. Chapter 10 argues for greater congruency between what Business Schools teach and do, and their African cultural contexts, as well as the importance of reciprocal networks and entrepreneurial ecosystems between nations inside and outside of the African context. Chapter 11 acknowledges the importance of psychological safety and respect for the human dimension in social enterprises. The hybrid orientation for social enterprises, together with its commitment to social value creation, are highlighted – by identifying such practices and their challenges in the manufacturing sector. Supporting entrepreneurs in the venture creation process is further illustrated in Chapter 12 by a study conducted in a business accelerator located in the disadvantaged area of Philippi Village in the Western Cape province of South Africa.

The third and final section delves into the micro-level foundations of entrepreneurial activities, deriving from both empirical and theoretical studies. Given the centrality of the entrepreneur's role in venture creation, it is not surprising that much attention is given to the 'entrepreneur.' Chapter 13, undertaking a mixed-method study in South Africa, examines entrepreneurial propensity and provides an index based on intrinsic and extrinsic factors that can be used to assess whether an entrepreneurial tendency will result in venture creation. In line with entrepreneurial propensity, Chapter 14 provides evidence for the relationship between the entrepreneur's locus of control and their happiness regarding entrepreneurial activities. It therefore argues that internality is linked to entrepreneurship and suggests that internals perform more efficiently in environments that allow control over their actions. It thus offers a 'best-fit' approach based on the entrepreneur's locus of control. Considering that the entrepreneur needs to relate to, and build relationships with, various stakeholders, Chapter 15 draws our attention to the importance of empathy and, in particular, self-empathy in fostering such relationships. Given that the entrepreneur needs to firstly rely on him/herself, the chapter offers the skillsets required for self-care. It does so by walking us through a case of an entrepreneur undergoing self-empathy coaching sessions, and providing recommendations for future practice. Building on the importance of coaching, Chapter 16 provides a qualitative study of how executive coaching becomes an entrepreneurial venture. From the perspective of the entrepreneur, it reveals the important components of building an executive coaching venture, namely networks, architecture, value proposition and financial support. Thus, providing the factors that contribute to a successful coaching business model. Chapter 17, which aims to provide a theoretical framework for micro-entrepreneurs and their start-up teams, focuses on the impact of emotions and the entrepreneurs' disposition to trust in the early stages of venture creation. Using the lens of 'person-in-situation perspective', the chapter draws from individual-level factors such as personality traits, emotions, entrepreneurial mindset, propensity to trust, and assessment of others' trustworthiness in order to provide a framework that takes into account the importance of entrepreneurial networks on venture creation, thus, providing a point of departure for micro-entrepreneurs and their start-up teams. Chapter 18 looks at the challenges in ensuring collaboration in the racially segregated spatial arrangements of South Africa, even when we know that diversity and inclusion are enablers of entrepreneurial ventures. The chapter also highlights the inadequacy of traditional training and education in preparing modern-day entrepreneurs, and calls for greater permeability of a myriad of traditional boundaries in the pursuit of solutions for social challenges. This section concludes with a micro-level lens on the personal journey of an immigrant entrepreneur in Cape Town. Through narratology, Chapter 19 explores the resilience, efficacy and achievement of African refugee entrepreneurs in South Africa and provides a unique perspective on not only factors that lead to success, but also the challenges and obstacles that are faced in the venture creation and growth process.

The book offers interesting and rich perspectives on parts of the African entrepreneurial ecosystem, through a number of lenses, from both local Africans as well as international researchers and practitioners who are passionate about the future of Africa. Many of the perspectives offered and insights from actual praxis on the continent can prove instructive to other parts of the world, particularly the developing and emerging economies around the globe.

Part I

Entrepreneurial Context: A System-Level Lens Towards Entrepreneurship

Chapter 1

Informality, 4IR and the Entrepreneurial State in Africa: An 'Economic Ecosystems' Perspective

Assoc. Prof. Camaren Peter

Abstract

This chapter argues that – by embracing the notion of the entrepreneurial state – African governments can harness the offerings of the fourth industrial revolution and green technologies to build sustainable local and regional economies, while addressing their pressing developmental challenges at the same time. Moreover, it argues that the role of the entrepreneurial state in Africa can be better appreciated through adopting an economic ecosystems perspective as it; (1) enables a holistic appreciation of formal-informal sector dynamics, and (2) places a specific focus on local and regional economies, which are more manageable scales of implementation. Hence, by adopting an economic ecosystems perspective the entrepreneurial state in Africa can play a key role in building capacity for transition through local and regional economic diversification that is sustainable and equitable. The economic ecosystems perspective can help build capacity to adaptively navigate the changes that the fourth industrial revolution will bring and leverage them for local and regional economies, while increasing resilience and minimising risks at the same time.

Introduction

According to Klaus Schwab, who founded the term "fourth industrial revolution", characterized it as the fusion between the "physical, digital and biological" spheres.[1] It is distinguished from the third industrial revolution by its "velocity, scope and systems impact". It is fast moving and emergent (i.e. complex and unpredictable), impacts all sectors of society and fundamentally changes the way in which systems operate (e.g. in terms of their functions, controls, processes, networks, and material and information flows). Hence, it is the rapid pace of change across multiple sectors at different scales and levels, and disruptive innovation emerging from the technological and informational convergence of the physical, digital and biological domains, that characterises the fourth industrial revolution.

---

1   Klaus Schwab, 2015.

The question of how the fourth industrial revolution (or "4IR") will impact the economies and societies of the 21st Century is currently a topical area that is characterised by a mixture of opinion, scholarship and debate. For the most part, the impact of the fourth industrial revolution on highly industrialised economies – whether in developed or developing countries such as those in Northern Europe or the Far East, respectively – remains the focus of such debates. Thus far, little attention has been devoted, however, to the question of what shape and form the opportunities afforded by the fourth industrial revolution may take in African economies, given their particularities, and consequently how best to support entrepreneurial growth and economic diversification in response to it.

The specific factors that characterise the African context include: high levels of unemployment, high infrastructure and basic service provision deficits, a low skills base, low levels of industrialisation, heavy economic dependence on resource exploitation or agrarian activities, high import dependency, a youth bulge characterised by severely high levels of unemployment, and the prevalence of dual formal and informal systems.[2] The complexity of African developmental challenges hence clearly cannot be approached from the same perspective as that of industrialised, developed nations.

Yet, the question of how African governments should respond to the fourth industrial revolution remains largely unanswered, with some of the emerging political discourse around it being devoted to three key issues. First, the prospect of increased unemployment across a variety of sectors. Second, the prospect of leveraging the 'vast transformative potential' that the fourth industrial revolution holds to leapfrog development on the continent. Third, the skills transition that is necessary to absorb and harness the impacts of the fourth industrial revolution.

How to respond to the fourth industrial revolution in Africa, or indeed other countries characterised by low levels of industrialisation, is an important one; not least because the fourth industrial revolution poses the threat of exacerbating and deepening existing inequalities, both globally and locally. Actualising an affirmative vision of the fourth industrial revolution in the African context requires that a contextually appropriate appreciation of how African economies are constituted is embraced, in particular, their dual economy (i.e. formal and informal) status. Identifying the opportunity space for engagement with the fourth industrial revolution must also take this duality into account.

---

2   UN HABITAT, 2014.

Moreover, it is important to understand what the role of the state is in shaping and guiding national and regional responses to the fourth industrial revolution in Africa. MinHwa Lee et al.[3] argue that responding to the fourth industrial revolution necessitates:

> "... the institutionalization of the role and function of the **entrepreneurial state,** which intensively and directly invests in fields whose social value is high **but not immediately shown,** such as renewable energy, social innovation, senior citizen welfare, environmental risks, and the resolution of disparities among ages, regions, and classes."

The entrepreneurial state,[4] as defined above, possesses precisely those goals that are appropriate for African countries, which are characterised by high levels of disparity between minority elites and the majority poor. The question of how to actualise the entrepreneurial state in Africa, however, requires a perspective that can accommodate dual formal-informal systems in the spirit of the definition tendered above.

Accordingly, this chapter proposes that an "economic ecosystems" perspective is more suited to the African context in respect of how African economies can respond to the fourth industrial revolution; especially in accommodating both formal and informal systems (see section on *Beyond neoclassical economics*). It accounts for African developmental conditions (see section on *The Fourth Industrial Revolution in Africa*) and provides a rationale for the developmental opportunity space (see section on *Implications for The entrepreneurial state in Africa*) that high levels of informality in African cities present in respect of the fourth industrial revolution (in combination with green technologies and systems). In doing so, the role of the entrepreneurial state[5] in relation to the fourth industrial revolution[6] in Africa becomes clearer (see section on *Critical Reflections on the "Economic ecosystems" approach*), pointing a way forward for African governments (and states) to leverage the fourth industrial revolution to; leapfrog their infrastructure and technology base, diversify their economic activities and stabilise and grow the African middle class. The chapter ends with critical reflections of the economic ecosystems approach in the African context (see section – *Critical reflections on the "economic ecosystems" approach*) and conclusions (see section *Conclusions and way forward*) in the chapter.

---

3   MinHwa Lee et al., 2018.
4   Mazzucato, 2013.
5   Ibid.
6   MinHwa Lee et al., 2018.

Beyond Neoclassical Economics:
An 'Economic Ecosystems' Perspective

Dual economies as "economic ecosystems"

The question of what kind of "lens" or metaphor is adopted to visualise African economies – especially the interface between formal and informal systems – is critically important in the (sub-Saharan) African context, where informality is the majority condition in most countries and regions (see section *Opportunity space for local economic diversification*). In this respect, this chapter makes the argument that: (1) formal-informal sector *duality* is critical to accommodate when considering what choice of economic 'lens' is appropriate for African economies. Moreover, in the quest to better appreciate the fluid boundaries between formal and informal systems, it is critical to (2) adopt a *systems perspective*. A systems approach enables the interconnectedness between formal and informal systems – as well as their dynamics – to be appraised as one system, comprised of two densely interconnected and overlapping sub-systems. The rationale for these two requirements is outlined as follows:

A post-dualistic perspective: Neoclassical economics largely treats formal and informal economic systems as *dualisms* (i.e. as distinct binary systems). In practice, this results in legitimacy being granted to formal systems, with informal systems treated as illegal or illegitimate at worst, or simply tolerated and quasi-regulated at best. At its core, however, formal and informal systems are neither distinct, nor are they always mutually reinforcing. Formal and informal systems are characterised by significantly 'grey' areas of overlap and porosity (where it is difficult to determine whether an activity is formal or informal), as well as significant levels of contestation (alongside cooperation) (e.g. Chakrabarti; Chen; Gastrown & Amit; Nadin & Williams).[7] Hence, it is more appropriate to regard formal-informal systems as *post-dualistic*.

A systems perspective: Whether adopting a systems perspective, or ecosystems perspective on a locality or region, it is imperative to acknowledge the importance of the functions, controls, processes and feedbacks in maintaining systems' identity, stability conditions and resilience. Here, the traditional dynamic systems perspective, which models how stocks, flows, leads and lags in the system interrelate, can act as any one or more of the aforementioned factors (i.e. functions, controls, processes or feedbacks). Understanding non-physical (e.g. socio-cultural) systems dynamics can also be enhanced through causal loop mapping, which focuses more on influences than physical flows in a system. Hence the systems approach is especially important in treating informal and formal systems as equally important, interdependent and

---

7   Chakrabarti, 2013; Chen, 2007; Gastrow & Amit, 2015; Nadin & Williams, 2012.

interrelated systems that compose a 'whole' system. Building on the systems perspective, the economic ecosystems perspective is evolutionary in its outlook (i.e. a complex adaptive systems perspective), as outlined in the next section.

Defining economic ecosystems

This chapter proposes that an "ecosystems" perspective be adopted as a "lens" or metaphor through which formal-informal systems dynamics can be evaluated and acted upon. In this respect, we adopt the definition of an economic ecosystem as proposed by Auerswald and Dani,[8] namely:

> "An [economic] ecosystem is defined as a dynamically stable network of interconnected firms and institutions within bounded geographical space."

In this perspective the reductionist, mechanistic neoclassical economic perspective is transcended by a heterodox biological economic perspective; namely one that coheres well with that of an institutional, evolutionary or "Schumpeterian" economics perspective. Many heterodox economists argue that economies in general are more akin to evolutionary, biological systems than they are to machines, precisely because they are *complex adaptive systems*.[9] That is, as complex adaptive systems they do not reside in equilibrium, but rather reside in stability that is far away from equilibrium, maintained by strong feedbacks. As such, they also exhibit emergence (i.e. unexpected, unpredictable, often non-linear change) that can be characterised as *disruption*. This aligns well with the Schumpeterian perspective on "creative destruction".[10]

The characteristics of economic ecosystems perspective are summarised in the sections below as follows.

Localisation and innovation

In its original conception by Alfred Marshall, who favoured the use of biological metaphor over that of mechanism in conceptualising economic systems, the two key factors that influenced this perspective is an emphasis on: (1) the "localization of economic activity" and (2) "invention and innovation in geographical localization".[11] More recently this has led to conceptualisations and studies that treat local or regional innovative systems as "ecosystems", prompted by an improved understanding of how real-world ecosystems and human systems function. That is, through the mainstreaming of "resilience theory",[12] as well as greater interest from policymakers and decision-makers.

---

8   Auerswald & Dani, 2018.
9   Hodgson, 1993.
10   Schumpeter, 1911, 1939.
11   Marshall, 1920.
12   Gunderson & Holling, 2002.

Differentiation and growth

In the economic ecosystems perspective used in this chapter[13] firms are more densely intra-connected than inter-connected. However, their inter-connection is significant enough to constitute an ecosystem. Varying degrees of inter-connectedness hence underlie the 'speciation' of firms.[14]

This speciation is also attributed to two other key factors. First, the notion of a "production algorithm" as the unit of analysis, which is analogous to that of biological genes in ecosystems. Genetic mutation is key to navigating its "fitness landscape", which is a visualisation of the reproductive success of a species against its genotype in two dimensions. Second, they de-emphasize the role of chance mutation in favour of bi-parental reproduction, that is, inter-connectedness drives speciation. This is analogous to Schumpeterian entrepreneurship and innovation.

Simply put, interconnections that produce a contextually 'fit' population of products enables the population to move beyond its neighbourhood, which is constituted of "adjacent genetic variants" (i.e. competitors), on the fitness landscape. Inter-connectedness (or 'bi-parental') mutation enables a fit population to reach parts of the fitness landscape that lie beyond its competitors, that is, adaptive capacity of the population is enhanced (see next section).

Adaptation and stability

By treating firms as organisms within ecosystems[15] the DNA of firms can be defined as "the economically relevant knowledge embedded within the firm on which the firm's survival depends". This constitutes the "production algorithm'" or "production recipe" of the firm.[16] These production algorithms or recipes are intimately linked to firms' *learning curves.*[17] Hence, in this conception the "evolutionary pathway" can be treated or understood as "an 'adaptive walk' or step-wise optimization process" that depends on learning and feedback. This conception of systems evolution clearly mirrors that of complex, adaptive systems, where stability is maintained far away from equilibrium conditions (i.e. in non-equilibrium) through strong, often multiple, feedback processes.

---

13   Auerswald & Dani, 2018.
14   Ibid.
15   Ibid.
16   Ibid.
17   Muth, 1986; Wright, 1932 in Auerswald & Dani, 2018.

Summary

Auerswald and Dani[18] state that characterising networked regional economies as ecosystems yields three key theoretical benefits, namely that it "provides analytical structure and depth to theories of": (1) "the sources of regional advantage"; (2) "the role of entrepreneurs in regional development"; and (3) "the determinants of resilience in regional economic systems".

In addition to these, the economic ecosystems perspective also enables both a post-dualistic and systems perspective on local formal-informal economies and their interfaces, because it is implicitly agnostic towards the question of institutional legitimacy. Rather, it prioritises a complex, adaptive systems perspective and focuses attention on: what generates local/regional competitive leverage; the dynamics of differentiation, co-evolution, production and reproduction; as well as adaptive capacity and stability conditions. Hence, in this framing (i.e. a complex, adaptive systems perspective) the question of whether these factors are formal or informal can hence be regarded as secondary to the question of what governs the evolution of an economic ecosystem as a complex, adaptive system.

African developmental needs and conditions

Africa's socio-economic developmental needs are paramount concerns for both governments and societies alike. High infrastructure and service provision deficits prevail across the continent, and especially the fast-growing cities of the continent.[19] At the same time, there is an emerging consensus around the need for the preservation of resources for future scarcity values, maintaining the natural environment, and boosting resilience and adaptive capacity to alleviate projected climate change impacts.[20]

The common, conventional view on African development, which has persisted throughout the latter half of the 20th Century is that beneficiation and industrialisation is required in order to transition African societies into modern industrial economies.[21] Yet, with the advent of the third and fourth industrial revolutions, there are indications that alternative ways of transitioning may emerge on the continent.[22] This is especially so when considering the contextual specificities governing the needs of African societies, as well as the commensurate opportunity spaces they open up for economic diversification, when considering new waves of technological development (in particular, green technologies and the fourth industrial revolution).[23]

---

18 Auerswald & Dani, 2018.
19 AfDB, 2011a; United Nations, 2014.
20 African Union, 2017.
21 United Nations, 2019.
22 WEF, 2017.
23 Peter, 2018.

The critical developmental necessities of emerging African economies and societies can be understood by considering the following phenomena and the socio-economic conditions that accompany them, as outlined in the following sections.

Urbanisation

Whereas the first global wave of urbanisation spanned 200 years, urbanised 400 million people and coincided with the industrialisation of the economies of the developed world (i.e. between 1750 and 1950), the second global wave of urbanisation is occurring over 80 years (i.e. 1950 – 2030) and is projected to urbanise around 4 billion people, most of whom will reside in the cities of the developed world.[24]

Africa's cities are growing at the highest rates in the world (the highest magnitudes are in Asia), and urban dwellers are projected to grow from 400 million circa 2014 to 1.26 billion in 2050, increasing its global percentage of urban dwellers from 11.3 per cent in 2010 to 20.2 per cent in 2050.[25] Two key factors are important to take into account when considering this urban growth: (1) that the majority (i.e. 75%) of urban growth is occurring in *small to intermediate cities* (i.e. 100,000 to 500,000, and 500,000 to 1 million, respectively),[26] and (2) that in contrast to the first wave of urbanisation, African urban growth is taking place *without significant levels of industrialisation.*

Africa's cities are especially vulnerable to climate change impacts such as spatio-temporal vegetation change, desertification, urban heat enclave effects, and extreme events such as drought, flooding, storm surges and cyclones. This vulnerability is due to the lack of adequate infrastructures (e.g. water reticulation systems, drainage systems), as well as the lack of adequate care and protection of natural habitats that strengthen resilience to climate change effects by buffering them (for example: coral reefs, mangrove forests, wetlands, adequate urban green spaces, forests).[27]

High infrastructure, service provision deficits

African human settlements, whether rural or urban, are generally characterised by high levels of infrastructure and basic service provision deficits (e.g. energy, water and sanitation, transport, healthcare, housing).[28] While urban areas enjoy greater access, due to high levels of urban agglomeration and population pressure, these deficits remain particularly significant and are reflected in the high levels of informality in African cities. Infrastructure and service provisions that are not (or inadequately and

---

24 Pieterse, 2010.
25 United Nations, 2008, 2014.
26 United Nations, 2010.
27 United Nations, 2014.
28 AfDB, 2011a; United Nations, 2014.

unreliably) met through centralised, bulk infrastructures are sourced through informal and private sector service providers, often at higher cost.[29]

High levels of informality

Informality goes beyond simply the proliferation of slums and informal settlements (which ranges between 60-80 per cent across West, Central and East Africa, for example).[30] Informal trade, employment, service provision (e.g. water, energy, food, transport, waste removal and management/recycling), land management and housing agreements characterise the African urban condition. High proportions of the continents large, youthful population base are absorbed into informal sector employment.[31]

The emerging African middle class 'precariat'

While a great deal of optimism has been focused on the continent, with the continent's highest performing 18 cities projected to reach a purchasing power of USD 1.3 trillion by 2030,[32] and significant GDP growth – occurring uniformly across sectors[33] – since the 1980s and 1990s, the emerging African middle class that is central to this transition requires closer scrutiny. Early projections are that by 2020 128 million households will have transitioned to 'middle class' status, that is; growing from 355 million people in 2010 to 1.1 billion in 2060.[34] Combined with a labour force that is set to grow to 1.1 billion in 2040,[35] it is clear that significant labour and consumer pools are growing on the continent.[36]

However, when one considers how the African middle class is defined, the picture is considerably less optimistic. The African middle class is defined as people living on between USD 2-20 per day and constituting around 34 per cent of the population circa 2011.[37] Around 60 per cent of this 34 per cent live on between USD 2-4 per day and are referred to as the "floating middle class".[38] Only around 4% live on more than USD 10 per day, constituting only 2% of the global middle class who earn between USD 10-100 per day.[39] Moreover, around half of the population live on less than USD 1.25 per day,[40] which is below the global poverty line.

---

29 United Nations, 2014.
30 Ibid.
31 Ibid.
32 Swilling, 2010; United Nations, 2014.
33 McKinsey, 2010.
34 AfDB, 2011a; United Nations, 2014.
35 McKinsey, 2010.
36 United Nations, 2014.
37 AfDB, 2011b.
38 Ibid.
39 Africa Progress Panel, 2012.
40 Ibid.

The precarity of the African middle class is thus clear, yet this group is key to closing the inequality gap on the continent. Stabilising the African middle-class households in particular requires interventions that target their expenditure. Around 50-70 per cent of household expenditure in African households – especially poor households – can be attributed to food, water[41] and energy[42] (including transport) costs. Hence, global developmental agencies refer to the food-water-energy "nexus" as a key point of intervention.[43]

The heavy dependence of most African countries on imports (e.g. food and energy) renders poor and middle-class households vulnerable to double and triple-squeeze effects. In particular, the "floating middle class" can find themselves oscillating between near poverty and poverty conditions to 'middle class' status from month to month. As they constitute a majority of the African middle class, stabilising these households against exogenous change effects is critical for ensuring the stability of the African middle class as a whole. Moreover, local authorities are unable to collect revenues due to the relative instability of these households, rendering them heavily dependent on central governments. Local economic diversification hence suffers, as local authorities are unable to re-invest strategically to boost local economic growth and are often subject to undue – often corrupt – influence from central governments in local decision-making.

The Fourth Industrial Revolution in Africa: Opportunity Space for Local Economic Diversification

A small-scale, high absorption infrastructure boom

So how can the fourth industrial revolution be leveraged to respond to Africa's pressing developmental challenges. In "reimagining sustainable urban transitions in Africa"[44] a significant opportunity space resides in the overlap between new and emerging green technologies and systems solutions, and the offerings of the fourth industrial revolution.[45] Perhaps the most under-appreciated, but most significant, factor in considering the emergence of new green technologies, infrastructures and systems solutions is that they are largely *semi-decentralised* or *decentralised*. They can hence be implemented without the need to link up to bulk infrastructures, although they can be linked to bulk infrastructures if necessary.

---

41 De Magalhães & Santaeulàlia-Llopis, 2018.
42 Kojima et al., 2016.
43 "Water, Food & Energy | UN-Water," n.d.
44 United Nations, 2014.
45 Peter, 2019.

While the majority of African cities are constituted by slums and informal settlements that are not and cannot easily be linked to bulk infrastructure provisions, the availability of semi-decentralised and decentralised offerings offers an opportunity to get essential services into households faster, and with significantly less cost and disruption than bulk infrastructures (which would require clearing away and entirely re-planning slums and informal settlements).

These semi-decentralised and decentralised systems can be scaled up and integrated at street, neighbourhood and higher scales (e.g. through micro-grids) in "in-situ" development schemes, and eventually linked to bulk infrastructures in an incremental and manageable manner, where progress on service delivery can be seen and experienced over the course of the socio-technical transition. That is, service delivery and absorption grows as the transition unfolds, and is not contingent upon establishing a large, centralised infrastructure first. In contrast, the costs of bulk infrastructures, which can escalate significantly over the short to medium terms, doubling or tripling, can prove prohibitive, notwithstanding the uncertainties and long duration of implementation and roll-out.

Green technology and 4IR for Africa

Green technologies and systems solutions that are relevant to the African context include, for example: solar panels, solar water geysers, renewable energy or mixed energy micro-grids, grey- and black-water recycling systems, biogas digesters (which can take organic waste and/or sewerage off grid), small-scale wind and hydro energy technologies, urban agriculture, hydroponic and permaculture operations, agro-industrial processing systems, waste recycling systems and public transit systems.

Moreover, these green technologies target precisely the food-water-energy-transport "nexus" that is key to stabilising middle-class and poor households in Africa.[46] By reducing the dependence of these households on exogenous change impacts, green technologies and solutions – which can be rolled out in African settlements without significant spatial intervention and re-planning – household budgets can be stabilised and rendered more resilient to nexus effects.

Note that many of these technology options are relatively low cost, small-scale solutions and do not require high skills levels to roll-out and maintain in comparison to bulk infrastructures, offering the opportunity to significantly boost SME growth and employment amongst the groups where it is most needed in the African context.

---

46 Peter, 2019.

The green technology – 4IR melting pot!

The emerging – and yet to emerge – offerings of the fourth industrial revolution are largely complementary to the opportunity space that green technologies and solutions offer up in the African context.[47] The fourth industrial revolution is largely characterised by the decentralisation of production, services, controls, functions and processes that underlie business activities, based on the availability of larger stores of detailed information, advanced analytics and the ability to make decisions in real or near-real time, greater interconnectivity, lower upfront transaction costs, lower resource requirements. It provides more degrees of freedom to customise systems and products to local contexts and 'wed' offerings more closely to implementation contexts.

Critically, the fourth industrial revolution hosts the potential to contribute significantly to boosting the rate of the required skills transition and certification that is necessary to roll out green technologies and solutions. Moreover it can help provide the financial, banking and micro-credit and credit services that low- and middle-income households require for the absorption of these technologies. Platforms such as Blockchain and Etherium enable new provisions to be developed without the need to develop 20th Century infrastructures (i.e. physical and organizational), reducing the transaction costs of delivering the aforementioned services, and rendering conventional service providers less agile due to their legacy infrastructures.[48]

The convergence of both green technologies and the offerings of the fourth industrial revolution also hosts vast potential for local innovation that customises products, systems solutions and offerings to meet the specificities of local contexts. By leveraging information, advanced analytics, decentralised production (e.g. 3D printing and additive manufacturing), for example, systems solutions that are tailored to local contexts and needs can be innovated and developed.

In this framing legacy infrastructures are a disadvantage, especially for inflexible, top-heavy organizations that are characterised by high levels of capitalisation but are inflexible and/or rigid in terms of their dependence on highly optimised linkages. Indeed, new actors in the banking space – e.g. Capitec ("South Africa's cheapest bank accounts: Capitec vs the rest," 2019) in South Africa, or mobile telecoms companies such as Safaricom in Kenya ("Mobile phones are replacing bank accounts in Africa | IOL Business Report," 2019) – are rapidly growing their offerings and outcompeting traditional, conventional financial services.

---

47 Peter, 2019.
48 Ibid.

Additional examples of fourth industrial revolution offerings that can help boost absorption of green technologies and solutions include: advanced revenue collection systems; sharing economy offerings; real-time data and information synthesis, analytics and visualisation; smart materials and nano-technologies; enhanced coordination of resource and material flows; automation, 3D printing and additive manufacturing; mechanisation and robotification; smart logistics; smart transportation; enhanced planning and spatial development, and recombination of technologies at regional/local scales (e.g. through 'smart' industrial symbiosis).

Spatial implementation considerations

A critical factor in respect of this opportunity space is the proliferation of small and intermediate sized cities on the continent.[49] These cities have typically grown along the corridors that connect larger urban metropoles (e.g. in West Africa, along the GILA corridor).[50] Moreover, the functions that these smaller to intermediate cities perform have also changed as they have diversified to exploit new opportunities for growth. These cities host significant potential to: (1) act as 'test-beds' for implementation of new, innovative solutions that straddle the green technology and fourth industrial revolution realms, and (2) accordingly serve as ideal locations for developing leapfrogging strategies that can have significant impacts in respect of lowering nexus vulnerabilities.

In this conception of the utility of green technologies and solutions and the offerings of the fourth industrial revolution, large overall impact on the future developmental trajectory of – especially urban – settlements in Africa can be achieved. By targeting the smaller to intermediate sized cities that host the vast majority of urban growth, large-scale impact can be achieved at lower risk. In turn, learning from these interventions (i.e. at smaller 'safe to fail' scales) can be transferred to rural locations, or scaled up incrementally in larger urban locations.

Implications for The Entrepreneurial State in Africa

So how can dual formal and informal systems of trade, service provision, employment, skills development, land, housing, financing and so forth be supported in their engagement with the developments of the fourth industrial revolution so that they benefit from its transformative impacts in the main? In this respect, the question of what kind of role the state can play in managing economic ecosystems is an important one.

---

49 United Nations, 2014.
50 Ibid.

Moreover, when considering the fourth industrial revolution the notion of an economic ecosystem acquires a significant online, digital dimension. This section hence also explores how leveraging the digital dimension in regional African contexts can significantly enhance the capacity of the state to actualise economic ecosystem dynamics that are appropriate for local/regional African contexts.

Introduction: An economics ecosystems perspective on the Entrepreneurial State in Africa

Informality and the State in Africa:

It is critically important to acknowledge the role of *power*, and particularly the state, in the African context. In the wake of over a decade of refreshing urban studies that grew a greater appreciation of the survival strategies and resourcefulness of informal sector activities (and their importance in maintaining every urban life),[51] recent urban studies and literature have begun to re-emphasize the importance of the state in shaping urban spatial, social, cultural and infrastructural dynamics.[52] Whether considering the *presence* or *absence* of the state, the state plays a key role in shaping everyday urbanism in Africa. It is not a neutral or simply ineffective force that can be ignored in the analysis and appreciation of how urban development in particular unfolds.

When considering the role of the state in Africa – and at multiple scales or levels of governance – it is important to acknowledge that it actively or de-facto presides over dual formal and informal systems. Moreover, that both formal and informal systems themselves can be regarded as societal or social institutions that have varying degrees of interaction with the state. The fluid/porous boundary conditions between formal and informal systems,[53] despite their distinctiveness in many respects, speaks to the need to enable a more holistic approach.

The Entrepreneurial State:

In appraising the role of the entrepreneurial state in the context of the fourth industrial revolution, Lee et al.[54] emphasize the need to institutionalise and strengthen the entrepreneurial state[55] in order to: (1) boost capital fluidity, (2) reform national taxation regimes, (3) leverage productivity gains to reduce working hours and increase wages, and (4) address safety and security risks of the fourth industrial revolution. Moreover,

---

51 De Boeck & Plissart, 2005; Simone, 2001.
52 Cirolia & Scheba, 2019; Gastrow, n.d.
53 Chakrabarti, 2013; Chen, 2007; Gastrow & Amit, 2015; Nadin & Williams, 2012.
54 Lee, Ramus & Vaccaro, 2018.
55 Mazzucato, 2013.

the entrepreneurial state has a role to play in (5) generating economic and innovation policy that is future-oriented, and (6) enabling education systems to be more adaptive to changes in respect of skills and knowledge base, and that (6) fiscal policy can be leveraged to decrease taxation on labour (i.e. by accentuating productivity-based taxation). It also has a key role to play in (7) facilitating cooperation and collaboration between business, government, academia and civil society in navigating the challenges and opportunities that accompany the fourth industrial revolution.

An economic ecosystems perspective:

While this appraisal of the entrepreneurial state is useful, it largely focuses on the role of the state in relation to formal sector activities. When an ecosystems perspective on the entrepreneurial state in the African context is adopted, however, additional depth and perspective on its role in holistically engaging the fourth industrial revolution can be garnered. Once the basic systems properties, features and interdependencies of a local or regional economic ecosystem are understood – e.g. whether through 'hard' dynamic systems models[56] or 'soft' systems models such as causal loop diagrams – the key question in respect of transition is: how can these be configured and/or supported to improve the ecosystem health and self-organising capacity so that the ecosystem inhabitants can transition to desirable regions of the fitness landscape? In endeavouring to answer this question, the economic ecosystems perspective[57] has a significant contribution to make in respect of the entrepreneurial state in Africa. The rationale for this is discussed in the following sections.

Shaping economic ecosystems' responses to change effects

Industry evolution in economic ecosystems is driven by both endogenous and exogenous factors.[58] Hence, the state can play a role in shaping or mediating how these impact on regional or local scale economic ecosystems (i.e. boosting adaptive capacity and resilience). Monitoring and evaluating both endogenous and exogenous (i.e. cross-scale, transversal) impacts from a systems perspective is hence key to understanding how a regional economic ecosystem is evolving i.e. 'what is influencing it, and how is it reacting to these influences?' Moreover, it is also essential so that local and other decision-makers have the requisite knowledge of when and where to intervene in the economic ecosystem in order to: (1) mitigate against undesirable effects, and (2) exploit opportunities for innovation and/or growth and diversification.

By developing mechanisms that boost adaptive and creative capacity (e.g. by promoting niche development, knowledge infusion programs, innovation support

---

56 Smit, Musango, & Brent, 2019.
57 Auerswald & Dani, 2018.
58 Ibid.

'hubs'), and provide support functions (e.g. skills development, micro-credit/credit, financial services, banking) where needed, the state can play a key role in shaping how regional ecosystems respond to endogenous and exogenous change impacts (i.e. increase resilience).

Diversifying the "product space" of economic ecosystems

Moreover, the state can also help identify opportunities for product and/or systems innovation that meets the contextual specificities of local and regional contexts (i.e. sources of regional advantage). Here, the 'product space'[59] (i.e. the networked "co-occurrence of products" of a region)[60] is important to consider.

Studies[61] show that the product space of developed countries are more diverse and densely networked than those of developing countries. Moreover, product spaces tended to be characterised by the prevalence of sophisticated products in "denser regions of the network",[62] while less sophisticated products occurred at the peripheries. That is, greater inter-connectivity drives more sophisticated 'speciation' whereas lesser inter-connectivity drives less sophisticated 'speciation'.

Additionally, the distribution of firms within economic ecosystems is not uniform, and the firm's location within the system plays a big role in its ability to produce and its evolutionary trajectory.[63] Locational advantage is important. Hence, a fuller appreciation of how interdependencies (both real world and virtual) may influence a firm's 'location' within an economic ecosystem is necessary.

In the African context, where formal and informal systems characterise local and regional economies, invoking a product space 'lens' on the economic ecosystem may yield greater insights into: (1) the diversity of products occurring over the formal-informal spectrum, and (2) where products of higher and lower levels of sophistication are emerging from in the networked product space that spans this spectrum.

In order to support entrepreneurial activities in the product space, the entrepreneurial state in Africa can help build in the means that enable entrepreneurs in both the formal and informal sector to exploit the products in the product space more effectively. That is, by developing mechanisms, feedbacks, processes, support functions and catalysts that help them "redeploy (human, physical and institutional) capital towards goods that are different from those currently under production"[64] the entrepreneurial state

---

59 Hidalgo, Klinger, Barabasi, & Hausman, 2007.
60 Auerswald & Dani, 2018.
61 Hidalgo et al., 2007.
62 Auerswald & Dani, 2018.
63 Ibid.
64 Ibid.

in Africa can play a role in the 'adaptive walk' of entrepreneurs and actors within a regional economic ecosystem, engendering diversification and facilitating transition at the same time.

Entrepreneurial dynamism and innovation

In respect of how novelty arises, where technological innovation and novelty are treated as resulting in a species of technology,[65] emphasize that novel technological species predominantly emerge as a result of the "purposive recombination of existing solutions". This indicates that it is not as much an evolutionary process as it is about "linking pieces that already exist (or pieces that can be created from ones that already exist)". They also emphasize that species co-evolution with other species is a critical aspect of the evolutionary 'adaptive walk'. That is, the inter-relationships between technological 'species' is an important factor in considering how the evolutionary pathway unfolds. Inter-connection is important.

Entrepreneurship drives economic change and transition[66] and, in turn, a whole ecosystem is required to help innovators actualise the full potential of their organizations.[67] In this sense, we can consider the importance of an "industrial infrastructure"[68] in seeding, catalysing and shaping innovation. Citing outlines this industrial infrastructure as:[69]

> "(1) institutional arrangements to legitimize, regulate, and standardize a new technology; (2) public-resource endowments of basic scientific knowledge, financing mechanisms, and a pool of competent labor; (3) development of markets, consumer education, and demand; and (4) proprietary research and development, manufacturing, production, and distribution functions by private entrepreneurial firms to commercialize the innovation for profit."

In the African context it is patently clear that this notion of an industrial infrastructure would not be entirely appropriate, largely because it is primarily focused on formal-sector activities that exist – in larger part – in developed economies. In the case of dual formal-informal economies in Africa it is important to draw on this characterisation of industrial infrastructure in a manner that clearly incorporates informal sector dynamics. A more delicate balance is hence required between regulatory and supportive functions that the entrepreneurial state imposes on formal-informal sector dynamics. This 'balancing act' needs to take into account the various

---

65 Auerswald & Dani, 2018.
66 Schumpeter, 1911.
67 Auerswald & Dani, 2018.
68 Van de Ven, Polley, & Venkataraman, 1999.
69 Van de Ven et al., 1999; Auerswald & Dani, 2018.

interdependencies, relationships and feedbacks that maintain formal-informal sector interface.

In this respect there is a clear need for the creation and support of national or local/regional *strategic intermediaries* in the African context that: (1) help seed, catalyse and shape co-evolutionary innovation mechanisms in economic ecosystems, (2) manage feedbacks and network evolution of economic ecosystems, (3) monitor and evaluate the institutional arrangements (as accounted for above) that fuel and regulate ecosystem competitiveness and effectiveness,[70] and (4) are sensitive to and can respond to formal-informal sector dynamics and evolution.

The broader state also has a critical role to play as dealmakers – or alternatively in supporting dealmakers in other sectors – who "act as brokers" whose functions are to "shape the network, manage structural holes, and 'connect disparate actors to social networks'".[71] They can, for example, take actions that enhance industry 'speciation' (e.g. through improving positioning and inter-connectivity), thus initiating new pathways for growth in the regional economic ecosystem that spans both formal and informal sector activities.

Maintaining stability and resilience through transition

Stability conditions of these complex, self-organising systems are typically generated by a small set of controlling processes, not from the interactions between very many variables and/or factors.[72] Nonetheless, they are also nested within larger systems spanning the regional to the global. Hence, being able to visualise and understand how the variety of transversal and cross-scale linkages may impact on an economic ecosystem remains important. Actualising an adaptive walk that does not proceed towards equilibrium conditions, but rather towards non-equilibrium stability conditions that are maintained by strong, manageable feedbacks, is desirable.

In the African context, resilience can be enhanced through lowered resource dependency (i.e. through green and sustainability-oriented infrastructures, technologies and systems solutions), as well as increased diversity that improves "capacity for algorithmic recombination". For example, by strategically increasing *redundancies* and *degeneracies* in the economic ecosystem and densifying inter-connectivity, more adaptation options to create the same outcome (i.e. equifinality) can be instilled in the economic ecosystem.

---

70   Chakrabarti, 2013; Chen, 2007; Gastrow & Amit, 2015; Nadin & Williams, 2012.
71   Feldman & Zoller, 2011 in Auerswald & Dani, 2018.
72   Cilliers, 1998.

In addition to these considerations, in the context of the fourth industrial revolution, it is important to acknowledge that the virtual realm (i.e. digital) plays a critical role. The digital realm is also characterised by the prevalence of both ecosystems (and nested ecosystems) as well as transversal and cross-scale linkages. In this respect the virtual realm extends the interdependence of local economic ecosystems far beyond its locality, while still allowing it to belong to an economic ecosystem that is recognisably bounded in some sense (i.e. through its inter-connectivity). That is 'bi-parental reproduction' can occur through remote inter-connections (i.e. involving exchange of materials, information, resources and ideas) and not just through local ones.

In the fourth industrial revolution paradigm it is hence conceivable that parts of that ecosystem may reside entirely in the virtual realm (i.e. digital) and that the random walk of an economic ecosystem would draw on its virtually enabled competencies, linkages and parts to innovate new production algorithms/processes that maintain its 'fitness trajectory' on the fitness landscape. In this sense, the ecosystem could resemble more of an open systems "assemblage"[73] than a tightly bounded system, and this could in turn impact on the number of variables and/or factors that ascribe the 'set' or array of controlling processes that keep the ecosystem stable.

Critical Reflections on the "Economic Ecosystems" Approach

Power, social institutions and context

While representing dual African regional economies as economic ecosystems is a useful framing, as illustrated in this section, there are nonetheless legitimate concerns about what is lacking in this perspective. As alluded to earlier, the economic ecosystems perspective is lacking in its appreciation of power. It's framing of economic performance is expressed in terms of "fitness" in relation to a changing environment and interspecies interactions. This is an expressly Darwinian perspective that is suited to natural systems.

In human systems, however, power is a critical factor that is not necessarily related to fitness in the evolutionary Darwinian sense. Power does not add to fitness or cannot always be a product of – or attributed to – fitness; but fitness can help acquire power! In highly unequal human systems power may *obviate* fitness as understood in the biological sense. Power acts to retain power, and in the case where social actors may enjoy power that is derived from sources other than fitness, they may view fitness as a threat, and seek to nullify it.

---

73   De Landa, 2006.

Hence, the notion that economies and society obey 'natural' laws and/or rules can be problematic in the sense that it remains a form of 'mechanistic' thinking. Human systems are both obeying and reproducing laws and/or rules and generating new ones at the same time. These processes are informed by a constellation of factors that are often contextual, and embedded in the finer, more detailed analyses of how local systems are driven by human actions and behaviours. Culture; social values, beliefs and norms; existing practices and processes; identity; networks; local, contextual specificities and opportunity spaces – all influence the exercise of power and the 'evolution' of these systems. This is especially the case with informality in Africa, but also – perhaps to a relatively lesser extent – in formal systems.

In this respect, it is important to emphasize the importance of *context* in regional economic ecosystems in Africa. It would be great folly to adopt an economic ecosystems perspective that is wholly dependent on the notion that 'natural' laws are in operation. The discourse on informality – especially with respect to urbanism – hosts great potential for revealing and contextualising informal sector dynamics, as well as that of formal-informal interfaces, overlaps and interdependencies. Locality and context are paramount in African localities and any serious attempt at enabling an economic ecosystems perspective must necessarily accommodate these adequately.

Notwithstanding the importance of locality and context, however, it must also be noted that the virtual realm locates power in an instantly accessible arena with high levels of proximity to a fluid, highly connected and diverse high-density pool of agents (whether human or non-human), services, organizations, processes, functions, controls and resource flows. This is an arena that is set to grow in importance as the fourth industrial revolution unfolds, critically as the digital realm increasingly merges with the physical, biological, and – critically – political realms; impacting every aspect of everyday life in a vast array of societies and sectors across the world.

Formal-informal "Edge Effects" and the Digital Realm

While a holistic perspective on dual formal-informal systems is desirable, it is also necessary to distinguish between them appropriately. In this respect, we can consider the "edge effects" in ecosystems:

> *"The greater the contrast between the habitats sharing an edge, the stronger will be the edge effect."*

It is imperative that any interventions that are derived from an economic ecosystems perspective for the entrepreneurial state in Africa adequately accommodates their impacts on trade, service provision, employment, skills development and cash-flow in both informal and formal sectors. Hence, while a holistic perspective is desirable in respect of formal-informal sector duality, it is still important to adequately account for how "edge effects" manifest between them.

However, it is important to point out that an overly spatial or physical reliance on conceptualising the "edge" or transition zone in terms of physical proximity is inadequate. It is important to accommodate how the virtual realm influences and shapes these transition zones, in respect of density, fluidity, connectivity and diversity,[74] but also in terms of power (as outlined in the previous section).

Conclusions and Way Forward

While acknowledging the limitations of the "economic ecosystems" perspective, this chapter discusses how an economic ecosystems perspective on African localities and regions can help understand how the entrepreneurial state can: (1) help mediate the impacts of exogenous change effects on local/regional economic ecosystems, (2) play a role in leveraging local/regional advantages while drawing on global connectivity, (3) stimulate entrepreneurial activity and growth while benefiting society as a whole, and (4) maintain stability and resilience through transition.

In respect of formal-informal sector duality, the economic ecosystems perspective offers a conceptual framework that can help bridge the formal-informal sector divide and engender multi-level economic activity. Moreover, its focus on local and regional economies closely matches the spatial developmental opportunity that exists in respect of African cities i.e. small to intermediate scale cities, which helps resolve the question of "where" it would be best implemented, tested and adapted. In these respects, the economic ecosystems perspective on the entrepreneurial state in Africa offers considerable hope for accommodating both formal and informal system dynamics in a holistic perspective, with the acknowledgement that more praxis-oriented research is needed to develop the concept further.

---

74   Stangler & Bell-Masterson, 2015.

Chapter 2

Collective Intelligence for Good in the Fourth Industrial Revolution

Dr. Anet Potgieter, Robin Koopman, Vincent Meurens and Matthys Potgieter

Abstract

The fourth industrial revolution (4IR) merges the physical, digital and biological worlds and integrates humans, societies, processes and things through massive communication networks into a 'hyperconnected world'. This hyperconnected world is decentralised in its nature due to a large number of distributed autonomous entities solving, in parallel, many various tasks based on intensive interaction among its participants. The integration of Internet of Things (IoT) technologies and software agents is called the Internet of Agents (IoA). Capabilities of software agents, namely learning, social ability, adaptability, collaboration, mobility and proactivity are ideally suited to join human communities and entrepreneurial ecosystems to solve the intelligence, interoperability and autonomy needs of the 4IR.

Emerging Internet of Agents platforms mostly implement autonomous agents that use extensive interaction protocols and social laws to control interactions in order to ensure that the correct automated behaviors result during run-time. In hyperconnected environments it is not possible to predict emergent interactions. For a complex system to be able to adapt in uncertain and non-deterministic hyperconnected environments, we propose the use of agencies consisting of simple software agents, which uses probabilistic reasoning to adapt to their environments. Our agents collectively implement distributed Bayesian networks, used by the agencies to control automated behaviors in response to environmental states. Each agency is responsible for one or more behaviors, and the agencies are structured into heterarchies according to the topology of the underlying Bayesian networks. We refer to our agents and agencies as Bayesian agents and Bayesian agencies. Due to the simplicity of the Bayesian agents and the minimal interaction between them, they are deployed as reusable components into our IoA platform.

We integrate our Bayesian Agencies into communities to promote Sustainable Development, adhering to the agenda of the United Nations. Using our generic IoA platform, we created a community safety ecosystem and a health ecosystem. The community safety ecosystem consists of our IoA platform integrated into control rooms and social media platforms, continuously monitoring video feeds and issuing early warnings of situations that endanger the safety of citizens in urban environments, human settlements and farms. The health ecosystem includes the use of our IoA platform in collaboration with the Stop TB Partnership, a UNOPS organization, to find missing patients in underserved communities. As an example, for TB alone, around 4 million patients are missed every year. Our platform provides a set of practical and cost-effective software agents to help find those missing patients, screen and enter those affected into a treatment program.

Background

The fourth industrial revolution (4IR) merges the physical, digital and biological worlds and integrates humans, societies, processes and things through massive communication networks into a 'hyperconnected world.'

These networks are enabling people, processes and things (e.g. vehicles, home appliances, etc.) embedded with electronics, software and sensors to connect and exchange data streams and messages through wireless networks and the Internet. In these highly connected environments there is a need for a new generation of intelligent tools that are context-aware, can make sense of their dynamically changing environments and the observed behaviors of animate and inanimate objects and processes in these environments. These tools must be context-aware and able to continuously extract new perishable insights from a variety of data sources. Context is any information that characterizes the environment of an entity (a person, group of people, a place or an object) relevant to the interaction of the application and the users. It means, understanding the whole environment and current situation of the entity.

Typically these tools must operate in high velocity and high-volume sensor and event streams and immediately harness these insights to modify processes in these highly connected environments in order to augment behaviors of objects. There is a further need for systems that learn from experience and become better in achieving their goals. This incremental learning capacity will improve behavior over time in dynamically changing hyperconnected environments. These evolving systems are called "complex adaptive systems".

What is emergence?

A complex adaptive system in nature "moves to" the "rhythms" and regularities in its environment by using agents, organised into adaptive aggregates (agencies), interacting with each other and collectively acting in response to environmental changes. Agents are the independent components of intelligence within a single creature in nature.

A complex adaptive system is characterized by emergence, which results from the interactions among individual system components (agents), and between system components (agents) and the environment. A complex adaptive system is able to adapt due to its ability to learn from its interactions with the dynamically changing and uncertain environment. It learns from, and understands patterns, extracted from these interactions and adapts its actions in order to better achieve its goals in the environment.

Emergence, the most important characteristic of a complex adaptive system, is the collective behavior of interacting system components. IoT applications can have tens of thousands and even many more communicating autonomous heterogeneous objects including data and services, software and information objects of social networks together with co-existing human societies, network of sensors, various real-world objects as well as cloud-based objects. These networked humans, societies, processes and things are characterized by emergence as these entities are interacting on a peer-to-peer basis generating emergent behaviors.

Emergence leads to holism.[1] A complex adaptive system is holistic, which means that the collective behavior of the system components is more than the sum of the behaviors of the individual system components, for example a flock is more than a collection of birds and a traffic jam is more than a collection of cars.[2] Minsky describes holism as a "lack of understanding" (of an observer) due to the unexpected emergence of a phenomenon that had not seemed inherent in the system components, showing that "the whole is more than the sum of its parts".

Agents and agencies

The system components of a complex adaptive system are called agents. Marvin Minsky describes the concepts of agents, agencies and heterarchies in his Society of Mind.[3] An agency consists of a society of simple agents. The intelligence lies in the behavior of agencies and not in the individual agents.

---

1   Baas & Emmeche, 1997.
2   Odell, 1998.
3   Minsky, 1988.

An agent is defined as a simple independent software component that communicates with and acts on behalf of a human or a thing (for example a sensor/video camera/object) or act upon emerging relationships between things in the networks of connected devices or things. In distributed systems the agents communicate and coordinate their actions by passing messages amongst themselves to achieve common goals. These agents are collectively adaptive in that they learn from experience and from each other. In order to become better at achieving their goals with experience, they change and improve their collective behavior over time.

An agency consists of a society of agents that inhabit some complex dynamic environment, where the agents collectively sense and act in this environment so that the agency accomplishes what its composite agents set out to accomplish by interacting with each other.[4]

The organization of agents in an agency can be hierarchical or heterarchical. According to Minsky,[5] a hierarchical organization is "like a tree in which the agent at each branch is exclusively responsible for the agents on the twigs that branch from it".

If agents in a society belong to more than one agency, the set of "overlapping" agencies forms a heterarchy. A heterarchy is a form of organization resembling a network or fishnet. Authority is determined by intelligence and function. Heterarchies are more powerful than hierarchies. If structured into a heterarchy, the agencies can collectively solve problems that are too complex for single autonomous agents.

Situatedness, embodiment, intelligence and emergence

Collective intelligence of agencies emerges through the interaction of the agents within the agencies. In the hyperconnected world, collective intelligence can be achieved through agents (humans, software agents, things, processes) that are solving, in parallel, many various tasks based on intensive interaction within the agencies.

Most Artificial Intelligence systems deployed in hyperconnected environments attempt to model the world, and then reason about it using complex control strategies. The control strategies can either be centralized or distributed. The traditional distributed control strategies employ computation units that are very complex and with a high communication overhead.

---

4   Potgieter & Bishop, 2001.
5   Minsky, 1988.

Brooks[6] argues that the world is its own best model, and it cannot be modelled successfully. An agent must be situated in the world and must react to inputs from the world, rather than attempt to model the world internally. Just as agents can be situated in physical environments, agents can be situated in the hyperconnected environment and they must be able to handle the dynamics and uncertainty in this environment.

Brooks[7] characterizes intelligence in terms of situatedness, embodiment, intelligence and emergence. Situatedness can be described as the state of being in the world. Embodiment is the method by which situatedness is achieved, namely to be in the world and to react to inputs from the world. Intelligence and emergence are tightly interwoven – intelligence emerges out of interactions between behaviors and the environment.

Highly interconnected environments are constantly evolving and are characterized by environmental conditions that cannot be predicted by static models. Machine learning systems employing pre-trained models that cannot adapt in real-time to high variety, volume and velocity streams, are not suitable for environments where operations are time-critical or communication infrastructure is unreliable. In these high-velocity and high-volume systems, delays due to latency caused by the round-trip to centralised automated reasoning facilities or inappropriate actions informed by non-adaptive machine-learning models, can have fatal consequences. Examples include physical security, where the prevention of life-threatening activities cannot afford the latency caused by round-trip to the centralised reasoning facilities or wrong decisions by reasoning using non-adaptive machine learning models.

To be able to adapt, machine learning models must apply transfer learning. In transfer learning, a model developed for a specific task is reused as the starting point on another one, mimicking the way humans generalize knowledge from one specialized task to another. This form of learning reduces the required size of training datasets.

Transfer learning is an adaptive machine learning strategy that enables situatedness and embodiment. Agencies using transfer learning can generalize in the presence of emergent conditions. Through transfer learning, agencies can adapt models at the edge. Bayesian learning and reasoning are ideally suited for transfer learning.[8]

Judea Pearl in his *The Book of Why* states:[9]

---

6   Brooks, 1991.
7   Ibid.
8   Karbalayghareh, Qian, & Dougherty, 2018.
9   Pearl, 2018.

"As much as I look into what's being done with deep learning, I see they're all stuck there on the level of associations. Curve fitting. That sounds like sacrilege, to say that all the impressive achievements of deep learning amount to just fitting a curve to data. From the point of view of the mathematical hierarchy, no matter how skillfully you manipulate the data and what you read into the data when you manipulate it, it's still a curve-fitting exercise, albeit complex and nontrivial."

According to Judea Pearl: *"To Build Truly Intelligent Machines, Teach Them Cause and Effect"*.[10]

Agents can be taught *"Cause and Effect"* through Bayesian networks. These networks provide a powerful Artificial Intelligence (AI) technology for probabilistic and statistical inference that can be used to reason with uncertainty in complex environments. These environments contain complex data sources such as surveillance, socio-economic and spatial-environmental datasets with multiple variables that have many hidden relationships, large amounts of natural variation, measurement errors, or missing values. A Bayesian network contains a set of predictor variables represented as nodes. The links between the nodes represent informational or causal dependencies among the variables. The dependencies are given in terms of conditional probabilities of states that a node can have, given the values of the parent nodes. Each probability reflects a degree of belief that encodes causal dependencies. The degree of belief in any cause of a given effect is increased when the effect is observed, but then decreases when some other cause is found to be responsible for the observed effect. Causal dependencies are derived from the knowledge of domain experts, or by mining the structure of the network from data by using unsupervised or supervised machine learning.

The internet of agents

Most Internet of Things platforms are not situated or embodied. These platforms employ centralised computing models that require an extremely large amount of data and computing power to be effective, which is costly and time-intensive. Cloud data centres are geographically centralized and they often fail to deal with storage and processing demands of billions of geo-distributed IoT devices/sensors. As a result, congested network, high latency in service delivery, and poor Quality of Service (QoS) are experienced.

Distributed Artificial Intelligence (DAI) using distributed software agents are best suited to cope with emergent behavior in hyperconnected environments. Integration of IoT technologies and software agents are called the Internet of Agents

---

10 Pearl, 2019.

(IoA).[11] Capabilities of software agents, namely learning, social ability, adaptability, collaboration, mobility and proactivity are ideally suited to solve the intelligence, interoperability and autonomy needs of the 4IR.

IoT platforms that use agent-oriented strategies, mostly implement autonomous agents that use extensive interaction protocols and social laws to control interactions in order to ensure that the correct behaviors result during run-time. In hyperconnected environments, it is not possible to predict emergent interactions. For a complex system to be able to adapt in such an uncertain and non-deterministic environment, we propose the use of situated and embodied agencies, integrated into an IoA platform, consisting of simple software agents, which uses Bayesian transfer learning to adapt to their environment.

The artificial mind engine

According to Minsky, "Minds are what Brains do".

A "Brain" in the IoA can be defined as the self-organizing, adaptive network formed by people and things and software agents in an IoA agency together with the information and communication technologies that connect them into a coherent system. The Global Brain is the self-organizing, adaptive network formed by all people on this planet together with the information and communication technologies that connect them into a coherent system.[12]

A "Brain" consists of hyperstructures that are higher-order structures that emerge from the collective behavior of the agents in a complex adaptive system. Complex adaptive systems use these hyperstructures for explanation and understanding in order to act ("do") in the real world.[13] The "brains" of complex adaptive systems are their internal models, consisting of these hyperstructures representing "regularities" in the information about the system's environment and its own interaction with that environment.

Gell-Mann refers to the information about the environment of a complex adaptive system and the system's interaction with the environment as the "input stream" of the system. All complex adaptive systems maintain internal models.[14] A complex adaptive system creates and maintains its hyperstructures ("Brains") by separating regularities from randomness" in its input stream.[15] Emergence occurs as soon as the regularities

11 Pico-Valencia, Holgado-Terriza, Herrera-Sánchez, & Sampietro, 2018.
12 Heylighen & Lenartowicz, 2017.
13 Gell-Mann,1994.
14 Holland, 1995.
15 Gell-Mann 1994.

identified in the input stream deviate from what is expected from the internal model maintained by the complex adaptive system.

In Minsky's *Society of Mind*, internal observation mechanisms called A-Brains and B-Brains maintain internal models consisting of hyperstructures called K-Lines. Each K-Line is a wire-like structure that attaches itself to whichever mental agents are active when a problem is solved or a good idea is formed.[16] The A-Brain has inputs and outputs that are connected to the real word, and the B-Brain is connected to the A-Brain. The A-Brain can sense and influence what is happening in the world, and the B-Brain can see and influence what is happening inside the A-Brain.

We implemented Bayesian agents that collectively implement distributed Bayesian networks as hyperstructures. These hyperstructures are mined through incremental transfer learning at the edge closest to data sources. These networks are used by the agencies to control behaviors in response to environmental states. Each agency is responsible for one or more behaviors, and the agencies are structured into heterarchies according to the topology of the underlying Bayesian networks. We refer to our agents and agencies as Bayesian agents and Bayesian agencies. Due to the simplicity of the Bayesian agents and the minimal interaction between them, they are deployed as reusable components into our IoA platform, called The Artificial Mind Engine (AME).

The distributed Bayesian networks continually evolve through incremental learning from feedback loops from processes and people. AME achieves intelligence through its A-Brains and B-Brains. A-Brain agencies are situated and embodied right at the edge closest to the data sources – tapping into the input streams in the hyperconnected environment and continuously inferring beliefs about and learning from the latest environmental states. B-Brains inspect the beliefs of the A-Brains and influence these beliefs.

Competence agencies actions are "Minds" in that they are making "Brains do". These agents form part of dynamic interaction with the interconnected entities in their environment (embodiment). These agencies are observed to be intelligent (intelligence). The intelligence of our agencies emerges from the interaction between the agencies and the hyperconnected environment, and between themselves and other agencies (emergence).

The artificial mind engine and cybersecurity

The IoT introduces additional complexity for security. The data traffic to and from

---

16   Minsky, 1988.

IoT devices in a network must be continuously monitored and anomalies must be detected as they happen. Perimeter-based solutions are not adequate in an IoA platform environment because users, things and agents apps can no longer be contained inside a company's network, behind a clearly defined protective wall.

The Artificial Mind Engine (AME) uses Blockchain's alternative approach to storing and sharing information. Using a distributed ledger, AME can increase security on three fronts: blocking identity theft, preventing data tampering, and stopping Denial of Service attacks.

AME's distributed ledger is illustrated in Figure 2.1.

A smart contract binds things and people together, defining context-aware publish-subscribe services between humans and things, defining what services are to be provided by "things" and AME's agents, continuous monitoring and early warning, protecting the community of things, humans and processes against unwanted participation and intrusion.

Services can be exchanged in virtual currencies or critical information, that cannot be intercepted by unauthorized parties.

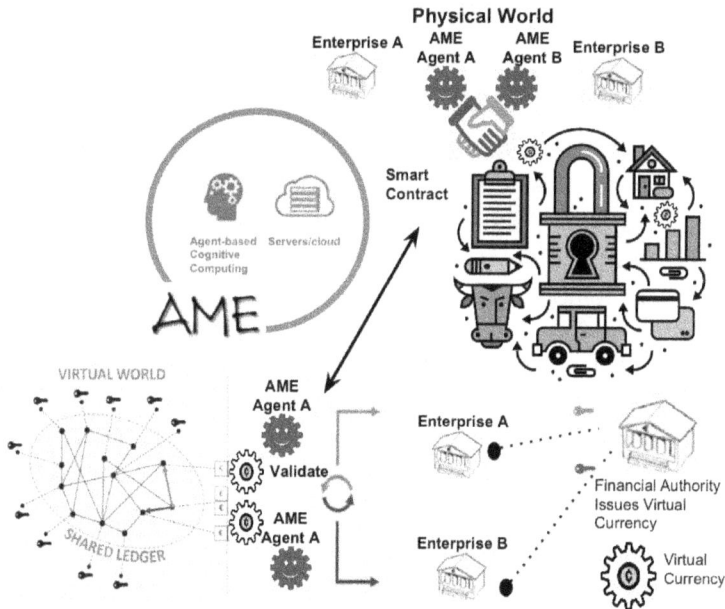

Figure 2.1: Distributed Ledger in The Artificial Mind Engine

Collaborative ecosystems in the 4IR

The Internet of Agents is decentralised, working through processes endlessly set in motion by triggering software agents and harnessing the power of massive communication networks. The implications for security, crowd control, traffic control, customs control and many other branches of social control – are staggering. It is however very difficult for entrepreneurs to achieve and sustain competitive advantage in the 4IR. Success often depends on access to specialized knowledge and resources that lie outside the entrepreneur's ownership or control or depends on the innovations, actions, relationships, partnerships or ecosystems of others who complement the entrepreneur's offer.

For entrepreneurs to optimally harvest the opportunities of the 4IR, they should be able to combine Internet of Agents platforms with trusted business ecosystems. Entrepreneurs must practice responsible entrepreneurship and responsible innovation in order to mitigate the risks of the 4IR. Integrating IoA platforms responsibly into human societies, the collective intelligence of humans, software agents, societies and things can work for the good of humankind, collectively working towards the Agenda for Sustainable Development.[17]

The best example of such an ecosystem that harvests opportunities of the 4IR is the global WEF-Accenture ecosystem. According to Klaus Schwab of the World Economic Forum (WEF), 4IR technologies have the potential to propel digitally-ready countries into a new age of unprecedented economic prosperity. In 2015, the WEF, launched their "Digital Transformation Initiative" in collaboration with Accenture, which will unlock "$100 Trillion for Business and Society from Digital Transformation".[18] In the Accenture-SAP ecosystem, Accenture and SAP are co-innovating and co-developing digital solutions, using distributed ledger technology, Artificial Intelligence, extended reality, and quantum computing.

Several South African government departments have adopted WEF-inspired 4IR strategies. President Ramaphosa encouraged South Africans to focus on new technologies that will revolutionise the world, and started a Presidential 4IR Commission in April 2019. Gauteng province is the first provincial government to set up a Department of e-Government as part of the South African government's drive to be a smart, innovation-driven, knowledge-based and digital economy. The key role of the Department of e-Government is the roll-out of a network infrastructure that will connect government facilities, including schools, hospitals, offices and economic zones. In addition, the Department of e-Government endeavours to stimulate the ICT

---

17   United Nations, 2015.
18   Accenture & World Economic Forum, 2018.

economy and encourages public and private partnerships for the development and roll-out of e-Government services.

With the ability to unlock value for business and society, reservations on 4IR in the South African context relate to its impact on employment and, more notably, the question of ownership and meaningful economic participation.[19] With foreign-owned technology companies leading investment and acquisitions in 4IR, pushing their platforms as comprehensive solutions, and potentially informing policy, Nkala's questions about 4IR in South Africa are especially relevant: *What will be the ownership patterns of the technology enterprises that emerge to dominate our economy? Will they be woven in the same patterns of ownership as the old industries in South Africa (grossly unequal and racially skewed)?*

New business models have and are emerging in the 4IR. The complexity of 4IR technologies, Artificial Intelligence, Big Data and Internet of Things calls for specialisation and sustainable collaboration among partner organizations. For the 4IR, the business model blends product purchases and provision or subscription to services. Competitiveness no longer depends solely on optimisation resources within a single firm, but on a value chain that spans innovation and supportive partner technologies across complementary firms, joint products, services and systems. With the aid of their partners, firms are creating inter-organizational value through innovation and trust, and produce value chains that operate in a local, regional and international collaborative business ecosystem.

Collective entrepreneurship in the 4IR

IoA technologies will cause a revolutionary shift from the knowledge-based economies to intelligence economies. Significant financial investment is needed to develop core technologies and applications for an IoA platform. Once developed, interdisciplinary skills, and trusted partner networks are needed to be successful in this emerging intelligence economy, impossible to achieve by any single player. Entrepreneurial ecosystems – communities of new organizations focused on the creation of new products and services – will be able to attain competitive advantage in the new intelligence economy. Agents managed by IoA platforms, integrated into entrepreneurial ecosystems (collectives), will contribute to the collective intelligence of these ecosystems, broadening firms to collectives in the 4IR. These ecosystems must be heterarchical, where entrepreneurs, agents, functions, controls and processes rise to authority depending on how the context evolves – a complex adaptive system.

---

19 Thanduxolo Nkala, 2019.

There are challenges to sustainable growth in IoA-based collectives. These collectives have to collectively maintain a chain of sustainability[20] in order to attain, and sustain competitive advantage in the knowledge, digital and new intelligence economies of the 4IR.

Applying Kurt April's chain of sustainability to collectives rather than firms, there are dynamic relationships between collective resources, the capabilities of the collectives and the competitive advantage of the collectives in the 4IR. This chain of sustainability continuously evolves from the interactions between the individual resources and the interactions between the resources and the dynamically changing hyperconnected environments.

The South African Technology Innovation Agency (TIA), Department of Science and Innovation, is a funding body that has the objective of stimulating and intensifying technological innovation in order to improve economic growth and the quality of life of all South Africans by developing and exploiting technological innovations. TIA facilitates the translation of South Africa's knowledge resources into sustainable socio-economic opportunities, providing South Africa with appropriate and effective support for innovation. These innovations must have high social and economic impact, supporting and enhancing technological innovation in Africa, and globally, through partnership initiatives. TIA provided funding for the Artificial Mind Engine 2016 - 2018, to develop this generic agent-based cognitive engine that is able to address the volume, velocity and variety challenges associated with the Internet of Things (IoT) and Big Data environments. Once developed, local and global entrepreneurial ecosystems were formed to successfully integrate the AME platform into the emerging 4IR.

Practising responsible entrepreneurship, we integrated our IoA platform into a local community safety entrepreneurial ecosystem as well as a global health epidemic control entrepreneurial ecosystem.

Community safety entrepreneurial ecosystem

One of the transformational visions of the United Nations, in their agenda for sustainable development is "a world free of fear and violence" and "a world where human habitats are safe, resilient and sustainable". According to Goal 11 of their agenda: "By 2030, provide access to safe, affordable, accessible and sustainable transport systems for all, improving road safety, ..., with special attention to the needs of those in vulnerable situations, women, children, persons with disabilities and older persons...". According to the World Health Organisation, more than 90% of road traffic

---

20 April, 2002.

deaths occur in low- and middle-income countries. Road traffic injury death rates are highest in the African region, and road traffic injuries are the leading cause of death for children and young adults aged 5-29 years.

Crime in South Africa is rising, and people feel unsafe – in their streets, their parks and their homes. The latest crime stats revealed 21 022 murders in the 2018/19 financial year – 686 more than the previous year, and an increase of 3.4%. President Ramaphosa commented that the situation in South Africa is "quite bad".

Our community safety collective, illustrated in Figure 2.2, consists of the AME IoA platform integrated into control rooms, continuously monitoring video feeds and issuing early warnings to control rooms and social media. These early warnings include situations that endanger the safety of citizens in urban environments, human settlements and farms.

IoT helps enabled security devices to deliver real-time security alerts, which can positively change the landscape of physical security protocols. The presence of IoT means that data about a particular physical environment can be processed and relayed much faster. If access control devices are able to communicate with surveillance cameras and other security deterrents, it means that community safety control rooms will receive risk alerts right when they happen.

Our community safety collective is a South African ecosystem that improves the safeguarding of citizens in their home or work environments. Our IoA platform provides automated assistance through "collector" software agents that tap into CCTV streams to constantly monitor the behaviors so as to timeously identify risk situations in order to safeguard lives. Our ecosystem consists of communities to be safeguarded, as well as different firms, specialising in the IoA platform, IoT devices and control rooms.

Our HUB is a Virtual Control Room that will seamlessly integrate into community safety command and control rooms, with the goal of maximising safety and minimizing opportunities for crime.

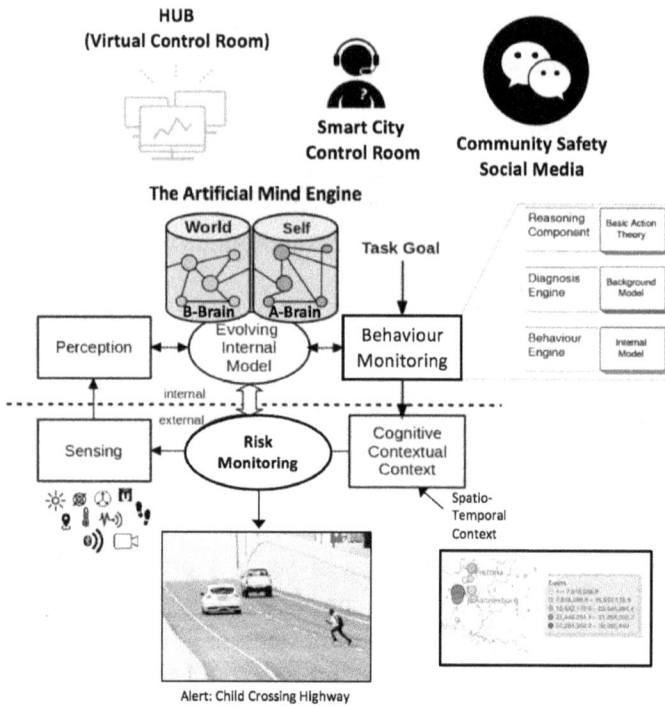

Figure 2.2: Community Safety Collective

Epidemic control entrepreneurial ecosystem

Our health collective includes the use of our IoA agents in collaboration with the Stop TB Partnership, a UNOPS organization, and multiple country health organizations to find missing patients in underserved communities. As an example, for TB alone, around 4 million patients are missed every year. Our platform provides a set of practical and cost-effective intelligent software agents to help find those missing patients, screen and enter those affected into a treatment program.

Epcon uses the IoA platform to learn from historical data, processes and things to add an intelligence component to augment reference data and variables. The platform uses distributed Bayesian reasoning methods and allows for the identification of cause-effect patterns in complex datasets spanning multiple variables that may have hidden relationships. Through this model, one can quantify risk at the population and individual level, enabling data visualization and inference queries on a set of observed variables from relationships learned from historical data.

Given contextual information and data generated from a region, the platform will dynamically produce program insights, recommendations and actionable output to enable more targeted case finding (CF), optimize country health resources and increase program yield. Such output is visualized at the program steering level or pushed towards stakeholders at all levels of the National TB Program office.

The complexity for the above mentioned collective is that it needs to interact with various stakeholders and parties active in the local health ecosystem. These members can be considered agencies who in turn may, or may not, deploy a set of agents interacting with different platforms, people, processes and things.

In this process, data privacy plays a role, IP, interoperability, ethical clearance, and potential sharing of income or costs.

Besides the legal, costs and interconnectivity challenges, underserved communities often add an additional complexity in terms of technology readiness. Some countries' health organizations may operate on paper-based survey or registration mechanisms, while others may use digital devices or connected agents. This challenge also offers great opportunities, as the low cost infrastructure to implement hyperconnected agents and sometimes limited regulatory requirements can hasten the process to implementation. Governments are often in favor of piloting projects that advance human development and health through technology. Similar events have taken place in the financial markets where the use of mobile money is more widespread in Low and Middle Income Countries.

Universal health coverage (UHC)

A main target in the Global Public Health domain is to provide Universal Health Coverage to all. This objective is not only challenged by economic inequality, but is also affected by the geographical realities and location-aware context in which people live. The IoA can help achieve this goal through its efficient use of distributed and hyperconnected agents and agencies. Applications, and connected medical devices, can operate autonomously, using patient sensors, location-aware context and distributed intelligence.

One such example in our health collective is the availability of computer aided diagnostics for chest x-rays. We provide this feature for free so that remote physicians and radiologists have the ability to receive an instant diagnostic result for a given chest x-ray through a mobile application.

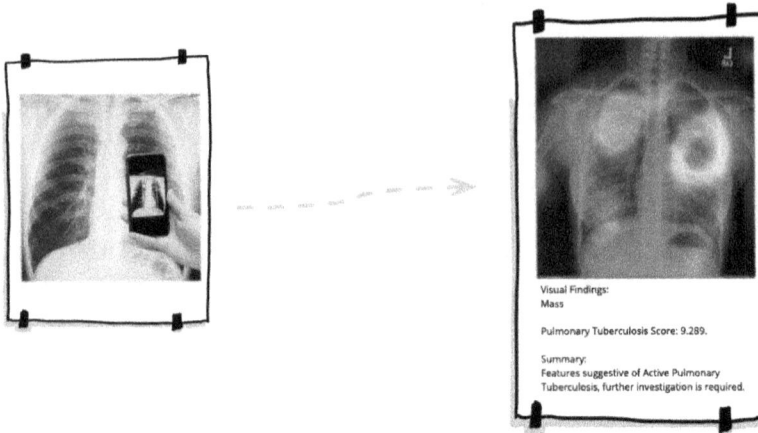

Visual Findings:
Mass

Pulmonary Tuberculosis Score: 9.289.

Summary:
Features suggestive of Active Pulmonary
Tuberculosis, further investigation is required.

Financial risks and return

For the private sector and entrepreneurs to be involved in the global public health collective, with a focus on social impact, the financial models are complex and the potential returns are minimal. As many financing mechanisms are focused on the building of local capacity and last mile health strengthening, the investment in the use of collective agents and the augmentation of reference data through intelligence and context is not widely accepted and/or recognized.

This requires creative financing mechanisms that make use of philanthropic funding, grants, innovation funds and ultimately local governments. Entrepreneurs and private sector collectives active in Global Public Health for social impact, ideally creating hybrid business models whereby part of the revenues can be generated through more sustainable segments, and part focused on lower margin, social impact budgets for GPH in Low and Middle Income Countries.

Conclusion

We described how we implemented Marvin Minsky's vision of "Minds are what Brains do" in the 4IR, through ecosystems of collective "Minds" that are collective "Brains" that are able to "do good" for humankind. We described how we implemented the Artificial Mind Engine (AME), an Internet of Agents platform. We implemented "Brains" that "do good" through Bayesian agents that collectively implement distributed Bayesian networks as hyperstructures that continually evolve through incremental learning from feedback loops from processes and people. AME achieves intelligence through its A-Brains and B-Brains. A-Brain agencies (collectors), are situated and embodied right at the edge closest to the data sources – tapping into the input streams in the hyperconnected environment and continuously inferring beliefs about and learning from the latest environmental states. B-Brains agencies inspect the beliefs of the A-Brains and do and act according to these beliefs.

The B-Brain competence agencies' actions are part of dynamic interaction with the interconnected entities in their environment (embodiment). The agencies are observed to be intelligent (intelligence). The intelligence of our agencies emerges from the interaction between the agencies and the hyperconnected environment, and between themselves and other agencies (emergence).

We have described the challenges entrepreneurs face to transform digital and knowledge economies to attain and sustain competitive advantage in emerging intelligence economies. We furthermore described how we practise responsible entrepreneurship in these emerging economies by integrating our Bayesian Agencies into communities and partner networks in order to "do good" in the 4IR.

Using our Artificial Mind Engine, we created a community safety ecosystem and a health ecosystem. The community safety ecosystem consists of our IoA platform integrated into control rooms, continuously monitoring video feeds and issuing early warnings to social media platforms of situations that endangers the safety of citizens in urban environments, human settlements and farms. The health ecosystem includes the use of our IoA platform in collaboration with the StopTB Partnership and country health organizations, to find missing patients in underserved communities.

Chapter 3

Social Enterprise and its Contextual Challenges

Ndidi Okonkwo Nwuneli

Abstract

There are growing communities of social entrepreneurs in Africa committed to addressing the Continent's most pressing challenges in the health, education, energy, sanitation, food security and nutrition, transportation, water and climate change landscapes. However, they face two key challenges: 1) obstacles to scaling linked to a range of contextual challenges, including the lack of credible data, the heterogeneity within and across countries, the fragmented ecosystems as well as significant talent, infrastructure and financing gaps; and 2) the poor enabling environment and support from the government which often frustrates the efforts of founders and their teams. The chapter explores these two challenges in detail and also introduces four prerequisites for successful scaling. These include a) developing compelling business models that are demand-driven, can demonstrate measurable impact, are simple, engage the community, leverage technology and are low-cost; b) attracting and retaining mission-driven high achievers; c) demonstrating investment-readiness by implementing strong governance, financial management and communication strategies; and d) building partnerships with key stakeholders in the public, private and nonprofit sectors.

By exploring the challenges and prerequisites for scaling in Africa, this chapter provides specific recommendations for governments, development partners and social entrepreneurs who are committed to build sustainable social enterprises. It also provides practical examples of successful scaling efforts that can serve to inspire and propel more strategic interventions to drive social and economic transformation on the Continent.

Introduction

There are growing communities of social entrepreneurs in Africa committed to addressing the Continent's most pressing challenges in the health, education, energy, sanitation, food security and nutrition, transportation, water and climate change landscapes. Some focus on issue areas, or regions, others on specific demographics such as women and youth, and they strive to leverage innovation and technology to deliver their services and enhance their efficiency, effectiveness and impact.

Many operate as nonprofits, others as for-profits or hybrids, and their work is being supported by international and local funders, educational institutions and networks including Ashoka, Acumen Fund, the Bertha Center for Social Innovation & Entrepreneurship, Draper Richards Kaplan Foundation, Echoing Green, Ford Foundation, LEAP Africa's Social Innovators Program. Lagos Business School's Sustainability Center, Schwab Foundation for Social Entrepreneurship, Skoll Foundation and others. Their work is being propelled by the rapid advances in mobile technology which facilitates m-health, m-education, payment systems and mobile money and they are gradually being supported by a range of initiatives including accelerators, hubs, prizes, and fellowships.

The biggest economies in Africa – Nigeria, South Africa, Egypt, Kenya and Morocco – boost a sizeable share of social enterprises and an emerging ecosystem to support their work. However, the largest concentration of social entrepreneurs is in Kenya propelled by the mPesa revolution and the innovative payment systems that it supports. In addition, at the last count, over 50 impact investors have operations in Kenya to provide support to these social entrepreneurs.

In spite, of these promising trends, social enterprises operating in Africa face two key challenges: 1) obstacles to scaling linked to a range of contextual challenges, as well as limited access to talent and catalytic capital; and 2) the poor enabling environment and support from the government which often frustrates the efforts of founders and their teams.

This chapter will explore these challenges in detail, and also provide insights into prerequisites for surmounting them in the African context.

Scaling challenges

Despite the growing number of social enterprises across the African Continent, the vast majority operate as micro, small and medium-sized enterprises, reaching hundreds of beneficiaries, instead of the millions that desperately need their high-impact interventions. Their small sizes also limit their ability to leverage economies of scale and command significant influence in shaping policies and exerting positive influence to address the root causes of problems that confront their communities and countries.

Contextual Challenges: While scaling challenges are not unique to African social enterprises, there are some contextual issues that further exacerbate the reality on the ground. As outlined in the book – *Social Innovation in Africa: A practical guide for scaling impact*, published by Routledge in 2016, African social enterprises face at least four contextual challenges.

- First, the **lack of credible data for local communities, countries and regions**, slows down the processes for planning, piloting and scaling social innovations and hinders the ability of key stakeholders to measure their impact on society. For example, many countries in Africa have not conducted a population census in decades, making it extremely difficult to understand where the pockets of needs are and how to design interventions to fill them. When high-impact interventions are made, it is difficult to measure impact given the dearth of credible baselines or data on control groups. Similarly, credible and comprehensive information on the number of social enterprises in a given country, the sectors in which they operate, and the focus of their interventions is largely unavailable. This makes it difficult for organizations to find each other and to explore collaboration opportunities. Funders also struggles to identify which organization to support, further worsening the financing gaps.

- Second, the **heterogeneity within and across countries**, which includes significant diversity in colonial histories, languages, religions, cultures, community assets, and social development, essentially means that there is "no single story," and "no one-size fits all," interventions. This essentially makes it difficult to scale interventions without understanding the context and adjusting the business model to fit community realities and needs. Innovations have to be tweaked or significantly altered to enable scaling from one community to another, which is not only more expensive, but also slows the scaling process. For example, Nigeria has over 350 languages, and each ethnic group has its own unique culture of engagement, and a distinct group of influencers. When a social enterprise is scaling its leadership program for young girls from one community to another, in Lagos they could offer the training in English but may need to engage with a government official for partnership approvals especially if they are working in public schools. In Katsina, the program may have to be offered as an out of school program and in the Hausa language. In addition, instead of a government official, a traditional or religious leader would need to offer a formal endorsement and support for the program for full legitimacy and success. These differences in program implementation and execution will definitely increase the cost of engagement (e.g. requirement for printing program materials in two different languages), and the time required to build the relationships. Social entrepreneurs working in most African communities have to contend with these realities to ensure high-impact and sustainable interventions.

- Third, the **fragmented ecosystems,** in almost every sector, especially the agricultural, education and health landscapes limit the ability of entrepreneurs to reach large numbers of people efficiently and effectively. Consider the agriculture sector, where there are at least 33 million smallholders operating on the continent.[1] This essentially means that social enterprises that want to scale in this sector can only do so by working with farmer clusters as opposed to individual farmers. The process of creating clusters of farmers takes time and requires significant efforts to build trust among these groups and financial resources to cover the costs of multiple engagements with the farmers. These same interventions are required in the healthcare and education sectors, especially in countries where there are more "private" and unregistered schools, pharmacies and hospitals than official government-owned or managed entities. Entrepreneurs attempting to lead change in these communities essentially have to identify and engage with them individually, convincing each stakeholder to work in formal or informal groups to reduce the costs of engagement.

- Fourth, there are significant **talent, infrastructure and financing gaps** which limit scaling on the African Continent. According to the World Bank,[2] 48 countries in Sub-Saharan Africa generate approximately the same amount of power as Spain. This significant power deficit has limited technology innovations that require electricity, spurring the emergence of off-grid solutions. In addition, only one-third of Africans living in rural areas are within two kilometres of an all-season road, compared with two-thirds of the population in other developing regions. This, in turn, makes it extremely difficult and expensive to extend healthcare, education, and agriculture innovations to communities in rural areas. Sadly, with underdeveloped distribution and marketing systems, social entrepreneurs essentially have to work along all aspects of the value chain, filling gaps that ordinarily would not exist in other markets to reach customers or beneficiaries.

Beyond the infrastructure gaps, **talent and financing gaps** frustrate the efforts of social enterprises. The weak educational system in many African countries essentially means that there is tremendous competition from multinationals, large indigenous businesses, and the government for the most qualified and

---

1   Plaizier, 2016.
2   Eberhard, Rosnes, Shkaratan & Vennemo, 2011.

competent graduates. Typically, social enterprises, with their limited budgets are unable to attract these individuals. This fight for talent has taken on new global dimensions, with countries such as Canada and Germany targeting Africa's best talent, and creating another brain drain. Social entrepreneurs that are committed to scaling have to develop creative strategies for attracting and retaining talent, instituting fellowship and rotational programs, and investing in local and international training and other perks to sustain the loyalty and commitment of their team members.

Many African social enterprises struggle to obtain financing to scale their efforts, when compared to their counterparts operating in Europe or the United States. There are a broad range of financing options available to social entrepreneurs, depending on whether they operate for-profit, nonprofit or hybrid organizations. These financing options range from fee for service and cross-subsidization models to external funding sources such as grants, awards, fellowships, challenge funds, crowd funding, impact investments and loans.

In-spite of the plethora of funding sources, most local social innovators struggle to obtain financing for their ventures, while funders complain that they cannot find initiatives that are investment ready. Indeed, external funders are only interested in engaging with organizations that have strong credibility, governance structures, financial management systems and controls and can demonstrate the ability to utilize the funds to achieve results.

Sadly, many African social enterprises are not "investment ready". They typically do not have clear theories of change and compelling business models rooted in credible measurement and evaluation systems. In addition, many lack financial management systems, annual audited financial statements and clear and transparent systems and controls. Many social enterprises have not developed and implemented creative communications strategies to tell their stories and leveraged local and international networks to enhance their visibility so that we can attract the same attention and support as our international counterparts.

It is also important to recognize that part of the burden of funding access also falls on the impact investors and development partners, who have to devote their time and energy to finding and supporting promising social enterprises through the process of becoming investment ready. These funders and investors have to step outside their geographic and racial comfort zones to ensure that they create a level playing field for African social enterprises, who often complain that they face discrimination and unfair biases versus Americans or Europeans operating in Africa.

Poor enabling environment

The primary responsibility of African governments in this context is to create an enabling environment for social entrepreneurs to establish and scale innovations that will transform communities and countries. They are expected to reduce the hurdles associated with registering entities, obtaining patents and trademarks, and ensuring intellectual property rights protection. In addition, their role is to minimize the corruption and red tape associated with normal business operations and to encourage development partners, the private sector and citizens to invest in social innovators and provide financial and in-kind donations to the social sector.

While a few African governments recognize this role and have even introduced innovation funds, challenge grants, incubators, technology parks and accelerators, in partnership with the private sector and civil society to spur social entrepreneurship and innovation, the vast majority have historically not supported social enterprises. In fact, many countries have neglected to shape policy on critical issues, such as intellectual property protection, and to provide support infrastructure and programs to ensure that social enterprises in their countries can survive and even thrive. In some countries, social enterprises are actually suppressed by governments who consider them a threat, especially those organizations focused on democracy and human rights.

For social enterprises to thrive on the African Continent, it is imperative that African governments recognize the critical role that they have to play in creating an enabling environment for social enterprises. This includes:

- Designing and implementing a transparent and credible process for identifying promising social innovations at the grassroots that need to be showcased and celebrated, and then working with the local government and state government agencies to identify opportunities for supporting these enterprises with their scaling efforts.

- Addressing the data gaps in many countries, by strengthening in-country national research capabilities to ensure regular and credible census, and human development reports which would provide effective information for designing relevant and timely interventions and baselines for measuring impact in the social and economic landscape.

- Creating effective regulations, including clear and transparent annual financial and activity reporting requirements for social entrepreneurs to minimize fraud and maximize impact, which will invariably enhance the credibility of the sector.

- Creating and implementing laws, regulations and tax incentives which encourage development agencies, companies, communities and individuals to invest in, donate to and partner with social enterprises. The governments need to develop and implement policies focused on tax, rebates or credits, subsidies and reporting requirements, including setting guidelines for banks and institutional investors to articulate the social and environmental impact of their investments. Clearly this can only be accomplished in an environment where there are high levels of tax compliance and the systems and structures are sophisticated enough to track and identify false claims.

In addition, African governments need to actively address some of the contextual issues raised above, including bridging the serious infrastructure gaps that exist in many countries. More specifically, they have to ensure energy access and road networks linking rural and urban communities and invest in primary and secondary education to ensure talent for the social enterprise sector.

Prerequisites for success

Engagement with over eighty of the most vibrant and high-impact social enterprises operating on the African Continent and funders in the sector, as part of research for "Social Innovation in Africa: a practical guide for scaling impact", reveal four critical prerequisites for surmounting the contextual and enabling environment challenges described above. They include the following:

1. **Compelling business models:** Social entrepreneurs who surmount challenges and scale have compelling business models defined by six critical components: they are demand-driven, can demonstrate measurable impact, are simple, engage the community, leverage technology and are low-cost. These six components, shown in Figure 3.1, differentiate initiatives which die at the pilot phase or when the donor funding ends from initiatives that are sustainable and able to achieve scale, spanning communities and even countries.

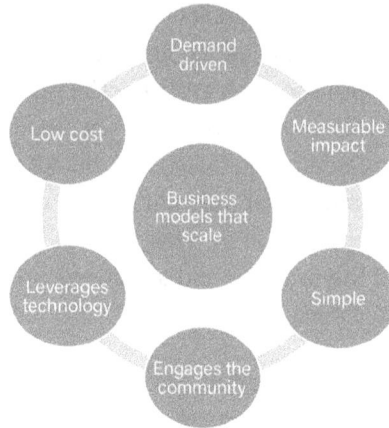

Figure 3.1: Components of Business Models[3]

Innovations that are demand-driven essentially meet the needs of individuals who value the product or service and are willing to contribute their time and financial resources, regardless of how minimal, to obtain it. In addition, the innovators have determined the most cost-effective approaches to deliver at scale and developed effective systems and structures to support their scaling effort. They often utilize simple payment mechanisms leveraging mobile technology, and support from microfinance partners, where applicable. These tools are highly dependent on robust data tracking systems to gauge impact and usage.

Two examples from the energy sector that demonstrate the power of demand-driven and sustainable business models are M-KOPA Solar and Off Grid Electric, which both operate in East Africa. They provide solar solutions to over 800,000 households using a pay-as-you go model and have demonstrated the tremendous potential at the bottom of pyramid.

2. **Talent for scaling:** Talent on the African Continent remains a huge constraint for all growth sectors given the weak education systems and the global opportunities that are available to the best and brightest. As a result, successful social entrepreneurs have to invest in attracting and retaining a dream team composed of mission-driven high achievers. They also invest in recruiting a committed and independent Board of Directors, and engaging volunteers, short-term consultants, and fellows.

    Organizations such as LEAP Africa in Nigeria, EDUCATE! in Uganda and Sanergy in Kenya have designed and implemented creative strategies for attracting, retaining, and developing talent. They have also invested in building cultures of

---

3   Nwuneli, 2016.

innovation and excellence, which attract individuals from the private sector to their organizations. They offer tailored training programs, travel fellowships and significant job responsibilities for their team members and have also developed modular approaches for scaling talent.

3. **Funding for innovation:** Social innovators operating in Africa who obtain financing work diligently to establish and communicate a strong business case and theory of change, backed by sound data that establishes a clear need and sustainable demand. They also amplify their impact work through creative communication strategies to raise broad-based awareness and effectively differentiate themselves. In addition, they demonstrate strong transparent systems and structures, a culture of ethics and accountability, attractive return on investment ratios and exit options for impact investors, where applicable. The One Acre Fund, the African Leadership Academy, Ashesi, mKOPA and Bridge International Academies are often referred to as "donor darlings." They have all successfully raised funds from local and international organizations by demonstrating their investment readiness, instituting strong governance structures and financial systems and controls, measuring and publicizing their impact and conducting annual external audits. Their fundraising success has also been linked to their ability to design and implement strong branding and marketing campaigns and to build strong local and international relationships.

4. **Partnerships with key stakeholders in the public, private and nonprofit sectors:** Social innovators cannot achieve impact and scale without cross-sector collaborations, rooted in shared values and a desire to achieve collective impact. This is especially relevant in sectors such as health and education that are highly regulated. Sadly, there are few examples of partnerships in the African context largely linked to significant distrust among actors, the intense competition for the perceived 'small pie' of resources and support structures and the fear of giving up control. Partnerships are also challenging in an environment where there is a high level of bureaucracy and red tape within government institutions which ordinarily should serve as catalysts for collaborations and innovations. In reality, social innovators who successfully collaborate in this context, actively map the 'ecosystem' determining which stakeholders can serve as champions, opponents or even beneficiaries. They then develop strategies for interfacing with all key actors, proactively shaping their ecosystems and forming strategic cross-sector collaborations that foster impact and scaling. Action Health Incorporated, a leading social enterprise in Nigeria was able to introduce sexuality education into secondary schools across Lagos and eventually in many states in Nigeria based on its strong partnership with the Ministry of Education at the state and national levels, and its ability to build trust with key stakeholders. Similarly, Ikamva

Youth in South Africa partners with key influencers and government officials in the education ecosystems in the communities in which it operates. These partnerships have enabled it to scale quickly and to have significant impact on the educational outcomes of its "learners".

Clearly, the ability to build strong business models, attract and retain talent and funding and build partnerships with other social enterprises, government agencies and the private sector have enabled social enterprises operating on the African Continent to surmount contextual obstacles and to scale their impact.

The future

With Africa's population projected to grow to 2.4 billion by 2050, over 70% under the age of 30 years old, with 60% in cities and towns, there is an urgent need for more social enterprises, operating at scale. These organizations will essentially need to develop creative and innovative solutions in the education, healthcare, economic development, gender, sanitation, security, energy, transportation, climate, food security and nutrition, and housing sectors to meet the needs of the masses of people.

These social enterprises also need an enabling environment to thrive, which requires that governments recognize their role as a critical third sector of the economy and institute the policies and programs required to support them. Ultimately, the founders and their teams will need to invest in building strong, ethical and transparent organizations that drive impact at scale, proving that African social enterprises can lead transformation in communities, and propel the growth and development that many of our countries desperately need.

Chapter 4

A Model for The Utilisation of Networks and Leveraging of The Economic Benefits of Migration Capital in Emerging Markets

Dr. Wanda Chunnett

Abstract

In trying to address the thorny issue of refugee integration into developing economies in a positive way, this chapter discusses a model that extends from the arrival of the migrant entrepreneur in the host country to the establishment of a sustainable, job-creating business. It examines both policy and practice and addresses the requirements of multiple stakeholders including the refugee, national and local authorities and potential local partners. The underlying assumption is that, contrary to the populist view that refugees are a burden on the communities where they settle, there is an alternative, mutually beneficial outcome where both refugee and local partner can synergistically develop and deliver economic benefits.

Introduction

South African migration and asylum policies post 1994 have been described as progressive but passive.[1] Migrants are allowed to enter the country but are not provided with settlement assistance and preference is given to local candidates for formal job opportunities by employers complying with policies such as the 2003 Broad Based Black Economic Empowerment Act (amended in 2013).

Bourdieu stated that an individual must have the requisite levels of economic, knowledge, legal and social capital to have the locus of power that will enable activities such as the establishment of a sustainable business.[2] However, as Nail noted, the often forced movement of migrants from their homeland "is not simply the deprivation of territorial status (i.e., removal from the land); it includes three other major types of social deprivation: political, juridical, and economic."[3] This implies that legal capital (political and juridical) must be established before social integration can

---

1   Handmaker, 2001; Landau & Amit, 2014 & Parker, 2013.
2   Bourdieu, 1985.
3   Nail, 2015:35.

take place and the migrant can attain the required economic capital to engage in entrepreneurial activities and create employment opportunities.

Rather than rejecting refugees and other migrants based on a lack of local, formal employment opportunities, a more equitable solution may, therefore, be to assess if these migrants can contribute to economic development and job creation in underdeveloped, high-unemployment regions of the country.

Understanding migration capital

While migrants as a source of job creation may be an aspirational ideal, the practicalities of how it can be achieved are not simple. The migrant influx into Sub-Saharan Africa is younger, less skilled and more culturally diverse than that found in other parts of the world.[4] Even so, researchers have identified viable economic networks among Congolese, Rwandese, Somalian and South-Sudanese refugee communities.[5] Members of these groups demonstrated considerable entrepreneurial skills within their own communities. These took the form of active trading networks and brokering interactions between refugees and their home country, including setting-up of systems to receive transfers of funds from family members.

The economic activity is not limited to within the migrant community, however. In their research on refugees in Tanzania, Kenya and Uganda, Betts & Omata[6] found that migrants spent an average of seventeen years in camps, which limited their economic activities in the host country. During this time the camps became mini cities in their own right and economies developed that benefited not only the refugees but also the villages and areas surrounding the camp and, in some cases, the broader, host country.

These examples highlight the existence of a potential for migrants to deliver economic benefit to their host country in addition to the more common notion of being a burden and drain on resources. Kloosterman & Rath[7] confirmed this when they found that the commonly held notion that migrant businesses are simple, labor-intensive, survival enterprises is being increasingly questioned as it becomes apparent that the migrants moving from less developed countries to more highly developed areas may well have skills that they can and do exercise, given the correct conditions.

---

4   Betts & Omata, 2015:3.
5   Crush, 2009; Whitaker, 2002; Verwimp & van Bavel, 2013; Verwimp & Maystadt, 2015; Betts & Omata, 2015.
6   Betts & Omata, 2015.
7   Kloosterman & Rath, 2003.

The migrants' exposure to and understanding of transnational opportunities and new, informal opportunities, for example, offer the potential for knowledge and economic capital transfer to local entrepreneurs within a business partnership relationship.[8]

In their study of women migrants from the DRC and Zimbabwe, Smit & Rugunanan[9] examined the challenges that respondents experienced trying to find employment opportunities. While their focus was on formal employment, they noted that the barriers to establishment of small businesses were far greater than the migrants had experienced in their home country. A lack of start-up capital and onerous permitting and licensing requirements were cited as the most significant impediments to start-up of businesses.

The proposition that it is possible to transfer and build on economic capital within migrant communities and between migrant and local networks is contentious, as Bourdieu claims that relationships are regarded as the outcome of individual power rather than the cause.[10] The possibility has, however, been raised by Atkinson[11] who notes that, in a world of "...international travel, global awareness and technological development where geographical movement has transformed the nature of societies, an additional capital needs to be added: a 'mobility capital' encapsulating differential capacity to move"

There are examples of other constrained entrepreneurs who are the beneficiaries of such networks. One such programme is the Siyakhula Programme, whereby the Women's Development Business (WDB) provides financing to rural women entrepreneurs who are considered to be "unbankable" by mainstream institutions. The programme is based on the Development Caravan model that was established by South African Women in Dialogue (SAWID) as part of their initiatives to achieve rural poverty eradication.[12]

While the Development Caravan programme targets poverty alleviation in rural, South African communities, many of the principles could apply to migrant community groups and the development of entrepreneurs as well. The model of a trained, trusted, community group advisor interacting with a family and providing the necessary linkages to local knowledge and resources reflects many of the requirements that the migrants have. This has significance for migrant groups, where people may, superficially, resemble each other, speak the same language and have migrated to the same place, but may react very differently to opportunities presented to them,

---

8   Kloosterman & Rath, 2003; Lucas, 2004; Orozco, 2008; Chrysostome, 2010; Betts & Omata, 2015.
9   Smit & Rugunanan, 2014.
10   Bourdieu, 1988; Atkinson, 2016.
11   Atkinson, 2016.
12   Ministry: Finance Republic of South Africa, 2008.

depending on the connections or links that they have to others within the group or environment. It also implies a requirement for the host country entity to scrutinise the individual and understand their relationship within the networks before engaging and committing resources.

Key enablers

The fact that a business has been started is no guarantee that it will add sustainable, economic benefit to the local, regional or national economy. Kloosterman & Rath[13] identified three requirements for sustainable migrant businesses:

1. There must be opportunities on the demand side.

2. The opportunities must be accessible and not require extensive capital inputs.

3. The opportunities must be "palpable" and embedded in the community where the migrant established the business.[14]

Waldinger et al.[15] emphasised the dynamic nature of these opportunities and that they require ongoing interaction between migrant and the host community, including access to information (social capital), as migrants must interact with the local community in order to have the scale of opportunity required to meet the Kloosterman & Rath requirements and are often language or culturally challenged when moving to a new country.

They also highlight training and skills requirements (knowledge capital), as many migrants have no exposure to even basic business skills before migrating.

In a study of sustainable constrained, migrant businesses in South Africa, Chunnett[16] has identified enabling characteristics that give migrant entrepreneurs the ability to move, in a phased fashion, towards business sustainability. In the process of doing this, the migrants followed the establishment sequence of conventional entrepreneurs, post an extended establishment phase. This is illustrated in Figure 4.1, which lists the variables (causes) and enablers within each of the phases over the lifetime of the migrant entrepreneur.

---

13 Kloosterman & Rath, 2003,
14 Ibid, 31.
15 Waldinger et al, 1990.
16 Chunnett, 2018.

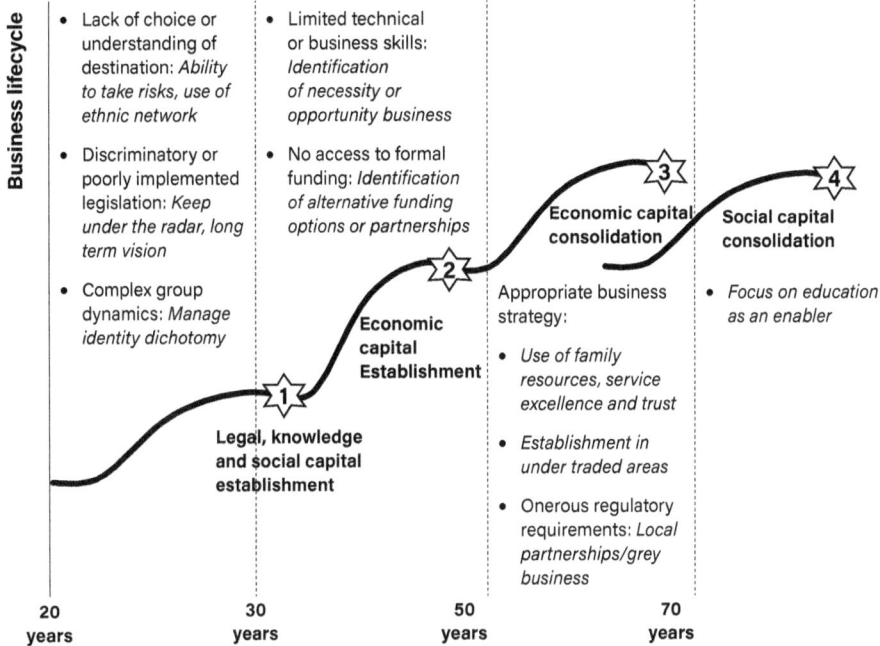

Business lifecycle

- Lack of choice or understanding of destination: *Ability to take risks, use of ethnic network*

- Discriminatory or poorly implemented legislation: *Keep under the radar, long term vision*

- Complex group dynamics: *Manage identity dichotomy*

- Limited technical or business skills: *Identification of necessity or opportunity business*

- No access to formal funding: *Identification of alternative funding options or partnerships*

Legal, knowledge and social capital establishment

1

Economic capital Establishment

2

Appropriate business strategy:

- Use of family resources, service excellence and trust

- Establishment in under traded areas

- Onerous regulatory requirements: *Local partnerships/grey business*

Economic capital consolidation

3

Social capital consolidation

4

- *Focus on education as an enabler*

20 years   30 years   50 years   70 years

Figure 4.1: Typical migrant business establishment continuum

It is not enough for a migrant to be determined, be technically able, have an appetite for risk, be able to identify or create an opportunity and have access to funding, as might be the case for a local entrepreneur in an emerging market economy.[17] The migrant entrepreneur requires an additional capital, termed 'migration capital', which offers the leverage potential for the host to realise economic benefit from the migrant. Migration capital is what allows constrained migrants such as refugees to survive extremely onerous conditions, where their lives, emotional well-being and safety may be threatened. It is built over time and, amongst other traits, allows the migrant to assess potential risk and react very quickly as well as identify transnational opportunities.

A defining feature of migration capital is that, unlike the capitals noted by Bourdieu,[18] not all the components that make up migration capital are held by the individual. While the view that the host country takes of any migrant should be based on individual merit, practicality, politics and experience, indicates that this is not necessarily the case. Instead capital, both positive and negative, is attributed to the individual, based on a stereotypical perception of the group. Migrants who may be highly technically competent but unable to speak the local language, may have their qualifications

---

17   Birch, 1987; McMillan & Woodruff, 2002; Alvarez & Barney, 2007; Block & Sandner, 2009 & Herrington et al., 2014.
18   Bourdieu, 1985.

and their entrepreneurial potential ignored by overworked local authorities who are processing hundreds of similar-looking applications, from members of the same group who do not generally have these competencies.

It is such individual characteristics that define migrant entrepreneurs, much as the actors within the network defined by Wellman & Berkowitz.[19] Characteristics of entrepreneurial capital that migrants may display include:

1. The ability to manage dichotomy and multiple identities that allows the migrant entrepreneur to transition back and forth between the host community and establish a mainstream business while managing the complex, cultural relationships within the migrant group.

2. A transnational mind-set that provides a platform for the entrepreneur to identify opportunities within a regional and, often, global context.

3. An ability to understand, survive and thrive on the edge of legality and to operate successfully in the grey zone that local entrepreneurs may not be able to understand.

Chunnett[20] found that the limitation on the degree of development of migration capital among the entrepreneurs depends on where they find themselves within the network, what opportunities are presented to them to create linkages outside of their immediate connections and their interdependencies within the group.

Leveraging migration capital

As the migrant entrepreneur is typically constrained by an extended pre-business establishment phase, the migration capital model, which is the proposed model of how the host country can unlock the value offered by the potential migrant entrepreneur, focuses on the social establishment and early business establishment phases. It focuses on a variety of public sector and private party network partnerships that leverage the migration capital of involuntary migrant entrepreneurs, both as individuals and as part of their group. The aim is to facilitate the creation of sustainable local migrant business partnerships that offer opportunities for accelerated economic growth for both the involuntary migrant and the local entrepreneur as well as local job creation.

The model relies on a series of weak and strong network connections that include national authority, local authority, NGOs, migrant group networks, local entrepreneurs and the individual migrant entrepreneurs, as illustrated in Figure 4.2.

---

19 Wellman & Berkowitz, 1988.
20 Chunnett, 2018.

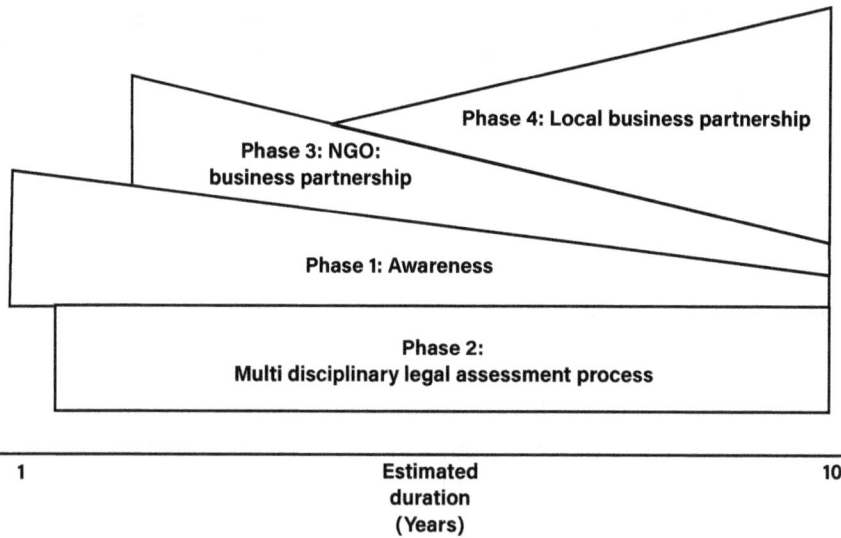

Figure 4.2: The migration capital optimisation model

The model comprises four phases, over the average 10 years that it would take a migrant to establish a business. Network connections emerge, come to prominence and fade, as and when required, to meet the requirements of both the migrant entrepreneur and the host country.

Phase 1: Raising awareness

The emphasis of much contemporary media reporting is on the burden that migrants place on host country resources. Current policies, populist press and political views are still driven by a donor view that favours exclusionist political agendas rather than encouraging integration. This is exacerbated by the substantial number of businesses that have based their operating models on providing refugee and involuntary migrant support in terms of aid programmes.[21]

Homan's[22] finding that networks will be maintained and social exchanges sustained as long as both parties see a benefit or potential benefit in the exchange, implies that if the notion of the "refugee burden", as termed by Zetter[23] will remain firmly rooted in the policy vocabulary of governments as public figures continue to gain more political mileage from expressing concern for the situation rather than embracing the possibility of migrants as potential economic contributors.

---

21 Fielden, 2008; African Union, 2012 & Zetter, 2012.
22 Homan, 1958.
23 Zetter, 2012.

Only once the concept that emerging market economies can realise economic benefit from the integration of involuntary migrant entrepreneurs is supported by political will, does the narrative change and the paradigm shift, as has been evidenced in countries such as Uganda and Tanzania.[24]

The ongoing process of raising this awareness at multiple levels provides the basis for the model and extends throughout the lifespan. The first partnership would be one between government institutions such as the African Union (AU), academic institutions or bodies and international or local NGOs.

Many local NGOs have credibility and, based on this, considerable influence in the very government departments that control the fate of the migrants. They also enjoy a high profile in the popular press, thereby allowing the transition of information from within the academic sphere into the public mind set.

Phases 2 & 3: Social integration

In order to overcome the shortcomings of the migrant networks and individual NGOs to meet the complex requirements of migrant entrepreneurs, the model proposes a multidisciplinary network partnership to provide the migrant with the local intelligence required and extract the maximum potential value for the host country.

The acquisition of the appropriate legal capital for the migrant entrepreneur is very important. When the migrant applies for an entry visa, there is very little to distinguish a potential entrepreneur from the hundreds of other migrants who are all trying to establish themselves in the host country. Similarly, there is very little guidance for potential entrepreneurs to distinguish themselves from other migrants. The most trusted sources of information for migrants are fellow migrants or the NGOs and the least trusted are the government authorities that are the very entities that deal with the processing of applications.[25]

Handmaker et al[26] proposed that localisation of the residence or visa application process that provides migrants with legal status in a country would improve the quality and delivery of service. Local authorities are better able to make contextual assessments, based on their understanding of local requirements for skills. However, Landau & Amit[27] highlighted that variations in competence at municipal and metro level are likely to have a significant impact on the implementation of an equitable application process.

---

24 Ruwakaringi, 2017.
25 Handmaker et al., 2011; Kavuro, 2015b & UN High Commissioner for Refugees, 2015.
26 Handmaker et al., 2011.
27 Landau & Amit, 2014.

To mitigate this risk, the model proposes implementation of a multi-disciplinary governmental partnership, with local NGOs providing balanced assessments and co-screening. This will mitigate the risk of lack of effective communication of visa option possibilities by authorities, who either do not recognize the potential of the migrants or choose not to disclose the possibility of alternative visa options. Entry options include:

The scarce skills visa

As a developing country, the South African economy is characterised by high rates of unemployment for unskilled or semi-skilled labor contemporaneously with a severe lack of skills in a number of professions deemed as critical for economic growth.[28]

Chunnett[29] found that migrants who had scarce skills such as engineers experienced significant difficulty in getting these recognised by local institutions, particularly if the academic institutions from which the migrant had graduated was not readily contactable or willing to furnish the required information. A combination of language issues and logistics often meant that technically qualified migrants were forced to take up semi-skilled or unskilled jobs for many years until they could requalify or establish a business for themselves. If migrants were offered local, business-centered assistance to prove the veracity of their qualifications in these skills had the option to remain in the country for the three years that a scarce skills visa permits, they should be able to get meaningful employment that does not impact negatively on local employment, be encouraged to establish small businesses if possible and create jobs.

The business visa

At first glance, the Business Visa application appears to be inappropriate for anyone but the most affluent migrants wishing to establish a business in South Africa and invest more than ZAR 5 million in the process. However, the wording of the application requirements[30] is open to interpretation and stipulates that the investment requirement may be waived if a compelling argument is forthcoming as to the benefits of the potential business venture. This could well be applicable to potential entrepreneurs who can create job opportunities and open new industries.

If there are opportunities for technically qualified, potential entrepreneurs to establish themselves as something other than asylum seekers, guidance on how to do this should be given as early as possible in migration, preferably before they enter the country.

---

28 Department of Home Affairs, 2017.
29 Chunnett, 2018.
30 Department of Home Affairs, 2014.

The entity that presents the options to the migrant should be highly credible, which is not the case at the moment.[31] The Department of Home Affairs is the custodian of visa applications and, logically, any partnership that would seek to improve the credibility and functioning of the visa system, would have to focus on supporting this Department.

Blaser & Landau's[32] report, presents a framework for local authorities to partner with credible Non-Governmental Organizations (NGOs) to assess individual migrant applications speedily, based on the developmental contributions that the migrant could make. Competence of the NGOs could be confirmed by implementing the assessment tool that Blaser & Landau[33] developed to measure municipal effectiveness.

Ideally, the partnership would be established at screening locations outside of the host country, to avoid the current situation where migrants must leave the country, return to their home country and apply for another type of visa. Practically, this might well not be possible and a compromise would be to use electronic conferencing facilities. If resourcing and competence is an issue, the respective Departments could appoint Technical Advisors to assist with the process until they have built up the appropriate capacity internally.

Cross-functional initiatives have had a somewhat chequered history in South Africa. Many politicians speak about them and the Departments of Health and Education have embarked on a number of cross-cutting initiatives, primarily to optimise the spending of capital funds. The extension of this approach into the realm of visa approvals would be a novel one, but possible, provided the roles and responsibilities are clear and the Department of Home Affairs remains the custodian of the process.

The presence of an independent NGO or legal advisor would be necessary to establish the level of trust required for migrants to interact with the new assessment process. The NGO can also serve the role of transferring information regarding potential entrepreneurs who have qualified to enter the country on either a Scarce Skills or Business visa to potential business partners. The inclusion of additional advisors in the screening process would allow for a more balanced approach as the Departments of Labour and Trade and Industry would present a commercial view of the applicant's potential to become economically productive in the scarce skills space or establish a viable business.

In Phase 3, the focus of the model moves from an NGO: government partnership to a migrant group: NGO partnership and thereafter to individual engagement in order to

31   UN High Commissioner for Refugees, 2015.
32   Blaser & Landau, 2016.
33   Ibid.

develop language and local knowledge capital. It is at this point that the development of the potential entrepreneur becomes a bespoke process.

Key for this phase is the development of capacity by the migrant entrepreneur to use their migration capital to identify business opportunities. During interviews with migrant entrepreneurs, Chunnett[34] was left in little doubt about the value that local NGOs add to the lives of migrants, assisting with legal issues and the search for employment. However, the activities of NGOs generally do not focus capacitating migrants as a possible providers of jobs. Rather they view their role as an aide for job seekers. While the NGO is willing to engage, the support focus remains legal compliance, or developing basic social skills such as language competence. Therefore, when potential entrepreneurs approach them for business-focused assistance, they cannot address issues such as partnering with local entrepreneurs or establishment of a business.

If NGOs were to partner or augment their skills with a business development forum, such as the Small Enterprise Development Agency (SEDA), that has a national footprint, supporting infrastructure and connections to government agencies that provide start-up and assistance funding for new ventures, this could form the intermediate bridge between formal state structures and the migrant community.

As local NGOs have credibility and an extensive network of contacts within the migrant groups, they would be well placed to lead the initiative to develop interactive migrant group: local NGO: local business development group networks, that will focus, at programme level, on entrepreneurial as well as social issues and provide the migrants with the necessary entrepreneur migration capital through:

1. Educating potential migrant entrepreneurs about the language and cultural complexities of the country and the specifics of geographic areas where they may wish to establish a business.

2. Assisting migrants with information about language classes, the local business regulatory framework, localisation requirements, financial controls and other business-related issues that will, eventually, impact on their ability to establish a sustainable enterprise.

Phase 4: Business establishment

If migrant opportunity entrepreneurs have access to viable entrepreneurial business opportunities in areas where these are under-represented in the local economy[35]

---

34 Chunnett, 2018.
35 Herrington et al., 2014.

these should provide opportunities for local economic growth as Chunnett[36] noted that, as identified by Waldinger et al.,[37] typical migrant business establishment strategies include:

1. Establishment in under-traded areas.

2. The identification of both creative and survival opportunities, dependent on skill.

3. An appetite for risk and ability to work on the fringe of legality.

4. Leveraging transnational opportunities.

The implementation of the facilitated partnership must be premised on an understanding of mutual benefit if it is to have any chance of success as both parties must understand that they have more to gain by success than by failure.[38]

Table 4.1 illustrates the value that the respective partners could bring into such a relationship. This demonstrates that there are definite synergies if they are correctly structured and supported by mentorship programs that address the respective partner weaknesses to the point that the business is fully sustainable.

Table 4.1: Partnership value analysis

	Involuntary Migrant Entrepreneur	**Local Partner**
Strength	Transnational experience Appetite for risk Technical skills Extensive exposure to entrepreneurial culture	Local context understanding (language, culture) Appetite for risk Access to funding Local citizenship benefits
Weakness	Limited local context understanding Lack of business experience Lack of citizenship/legal status	Possible lack of technical skills Lack of business experience Lack of exposure to entrepreneurship

A customisation of the Development Caravan principles[39] could accommodate potential business migrant:local partnerships based on the following:

---

36 Chunnett, 2018.
37 Waldinger et al., 1990.
38 Homans, 1958.
39 Silinda, 2008.

1. Facilitators should be sourced from within the target, migrant community by NGOs or Group representative business organizations, where these exist. The credibility of these facilitators is key and they should have no role in the project other than facilitation.

2. Facilitators should be trained to understand what the requirements for a viable business are, including:

    a. Identifying locations or opportunities that would be suitable for migrants to partner with local entrepreneurs or potential entrepreneurs (done in partnership with the entrepreneurial business development agency).

    b. Identifying groups of migrants or individuals that could create opportunity businesses, given an enabling environment.

    c. Rapidly screening potential opportunity entrepreneurs, including an understanding of their existing technical and business skills.

    d. Supporting the pre-screened migrants to develop their business cases for funding submission.

3. The business development agency should source local entrepreneur partners, based on compatibility of technical and business skills and level of business maturity and any other criteria required to obtain financing.

4. The business development agency should draw up the partnership contract, which is vetted by legal resources nominated by the facilitators.

5. The business development agency would be responsible for developing a three-to-five-year development plan for the migrant/local partners that develops both and recognises the strengths and contributions that both could bring to the relationship.

6. It should be possible, at the end of the five-year period, for either of the partners to leave the partnership with a better set of skills, able to create two independent and functioning businesses, should they choose to do so.

Conclusion

If implemented holistically, the migration capital model could add up to fifteen years of economic benefit to a developing country through the accelerated establishment of sustainable businesses started by migrant entrepreneurs who have access to:

1. A host country that recognises that they can add value.

2. Support with the correct, appropriate legal application process.

3. Local intelligence about entrepreneurial opportunities that overcomes language barriers and identifies potential local partners.

4. Guidance in the sustainable establishment of local partnerships.

Chapter 5

Mobilizing Values and Action through Framing Strategies in Creating a Regional Bio-energy Niche

Dr. Raymond Loohuis, Assoc. Prof. Michel Ehrenhard and Prof. Carla Millar

Abstract

Which type of framing strategy helps to develop a regional bio-resource market, and what lessons can we draw for emerging markets? Building on the literature on the social construction of niches in renewable energy technology, we examine how the enactment of a number of distinctive framing strategies (diagnostic, prognostic, and motivational) influences how a niche is shielded against competing bio-resource niches and current energy regimes, how mobilization and learning unfolds, and how they pre-determine the strategies underlying the empowerment of a niche. In a comparative study, we evaluate two regional bio-resource projects aimed at developing a sustainable bio-resource market for small-scale combustion in the Netherlands in the period 2009 until 2014. Analysis of the first project showed that a diagnostic framing strategy that emphasizes the sustainable character of a project is important for shielding a bio-resource project as well as developing exposure and legitimacy. However, it constrains mobilization and learning processes and requires a radical transformation of existing logics and practices. In the second project, we found that prognostic and motivational framing strategies are useful to spur nurturing in terms of mobilization and learning because such strategies provide a rationale for action especially when such strategies account for the individual economic and image benefits of participating parties. Overall, our study suggests that a diagnostic frame is important to justify a bio-resource project but should not overshadow the processes that support the nurturing and empowerment of a bio-resource niche. This chapter purports to contribute to scholarship in the social construction of renewable energy niches by showing how framing strategies influence the development of niches. Furthermore, we offer interested renewable energy practitioners a taxonomy of framing strategies that can be used for shielding, nurturing, and empowering their ideas and offer some recommendations for emerging markets.

Introduction

In the Netherlands there is a growing need for the adoption of renewable energy technologies, like wind power and bio-resources, to deal with the urgent problem of climate change. Despite this need and the urgency thereof, various scholars have argued that renewable energy transitions require a long period of time and involve structural change.[1] Energy transitions implicate a sensitivity to existing practices and frequent adjustment of goals to overcome the conflict between long-term ambition and short-term outcomes.[2] One important challenge that entrepreneurs, who have a novel idea, need to deal with, are the barriers of often 'taken-for-granted' socio-cognitive frames and values related to the traditional use of energy[3] and path dependencies.[4] To overcome these barriers, scholars have pointed to the importance of protected niches in the development of renewable energy technologies[5] – sometimes with the help of policy[6], sometimes based on crowd-funding-based investments of new technologies.[7] Shielded from existing regimes and practices, niches can nurture the technology by learning, mobilizing values and social networks, collect and manage expectations of users, stakeholders, and policy makers, and further collectively empower the new technology by transforming existing practices if considered competitive enough.[8] In this regard, the entrepreneurship literature highlights the importance of national cultural values that influence the level of entrepreneurial activity in a country (for a review, see, Hayton, George & Zahra[9]). Furthermore, Harmeling, Sarasvathy and Freeman,[10] have pointed out how contingencies play a large role in the creation of value and new values, which are very much applicable to the example of the creation of sustainable energy initiatives.

In order to propagate new values in the creation of such initiatives, social movement literature stresses the importance of framing strategies usually practised by activists,[11] but also by entrepreneurs,[12] to frame and mobilize "hot causes"[13] – for instance, through contentious politics[14] or by enacting cultural codes.[15] Thus, whereas protected niche literature focuses on the processes and practices to shield, nurture and empower a

---

1   Geels & Raven, 2006; Jacobsson & Bergek, 2004; Verbong & Geels, 2007.
2   Kemp, Rotmans, & Loorbach, 2007.
3   Sengers, Raven, & Van Venrooij, 2010; Unruh, 2000.
4   Kemp, Rip, & Schot, 2001.
5   Kemp et al., 1998 & Kemp et al., 2001; Raven, 2005.
6   Verhees, Raven, Kern & Smith, 2015.
7   Vasileiadou, Huijben & Raven, 2016.
8   Smith & Raven, 2012.
9   Hayton, George & Zahra, 2002.
10 Harmeling, Sarasvathy & Freeman, 2009.
11 Benford & Snow, 2000.
12 Van den Broek, Ehrenhard, Langley & Groen, 2012.
13 Rao, 2009.
14 Tarrow, 2011.
15 Weber, Heinze & de Soucey, 2008.

niche, social movement literature concentrates on the tactics and framing strategies to position their cause vis à vis existing practices. Looking at the current developments of new "bio-based" renewable energy technologies, it is clear that renewable energy entrepreneurs are concerned with both deliberate efforts to develop their renewable energy niches and at the same time with framing their idea against the backdrop of traditional carbon-related energy practices, which are often portrayed as damaging for society. Combining both theoretical perspectives broadens the scope of the study of the emergent renewable energy initiatives, and as such, can be advantageous for the development of both theory and practice.

The use of bio-based resources (organic material) in the Netherlands is low in comparison to other EU countries. Bio-based technologies such as pyrolysis, digestion, or combustion require specific bio-resource materials.[16] Despite the interest in technology development, projects, especially smaller scale 'bottom-up" projects, encounter difficulties in achieving the critical mass needed for market acceptance of the renewable technology.[17] For instance, in a study of the emergence of bio-resource gasification projects, Negro, Hekkert, and Smits[18] concluded that there are periods of intensive entrepreneurial activity performed by enthusiastic pioneers but it remains difficult to mobilize a persistent group of actors to push forward the technology. Others have argued that a deep engagement of local policy actors in the context of biofuel projects may help to support the emergence of local entrepreneurial processes.[19] Given such challenges, there is a need for insights into the framing strategies deployed by enthusiastic renewable energy pioneers to position their ideas against traditional practices and in doing so, succeed in creating new paths and mobilizing communities and local political actors as well as third parties.

We address this by examining how framing strategies shape the development of a small-scale bio-based energy project, from shielding and nurturing to empowerment, and with what result. In this chapter, we report on the development of two bio-based energy projects in the eastern part of the Netherlands. The aim of both projects was to initiate the regional exploitation of bio-resource (plant) material harvested by agricultural associations which undertake landscape maintenance work using small-scale direct combustion. The first project named "Local Green Energy" started in 2009 and ended in 2012. The second one, called "Smart Local Green Energy Cooperation" started in 2012 and ended in 2015. Through our long-term research involvement, we were able to capture in-depth insights into the framing strategies deployed by members of both projects, including the effect on the development of their bio-based energy niches.

---

16   cf. Bastin et al.,2019.
17   Raven & Geels, 2010.
18   Negro, Hekkert, & Smits, 2007.
19   Van der Laak, Raven, & Verbong, 2007.

The chapter is structured as follows: first we discuss the literature on framing strategies and mobilization processes, which so far has been particularly in the domain of social movement scholarship. After that, the literature on framing strategies is integrated in the niche development literature from a socio-constructionist perspective. Next, we present the methodology and provide some background to each project, followed by a cross-case comparison and analysis. In the final section, we conclude the chapter, discuss implications, contributions and limitations of the study and propose applications to emerging markets.

Framing strategies

The social movement literature points to the importance of framing practices as a key activity of social movements to induce and legitimatise collective action.[20] Frames denote *"schemata for interpretation"*[21] that enable people to experience the world differently. Framing processes contribute to the development of a shared understanding of emotions related to a problem and the discursive practices needed to make new solutions more relevant, in comparison with alternatives.[22] This regularly happens by naming and shaming[23] or by praising.[24] Following Snow and Benford,[25] we can distinguish three interrelated core framing moves – diagnostic, prognostic, and motivational framing. Diagnostic framing refers to problem identification and assignment of blame. Prognostic framing refers to the offering of solutions, strategies, and tactics to solve a problem. Motivational framing helps to provide a rationale for action. Rather than offering shame and blame critique to incumbent actors and existing practices only, social movements can also enable favourable conditions and rationale for action for incumbent actors to set up new practices in sustainable markets. Therefore, social movements are deeply engaged in the deliberate activities involved in de-institutionalization of existing practices. In the context of sustainable practices, various studies reveal how social movement activists create new paths through framing strategies and tactics, for instance, in the recycling industry.[26] Weber et al.[27] showed how activists/entrepreneurs created space for sustainable meat and dairy products by using semiotic cultural codes of authenticity, sustainability, and naturalness which served the motivational, diagnostic, and prognostic functions of framing.[28]

---

20 Benford & Snow, 2000; King & Pearce, 2010.
21 Goffman, 1974:21.
22 Rao, 2009; Snow, Rochford Jr, Worden, & Benford, 1986.
23 Tarrot, 2011.
24 King & Pearce, 2010.
25 Snow & Benford, 1988.
26 Lounsbury, Ventresca & Hirsch, 2003.
27 Weber et al., 2008.
28 Benford & Snow, 2000.

In the wind power industry, Sine and Lee[29] revealed how social movements use transformative framing practices and encourage entrepreneurial activity by altering the taken-for-granted values about the material-resource environment, that is, altering the meanings and values of existing practices. These studies show that social movements can influence entrepreneurial activity and progress by moderating the effect of supply and demand sides and shape the material-resource environment.[30] In sum, framing strategies prove useful to attract attention to a problem and provide schemata for interpretation, but also help to provide strategies and tactics to find solutions, including a rationale for action either through diagnostic, prognostic, or motivational framing strategies. While framing as a term is usually associated with social movements and their representatives such as activists, in this chapter we examine the framing strategies of actors in the development of a niche in the context of renewable energy. In the following section we discuss in more detail the relationship between framing strategies and the successive steps in the development of a niche.

Framing strategies and the social construction of niches

Niches are identified as an important source of path-breaking innovations.[31] Smith and Raven[32] point to the importance of three interrelated, yet analytically distinct properties of niche construction: shielding, nurturing, and empowerment. Niches provide so-called protective spaces to nurture a new technology by shielding it from existing regimes.[33] Selection pressures are less felt in some passive niche spaces. For instance, some rural areas in Germany that are located outside the scope of actors in the natural gas regime provide opportunities for actors to experiment with renewable technologies. Niches can also be deliberately created through classic supply and demand side measures (subsidies, campaigns) on the basis of national policy regulations.[34] Other measures are those initiated by non-political actors, for instance, resourceful entrepreneurs or so-called 'business angels',[35] who temporarily protect actors with a novel idea from market forces. According to Schot and Geels,[36] the key processes underlying nurturing within protective spaces are experimentation, management of expectations, networking, and learning. These processes should contribute to resource commitments of business and political actors, collecting facts, and socio-technical implications, but should also include second-order learning.[37] In

---

29 Sine & Lee, 2009.
30 Scott, Ruef, Mendel, & Caronna, 2000.
31 Kemp et al., 2001; Kemp, Schot, & Hoogma, 1998; Smith & Raven, 2012.
32 Smith & Raven, 2012.
33 Geels & Raven, 2006; Rip & Kemp, 1998.
34 Smith & Raven, 2012.
35 Aernoudt, 1999.
36 Schot & Geels, 2008.
37 Ibid.

so doing, actors can experiment with the new technology, learn, and manage the expectations regarding the use of the technology.[38]

Protective spaces are important to nurture an innovation but, at some point, the innovation must become competitive enough to fit in and conform to existing practices or be able to stretch and transform established practices.[39] 'Fit and conform' empowerment refers to making the innovation competitive with mainstream socio-technical practices. This in contrast to a 'stretch and transform' strategy which undermines regimes and requires influencing of ongoing change processes towards more sustainable forms and building on broader trends in society.[40] Stretch and transform requires substantially more resource mobilization and political commitment[41] and might indeed be supported by social movements (activists) to create an opening for sustainable entrepreneurial action.[42] Logically however, actors must first perform specific actions to shield the innovation from regime pressures, followed by the activities necessary to develop the innovation in such a way that it can be implemented when considered competitive enough. Thus, the linkage between the new technology and traditional "regime" practices is reflected in the "fit and conform" and "stretch and transform" dichotomy.

At the same time, we have identified the use of framing strategies as an important activity in the development of a niche in renewable energy in multiple ways. First, deploying specific framing strategies may impact how shielding and nurturing turns out in the development of a niche. For instance, a motivational frame may be more effective than a prognostic frame in mobilizing others in the nurturing phase than a prognostic frame. Secondly, framing strategies may also impact the way empowerment of a niche occurs and thus how a new idea is positioned against existing practices. For instance, a diagnostic frame might stipulate a "stretch and transform" strategy whereas a motivational framing endorses a 'fit and conform' strategy aimed to seek a match between new and existing practices.

Methodology

We conducted a multiple case study[43] through a five-year in-depth involvement with both projects based on participative observation.[44] In the first project the role of the first author of this chapter was to conduct market research and provide recommendations. In the second project he became a member of the project advisory

---

38 Kemp et al., 1998; Schot & Geels, 2008.
39 Smith & Raven, 2012.
40 Ibid.
41 Kemp et al., 2007.
42 Sine & Lee, 2009; Weber et al., 2008.
43 Miles & Huberman, 1994.
44 Czarniawska, 2004.

board and provided advice on how to position the project in the region and on drafting a business model. Throughout, he ascertained which values were believed to be effective in communicating the project.

The cases consist of two regional bio-resource energy projects initiated in a region called "De Achterhoek" in the eastern part of the Netherlands. The overall aim of both projects was to endorse and develop a market for the use of locally harvested bio-material for bio-based heating for users in the region. For ease of language, we changed the names of the projects. As stated in the introduction, the first project named "Local Green Energy" started in 2009 and ended in 2012. The second one, called "Smart Local Green Energy Cooperation" started in 2012 and ended in 2015. Below we describe each project in terms of the duration of the project, the aims of the projects, how they were funded and the key players involved.

Table 5.1: Project description

	Local Green Energy (LGE)	**Smart Local Green Energy Cooperation (SLGEC)**
Duration	2009-2012	2012-2015
Project targets	1. Increase the economic value of hedgerows: if owners get a better price for their prunings, they will invest more in landscaping and encourage the investment in new landscape elements. 2. Improving the ecological value of landscape elements for cultural heritage and also the biodiversity in the region 3. Setting up a management system to conduct landscape work more efficiently. 4. Creating a local outlet for wood-chips by encouraging collaboration between landowners and land managers for the marketing of wood-chips 5. Providing information to local businesses and individuals on effective and cost-effective wood-fired heating systems.	1. Maximum regional utilization of the economic value of wood-chips to finance the maintenance of the regional forest, hedgerows, etc. of all the members involved (see key actors). 2. Maximum utilization of the energetic value of wood-chips from "de Achterhoek" for regional generation of heat. 3. The development of a professional and efficient system to arrange demand and supply in a responsible way.

	Local Green Energy (LGE)	Smart Local Green Energy Cooperation (SLGEC)
Duration	2009-2012	2012-2015
Funding	100% by Euregio (INTERREG), Dutch and German municipalities	Members, volunteers, small subsidy application for pilot plant
Key actors	Consultants (Environmentalist), Agricultural associations, NPO (Natuurlijk Platteland Oost)	Joint agricultural associations (VALA), Ver. Natuurmonumenten, St. Landschapsbeheer Gelderland, Geldersch Landschap,Waterschap Rijn en IJssel, 10 regional municipalities,

Data collection

In each project, we conducted in-depth interviews with key members, we interviewed experts in bio-mass exploitation and agricultural interest, we took field notes during the various project meetings and attended various exhibitions that the project members arranged in the region. In Table 5.2, we describe the data collection techniques and quantities in each project.

Table 5.2: Data collection techniques for each project

	LGE	SLGEC
Research period	2009-2012	2012-2015
Interviews	20 unstructured in-depth interviews with: • Project manager (8) • Coordinators of the six agricultural associations involved in the project (16) • Regional agricultural experts (2) • Policy makers from regional municipalities (2) • Targeted users of bio-based technology (2) (approx. 60 hours in total)	13 unstructured in-depth interviews with: • project manager (3) • Coordinators of the six agricultural associations involved (same as in SoS) (6) • Regional agricultural experts (1) • Policy makers from regional municipalities (2) • User of bio-based technology (1) (approx. 35 hours in total)

	LGE	SLGEC
Research period	2009-2012	2012-2015
Observations	90 hours total during: • Project group meetings (13) • Advisory board meetings of agricultural association (4) • Road-shows in the local community/exhibitions (2) • Site visits of targeted users (1) Field notes based.	30 hours total during: • Project group meetings (4) • Advisory board meetings of agricultural association (5) • Excursion to Germany (1) • Site visits of targeted users (1) Field notes based.
Documents	Agenda and minutes of the project group meetings, action list, documents of comparable projects in Germany.	Agenda and minutes of the project group meetings, action lists, position papers (drafts).

During the interviews, we did not explicitly use the term "framing strategy" or mention the phases of the niche development. Instead, we basically asked our informants which values they believed were effective in communicating the project to mobilize the public and specific stakeholders to advance their project. In this way, we believe that the interviewees could respond spontaneously without thinking of how they framed their project. Based on this information, we then could make the translation to the dominant framing strategies (diagnostic, prognostic or motivational) used in each phase of niche development (shielding, nurturing, and empowering). From there on, we could make sense of the data by structuring it into the developmental phases (shielding, nurturing, empowering) of niche emergence, i.e., which data pertained to each of these phases. Finally, we categorized the framing strategies of the key members in each project for each of the phases. We used the definitions of the framing strategies as offered by Snow & Benford,[45]: "diagnostic framing" referring to problem identification and assignment of blame; "prognostic framing" referring to the offering of solutions, strategies and tactics to solve a problem; and "motivational framing" which helps in providing a rationale for action.

Results

Although the aims of both projects were rather similar, we observed differences, and concluded that distinctive framing strategies were used in each of the projects, yielding distinctive outcomes for the development of their niches. In Table 5.3 we have summarized the framing strategies used by project members in each phase of niche development followed by an elaborated description of each project.

---

45 Snow & Benford, 1988.

Table 5.3: Results

NICHE DEVELOPMENT:	LGE – framing strategy: diagnostic and prognostic	SLGEC – framing strategy: prognostic
Shielding	**Passive shielding:**	**Active shielding:**
Passively (pre-exist deliberate mobilization) Actively (deliberate and strategic creation)	Shielding is ensured by subsidies. Diagnostic framing: "the cultural value of the regional landscape is in danger". Prognostic framing: "use of regional harvested biomass material contributes to the cultural value". Is different as opposed to alternative bio-resource projects in the region. Engagement of Wageningen and Twente Universities to collect "evidence" about the feasibility of the project as well as to increase the legitimacy of the project.	Shielding is ensured by securing the amount of potential biomass area (landscape elements of participating parties in the project) which is necessary to protect material from competing bio-resource niches or "regime" actors (i.e., Bruins & Kwast) Diagnostic framing: less emphasized (there is a common regional problem) Prognostic framing: persuasive strategies, used to promote becoming a member of a concrete regional high-status project that solves a common problem
Nurturing		
A process that supports the development of path-breaking innovations (Learning processes, articulating expectations, networking processes	Learning: collecting facts and figures about amount of biomass material and subsidies for labour work in the field. Lessons learned from the German counter parts. The management of expectations is in line with diagnostic and prognostic frames (shielding continues). Especially transforming the meaning of 'biomass' from waste to valuable resource	Learning: what is needed for the development of a bio-resource market? (i.e., resources, technology, money, activities, partners, value proposition, customer segments.) Collecting and managing the diversity of expectations of members and potential contributing parties and lead users. Mainly on the basis of earlier prognostic and motivational framing (what is the rationale for participating?)

NICHE DEVELOPMENT:	LGE – framing strategy: diagnostic and prognostic	SLGEC – framing strategy: prognostic
Shielding	**Passive shielding:**	**Active shielding:**
	Networking process mainly oriented towards mobilizing local policy makers and identifying a possible pilot plant (lead user)	Networking processes focused on strengthening commitment of powerful regional partners (i.e., AGEM) to advance legitimacy further.
	Roadshows, workshops, with a strong focus on "doing good" for the landscape.	
	Motivational framing "rationale for action" was ambiguous (how to calculate and compare between alternatives?)	
Empowering		
Developing widespread competitiveness	**Stretch and transform** strategy to frame existing natural gas and traditional bio-resource regimes as bad whilst emphasizing theirs as good because it is sustainable.	**Fit and conform** to existing practices. Emphasizing the importance of infrastructure, cost and efficiency as in current traditional energy regimes and yet, provide a sustainable alternative to multiple stakeholders including users.

LGE project 2009-2012

In the LGE project, we mainly observed how the members relied on diagnostic and prognostic framing efforts to spur the local use of bio material for heating purposes. The assignment of blame – a feature of diagnostic framing – was primarily oriented to highlighting the unsustainability and footprint caused by the use of large-scale collection of biomass material from eastern Europe. Some farmers in the region indeed purchased this material for heating purposes and the message was mainly intended to convince them of the negative consequences of this practice. Diagnostic framing was also directed towards the issue of natural gas being considered as carbon energy with high emission rates, a message intended for the region in general. Through this diagnostic framing strategy, key members managed to set themselves apart from other practices by highlighting the green character of their local initiative. The solution offered through the use of prognostic framing was that the cultural value of the region could be preserved should plant material be used from locally harvested coppices. These framing strategies were consistently presented in the nurturing phase in which members attempted to mobilize municipalities and users to learn from a similar project run simultaneously in Germany. Given the frame chosen, empowering this niche took the form of a stretch and transform strategy intended to change the taken-for-granted beliefs of the public in the region and other stakeholders such as municipalities or agricultural associations. However, motivational framing, that is, providing a rationale for action to participate in this project for instance by municipalities, harvesters or users, was underrepresented in this project. Consequently, potential stakeholders could not recognize how they would benefit from joining this initiative other than "doing good" for the region.

SLGEC project 2012-2015

In contrast to the LGE project, its successor, the SLGEC project, relied on a prognostic frame by highlighting the importance of exploring a solution to create a regional market for bio-material. In doing so, this team started to "secure" the forests of landowners and municipalities for their potential role in suppling plant material derived from forest maintenance work conducted by agricultural associations in the region including its potential for the economic benefits to be obtained. As a result, almost 65% of the regional landscape elements and potentially exploitable bio-resource material was pre-secured to the SLGEC project. This power structure was considered as an important shield to protect it from large-scale biomass material buyers. As a result, other parties too became interested in joining the project and this helped to legitimize the project to policy makers and other "green" initiatives and platforms in the region. Nurturing was basically driven by exploring a rationale for action for each member to join the project either as user, harvester, municipality, or landowner. Besides exploring the economic benefits for each party and how to arrange supply and demand in such a way that it contributes to sustainable harvesting and use of bio-material, the parties who become involved in this project jointly designed a business model that depicted how value is created to users, harvesters and municipalities, based on each one's interests. An important observation during the creation of that business model was that parties were keen on exploring sustainable solutions and activities without the need for subsidy. A key feature of this business model is that supply and demand are well orchestrated to avoid oversupply or shortages through storage facilities. In contrast to the LGE project, the empowering strategy of the SLGEC project was based on a fit and comfort strategy. This implied that, unlike the use of natural gas, efficiency and economic aspects of renewable energy were considered as important as the sustainability ones.

Conclusion

We examined the link between framing strategies and the emergence of a renewable energy niche. We asked how framing strategies shape the development of a small-scale bio- based energy project from shielding, from nurturing to empowerment, and with what result. We found that, in general, the use of framing strategies is critical in developing a niche and also that they are path dependent. By that we mean that a diagnostic frame created to shield a niche and identify a problem influences the mobilization process of potential stakeholders in the nurturing and empowering process. In the first project, we found that mobilizing potential stakeholders by relying on this frame was less successful. For the members of this project it was difficult to define a sufficiently motivational frame to attract and mobilize other relevant parties in the project to experiment with a potential regional market that would also economically benefit them. This was different in the second project where key members started with prognostic framing practices after they secured commitment of potential stakeholders on the basis of a motivational frame that could be explored further in the nurturing and empowering process. In sum, our study suggests that deliberately thinking of which framing strategy would help, in each phase of the project, is critical due to its path-dependent character (once a frame is set, it is difficult to undo). Furthermore, the results indicate that it appears to be critical to change a framing strategy on a timely basis. For instance, in the first project we observed that members kept on practising a diagnostic framing strategy and in doing so failed to provide a rational for action to the regional stakeholders for joining the project and as such missed out the thrust needed for niche development.

Limitations

A theoretical contribution, that at the same time could be a practical limitation, is that theoretically the various framing strategies can be used in a number of phases of the project. However, in this chapter we have only looked at an application in one environment (De Achterhoek) and in one type of context (the re-use of bio material/wood residue) in two timewise subsequent cases. A theoretical limitation is that the current study only looks at the application of the three types of framing[46] providing insight and case study results, but that wider applications, in other regional environments and/or in different contexts has not yet been carried out.

---

46 Snow & Benford, 1988.

Relevance for emerging markets

This chapter discussed the development of a market for locally harvested biomass material – an issue that became a hot item in the Netherlands as subsidies were withdrawn. We expect the topic to be of relevance too for emerging markets and we offer the following observations:

1. There may be a difference between what a developed country observer would see as the appropriate diagnostic framing and what the emerging market participant would see as the priority. Depending on the economic level of the country, alternatives to regular/current sources of energy may well be required to be cheaper, rather than necessarily sustainable, and there would may be many differences amongst the various emerging market countries.

2. Emerging market environments are much richer in motivational drives – not just in terms of money but also preserving heritage, displaying success/wealth/status, and building political power on the back of achievements in other fields. Hence motivational drivers are not just different, but often anchored in local/national culture. Unlike in the West where such products are sold on the open market, commonly owned biomass materials can also be used themselves as a common source of energy, i.e. a common good instead of a sales product.

3. The existence of a developed country preoccupation with a subject such as sustainability will affect the framing of that same subject in the emerging markets. Depending on the confidence of the country (leader or follower) and its geo-political aspirations, there may be positive or negative impacts arising from the adoption of environmental goals arising in other markets. And again, there is much variation amongst emerging markets.

4. Eco-tourism and building on it (or not deterring it) may be a variant on the framings – and one which combines diagnostic with motivational.

Chapter 6

Restoring the Agency of Voice through Video-led Cases for "Values-Driven Entrepreneurship and Societal Impact"

Prof. Martin Hall

Abstract

This chapter explores how video-led case studies can widen and strengthen the impact of curriculum design and delivery across education by restoring the agency of voice. Although counterintuitive, given the acknowledged dominance of visual communication across social media, video remains an underappreciated means for developing and transforming a curriculum. I argue that for education, and specifically for widening the impact of values-led enterprises, the potential of video rests on two key attributes: its democratisation through affordable mobile devices and its ability to change the subject position – to allow people to speak for themselves.

I develop this argument, and the broader case for curriculum transformation, by drawing on five prototypical video-led cases designed and developed in partnership with the Centre for Values Based Leadership at the University of Cape Town Graduate School of Business. By drawing from the substance and design of these five cases, I show how video can restore the agency of voice. I draw on theories of photography and particularly Margaret Olin's concept of "empowerment photography", which subverts the objectification of traditional documentary formats by inviting the viewer to look through someone else's eyes, with the aid of a facilitator, rather than learning about people under the authority of an instructor. Examples from each of the five video-led cases are used to exemplify Olin's earlier conceptualisation.

By way of conclusion, I look at the more specific opportunities for using video-led cases for exploring values-driven entrepreneurship within professional education, Masters programs and other kinds of courses offered by universities. I note that, with the rise of digitally enabled "platform economies", emphasis is shifting from respecting and acknowledging the university as the seat of expertise and authority to requiring assurance that universities can be trusted as intermediaries for information and perspective. Video-led cases can enhance trust by combining the text-based authority of resources and sources of information with direct, visual communication with key figures within the curriculum's narrative.

Introduction

The question behind the title of this collection of chapters is: how can values-driven entrepreneurship achieve societal impact? In this contribution, I narrow this broad scope to the curriculum design; the knowledge that is intended to be transferred by means of a course of study and also the context and apparatus for its delivery. Education of all kinds is a primary and expanding mechanism for both reaffirming and transforming the array of learned traditions, assumptions, beliefs and insights that, together, constitute the social world. As with other sectors in the knowledge economy, education is undergoing massive and rapid transformation which is also widening its accessibility.

Focusing on the curriculum has the potential to contribute to the societal impact of innovation in two ways. Firstly, and given the high and rising levels of educational participation, learners are in themselves a significant proportion of society. Secondly, many learners become influencers, incorporating newly-acquired knowledge into their daily practice and advocating to others. In this sense, and in a world where long-established sources of authoritative information and opinion are dissipating, people in themselves become the most viable channels for communicating new knowledge. Consequently, investing in the development and transformation of the curriculum is becoming an increasingly powerful means of achieving societal impact.

Within this frame of the curriculum, I focus on the use of video in learning and teaching, on the basis that video remains an underappreciated means for developing and transforming a curriculum. This may seem counterintuitive; video is everywhere from social media to an explosion of online platforms; video traffic was 75% of all data traffic in 2017 and is predicted to grow to 82% of all data transmitted via the internet by 2022.[1] But, in most academic curricula, video is an afterthought that is used to complement textual sources.

This nostalgia for traditional media of instruction misses out on two significant opportunities.

Firstly, the democratisation of visual media is, arguably, one of the more significant achievements of the digital innovation. Until quite recently, making a film was a big budget item, requiring professional videographers and editors. Today, acceptable quality video segments can be assembled by anyone, with a minimum of self-training, using a phone and a readily available editing application. This provides for a compelling immediacy in producing curriculum materials, that is in step with the pace of innovation and change in our contemporary world.

---

1   Cisco, 2019.

Secondly, video provides the curriculum designer with the opportunity to change the subject position; to let people speak for themselves. Traditionally, as academics, we write and teach "about" people. This applies whether or not we take a position on the issues covered in a curriculum; we still end up describing and analysing what we believe other people have experienced, what they feel, and what they want. Visual media allow those who are part of what we teach to be heard directly. In turn, this shifts the locus of power in the transmission of knowledge. Rather than self-representing as the definitive authority, whether by intent or default, the academic/teacher becomes more of a facilitator, orchestrating the assembly of the curriculum.

In the rest of this chapter, I will make this argument through reference to five experimental, video-led case studies developed as part of the work of the University of Cape Town Graduate School of Business's Centre for Values Based Leadership. These cases are very different, on a spectrum from a for-profit company developing online courses for international enrolment, to a NGO campaigning for the right to basic healthcare, they share a commitment to the primacy of values, understood as "principles, standards, or qualities considered worthwhile of desirable".[2] In turn, these values have shaped the ways in which each enterprise is run; "management by values", "a managerial philosophy and practice whereby focus is concurrently maintained on an organization's core values and aligned with its strategic objectives".[3] Each of these cases is available online, under a Creative Commons licence,[4] allowing readers to see for themselves.

> There are three values-based video cases, which are discussed in the chapter: 'Sokari Douglas Camp', 'Sam Paddock', and 'Mandla Majola', and which have already been uploaded to the website of the Allan Gray Centre (https://www.gsb. uct.ac.za/allan-gray-centre).
>
> The 'Communicare' and 'Kassahun Checole' video cases are in development, and will be published on the website of the Allan Gray Centre (but additionally discussed here in the chapter.

Enabling the power of speech

Communicare is a speech and language therapy practice based in Massachusetts, USA, that specialises in Augmented and Alternative Communication (AAC). AAC works with people who require assistance to speak, and primarily with children and young adults who have speech and language disorders. In their work, Communicare's

---

2   McNamara, 2012.
3   Dolan, Garcia & Richley, 2006.
4   Allan Gray Centre for Values-Based Leadership, 2021.

clinicians emphasise that AAC is, in itself, a form of language, with sets of rules and symbols that enable communication without speech. The technologies deployed to achieve this end range from pen and paper to sophisticated eye-gaze technology, in which the user communicates by looking at symbols on an interactive digital display:

"We love what we do! We specialize in Augmentative and Alternative Communication (AAC), Assistive Technology (AT), Applied Behavior Analysis (ABA), Speech-Language Pathology, and Special Education. We provide comprehensive services in the areas of assessment, intervention, consultation, training (professional development), and tele-AAC. We strive to empower our community through authentic connections and high-quality, evidence-based service provision."[5]

As an enterprise, Communicare works at the intersection between the state and the commercial sector. The majority of Communicare's clients are public schools. Over the past decade, the State of Massachusetts has outsourced significant elements in special needs education to private practices in order to reduce costs, while at the same time preserving the right of access to special needs support for people under the age of 21. Over the same period, the increasing pace of digital innovation has created a specialised industry in digital devices and applications to provide those in need with access to AAC. As with many forms of clinical practice, this creates a tension between the need for the practice to maintain and improve margins in order to run the practice as an enterprise and the ethics of providing clients with the solutions best suited for their needs. For example, in some cases "light tech" solutions – crayons and poster boards – may be a better technology for a specific need than the purchase of a sophisticated, and expensive, digital device.

These values come through strongly in the positions taken by Communicare's clinicians and in the video-led case that serves as the example here; in the work of their annual summer camp for AAC-users and paramedics; and in the commitment for getting the appropriate mix of solutions in place for each client and their family, irrespective of the technology.

A passion for spreading the word

Together, Africa World Press and GetSmarter span more than four decades of publishing, exemplifying the transition from books to fully online courses.

Kassahun Checole was born in Eritrea, then occupied by Ethiopia. Expelled from university in Addis Ababa in 1969 for political activities he moved to New York and returned to his home city of Asmara. In 1971 he was able to travel to New York, gaining

---

5   Communicare 2019.

a Masters degree in Sociology and an academic post at Rutgers University. In 1983, inspired by activist academics in Mexico, Kassahun founded Africa World Press from his apartment in Trenton, New Jersey.

In this video-led case study, Kassahun sees his three decades in publishing as shaped by a series of four definitive challenges: establishing a market for African books; his commitment to a free Eritrea; his resistance to the domination of US trade publishers; and the survival of Africa World Press in the digital age of Amazon.

Kassahun had been inspired to launch Africa World Press by the spirit of self-determination that he had experienced in Mexico, which resonated with his commitment to Eritrean independence. He defines this as a mission to offer Africa-centred books: "Africa is the world and the world is Africa". This was refined through a set of editorial themes: religion, sociology and economics, and African literatures. But, in approaching the established trade book stores, he was told that there was no market for books from or about Africa because "black people don't read". Faced with this resistance, Kassahun set up his own distribution company, Red Sea Press, and worked with others to create a market by setting up independent book stores across the US. By the end of the 1980s Africa World Press was well established, with a strong list of titles and a clear identity, supported by a network of independent book stores.

Kassahun had been actively involved in politics since his university days in Addis Ababa. When he left home in 1971 he had joined the Eritrean Peoples' Liberation Front (EPLA); he continued to support the EPLA in its opposition to Ethiopia's occupation of Eritrea throughout the time he was living in the US. In 1991, Eritrea achieved its independence and Kassahun decided to return home, arriving back in Asmara the following year. His vision for Eritrea was the establishment of a modern printing press that could meet the needs of both Eritrea and the broader East African region, particularly in providing books for education. He succeeded in establishing the press, which is still running today. But in May 1997, war had broken out between Eritrea and Ethiopia. Fighting continued until 2000, but with no political settlement. Vehemently opposed to the policies of the Eritrean government, Kassahun was again forced into exile in the USA.

Returning to his home in Trenton in 2001, Kassahun set about rebuilding Africa World Press. Trade book sellers such as Barnes and Noble had now realized that there was a market for books from and about Africa and used their competitive advantage in discounting to put many of the independent book stores out of business. Trade sellers would hold stock for many months for display purposes and then return books unsold, with no revenue for the publisher. Africa World Press's book distributor became insolvent, resulting in the loss of a large amount of stock. Kassahun responded to this crisis by turning to new and innovative processes of digital printing, allowing small print runs and reprints on demand, avoiding large capital outlays and warehousing costs. Kassahun sees this innovation as saving Africa World Press from collapse.

The challenges from trade book stores had been accentuated by the growing reach of Amazon.com through the 1990s. In rebuilding Africa World Press, Kassahun realized that working with Amazon would be essential. While commercial publishers could offset the discounts on mass-selling titles through very large print funds and lower unit prices, this option was not available to the small publishers that were now using digital technology to print on demand. Kassahun's strategy was to depend on Amazon for individual titles but to insist that bulk orders from college and university book stores are purchased directly from Africa World Press. Kassahun also had the foresight to keep some of his warehousing facilities for his direct sales. As a result, today about 30% of AWP's sales are through Amazon, and 70% are dispatched directly, free of the high discounts that Amazon demands. Africa World Press has a catalogue of over 1 000 titles, bringing out new books every year.[6]

Enterprises such as GetSmarter are both the antithesis and the natural successors of book publishers like Africa World Press. As online publishers – in this case of education courses – their business models are built on the possibilities and promises of the digitally driven "platform economy" of which Amazon is the early exemplar.[7] In this, GetSmarter is the nemesis of traditional publishing. But as natural successors, online publishers have the opportunity to build on the legacy of those book publishers driven by the values of opening knowledge to all. Between 2008, when GetSmarter was founded by brothers Sam and Rob Paddock, and 2016, when the company was sold, GetSmarter grew from under 400 student registrations a year to over 17 000 – a fifty-fold increase in the dissemination of knowledge.

Sam Paddock saw the possibilities of online education in 2004, when he was studying Business Science Information Systems at the University of Cape Town: what would it be like to be able to study entirely online? Sam's father had pioneered the introduction of flexible learning opportunities for lawyers specializing in property management and this resonated with the emerging possibilities for online learning. Sam founded GetSmarter in 2008 with his brother Rob. Their first course was in partnership with the University of Stellenbosch.

The opportunities in online learning are closely linked with digital innovation and the exponential-like increase in digital capacity. Increases in access to connectivity has combined with key digital innovations in processing power, bandwidth, transmission

6   Africa World Press 2019.
7   McAfee & Brynjolfson, 2017.

speeds and the declining cost of cloud storage, resulting in a striking increase in the global generation of digital information. Back in 2004, when Sam was building a model for a virtual classroom as a UCT student, the world was producing about 0.1 zettabytes of new digital information annually. By 2017, the production of digital information had increased two-hundredfold, to about 20 zettabytes each year, or the equivalent of three terabyte drives of new information for every living person in the world.[8]

Over its first four years, GetSmarter was strikingly successful in building on these opportunities. The number of students enrolled across all courses had increased tenfold. Course presentations had increased by a factor of twenty, from three in 2008 to 60 in 2012. And the team had grown from just three in the company's first year to 75 in 2012. But, as Sam explains in the ChangeMaker case study, the business had hit a wall, finding it increasingly difficult to deal with the consequences of rapid growth and the expectations of their partner organizations. GetSmarter's big strategic leap, made after two years of introspection between 2012 and 2014, was to offer only short courses.

GetSmarter also decided to move into the international arena, with initial partnerships that included the Cambridge Institute for Sustainability Leadership, Goldsmiths College, University of London, the University of Chicago and the Massachusetts Institute of Technology. By June 2016, GetSmarter had more than 1 000 international students from across the world. But, because GetSmarter's business model required that the company undertook almost all course development costs, and also underwrote the consequences of student enrolments not meeting targets, the scale of this expansion also increased the level of financial risk to the business. It was necessary to capitalize the business and this resulted in the decision to sell GetSmarter to 2U Inc., a large online program management company in the US.

Over these years of growth, from start-up success to substantial business, GetSmarter had pioneered the use of online provision to expand educational opportunity in South Africa. The apartheid years, which had ended with the first democratic government of 1994, had left the persistent legacy of a discriminatory and under-resourced educational system that had prevented many people with ability and potential to get access to the schooling that they deserved, or to gain university-level qualifications. High-quality online courses, certificated by leading South African institutions such as the universities of Stellenbosch, the Witwatersrand and Cape Town, enabled people in employment to smash against glass ceilings. Completion certificates were used as evidence for specific competences required by employers, or to provide the basis for alternative routes into graduate programs – the "recognition of prior learning" permitted in terms of South Africa's regulations for admission into higher education.

---

8   Meeker 2018.

Africa World Press and GetSmarter have been, from their inception, enterprises that have been driven by sets of core values. In this, both Kassahun Checole and Sam Paddock meet widely-accepted criteria for "transformational leadership": a clear, articulate and credible vision for the future direction of their organizations; "social architects" who orchestrate shared values and a distinctive institutional culture; leaders who establish by making their own positions and commitments clear; and a strong sense of self-awareness and how to use their own strengths and weaknesses.[9] Despite the tensions inherent between traditional book publishing and online provision, they share a driving concern to make knowledge and expertise available to as many people as can possibly be reached within the means of the mechanisms available to them.

Driven by a passion for justice

At first sight, Mandla Majola and Sokari Douglas Camp could not be more different: a health rights activist born and raised in a South African township; a sculptor born in Nigeria, working from her studio in London and widely recognised for the striking aesthetics of her art. What unites them in the ChangeMaker case studies is that they are both driven by the values of fundamental human rights and social justice, and that these values have shaped and directed their work over many years.

Mandla Majola was born and brought up in the Cape Town township of Gugulethu. When his aunt died painfully in 1999, Mandla became aware of the devastating HIV and AIDS epidemic that was sweeping across South Africa. For the next 15 years, Mandla was part of the TAC's national leadership.

AIDS was formally defined by the US Centre for Disease Control and Prevention in 1982. Since then, this global epidemic has taken about 35 million lives, and some 70 million people have been infected with the HIV virus. Africa is the most severely affected region, with nearly two-thirds of all those with HIV living in the continent: about 1 in every 25 adults.[10] By the early 1990s, it was clear that AIDS was reaching epidemic proportions in South Africa, with the South African National Health Department reporting that the number of recorded HIV infections had grown by 60% in the previous two years and was expected to double in 1993. But at this time, medical options were limited and prohibitively expensive. Despite initial optimism, early treatment regimens were disappointing. There were well-promoted claims for alternative treatments, and scepticism about the very existence of AIDS.[11] The Treatment Action Campaign was founded in December 1998 to campaign for access to treatment for HIV and AIDS in South Africa.

---

9   Bennis & Nanus, 2007; Northouse, 2019.
10 WHO, 2018.
11 Mbali, 2005.

Looking back, Mandla tells the story of the TAC as three major campaigns: the fight against Pfizer patent rights for fluconazole; the campaign for healthcare to prevent mother-to-child transmission of HIV; and the push for universal access to medication for those living with HIV and AIDS.

The Treatment Action Campaign's fight for access to fluconazole was set in the larger international context of patent rights, the pricing of drugs, and rights of access to generic medicines. Fluconazole had initially been developed by a team at Pfizer Central Research in the UK in 1981 and was protected by a patent awarded to Pfizer. The drug was approved for use in the USA in 1990, and was marketed by Pfizer as Diflucan.

As in many other parts of the world, patented drugs such as Diflucan were too expensive in South Africa to be made available to all who needed them through the public health system.

South Africa's new Constitution of 1996 had set the principle of the right of everyone to have access to health care and a new Medicines Act, passed by Parliament in 1997, was intended to give effect to this provision by allowing the parallel production of generic drugs that could be made available at prices far lower than their branded equivalents. But in early 2000, when activist Christopher Moraka died from cryptococcal meningitis and the TAC launched a campaign in his name, the Medicines Act had not been enforced.

In April 2000, after protests at Pfizer's offices in Johannesburg and Cape Town, the company announced that it would donate Diflucan to AIDS patients in South Africa, in collaboration with the Ministry of Health. But this did not meet the TAC's demand that the price of Diflucan should be lowered to the level of generic production. The TAC continued with the campaign, announcing at an international AIDS conference in July 2000 that it would "smash Pfizer's patent". TAC leader Zackie Achmat made the comparison with Thailand, where a generic version of fluconazole was legally available at a fraction of the price of Diflucan in South Africa. Later that year Achmat, in an act of public defiance, illegally imported 5 000 doses of generic fluconazole from Thailand, distributed them in South Africa without charge and then "confessed" his crime to the police.[12]

Prevention of mother-to-child transmission (PMTCT) programs provide HIV-positive pregnant women with antiretroviral treatment to reduce the risk of their unborn babies acquiring the virus. If HIV-exposed infants are given antiretroviral treatment within their first 12 weeks of life, they are 75% less likely to die from an AIDS-related

---

12   Cullinan, 2000; PharmaLetter, 2000.

illness. The TAC argued that pregnant women had the right of access to a short course of the drug AZT to reduce the risk of their child being infected with HIV during and after birth. The TAC widened its scope to include access to a second antiretroviral, Nevirapine which works to prevent the multiplication of the HIV virus, and complements AZT where women breast-feed their babies. In response to the TAC's case, the government stated that AZT and Nevirapine were too expensive to be provided through the public health system and – in an argument led directly by President Thabo Mbeki – that the relationship between HIV and AIDS was unproven. The TAC took legal action against the government, winning its case in the Pretoria High Court in December 2001. Following the government's appeal against the High Court ruling, the TAC took its case to the Constitutional Court, which ruled in favour of the TAC and the right of access to healthcare services in July 2002.[13]

Following the success of the PMTCT campaign, the TAC decided to push for all of those living with HIV and AIDS to have the right to appropriate treatment through the public health system – "universal access". This campaign was launched in February 2003 with a protest by 20 000 people in Cape Town, on the day that President Thabo Mbeki was delivering the annual "State of the Nation" address in Parliament.

The objections to providing a national treatment plan for HIV and AIDS were twofold. Firstly, the government deemed universal access unaffordable. But, while it was indeed the case that low-cost generic alternatives to patented medicines were still not available in South Africa, the lack of affordable treatment was also because the government had systematically refused price reductions and donations of drugs by multinational companies, and had blocked international aid to provide medication.[14] These actions are explained by the second reason that the government refused to contemplate a national action plan: AIDS denialism. While there had long been an alternative view that the connection between HIV and AIDS was unproven, these arguments had, for the most part, not derailed the steady advance of effective public health policies in other countries. But, uniquely in South Africa, denialism was enthusiastically embraced by the government and the ruling party, and explicitly by the head of state: Thabo Mbeki, South Africa's President from 1999 until 2008. Faced with this wall of opposition, the TAC decided to sharpen its tactics with an explicit campaign of civil disobedience, launched on 21 March 2003 – Human Rights Day – with the occupation of police stations across the country in an attempt to lay charges of culpable homicide against Health Minister Manto Tshabalala-Msimang and Trade and Industry Minister Alec Erwin.[15]

---

13 Mbali, 2003; Heywood, 2009; AVERT, 2018a.
14 Chigwedere et al., 2008.
15 Mbali, 2005.

The following five years saw a series of incremental victories as a broad alliance of activists, health care specialists and workers, civil society movements, international organizations and a broad swathe of the South African public pushed against the obdurate denialism of Thabo Mbeki, Manto-Tshabalala Msimang and other senior figures in the ANC government. Finally, and in 2007, the TAC was able to engage with government to draft a national plan for HIV and AIDS, which was endorsed by the Cabinet on 4 May 2007. By March the following year, when the TAC held its National Congress, 450 000 people were receiving treatment for HIV and AIDS through the public health sector.

The effects of the AIDS denialism of President Thabo Mbeki, Health Minister Manto Tshabalala-Msimang and other senior government officials has been calibrated through a sophisticated statistical model published by Harvard University's School of Public Health. This study estimated that 330 000 lives, or approximately 2.2 million person-years, were lost because a feasible and timely ARV treatment program was not implemented in South Africa. An estimated 35 000 HIV-positive births could have been avoided if the required mother-to-child transmission prophylaxis program had been introduced in South Africa at the time that it was first available. In comparison with South Africa, neighbouring Botswana, under the leadership of President Festus Mogae, introduced a PMTCT program in 1999, followed by national ARV access in December 2001. By 2005, Botswana had 85% ARV treatment coverage, as opposed to 23% ARV coverage in South Africa.[16]

As a direct consequence of the work of the Treatment Action Campaign and allied organizations, South Africa now has the largest antiretroviral therapy program in the world. As a result of universal access to antiretroviral therapy programs – the focus of TAC's successful civil disobedience campaign – overall life expectancy is steadily increasing, from 61.2 years in 2010 to 67.7 years in 2015. And in 2015, South Africa met the World Health Organisation's global target of reducing mother to child transmission of HIV by 90%. But the challenge of eradicating HIV and AIDS is still formidable, with 18.9% of the South African population infected.[17]

After standing down from the TAC's leadership group in December 2015, Mandla Majola completed his Master's degree in Public Health at the University of Cape Town and graduated in March 2016. He then joined the School of Public Health at the University of Cape Town, with the role of coordinating community projects, working in the Cape Town townships of Gugulethu and Khayelitsha. Using his experience in strategy, learned through his years with TAC, Mandla realised that better progress could be made by forming a coalition of community-based organizations. He founded the Movement

---

16   Boseley, 2008; Chigwedere et al., 2008.
17   AVERT, 2018b.

for Change and Social Justice, bringing together some fifteen groups with shared objectives, and continues to campaign for the constitutional right of everyone in South Africa, irrespective of their circumstances, to equitable and affordable health care.

Sokari Douglas Camp was born in Buguma, a coastal town in Nigeria's Rivers State that is the seat of the Kalabari Kingdom. In 1967, at the outbreak of the Nigerian Civil War, she moved to Britain to complete her schooling, but returning frequently to her home town. She studied art at the California College of Arts and Crafts (1979-1980), at the Central School of Art and Design in London (1980-1983) and at the Royal College of Art (1983-1986). She has lived and worked in Elephant and Castle, London, for more than thirty years. Her work has been recognized in many awards, including a CBE in 2005, an Honorary Fellowship of the University of the Arts London in 2007 and a Fellowship of the School of Oriental and African Studies, University of London, in 2017.

Rivers State's capital, Port Harcourt is the centre of Nigeria's oil industry. Commercially viable crude oil and gas reserves were first discovered in 1956; today's Rivers State has two major oil refineries, port facilities, airports and industrial estates and produces more than 60% of Nigeria's total oil output, a sector accounts for about 8.5% of Nigeria's GDP. Shell, in partnership with the British government, began oil production in the region in 1958. Between 1976 and 1991, some 3 000 oil spills were reported in the area, totalling about 2 million barrels and about 40% of Shell's oil spills across the world as a whole. In 2011, the United Nations Environment program reported that, as a result of oil spills, the alluvial soils of the Niger Delta are no longer fit for cultivation. UNEP has estimated that rehabilitation will take some 30 years.[18]

Protests against pollution and the destruction of the rich ecosystem of the Niger Delta were led by Kenule Saro-Wiwa, a writer, television producer and founder of the Movement for the Survival of the Ogoni People.[19] Saro-Wiwa was imprisoned by the Nigerian military government in 1994 and, with eight others, was sentenced to death and hanged on 10 November 1995.[20] The execution of the "Ogoni Nine", along with accusations of complicity with Nigeria's military dictatorship, brought international attention to Shell's record of environmental pollution, the exploitation of local communities and alleged human rights abuses. Legal cases against Shell have been brought continuously since 1996.[21] In November 2017 Amnesty International published a review of internal Shell documents, as well as records from its own archives, relevant to events in the Ogoniland region during the Nigerian military dictatorship. Amnesty's allegations have been denied by Shell Nigeria.[22]

---

18 Crayford, 1996; UNEP, 2011.
19 MOSOP, 1991.
20 Lewis, 1996.
21 Mouawad, 2009.
22 Amnesty International, 2017; Shell Nigeria, 2018.

Sokari's work as an artist has been focused and directed by the environmental destruction of the Niger Delta, by the actions of the Nigerian government and by the seeming complicity of Shell. Many of her sculptures are inspired by the Kalabari masquerades that are performed across twenty-year cycles to portray and invoke water spirits that are found in the mangrove swamps.[23] Sokari's "Battle Bus: Living Memorial for Ken Saro-Wiwa" was completed in 2006. This full-size sculpture travelled across Britain for nine years before being dispatched to Lagos in 2015. The planned tour of Nigeria was at the request of the Ogoni Solidarity Forum-Nigeria and other Nigerian organizations, both to continue the campaign to clean up the Niger Delta and to mark the 20th anniversary of the execution of the Ogoni Nine.[24] However, the Battle Bus was impounded by Nigerian customs at Lagos and has yet to be released.[25]

A second theme, running through Sokari's more recent work, is the legacy of slavery. The Act for the Abolition of the Slave Trade was passed by the Parliament of the United Kingdom in 1807 and prohibited the slave trade in the British Empire. The bicentennial of this landmark legislation was marked in a range of exhibitions and art commissions across Britain, inspiring a continuing strand in Sokari's work as an artist.

Here, Sokari's work is best represented by "All the World is Now Richer". This installation comprises six striking life-sized figures, welded in steel and representing stages in the legacy of history: a figure in West African robes prior to the devastation of the slave trade; a plantation worker and a domestic slave; a nineteenth-century liberated ex-slave in the distinctive dress of the time; a twentieth century executive in a suit and tie; and a relaxed figure – "Tee-shirt Man" – in casual clothes, looking for his heritage. Together the group stands on a grid composed of the words of a liberated ex-slave, William Prescott: "they will remember that we were sold but they won't remember that we were strong; they will remember that we were bought but not that we were brave."

"All the World is Now Richer" was exhibited in the House of Commons in 2012 and then in Bristol Cathedral, Norwich Cathedral and St George's Hall in Liverpool. It was shown again in St Paul's Cathedral, London, in 2014 and as part of the Diaspora Platform project during the Venice Biennale 2017. Sokari sums up her objective for this work: "How do you show that the people of slave heritage are brave and have dignity and strength? How do you show the social and economic legacy that has benefited the world from their suffering?"[26]

---

23 Brighton Museums, 2015; Sokari Douglas Camp, 2019.
24 Platform, 2018.
25 Rustin, 2015.
26 Diaspora Pavillion, 2017; October Gallery, 2019.

As with Mandla Majola's steadfast commitment to the provision of affordable and humane health care, so Sokari's advocacy as a sculptor has consistently pushed for basic human rights, environmental justice and recognition of the continuing legacies of slavery. Both are powerful expressions of values-based leadership.

Empowerment photography

A key point – and the focus for this paper – is that video-led cases, of the kind represented by Communicare, Africa World Press, the Treatment Action Campaign, Sokari Douglas Camp and GetSmarter, can achieve greater impact than conventional, text-led curricula by restoring the agency of voice. More specifically, this is achieved through two mechanisms: the democratisation of video as a medium of communication; and the shift of the focal point, transforming traditional subject of academic discourse into an active agent in the curriculum.

This point can be expanded, figuratively and literally, through returning to the Communicare case. The democratising of video stems from the ubiquity of video functionality on smart phones. Working with children and young adults at Camp Communicare demonstrated repeatedly that the phone is the device of choice in capturing and communicating narratives for children with special needs. Often, and whether or not deliberately, children with special needs become objects of pity in text-led cases and traditional documentary formats; a narrator or expert talks about them and paraphrases what they cannot do. In contrast, the intimacy of the phone medium allows both closeness and trust, both because the technology is far less intrusive than specialised videography equipment, and because the phone is now a familiar artefact, worth barely a glance.

This ubiquity of mobile devices brings significant practical benefits to a values-led organization such as Communicare, since accessible technology and easily usable editing applications remove many cost barriers. In turn, lower production costs encourage and allow more rapid renewal of curriculum content, improving the quality of continuing professional development for practitioners and, from this, the provision of better quality care. As part of their ongoing practice, and in order to support their work in Continuing Professional Development with the American Speech-Language-Hearing Association (ASHA).

Again – and literally as well as figuratively – AAC as a language directly restores the agency voice to those who have previously been denied speech. As with other forms of agency, empowerment has two requirements: the technical competence of the agent, in this case children and young adults learning AAC as a new language; and adaptation to, and acceptance of, AAC as a language by communication partners.

The ChangeMaker case explores both sides of this coin in depth. The intimacy of the video medium shows the compelling ability of AAC users, some under the age of 10, to master grammatical structure and vocabulary using technology as the medium. In parallel, the visual narrative provides a visceral sense of how we need to abandon unfounded assumptions and address what Dolly Chugh has termed the "unintended biases of good people".[27] In this Communicare's values-driven mission is to work within the opportunities afforded by the Massachusetts public schooling system to empower children and young adults in need by both teaching them to communicate using augmented and alternative instruments, and by removing the prejudices and social barriers that prevent them from being heard.

In a more general and abstract sense, the massive popularity of video enabled by ever more accessible technologies and social media reaffirms some earlier insights about photography and, in particular, Margaret Olin work on "empowerment photography". Olin sees photography as "gestural practice": "just as a painter gestures with brushes at a canvas to describe space, objects, people, and ideas, and lecturers gesture at audiences to describe ideas or to connect to their listeners, so photography's gestures function to describe ideas and things and to connect people".[28] This connection is dependent on the role of a facilitator: "all these ways of disseminating photographic activities to people(s) who are suppressed, oppressed, or voiceless, or who belong to an unrecognized nationality dispersed in a diaspora, entail an interaction between a community and a teacher who comes armed with a belief in the empowering potential of photography".[29] For Olin the key distinction is that, where documentary photography asks the viewer to look at a subject, empowerment photography invites viewers to see through someone else's eyes. The distinction is not in the images themselves, but in the intention for their use. Applying this to the Communicare ChangeMaker case, the intention is not to offer a documentary about children with disabilities, but rather to see the world through their eyes, mirroring the inadvertent prejudices that may prevent us from hearing their voices.

Olin's metaphor of the gesture serves well to describe the approach to making the other four ChangeMaker cases described in this paper. None were scripted. In each case, the request was to tell the story of the enterprise and of the objectives and values that gave it momentum; in Olin's terms the viewer is invited to "look through someone else's eyes" rather than to watch a "subject". In each case, this dialogue approach prompted new insights and forms of expression: for Sokarai, of her art as "her way of writing"; in Sam's case, of strategy as "people doing things"; for Kassahun, reflection

---

27 Chugh, 2018.
28 Olin 2012: 11.
29 Ibid, 136.

on the writers who have shaped his thinking; and for Mandla the recollection of being abused by police during the TAC campaign for universal access.

Professional is personal

How, then, does this "gestural practice" shift the needle in producing video-led cases for values-based leadership?

A first common point across the ChangeMakers prototypes is that the distinction between professional and personal personas blurs into irrelevance. This is particularly relevant to understanding how, in some enterprises, values come first. Africa World Press was initially shaped and defined by Kassahun Checole's experiences in Mexico, and the ways in which literature shaped national identity. This resonated with his commitment to Eritrean independence and inspired his curtailed return to Asmara in 1992. In rebuilding the business from 2001, Africa World Press has consistently prioritised the significance of a manuscript over its sales potential, in sharp distinction with the large majority of other publishers. While this may have reduced profitability, this values-led approach has resonated with a significant global community of partners and readers. Combined with Kassahun's innate qualities as an entrepreneur, Africa World Press has defied the odds and now has a unique position as a progressive, pan-African, publishing house.

In different ways, the values that have propelled both Sam Paddock's and Mandla Majola's work originated in their families. In some respects, these personal backgrounds could not be more different; the Cape Town township of Gugulethu and the affluent suburb of Rondebosch on the slopes of Table Mountain; a geography set by the institutionalised segregation of apartheid. Yet, when given the voice to shape their stories and priorities, both start with their families. Mandla traces his commitment to fighting for rights to basic healthcare to his aunt's death and to his dismay that his family was unable to talk about a sexually-transmitted disease. This has shaped a determination to fight back against prejudice and, in his reflections on camera, hones his anger and dismay at President Thabo Mbeki's AIDS denialism and its consequences. Sam attributes his commitment to education – GetSmarter's "audacious goal" of "changing a million lives" – to family values and to his father's determination to overcome the University of Cape Town's inherent conservatism and reluctance to open up access to education.

Sokari Douglas Camp's values-based leadership comes from a combination of the political imperative of moving beyond the legacies of empire and colonialism and her family context. Her sculptures and aesthetics have been shaped by her childhood memories of Kalabari masquerades and their ever-changing and evolving modalities.

Her political commitment to environmental justice originates in her dismay at Shell's devastating and cynical destruction of the rich ecosystem of the Niger Delta; in her visual narrative, she vividly recalls driving from Lagos to Port Harcourt and seeing the horizon black with smoke from the refineries and burning oil spills. She attributes the second theme that runs through her work – the legacy of slavery – to the right to dignity, an approach that rejects the dominant documentary trope in which slaves are objectified as victims. This is why she often returns to the single recorded phrase from a otherwise unknown slave, William Prescott: "they will remember that we were sold but they won't remember that we were strong; they will remember that we were bought but not that we were brave." Here, Sokari's values-based leadership is her continuing push for public sculpture in London that commemorates slavery through strength and bravery rather than as victimhood.

Their way of writing

A second common attribute across this diverse set of ChangeMakers is that, as unscripted conversations, they tend towards the teleological. Such narratives selectively interpret the past from a present condition, parsing away circumstances and events that at the time could have been significant, but which have subsequently proved irrelevant. This, in turn, attributes causality, whether explicitly or by implication. Sam Paddock is explicit in this in telling GetSmarter's story. Looking back, he is clear that the difficult, high-risk decision to focus on short courses for working professionals, and to abandon other business directions, allowed the company to reach many more students without the encumbrance of the regulations that apply to accredited qualifications. However, he also acknowledges that this clarity comes with hindsight; getting to the decision point took two years of arguments, debates and false starts.

Both Kassahun Checole and Mandla Majola attribute their circumstances at the point of their interviews to a logical chain of campaigns. For Kassahun this is fourfold: the founding of Africa World Press, the return to Eritrea, the fightback against the trade book stores, and achieving an accommodation with Amazon and the new world of publishing. Mandla's campaign history with the TAC is the fight for generic patents followed by the push for medication for pregnant women, leading to the victory in the Constitutional Court and universal access to medication.

Sokari presents a more nuanced narrative, appropriately so, given the nature of her work. As an artist her reach extends beyond words, encompassing the aesthetics of her sculptures and their interpretations of shapes, textures and colours. As such, this is her "way of writing", that will be diminished by any attempt to reduce the work to words alone. In her case the teleological effect comes from her choice of which works to choose from an extensive catalogue; the story of the Battle Bus from conception through until its confiscation by Nigerian customs authorities; the individual sculptures and their imagined histories that, together, comprise the "We were Brave" installation.

In the traditional, more academic, documentary mode teleology is "one-sided", "biased", "subjective", requiring counter-balancing points of view. But to go down this road is to return the authority of voice to the third-person narrator who stands outside and above the conversation as adjudicator; the umpire in an intellectual tennis match. This runs contrary to the primary objective of the ChangeMaker cases – the restoration of the power of voice. For many applications of "empowerment photography", that make use of the new and still-emerging opportunities of digital video, restoring voice is an end in itself. But for cases such as the ChangeMaker series, that are intended for use in the context of formal curricula, the objection of subjectivity and bias has to be addressed in order to project the validity of these new style narratives.

The approach adopted in producing and publishing these protypes has been to accompany each visual narrative with signposts to sources that both provide material that is complementary to the visual narrative, and which present counterarguments and contrary points of view. It is then left to those making use of the ChangeMaker cases to find out for themselves and to make up their own minds. Clearly, it would be naïve to claim that there is neutrality in this device. Just as the facilitator is central to Olin's concept of empowerment photography, so are these visual narratives shaped from the point of filming, on through the processes of editing, and into the selection and publishing of complementary materials. But necessary facilitation of this kind is distinct from both documentary reportage and from the traditional academic mode of writing, in which an all-knowing expert presents a "correct" version of events.

Beyond words

Like Sokari Douglas Camp's striking, life-sized steel sculptures, leadership is often about presence. Leadership presence can be dominant and pervasive; the personality that fills a room and a persistent theme in theories of leadership. Equally, though, leadership can be a subtle presence that invigorates others; the "servant-leader" tradition.[30] Presence can also be asserted indirectly, and negatively. For Sokari, the continuing presence of Nigeria's General Sani Abacha, in both his life and after his death, is part of her continuing journey. The communication of these various forms of leadership invariably extends beyond the limits of words. Dress codes and uniforms; mannerisms and music; ceremonial representations of authority. These visual dimensions of leadership make up a third and common strand across this set of ChangeMaker cases.

---

30 Northouse, 2019.

Non-verbal forms of communication are all the more significant for values-based leadership. The concept of "organizational values" is a clumsy shorthand, and institutional values that exist only as words are generally seen as meaningless and vacuous. Values that work are invariably embodied in real people and are often augmented by anything from facial expressions and body language through to settings, workplaces, architecture and landscapes.

This embodiment gives power to the visual and is a source of rich opportunities for photography in general, and for video. The power of photography, both benign and threatening, was peeled apart by Susan Sontag in her formative set of essays, "On Photography", first published in 1977. Here's an extract from "The Image-World":

"Photographs do more than redefine the stuff of ordinary experience (people, things, events, whatever we see – albeit differently, often inattentively – with natural vision) and add vast amounts of material that we never see at all. Reality as such is redefined – as an item for exhibition, as a record for scrutiny, as a target for surveillance. The photographic exploration and duplication of the world fragments, continues and feeds the pieces into an interminable dossier, thereby providing possibilities of control that could not even be dreamed of under the earlier system of recording information: writing".[31]

For this ChangeMaker series, non-verbal communication is evident across the cases, from Mandla Majola to Sokari Douglas Camp.

Mandla Majola's presence does not come across strongly in the reflective, narrative mode of the primary conversation. This makes the switch to the short clip of him leading a demonstration in Canada against Health Minister Manto Tshabalala-Msimang all the more compelling. Here, we see and experience the presence and charisma of the activist and community leader, and we are fully able to understand why he was effective, over some fifteen years, as a national leader of a widely recognised and acknowledged, values-driven NGO.

Sam Paddock's leadership style epitomises the embodiment of values. This is evident from the opening sequence of the ChangeMaker case, as he orchestrates the movements and expressions of the entire GetSmarter team. Here, and elsewhere in this narrative and in numerous other clips of GetSmarter at work, we can see how embodied leadership becomes an integral part of the day-by-day behaviors of the team as a whole; the shorthand of "organizational values", at the enterprise level.

---

31 Sontag 1977: 156.

For the Communicare ChangeMaker case, the rich sense of the learning and communication environment could not be achieved with verbal representations alone. Here, the video medium and the depiction of non-verbal communication is essential. The field of practice of Augmented and Alternative Communication depends on visual images, whether through use of minimal technologies, such as paper and crayons, or via sophisticated computer screens. In addition, voice simulation depends on sound. Consequently, the non-verbal properties of video serve both to express what Communicare is about and also to counter the inadvertent biases that prevent people from hearing those who are trying to communicate in these ways.

Sokari Douglas Camp is, not surprisingly, the most comfortable in moving beyond words and her explanations of her art are quiet, self-depreciating, almost reluctant. This serves to push the visual and tactile qualities of her sculptures into the foreground, refusing the reductionism of words alone. This is evident in her presentation of "Europe supported by Africa and America", a life-sized composition of three female figures. This sculpture was inspired by William Blake's 1796 print, made in support of the abolition of slavery. In Sokari's interpretation, the women are dressed in contemporary clothing. The central figure holds a wreath that morphs into a fuel hose; part of a rich and complex set of references to the contemporary issues that drive Sokari's work as an artist.[32]

Restoring the agency of voice in vales-driven entrepreneurship

To end, and by way of conclusion, how can the approach set out here – video-led cases – contribute to the societal impact of values-driven entrepreneurship? Here, I will stay with the field of the curriculum while again narrowing the scope, now to the design and delivery of programs offered to influencers in graduate programs and courses, ranging from full Masters degrees through to short courses. Overall rates of participation in higher education are still growing. UNESCO estimates that global enrolments grew from 32.6m in in 1970 to just under 100m in 2000, a 206% increase over three decades. By 2015, global enrolments had doubled to 214.1m and UNESCO predicts that just under 600m students will be enrolled in universities and colleges across the world by 2040.[33] Clearly, promoting change through the higher education curriculum is an effective means of reaching a very large number of people.

---

32 Houghton, 2016.
33 Calderon, 2019.

While growing, higher education is also changing in step with all other aspects of the knowledge economy. These changes can be conceptualised in terms of the "platform economy".[34] The distribution of many goods, and particularly digital services and products, is increasingly mediated by digitally enabled platforms that are vertical, in the sense that they are becoming essential intermediaries between products and services, on the one hand, and customers on the other. Amazon is the exemplar here, and Kassahun Checole's work in refining Africa World Press to enable it to survive in this new economy is exemplary of the realignment imposed on traditional businesses. As universities move increasingly into blended and fully online learning, whether out of choice or financial necessity, they are becoming less like traditional, bounded, campuses and more like digital platforms. Indeed, this insight was the basis of GetSmarter's success; as Sam Paddock describes it in the ChangeMaker case, GetSmarter learned that a university's brand value is sometimes more important than its formal degree-awarding powers.

A consequence of the emergence of the platform economy is a shift in emphasis from authority to trust. The exponential expansion of digital media makes it difficult, and sometimes impossible, to establish the value and authenticity of new insights and exemplars in terms of their own merits, particularly when there are multiple claims, and false claims, to authority. In these circumstances, the reputation of a university, represented by its brand, serves as a proxy for trust. When incorporated into the curriculum of a trusted university, video-led cases will further enhance trust by combining the text-based authority of resources and sources of information with direct, visual communication with key figures within the curriculum's narrative. For example, and drawing on the protype cases that have been described here, Sokari Douglas Camp's video-based narrative, along with the visual power of her art, engenders trust in the sincerity of the long campaign for environmental justice for those who bear the direct brunt of fossil fuel extraction.

This agency of voice gains its valency – its societal impact – through the reach and richness of widely available, and affordable video. In turn this empowers what Walter Mignolo calls "border thinking" – the values and insights of those on the margins of traditional methods of knowledge creation and distribution.[35]

---

34 McAfee & Brynjolfson, 2017.
35 Mignolo, 2011.

In this set of prototype ChangeMaker cases, access to "border thinking" gives Mandla Majola and Sokari Douglas Camp platforms to advocate powerful and alternative perspectives to the institutional narratives of global corporate institutions, in particular the pharmaceutical and oil industries. Sam Paddock thinks and talks from the edge of curriculum innovation, pushing universities to widen access to knowledge and opportunity. Kassahun Checole makes the case for independent publishing in the wake of Amazon's gigantean path. In a contrasting frame, Camp Communicare's video-led agency allows some of those consigned to societal border zones by prejudices against "disabilities" to push back against the hubris of the assumed normal.

Part II

Organizational-Level Activities in Entrepreneurial Developments

Chapter 7

B Corps on the African Continent: A Source of Socio-Economic Hope?

Dr. Ann Armstrong

Abstract

This paper discusses the possible impact of the diffusion of the B Corps movement on the African continent. It examines what being a Certified B Corp entails and addresses how the ideology of business as a force for good, B Corps' defining principle, is an antidote to rapacious capitalism. While B Corps ecosystem on the continent is tiny, B Corps could become one possible model of inclusive business for the continent. It concludes with the caution that if the B Economy is to grow on the African continent, it must be indigenized to the local contexts.

Introduction

In this paper, I examine the value (if any) of amplifying the movement towards B Corps on and for the African continent. B Corps are gaining traction globally as one way to address the vicissitudes of today's capitalism. In the face of rising inequalities, even mainstream capitalists are wondering if capitalism has gone too far on the 'greed is good' mantra. Larry Fink, CEO of the hedge fund BlackRock, in a recent letter to CEOs, challenges them to become committed to purpose as well as profit. He argues "To prosper over time, every company must not only deliver financial performance, but also show how it makes a positive contribution to society,...". [1] Scholars such as Roger Martin[2] have argued that capitalism is broken and needs a significant re-examination and fix. Here, I examine if B Corps are a significant fix for a continent that has varied and complex histories and many grave post-colonial challenges.

To that end, I describe briefly the B Corps movement, the B Economy, and then delve into the B Corps that are currently operating on the continent. I will discuss whether the B Corps ideology of 'business as a force for good' is a fix for capitalism or if it is merely capitalism with a tweak. I conclude by addressing if the diffusion of the B Economy would in some way help to provide socio-economic hope to a continent that has endured so much corruption, false hope, and exploitation.

---

1   Norton, 2018.
2   Silverthorne, 2011.

B Corps as a movement

B Corps are not only a manifestation of marrying purpose and profit but were explicitly created to change the nature of capitalism. B Corps are designed to integrate profit and purpose. B Labs is a non-profit organization that essentially catalyzed what is now the B Corps movement. It is important to distinguish between benefit corporations and Certified B Corps. Certified B Corps "...are companies that have been certified by the nonprofit B Lab to have met rigorous standards of social and environmental performance, accountability, and transparency".[3] The organizations must be re-evaluated every three years to maintain their certification. There are over 2 500 B Corps in over 60 countries in 160 industries.[4]

The B Corps movement is gaining considerable traction now and is expected to continue. Among the best-known B Corps are Patagonia Inc., Me to We, and Ben & Jerry's (now owned by Unilever). Paul Polman, former CEO of Unilever, lauded as a 'conscious capitalism hero', notes:

> Business needs to be part of the solution, not the problem. We cannot be bystanders. We need to be a giver, not a taker in a society that gives us life in the first place. It is – after all – not possible to have a strong, functioning business in a world of increasing inequality, poverty and climate change.[5]

At the core of the B movement is the vetting and auditing process that B Lab has designed to certify and re-certify organizations. The B Lab is a non-profit organization that has global partners, including B Lab East Africa. The B Lab Directory of B Corps provides important information about all Certified B Corps. It has five elements to its scorecard or B Impact Assessment Report. The questions in the B Impact Assessment are organized into five Impact Areas: Governance, Workers, Community, Environment, and Customers. To be certified, an organization must have a score of 80 or above, out of a maximum of 200. B Lab estimates that the median score for an 'ordinary business' is 50.9.

The B Impact Assessment is customized to a company's size, sector, and geographic market. However, within those parameters, there are still questions included in the B Impact Assessment that might not be relevant to a particular company. In cases where a question is not applicable, the potential points available for that question are instead earned based on the performance of the company on the other topics relevant to the stakeholder.[6]

---

3   Honeyman, 2014.
4   B Corporation, 2018a.
5   Schwabel, 2017: 2.
6   B Corporation, 2018b.

The B economy

The B Economy is not limited to Certified B Corps. There are benefit organizations and, more importantly, those organizations that use the certification methodology to audit their own performance on the five criteria but do not go forward to the actual certification stage. B Lab "collaborates with leaders across all sectors of society to build a broader global movement of people using business as a force for good."[7] The B Economy encompasses people and organizations that engage in some way within conscious capitalism, doing business differently. The vision is that "one day there will be no B Economy—just a global economy that aligns its activities toward achieving our common purpose of a shared and durable prosperity for all".[8]

As noted earlier, Me to We is a Certified B Corps and is a subsidiary of WE Charity. Me to We is a social enterprise that operates in the consumer goods, voluntourism trips, and training and leadership sectors. It was first certified in November 2015 and has the following 2018 Impact Assessment Scores: Governance 11.7, Workers 17.1, Community 46.7, Environment 8.3, and Customers 24.2 for a total of 108. It was honoured by B Lab, in 2018, as Best Overall, Best for Community and received the same recognition in 2017.[9] Many of its consumer goods are made in Africa and many of its voluntourism trips are to Africa, principally Kenya. In addition to the overarching concern if Me to We exemplifies the white saviour complex, Me to We has faced some considerable controversy about its practices in 2019. Allegations include that its supply chain is tainted with child labour; its many corporate partnerships include companies doing 'bad business'; and that WE Charity resembles a cult.[10] WE Charity denies these allegations categorically and has sued the news organization that published them. It is too early to tell what impact (if any) the controversy will have on its future re-certification audit by B Lab. (In 2020, WE was felled by scandals.)

B Corps on the continent

According to the B Corp Directory, there are 30 Certified B Corps in seven African countries: Egypt, Ghana, Kenya, Rwanda, South Africa, Uganda and Zambia. Egypt has one, Ghana two, Kenya 15,[11] Rwanda one, South Africa eight, Uganda two, and Zambia one. Table 7.1 provides a summary of the 30.[12] Stephen Smith, a managing director at South Africa's IQbusiness, comments that "For us, to have a movement

---

7   The B Economy, 2019: 2.
8   Ibid.
9   B Corporation, 2018c.
10   Kerr, 2018 & Kerr, nd.
11   The 15 in Kenya do not include Me to We as it is a Canadian Certified B Corp.
12   There is a discrepancy between the directories of B Lab & B Lab East Africa as to the number of certified B Corps on the continent. As well, the B Lab East Africa includes one in Ethiopia, Oliberté, that shut down in 2019.

which is proving and driving the impact we have on the community broader than ourselves, we think, is critical".[13]

Table 7.1 – Africa's Certified B Corps (as of June 2019)

Country	B Corp Name	Location	Industry/ Sector	Month/ Year of Certification	Overall Impact Assessment Score
Egypt	Danone Egypt	El Obour City, Cairo	Food Manufacturing	April 2019	81.6
Ghana	GROWTH Mosaic Inc	Accra	Venture Building, Acceleration	October 2018	123.3
	PEGAfrica	Accra	Solar Home Systems	November 2015	131.2
Kenya	Let's Create Africa	Nairobi	Creative Agency	October 2018	84.7
	CoolCap Limited	Thika	Financial Services	May 2019	125.3
	TruTrade Africa	Westlands, Nairobi	First Mile Sourcing	October 2018	87.6
	Insurance for All (IFA)	Nairobi	Insurance and Loans for Small Income Earners	October 2018	81.6
	Aqua Clara Kenya	Keroka, Kisii	Water Solutions	October 2018	118.2
	Strauss Energy Limited	Nairobi	Solar Tiles, Panels, etc.	August 2018	90.6
	Vava Coffee Limited	Nairobi	Coffee Exporters and Roasters	August 2018	104.5
	Olivelink Healthcare	Nairobi	Primary Healthcare services	July 2018	102.3
	Kuza Biashara Limited	Nairobi	Micro Learning	June 2018	104.2
	Soko Inc.	Nairobi	Jewelry and Private Label	May 2018	80.1
	Sustainable Business Consulting	Westlands, Nairobi	Consulting	September 2017	85.5

---

13   Pisanello, 2018: 2

Country	B Corp Name	Location	Industry/ Sector	Month/ Year of Certification	Overall Impact Assessment Score
	Greyfos	Nairobi	Green Branding/ Advising	August 2017	80.2
	Daproim	Nairobi	Data Outsourcing	January 2015	101.3
	Eco2librium	Kakamega	Emission Reductions, Job Creation	October 2014	180.1
	EcoZoom	Nairobi	Ecological Products	January 2012	86.1
Rwanda	Karisimbi Business Partners Limited	Kigali	Consulting	June 2018	85.3
South Africa	Lubanzi Cape Venture Wine Company	Cape Town	Wine	December 2018	82.4
	Simanye	Johannesburg, Gauteng	Impact Investing, B-BBEE Verification	September 2018	80.7
	Chris Bertish Impossible	Cape Town	Speaker/Author	June 2018	107.8
	IQbusiness	Johannesburg, Gauteng	Consulting	September 2017	93.4
	Imani Development	Cape Town	Consulting (Economic Development)	May 2017	80.3
	LifeCo UnLtd Investment	Gauteng	Human Development and Management Services	March 2017	130.9
	Ecolution Consulting	Cape Town	Sustainability Consulting	October 2016	95.8
	Zoona	Cape Town	Mobile Payments	October 2014	113.8
Uganda	Solar Now	Kampala	Solar Systems	January 2019	142.2
	Pearl Capital Partners	Kampala	Equity, Quasi-Equity, Debt Investments	August 2017	105.1

Country	B Corp Name	Location	Industry/ Sector	Month/ Year of Certification	Overall Impact Assessment Score
Zambia	BioCarbon Partners	Mfuwe, Mambwe	Offsets	July 2017	177.3

As Table 7.1 makes clear, the B Corps do vary by industry/sector, certification dates, and by impact assessment scores. Even so, there are a notable number of B Corps in the solar and consulting sectors, some of which have very high impact assessment scores.[14] Few B Corps anywhere attain such scores as BioCarbon Partners has earned. It will be vital and informative to conduct long-term research to see what changes (if any) occur in the mission and margin mix of these B Corps.

Zoona, in South Africa,[15] is one of the oldest B Corps on the continent. The co-founders of Zoona (the Magrath brothers) are building an inclusive business to enable financial participation from previously underserved communities. Zoona was founded in 2009, was certified in 2014, and has maintained an impressive B Impact Assessment score. Zoona is a fintech company whose mission is "[to] bring together the drive of young entrepreneurs and the power of cutting-edge technology to bring safe and reliable financial services to underserved communities all over Africa.[16] Zoona has three "wildly important" goals – (1) To develop products and services that improve the financial health and well-being of one *billion* people; (2) To empower emerging entrepreneurs to build profitable businesses that create one *million* jobs; and (3) To prove that a purpose-driven business can be a global model for growth and impact.[17]

Zoona's co-founders place considerable emphasis on building a culture of inclusion. They seem to believe the adage, attributed to Peter Drucker, that 'culture eats strategy for breakfast.' They use 'Founderisms' to re-inforce the culture that they want to establish. Their book, *Founder isms* (sic), is replete with their culture-shaping ideology.[18] One theme throughout is be *real*, which is what the word *zoona* means. To illustrate a few... (1) Be bold and be brave; (2) Say no; and (3) Knowledge is the enemy of learning.[19]

---

14 Of course, there is no (misguided) attempt here to generalize about B Corps across the seven African countries in which they operate.
15 Zoona might be more accurately classified as a Zambian Certified B Corp. It is based in Cape Town but Zoona works primarily in Zambia & other Sub-Saharan countries.
16 Zoona, 2019a.
17 Zoona, 2019b: 1
18 Zoona, 2018.
19 Tsele, 2017.

Since its start, Zoona has received considerable recognition, not only for its business model, but also for its social impact. In 2011, Zoona received the Best Mobile Money Start-up Award and, in 2014, it was selected as one of ten companies worldwide best suited to taking women and girls out of poverty,[20] to highlight only a few of its accolades. Zoona appears to be on a successful growth trajectory and continues to expand geographically. In short, Zoona seems to be successful at marrying purpose and profit.

In light of the tiny size of the B Corps ecosystem in Africa, it is not surprising that there is little written about the B movement. The few papers tend to be messianic and anecdotal. It seems advisable, therefore, that organizations on the continent not get caught up in the current hype about the B Corps movement. As noted earlier, one well-known – perhaps best known – B Corp on the continent,[21] Oliberté shut down in March 2019. In 2009, Oliberté started as a small shoe company partnering with suppliers and factories in Africa. In 2012, it was able to launch its own factory in Addis Ababa, Ethiopia and in September 2013, it became the first shoe manufacturing company in the world to receive the FairTrade Certified designation.

The social enterprise continued to expand from 15 to 120 workers, most of whom were women. Oliberté opened another factory in Debre Marcos with the goal of making specialty shoes for people suffering from Podoconiosis.[22] However, in the last few years, Oliberté was losing money, about $500,000 annually. The founder, Tal Dehtiar, a Canadian, mortgaged his house and the shareholders invested considerable amounts to keep Oliberté afloat. Even so, in late 2018, Dehtiar made the decision to close down the company.[23] The company worked successfully with the in-house union to find work for most of the employees in the shoe industry.

Its final overall B Impact Score was 112.8 and it had been certified since June 2012.[24] While it may be premature to draw any definitive conclusions about what went wrong, the rapid rate of expansion is a likely factor. In addition, while the second factory focused on Oliberte's purpose, it may have been a drain on its profits. Oliberté may represent another failed capitalist experiment on the African continent by yet another 'white saviour.'

---

20 Zoona, 2019c.
21 Oliberté was technically a Canadian Certified B Corp but is included here as its impact in Ethiopia was considerable & it was heralded as a stellar example of a new way of doing business.
22 Podoconiosis is a geochemical disease occurring in individuals exposed to red clay soil of volcanic origin. This Neglected Tropical Disease is highly prevalent in Ethiopia (Deribe et.al., 2017).
23 Oliberté, 2019.
24 B Corporation, 2018d.

Africa as the world's next economic opportunity

In a recent McKinsey report, Leke, Chironga, and Desvaux[25] describe the considerable economic potential that exists in Africa which they describe as a giant awakening. Their claim of Africa's considerable growth potential is supported by the following data: (1) Africa is a 1.2 billion person market; (2) hundreds of multi-national and local companies are already doing business there; (3) Africa has considerable unfulfilled demand for products and services, estimated to be worth US$5.6 billion; (4) there are 122 million active users of mobile financial services; and (5) 54 countries are expected to create the world's largest free trade area. In short, there is rapid urbanization coupled with increased spending power.[26] Africa continues to have strong agriculture, mining and oil and gas sectors.

Africa however also has significant challenges: they include poor infrastructure, acute poverty, corruption, uneven education and health care, and profound inequalities, often based on racism. It is critical to see Africa not simply as a place to do business but as a place to do good business by using business as a force for good.[27] According to Ngozi Okonjo-Iweala, the former Nigerian Minister of Finance, companies must invest in the local communities if they are to be successful in Africa. She notes:

> You need to build trust with whichever community you're in, ... If the community lacks transport and there's a way you can help build a railroad where you are, why not? Because, in the end, the community will surround you, protect you, and love you.[28]

Similarly, Mark Bowman of SABMiller argues that companies must be constructive partners to government as well as good corporate citizens. SABMiller therefore positions itself as a co-collector of tax so that it has "a place at the table with senior government leaders and a voice on critical business issues".[29]

Whether the African continent is the 'awakening giant' or not, it is clear that there are significant opportunities to create inclusive economic models that rely on entrepreneurial imagination rather than on aid. *How We Made it in Africa: Learn from the Stories of 25 Entrepreneurs Who've Built Thriving Businesses* highlights various entrepreneurs who have created opportunities for themselves and their communities. All are candid in their discussions of the challenging contexts in which they operate.

---

25 Leke, Chironga, & Desvaux, 2018.
26 Ibid.
27 McKinsey itself has been involved in bad business practices in Africa. It advised Libya's former president, Muammar al Gaddafi and, more recently, was involved in the Eskom scandal in South Africa (Bogdanich & Forsythe, 2018).
28 Leke, Chironga & Desvaux, 2018: 150.
29 Ibid, 151.

Even so, they took risks and have enjoyed success in the longer term. For example, Addis Alemayehou, founder of Ethiopia's 251 Communications which employs over 40 full-time staff, comments:

> Businesses did not enter Ethiopia in 2001, it was a crazy thing to do. Nobody launched an English FM station at the time... Now we are experiencing a fairly exciting time because it is possible to adopt what has worked elsewhere and bring it to Ethiopia.
>
> There is a lot more to do, not just in Ethiopia, but elsewhere on the continent, too. I think we have not even scratched the surface as far as opportunities in Africa go.[30]

B Corps as a remedy?

While there is much buzz about the B Corps movement, it is not without its critics. First, there is the issue of whether it is a movement or simply a small number of businesses doing business somewhat differently than before. The claim that it is a movement may be more an echo chamber effect than any empirically demonstrable fact. More damning though is the critique that B Corps are nothing more than another glossy market-based solution to address social and economic injustice. Giridharadas[31] sees B Corps as simply a variation of capitalism that does not in any way change its power dynamics. Rather, he sees B Corps more as a kinder, community-focused capitalism. He sees current social change initiatives such as social enterprises, social venture capital, impact investing, and others as similar manifestations of capitalism. In other words, they do not create and substantive systemic change. Or as he puts it, "Many of them believe that they are changing the world when they may instead – or also – be protecting a system that is at the root of the problems they wish to solve".[32] One of the co-founders of B Lab, Jay Coen Gilbert, in addressing the concerns raised by Giridharadas, observes:

> I know that we test our core assumptions to ensure that we are challenging existing power structures to "fundamentally question the rules of the game – [and] alter . . . behavior"; first our own, and then, hopefully, others".[33]

Even so, Coen Gilbert does acknowledge that the question remains if the B Corps movement has gone far enough in trying the right the wrongs of capitalism.

---

30 Maritz, 2018: 98.
31 Giridharadas, 2018.
32 Giridharadas in Coen Gilbert, 2018: 7.
33 Coen Gilbert, 2018: 4.

Further, Giridharadas is concerned that MarketWorld, i.e., "...an ascendant power elite that is defined by the concurrent drives to do well and do good, to change the world while also profiting from the status quo",[34] has taken over what should remain in the public sphere. He argues that billionaires, in particular, should pay their taxes so that government and civil society can address social injustices. He criticizes them for engaging in dramatic and public acts of philanthropy often in sectors about which they have neither the knowledge nor the experience while enjoying significant tax benefits. Such acts of philanthropy can be seen as an example of what Marcuse defined as repressive tolerance. According to Marcuse, repressive tolerance has two forms:

> (i) the unthinking acceptance of entrenched attitudes and ideas, even when these are obviously damaging to other people, or indeed the environment...; and (ii) the vocal endorsement of actions that are manifestly aggressive towards other people....'[35]

Marcuse believes that genuine tolerance is only possible when real freedom is not limited, i.e., where we are intolerant of limits to freedom.

On the other hand, there are some benefits from the B Corps movement. B Corps are likely to have less toxic workplaces than other organizations, for example. What is valuable about the movement is its focus on measurement as there is much experience that shows that 'what gets measured gets done'. While the focus on measurement does not serve as a fix to capitalism, it does move organizational accountability to the forefront of its practices. The measurement process is explicit and public, so greenwashing, for example, is less likely to occur. We can have more confidence that the organizations are not merely engaging in a branding exercise but are having some sort of social, economic, and environmental impact, however modest. As Muira[36] notes,

> For business to be an agent of change, credible standards and public transparency are necessary for customers, investors, policy-makers and workers to differentiate good companies from just good marketing. Credible standards hold businesses accountable and transparent about their impact performance.

B Corps are therefore likely to engage in – and encourage – better governance. That alone may be a significant contribution to addressing the alarming consequences of today's capitalism.

---

34 Giridharadas, 2018: 58.
35 Oxford Reference, 2017: 1.
36 Muira, 2019: 7.

B Corps in Africa

As noted earlier, the African ecosystem of B Corps is tiny; as a result, the B Economy's impact will be small. However, there are some useful practices that organizations on the continent can take from the B Economy. Most importantly, companies can use the measures developed by the B Lab without any requirement to become certified. Not only can they score themselves on the five Impact Areas – Governance, Workers, Community, Environment, and Customers – they can consider them in the design of their organizations. The Impact Areas would be useful to founders of start-ups as they begin their entrepreneurial journeys and as their organizations grow.

However, it is essential that the B Corps movement on the African continent be driven by an unwavering commitment to local communities by creating a relationship of mutual trust between the company and the local context. There are many diverse communities and economies in Africa that work well. For example, there are various rotating credit and savings associations (ROSCA) such as the well-known stokvels in South Africa that support economic empowerment and may help to support inclusive business practices.[37] Further, it is important to remember that capitalism was seen as colonialism redux in many African countries at the time of their independence. Capitalism is *not* considered to be the only economic model and some African states turned to socialism, as an attempt to indigenize their economies.[38]

If B Corps are to diffuse across the continent, they must demonstrate their understanding of the diverse economies already working in Africa and demonstrate the value of measurement as a force for doing business better, even if they cannot achieve their self-proclaimed belief that business is a force for good.

---

37 Armstrong, forthcoming.
38 Akyeampong, 2018.

Chapter 8

Collaboration Over Competition

Dana Rissley

Abstract

Entrepreneurship has taken center stage as a leading initiative for economic growth on the Southern African continent. Startup success stories provide insights into what is required to 'make it' in the startup world. However, in many cases, the path to profitable revenue growth may seem elusive, even unattainable, at times, particularly when a business is resource constrained This chapter will explore ways to use a collaborative approach to business growth to achieve success. A collaborative approach is particularly helpful for businesses that may be under-resourced or stretched too thin. It can also act as a catalyst to reignite a stagnant business or give a boost to an already successful organization.

First, I will share what I mean by collaboration, which ties into the African collective approach to life. Secondly, I will outline what resources are typically needed to launch, grow and sustain a business. Thirdly, I will share examples of successful collaborations that have occurred on the African continent. Finally, I will introduce a framework to assist with understanding where collaborations may exist, to assist entrepreneurs and established business owners.

Introduction

A challenge for many start-ups and established businesses globally, is resource constraint. Like start-ups in other geographies of the world, this challenge exists in Southern Africa and depending on where the start-up founders are positioned geographically and socioeconomically, it will vary widely. The continent is also challenged by a lack of skills and readily available start-up capital. While it may sound like a non-starter to launch a business, the fact is that it's actually rife with opportunity. Africa has one of the youngest populations, some of the world's fastest growing economies, and is developing solutions to world problems that everyone can learn from – a phenomenon known as the Leap Frog effect. Rather than look at lack of imminent resources as a challenge, it is actually an opportunity to be creative, collaborate, and grow values-driven, inclusive company.

After spending time with entrepreneurs on the African continent, I realized that they approach entrepreneurship with a 'find a way' mentality. Their business models generally incorporate some kind of social impact, whether that is looking after their employees, finding a way to provide products or services to an underserved population, or impacting their communities. More often than not, success is measured by the number of jobs created or the number of family members that can be supported, with less focus placed on the bottom line. These measures focus on the impact on the whole rather than on the individual.

Thus, many entrepreneurs in Africa tend to favor collaboration rather than competition by way of life. What can be learned and expanded upon, is how this collective or collaborative approach can touch many areas of a business. When a business may seem resource constrained, an entrepreneur can leverage the collaborative approach to impact their resource position.

At its core, collaboration is bringing various parties together to work collectively to achieve either a shared goal or an individual goal that aligns with a broader goal. Collaboration can take many shapes, whether that be a business partnership, a joint venture, fractional employment, collective marketing, or industry awareness. The list will continue to grow, and companies are finding new ways to collaborate each day.

Collaboration can be both a long-term effort or a shorter, once-off event. The notion is really to find a way to come together with another party to have an exponential effect, meaning the two parties together can achieve more than what either party could achieve on its own. Perhaps the collaboration starts off as a one-time event, but based on the success from the venture, it becomes a longer-term partnership. The point here is to start to open the mind to thinking of ways in which two separate entities can find a way to collaborate for improvement not only for themselves, but also for their communities and society.

With regards to resources required by entrepreneurs, most companies, at one stage or another, will need one (or more) of the following resources: funding, employees, customers, suppliers, mentorship or access to networks. The list can feel overwhelming, especially when sufficient funding is not available to procure all of the other items on the list.

Before I move into the discussion of examples of collaborations, I want to elaborate more on the list above. In the table below, I have included the type of resource needed, a description of the resource and the typical approaches to finding the resource.

Table 8.1: Collaboration and resources needed

Resource	Description	Source
Funding/ Financial Capital	Typically, one thinks of start-up funding as the only resource required. However, even once the business has been launched, it will need growth capital and a steady stream of working capital.	• Bootstrapping/ founder's funds • Venture capital • Crowdfunding • Revenue generation
Employees	Companies require skilled employees that are a culture fit for the company. At times, finding the correct person may be challenging. Hiring an employee enables a company to grow and share tasks. However, it creates a financial obligation for the company and also requires ongoing support and mentorship.	• Referrals from friends/family/ colleagues, employees • Online job postings • University recruiting
Customers	A solid, and growing, customer base is required to build a successful company. A rapidly growing customer base is exciting for any company and a sign of success. Maintaining and expanding that customer base is where the challenge comes in for many companies.	• Traditional Marketing • Social media • Word of mouth/ referral
Suppliers	Reliable suppliers are essential to the development and long-term success of a business. Similar to employees, finding the right mix of skills and cultural fit can prove challenging for a business. However, once the right suppliers are found, it can make the business run like clockwork.	• Bidding process • Online resources • Referrals
Networks	Access to networks can take a business to the next level. Finding the right people to connect you with a decision maker can open doors that may have seemed closed.	• Family • Friends • Work colleagues • School colleagues
Mentorship	Mentorship provides the emotional and psychological support that many people, not only entrepreneurs, often underestimate. Having a mentor to call and check in with helps vet new ideas, works through challenges, and shares in the celebration of wins.	• Family • Friends • Work colleagues • School colleagues

Now with both an idea of what is meant by collaboration and an idea of where resource needs to lie, let's look at some real-life examples of building businesses in Africa using a collaborative and collective approach.

For our first example, I am going to share my personal experience of building a social impact software and consulting company. In this example, my partner and I used a collaborative approach to solutions for our employee needs, supplier needs, network needs, and customer needs.

Our company set out with a broad mission, to positively impact the lives of others through positive social change. The long-term goal is to be the leader in the African market for all social impact needs. Our first order of business, a large undertaking, was to develop a social impact software that measures multiple levels of impact of a social intervention. Starting with an idea and a passion, we basically needed every resource on the list above.

A typical approach would be to understand funding required which would include software development fees, marketing efforts, renting an office space, hiring staff, etc. However, we decided to approach it a bit differently, combining both a collaborative approach and the 'find a way' mentality.

Firstly, we set up shop in an existing office space that is leased by a sister company. Rather than hire an entire administrative staff, we began sharing personnel resources with the sister company. We found that the staff enjoyed the new challenges and was eager to get involved with our new project.

Rather than follow a typical marketing approach, we identified members of our existing networks, which came from mentors, school colleagues, friends, and family. These individuals were able to help get us in front of key decision makers that would be buyers of our product. For our initial meetings with potential customers, we knew we needed to gain an understanding of potential clients' needs as we envisioned bringing our software to life. So rather than try to immediately sell them new software, we took a collaborative approach to piloting new projects. As a result, both the client and our company learned from our joint projects.

One of the biggest challenges for us was finding the data required and the software development skills available within our start-up budget. Again, utilizing our networks we found data scientists that could accommodate the large amount of data needed. We also found a software developer that understood our vision and had a passion for our project. Due to resource constraint, we could not afford to hire the developer full time. Our solution to this was to pay for the fractional use of the developer's time required to complete our project. Indirectly, we collaborated with other customers of the developer to achieve our business goal while they achieved theirs.

There are numerous examples of start-ups and existing companies taking a collaborative approach to solution for resource constraint or simply to grow their businesses at a more rapid or inclusive rate than they would have independently. Further examples of typical start-up challenges I've encountered, either in my personal experience or from start-ups that I've mentioned, are included below. They aligned with the resources above, to give examples for each type of potential resource needed.

Funding

Challenges: Often times, start-ups have a need for funding, but don't know where to look, who to reach out to, or how to talk to 'investors'. Then, if interested investors are found, the capital required is below the minimum investment amount.

Collaborative approach: To identify funders, companies should look to similar companies (either in industry or customer base) to find out who funded their company. Often times this information is found on the company's website. Other times, it's a simple question to the founder. Surprisingly, many founders are eager to connect and share their stories, it's just a matter of asking the question. The other start-up founder is also an excellent resource for coaching on how to speak to the investors, in terms of what documents are expected and what content to include.

In the case of our social impact start-up, we looked at other software companies in the social impact space to understand where their initial funding came from. Once we understood potential source of funds, we had conversations with individuals within organizations that received funding from our target sources. They were a wealth of information on how to position our company and what approach to follow. Rather than look at us as competition for funds, the other organization saw it as an opportunity to demonstrate more need for this type of funding, thus securing a future pool of funds for us all to draw from.

To achieve the minimum funding amount, start-ups should join together to form a pool of companies that an investor can tap into. Rather than individual companies charging down the same path, they can leverage each other's identified investors, synchronize their pitch decks, and raise their total investment amount required to meet the minimum investment amount.

Employees

Challenges: Finding the right people at the right price is an ongoing and ever-evolving challenge, both for start-ups and established companies. As the world continues to progress and more knowledge workers are needed, the gap will continue to grow between skills required and skills available. Outdated education systems are failing to equip people with the skills required to step into vacant roles.

So, we are sitting with a growing population of unemployed or underemployed workers, and a list of vacant jobs that cannot be filled. Further, if we layer on the potential effects of the 4th industrial revolution, the job and career dynamics can seem impossible to navigate.

Collaborative approach: What is described above can seem overwhelming both for companies and potential employees. But, there are solutions! In this category, the collective approach to focus on the benefit to the whole, rather than the individual, is imperative. Firstly, start-ups should focus on the skills required and the values of the individual they are hiring, rather than trying to fill a full-time role. Shared resources, where time and therefore expense are shared are becoming increasingly common. In my experience, this has worked well for project-based jobs, including software development, communications strategy, and social media marketing.

Additionally, as a helpful solution to the development of longer-term resource needs, start-ups should consider offering internship positions. Many times, the short-term period and lower costs associated with an intern are beneficial to start-ups. Further, the employment of interns benefits not only the start-up, but also benefits the larger labor pool. By providing work-ready talent to the marketplace, the start-ups are working toward the greater good.

Customers

Challenges: Many start-up founders turn over in their minds how they are going to land their initial customers. For start-ups that saw initial success in developing a client base, their next push is to grow their customer base and deliver value and impact lives of their expanding circle of influence. Often times, a full-time marketing resource is outside of a company's budget, or they have other pressing needs for their restrained cash flow.

Collaborative approach: The message here is that a company does not have to go it alone! Almost every company shares a similar customer profile with another company. A first step for any company is to articulate their value proposition and define their customer profile. Once understood, they can use that information to identify other brands that share that customer profile to jointly target their customer base.

For a business development consulting firm I was building, I identified my target client type (B2B, small to medium sized). Then I partnered with other service providers that would target the same type of company. This group included lawyers, human resource professionals, and accountants. By creating this network of service providers, we had multiple sources of customer referrals and also became a 'one stop shop' for the small- to medium-sized businesses. We found this offering to be a differentiator; now management of our clients did not have to shop around for a variety of services they required.

Suppliers

Challenges: Similar to that of finding the right employees, partnering with suppliers that meet your needs and share your values can be challenging. Especially as a start-up or small business, the supplier base that supports larger corporates may not align well with your business for a variety of reasons. Their minimum order quantity may be too high for you, they may not be flexible on pricing due to the lower order quantity, and they may not offer flexible payment terms. All of these seemingly small issues can make building your supplier base seem very overwhelming.

Collaborative approach: This approach may sound simple, and sometimes that is what we need to just make things work. Find suppliers that are 'your size'. While we tend to think of the traditional supplier base to meet our needs, there are hundreds (if not thousands) of smaller suppliers that will make things work for you. Take the focus off of fitting into what the supplier wants from a customer and start searching for a supplier that may not have the same big-name brand recognition, but can deliver quality products, on time, and within your budget. Trust me, they are out there.

I really love the approach to finding the solution to this challenge, because it is truly collaborative. While you are building your business, you are also enabling other small businesses to grow and find the market they can best serve. As more businesses look to non-traditional suppliers, the impact on small business growth will become exponential.

In my experience, this has worked well, particularly for software development. Rather than go through a traditional software development company that layered on overheads and other management costs, we chose to work directly with a developer that could still deliver a high-quality product, within our required time frame, and at a cost that was within our start-up budget.

Networks

Challenge: A major challenge I often hear is that you need to know the right people to open doors and make the right connections. Often times this is true in finding funding, finding your early adopter customers, and landing top employees or contractors. Looking around, it seems that everybody who has made it, has had a strong network to help them out. And while it is true that networks do help, often times we don't know who we know until we ask.

Collaborative approach: In this case, it's comes down to reaching out to those around us. While, yes, some people do just have amazing networks, we all have social spheres we operate within that have the potential to also double as commercial networks. Just think of all of the 'networks' you have been part of in your life, whether that be from secondary education, tertiary education, community groups, church groups, former work colleagues, or current work colleagues. You know more people than you realize.

Now that we've established that we know people, it's time to start talking to them about what you are working on. Set up coffee meetings, offer to present to a group, attend a reunion event, the way to get in front of people is endless. You will be amazed by how quickly people want to learn more about what you're working on and share it with their networks.

When my partner and I were trying to find early adopters and partners for our social impact software, we sat down and brainstormed who within our networks would want to learn more and know of collaborative partners. We short listed a few individuals and set up a time to meet with them and share what we were working on. As a result of those meetings, we have five meetings with potential end users/early adopters that are eager to partner with us and further develop our software. It may seem like we have an extensive network to get us in front of potential clients, but really it is our connections to the networks that we needed to find – and we all have them.

Mentorship

Challenge: One of the often underappreciated but extremely necessary aspects of entrepreneurship is finding mentors that have the passion, knowhow, and time to support your business. It isn't a widely advertised role, is generally unpaid and the relationship develops naturally over time. However, in these relationships, sometimes the best advice and most genuine support is found, because it tends to come from the heart.

Collaborative approach: Many times, the solution to this one is just asking someone you admire or aspire to be like, to give you some advice. That initial conversation leads to further conversations, and eventually a mentor/mentee relationship begins to develop. These potential mentors can be found at start-up events, incubator or accelerator programs, or even online. With the technology available to us, we can find individuals who have succeeded in our industry, or geography or even more broadly, at entrepreneurship. Using online tools, such as LinkedIn, we can start dialogues and set up telephonic or in-person meetings with these target mentors.

By nature, mentorship is collaborative. Mentors are eager to collaborate with start-up entrepreneurs who share the same values as them. Often, mentors are spending time with other start-ups, thus positioning them to leverage ideas from one start-up to benefit another. Typically, since it's an unpaid position, mentors come from a space of a truly collective attitude, putting the good of the whole above their own monetary gain.

I have been fortunate enough to have a few strong mentors in my life. A couple were mentors for a specific project or period of time, but others have stayed with me as I have progressed through different stages in life. They have been invaluable in my development. Typically, they started out as mentors for once-off projects which then developed into long-term relationships.

Now that we have run through examples of challenges and the collaborative approaches to resources required for entrepreneurship, let's look at a framework to help you start to find the resources for your business.

The goal of the framework is to present a 3-step approach to identifying resources required, where and how to find them.

The first step is to understand what resources you have and what resources are needed. In the table below, you can write what resources you already have in each category. Next, write the resources you know you need but don't have. The key here is to be specific. For example, under 'Funding', rather than stating 'money' or 'cash', state 'funding for computers', 'funding for software development'. Being specific will help with finding sources at a later stage.

Another example is in 'Networks'. Rather than simply say you need a network, list the networks you have such as 'colleagues from Company ABC' or 'alumni from University'. Then list networks for what you feel you may lack access to at the moment.

Table 8.2: Resources required

	Funding	Employees	Suppliers	Customers	Networks	Mentors
Have						
Need						

The second step is to determine where they may be overlap in 'Needs' from various types of resources. For example, if you listed 'software developer' in employees and 'software support' in suppliers, there may be an opportunity to combine those needs into one need, making the list shorter and the search a bit easier. You'll notice that we excluded 'Networks' and 'Mentors' from this step of the exercise. You'll see why in the final step.

Table 8.3: Resource consolidation

	Funding	Employees	Suppliers	Customers
Employees				
Suppliers				
Customers				

Now, in the final step, we will start to brainstorm where from networks or mentors these resources can be found. This step should bring the brainstorming and planning process full circle by finding solutions to the gaps that you may feel exist to move your start-up forward. Bonus if you add the specific network or mentor where the resource will come from.

Table 8.4: Resource mapping

	Funding	Employees	Suppliers	Customers
Network				
Mentors				

So, there we have it, an approach to leveraging a collective & collaborative approach to launching a business on the African continent. While it may seem overwhelming to launch a business, anywhere in the world, when broken down into actionable steps, it is an achievable goal. The African continent, with its energy, excitement, and massive potential, is the perfect launching pad for an inclusive, values-based business.

Chapter 9

Lessons Learnt from Supporting Early-stage Ventures at an African Business School Incubator

Sarah-Anne Alman

Abstract

This book chapter addresses the core question: how do you best support entrepreneurs on their journey from idea to viable business? To put it in another way, what do entrepreneurs need in order to develop their idea, test their product in the market and establish a viable business? What are the optimal conditions for new ventures that assist with their growth and development?

As part of the research to answer this question, interviews were carried out with start-up founders and ecosystem contributors who participated in two pilot venture incubation programs. Use was also made of anonymous surveys during and after incubation support. At the end of each month, multiple feedback forms were collected to benchmark the success of the program and to identify what worked and what didn't. Approximately 50 semi-structured interviews were conducted with the participating founders, mentors, industry and program partners. The information collected was reviewed to reveal a few key lessons, or reminders, for incubation.

These lessons will be valuable for industry bodies, individuals or universities who want to launch or improve programs working with early-stage start-ups and for founders looking for support from incubators.

Understanding the key needs of start-ups

A start-up is a temporary organization formed to search for a repeatable and scalable business model.[1] Individual start-ups have specific needs that must be met as they develop their idea into a viable commercial enterprise. Entrepreneurs might need support, advice, mentors who have walked the same path, a sense of community, funding, skills and human capital to support them as they scale. They also need specific skills and expertise to help them address particular problems unique to their own context. Nesta's research[2] identified eight most cited needs mentioned by start-

---

1   Blank, 2013.
2   Miller & Stacey, 2014.

ups. These included a clear understanding of a problem, potential customers, advice for the basics, strategic advice, people to work with who have complementary skills, early-stage finance, and space to work.

Before launching the pilot venture incubation program, a co-working space was initially launched to engage with early-stage entrepreneurs on a daily basis in order to understand their pain-points and most important needs. Interestingly, surveys and focus groups with entrepreneurs revealed needs that focused on funding and services. On the other hand, observations and interactions with entrepreneurs in the co-working space identified key needs involving guidance and advice, time management, prioritisation and access to relevant networks. It became apparent that first-time founders were not always aware of, or the best placed to identify, their most important needs.

What also became clear from this phase is that there is no one-size that fits all. Context is critical, where needs varied according to the entrepreneurs' previous entrepreneurship experience, the venture's stage of development and overall access to other resources. An incubator has to clarify its intended target audience and its overall goals and objectives. We saw important differences between founders who had started other businesses and those who were starting a venture for the first time. There were also major differences between those that lacked access to additional resources and networks compared with those who had some ability to self-fund or draw on personal and professional networks. For incubators based in countries that have high levels of poverty and inequality, it is particularly important to pay closer attention to the less apparent needs of entrepreneurs. There is growing evidence[3] that suggests that successful incubators start with identifying the needs of their target group and matching the services and adapting as the target group needs change.

Through daily interactions with entrepreneurs working in the co-working space and recent graduates who had founded a company – along with desktop research, surveys, focus groups and face-to-face interviews – we identified six core elements for an incubation program as particularly important to the local context and target audience. These will be discussed further under the section entitled 'Pilot venture incubation program'.

Early-stage entrepreneurship support systems

The last decade has seen a surge of activity in entrepreneurship and innovation across the African continent. Hubs, co-working spaces, labs, incubators, accelerators, hackathons, competitions or challenges and the like abound. While different in

---

3   Miller & Stacey, 2014.

their objectives and delivery, these start-up support programs aim to bring critical resources, skills, funding and networks to support the creation of new ventures. What is the different role of all these start-up support programs? And how does incubation fit within this landscape?

Through desktop research and feedback from key stakeholders in the wider entrepreneurship ecosystem, the diagram below was developed as a working typology of early-stage entrepreneurship support programs. This will enable entrepreneurs to further understand the primary characteristics and value proposition of each initiative. There is a huge range of early-stage entrepreneurship support programs. The table below draws a comparison between the five types that dominate the arena: competitions, programs, co-working spaces, incubators and accelerators.

Table 9.1 Early-stage entrepreneurial support systems

	COMPETITION	PROGRAM	CO-WORKING	INCUBATOR	ACCELERATOR
BACKGROUND	Designed to stimulate new innovations and find talented entrepreneurs.	Originally focused on business plans and execution, there has been a more recent shift to focus on how to search for the uncertainties and unknowns in new ventures.	The use of an office environment typically so as to share furniture, equipment, ideas and knowledge.	Originally designed for capital-intensive start-ups or formal IP-based technology spin-offs. Typically one to two years.	Initially designed for digital ventures early in their lifecycle, using lean start-up methodology. Typically three months in length, often ending in a demo day.
ORIGIN	Peter Diamandis founded the first incentive competition – the X Prize – to inspire the creation of space travel (1994).	Myles Mace taught the first entrepreneurship course – the Management of New Enterprise – at Harvard Business School (1947).	Jonathan Robinson created one of the first social innovation hubs – the Impact Hub – as a workspace dedicated to social innovation (2005).	Joseph Mancuso started the first business incubator – the Batavia Industrial Centre – in New York (1959).	Paul Graham, Jessica Livingston, Trevor Blackwell, Robert Morris started the first accelerator – Y Combinator – in Cambridge, Massachusetts (2005).

	COMPETITION	PROGRAM	CO-WORKING	INCUBATOR	ACCELERATOR
ARCHETYPES	Contests vary in their objectives: 1. Identify excellence 2. Influence public perception 3. Mobilise capital 4. Strengthen a community 5. Improve education and skills	Programs typically aimed at two distinct forms of enterprise: 1. Highly scalable and high-growth potential start-ups 2. Small and medium enterprises	Can vary in membership profile: 1. Freelancer 2. Creative 3. Young Professional 4. Entrepreneurs 5. Technology	Business support varies greatly based on where an entrepreneur is in the entrepreneurial process and profile of entrepreneur and new venture. Most offer: 1. Facilities 2. Business services	Varies based on objectives: 1. Investor: bridge equity gap 2. Matchmaker: new services to customers/stake-holders 3. Ecosystem: stimulate start-up activity within a special region or domain.
CHARACTERISTICS	1. Online application form designed to test certain aspects of business or entrepreneur. 2. Selected entrepreneurs participate in local pitch (regional). 3. Sometimes intervention includes week-long course or academy. 4. Final presentation and gala dinner or award ceremony with top finalists.	1. Typically focuses on either business model discovery phase, or basic business skills. Niche focuses include intrapreneurship, social entrepreneurship, high growth. 2. Combination of theory and practical 3. Culminates in written business plan or presentation.	1. Flexible desk and meeting space. 2. Opportunities to meet other freelancers, consultants or entrepreneurs. 3. A limited program of events or learning to support ventures. 4. Open application process. 5. Variety of membership fees for founders or freelancers based on level of usage. 6. Additional revenue streams from events and/or catering.	1. Typically does not invest directly in the company. 2. Longer support (12-36 months comprising support services). 3. An application process that is 'in principle' open to all, yet highly competitive. 4. Business support consulting, IP, Legal, Marketing, HR (develop management team), external financing. 5. Focus on enterprises reaching sustainability. 6. Less clear on exit or graduation criteria.	1. Possible offer of upfront investment ($10k – $50k), usually in exchange for equity (5–10%). 2. Time–limited support (three to six months comprising programs, events and intensive mentoring. 3. An application process that is 'in principle' open to all, yet highly competitive. 4. Cohorts of start-ups rather than individual companies. 5. Mostly focus on small teams, not individual founders. 6. Periodic graduation with a Demo Day/Investor Day.

Incubation

Incubators have been seen as one way to meet the needs of new ventures, and have been in existence for over 50 years. While they became mainstream in the late 1990s through supporting capital-intensive hardware businesses, they have more recently gained a poor reputation largely due to the long timelines of support, lack of company exit policy and reliance on long-term public funding. Incubators have an essential role to play within the entrepreneurship ecosystem, but the terminology has become widely used, leading to different interpretations.

Hackett and Dilts[4] define incubation as: *"...a shared office–space facility that seeks to provide its incubatees with a strategic, value–adding intervention system of monitoring and business assistance."* While Miller and Stacey describe incubation as: *"... a collection of techniques that can be used to prove an idea, develop a team and de-risk ventures for later- stage investors. It happens in accelerator programs, co–working spaces, social venture academies and learning programs, competitions and through the work of very early–stage investors."* [5]

Studies regarding the impact of incubation programs have also varied. Some show neutral to negative impacts of incubation; others reflect positive impacts on survival rate, job creation and revenue growth. To test and evaluate the pilot venture incubation program, the overall concept of 'incubation' was broken apart into smaller components. This enabled each of the identified six elements to be tested in order to understand how valuable each one was for early-stage ventures.

Pilot venture incubation program

The primary audience for the pilot venture incubation program was business school graduates, recent alumni and students or alumni from the wider university network. The decision to focus on this initial target audience was based on observing the high volume of activity in the local ecosystem that existed locally to support entrepreneurship at the aspiration and intention stage (events, hackathons, start-up weekends, competitions), and early-stage and late-stage ventures (accelerators, scalerators, venture capital). A gap was identified at the business model discovery phase and the start-up launch phase where very few support mechanisms were available post-classroom and pre-first investment or accelerator. The aim of the pilot program was to change that and support the development of viable businesses and reliable entrepreneurs. Viability was defined as either sustainable growth or an investable business case.

---

4   Hackett & Dilts, 2004.
5   Miller & Stacey, 2014.

In trying to answer the question: "What are the optimal conditions for new ventures that assist with their growth and development?", a 'hybrid' incubation model was developed which aligned with the needs of the entrepreneurial ecosystem in the local context rather than trying to fit pre-defined classifications of incubators or accelerators. This hybrid model used some elements of the accelerator – which comprises a highly competitive selection process, a cohort base, and has a time limit of three months as well as some elements of an incubator. The latter provides access to critical resources, workshops, networks with no equity taken and has six-months' post- program support for successful ventures.

The key elements for the pilot venture incubation program included:

1. Co-working space: hot-desks, meeting rooms, and community meet-ups and check-ins

2. Mentorship: founders were assigned a mentor who was an experienced entrepreneur

3. Workshops and structured guidance: based on a lean start-up curriculum

4. Advisory services: partnerships with corporates to offer pro-bono advice or clinics

5. Events: regular events to provide information, feedback and networking

6. Access to networks: facilitated introductions to a network of alumni, entrepreneurs, and the broader ecosystem

The following sections further describe the support provided for each element, then summarize and unpack the key lessons learnt for each element.

Co-working space and community

A co-working space in the business school was available 24/7 for entrepreneurs who were part of the pilot program and for graduates of the program. The aim was to provide start-ups with physical work space and meeting rooms, and create a vibrant community of entrepreneurs.

The pilot identified a few important lessons for building start-up communities:

- Cohort cohesion was an asset to the program's success. However, trust and respect were crucial to facilitate peer mentoring. Incubators should be intentional about how they go about fostering trust amongst founders in their community.

- Driving engagement opportunities for start-ups to discuss their business and key issues or challenges created more value for founders in contrast to social mixers or general networking amongst peers.

- Situating a co-working space within a business school provided entrepreneurs with additional credibility through association with a reputable organization. This in turn unlocked further opportunities, networks and resources for the start-ups.

Overall the co-working space was found to be extremely valuable and aided the building of community amongst the start-ups. The pilot found that physical proximity increased collaboration and knowledge exchange between start-ups who supported each other throughout the program. Entrepreneurs associated less value with the physical office space than with a strong community of peers. The latter added the most value to the founder – above even mentorship. While the first pilot saw founders frequently drawing on each other for emotional support, advice and skills exchange, founders in the second cohort interacted less. The first cohort feedback revealed peer mentoring to be the most valuable aspect of the program. Founders who were a stage ahead of other founders were able to provide guidance and advice for common issues. The first cohort had a high degree of social cohesion, community and underlying trust compared to the second cohort, where peer mentoring did not even feature in feedback provided.

A strong community of co-founders also created opportunities to facilitate peer learning and skills exchanges (for example, legal advice, financial modelling or technology knowledge). Regular group check-ins with the founders aided peer learning where start-ups had to critically and honestly assess each other's business models. The pilot showed that when regular weekly check-ins with the cohort were conducted, this almost certainly increased peer pressure to make progress. It also enabled regular interactions and understanding of the issues each founder was grappling with. While it was time-consuming for the cohort to listen to each venture, when the group process was abandoned in favour of one-on-one sessions, the sense of community and commitment to the group was severely impacted.

Situating the co-working space within the business school had the additional benefit of aiding connections across the business school and the broader university. This was particularly beneficial for start-ups where there was direct alignment with faculty expertise. The association with a university also gave entrepreneurs additional credibility. This was extremely valuable as new ventures don't have a track record or reputation to fall back on. The pilot showed that entrepreneurs were able to secure meetings with potential clients or advisors more easily, in contrast to when they didn't have an association with a reputable organization like a business school.

Mentorship and guidance

Founders were assigned a mentor who was an experienced entrepreneur or industry expert to work in a milestone-driven system. Founders received strategic advice in weekly check-ins with their mentor, and bi-weekly check-ins with an Entrepreneur-in-Residence (EiR) who met with all the founders. The aim was to connect start-ups with an experienced entrepreneur who could guide them in their testing of their business model and provide 1:1 support that was not always possible in a training or workshop environment.

The pilot identified a few important lessons for mentoring entrepreneurs:

- Experienced entrepreneurs were found to be an invaluable asset to an incubator and provided additional benefits to founders.

- However, multiple mentors for early-stage start-ups was not beneficial as conflicting advice often led to indecision and confusion among founders.

- Chemistry between mentor and mentee was vital for a productive relationship to continue beyond the life of the program.

- Founders needed to be coachable and open to advice in order to benefit from the program.

Both pilots revealed the most valuable aspects of the program to be access to experienced entrepreneurs that provided guidance, support and advice. Entrepreneurs were matched to mentors who had previous experience running a business. The mentorship model was a milestone-driven system by which entrepreneurs progressed through a development plan for the duration of the program together with their mentors. The program ensured that both mentor and mentee understood the expectations of the other, as well as their own role. Aside from the guidance and support, founders highlighted the valuable aspects of mentorship which were having 'one person' cheering for you, strategic advice and key introductions.

The first pilot program had multiple mentors per start-up. This was found to be unhelpful for this stage of a new venture as too much conflicting advice sometimes led to indecision by the founder. Founders needed to be prepared to make the final call on their decisions, but to think through advice and guidance offered by mentors. For the second pilot, only one mentor was assigned to an entrepreneur, and an entrepreneur-in-residence was introduced to the program in order to provide consistent guidance to the start-ups as they progressed. The entrepreneur-in-residence role was found to be helpful where mentors did not always follow through on commitments made. It also helped to assess the overall quality and consistency of the mentors.

Chemistry between mentor and mentee was also found to be vital. Founders on the program met with each of the program's mentors and selected the individual who they felt would align with their own vision and values. Likewise, the mentors indicated their preference of founder. The chemistry between mentor and mentee needed to be right to ensure success. The pilot showed that where there was a good match, the relationship often continued beyond the life of the program into a more formal advisory or governance role. Mentoring was far less productive when there was not a direct match, with some mentors not making time to meet with the assigned venture at all.

Start-ups and ideas can have great potential. However, if the founder was not open to being coached and receiving advice, the value they derived from the program was found to be minimal. The pilot revealed that selected start-ups must be coachable to ensure they derive value from the program. This became an increasing focus in the selection and evaluation criteria as mentors became frustrated and unwilling to contribute towards the program on an ongoing basis when they saw that an entrepreneur was unwilling to consider and explore advice given.

Training and workshops

Regular training and workshops focused on a lean start-up curriculum to provide direction to the iterations the start-up would go through on the program. Lean start-up methodology uses hypothesis-driven experimentation, iterative process and validated learning to develop business models. The aim was to provide a methodology that would guide start-ups in testing their business models.

The pilot revealed a few important lessons for developing entrepreneurship training and workshops:

- Lean methodology helped entrepreneurs quickly test their assumptions and accelerated quick learning which was key for a start-up with limited resources and time.

- Requiring entrepreneurs to apply what they learnt in the workshop to their own business helped to create accountability and ensure the start-up was making consistent progress.

- Practical 'hands on' workshops that require entrepreneurs to apply what is being learnt to their business were seen to be more valuable compared to traditional 'chalk and talk' lectures.

The early stages of a start-up are full of questions and unknowns. Who is my customer? What can I do for my customer? How do I make money? How do I scale? The workshops aimed to help entrepreneurs answer these questions and identify and validate the foundational assumptions of their business model. Using a 'lean' methodology to test assumptions and build a minimum viable product (MVP) was very useful to the early stage start-ups. It was clear that many entrepreneurs were not familiar with the lean start-up methodology. Where a start-up is operating on limited resources, teaching the method of testing a market's reaction to an assumption or basic product is incredibly valuable. A business plan and a large capital investment in what might prove to be the wrong product and ultimately lead to the start-up's failure is not. This training approach facilitated short feedback loops and quick learning, key to developing new business models in a short space of time.

The first pilot revealed a need to restructure the curriculum to maximise its effectiveness. This included facilitating smaller learning circles amongst peers in order to apply what was being taught in each workshop and receive feedback on how they had applied this to their business. In the second pilot, the curriculum was restructured around an 'input' and 'output' model. For example, following the input of a social media strategy class, entrepreneurs were expected to set up and plan a social media platform. This output was presented to their peers in order to receive feedback from the cohort and an expert in this area. While this approach was useful to ensure entrepreneurs applied what was being taught, the pilot continually faced a tension in how fast to move new ventures through the program's key milestones. Too fast might break the business. Moving too slowly would not apply enough pressure for them to learn how to make rapid progress. The pilot showed that start-ups were often dealing with different priorities depending on their specific context. Forcing an entrepreneur to spend time working on an area of their business which they didn't view as critical was not always helpful. Resistant entrepreneurs did, however, reflect that this structured processed compelled them to complete certain tasks they might not otherwise have gotten around to doing.

One thing that all entrepreneurs had in common was limited time. Entrepreneurs would quickly switch off and start doing more urgent tasks in workshops that did not add direct value. The pilot found that entrepreneurs tended to favour working on their start-up rather than taking advantage of training even when needed. Following the first pilot, the program was restructured to incorporate more 'hands on' workshops where workshop facilitators were instructed to implement a principle of 20% time allocated to theory and 80% towards a clinic environment where entrepreneurs applied what was taught to their business and received feedback. This format worked much better where entrepreneurs could see the relevance for their business and receive additional feedback based on their particular scenario.

Advisory services

Corporate partners were approached to partner with the business school and provide pro bono advisory services to entrepreneurs on the program on a limited time basis. The aim was to provide additional services, for example legal, intellectual property, technology and venture capital that are essential for building a business.

The pilot identified a few important lessons for incubators offering advisory services:

- Advisory services are less relevant for early-stage entrepreneurs and were only utilized at a later stage, often post program once the start-up had defined their business model.
- Freelancers that provide relevant services to start-ups can bring additional benefit to co-working communities.

The pilot revealed that early-stage entrepreneurs didn't need as many resources as one might think, mainly because the majority of start-ups were at the business model discovery stage and were focusing on defining their business model rather than building a company. Advisory services were utilised far less than initially anticipated. The pilot helped to clarify that companies that were still on the journey of establishing product/market fit needed many of the additional resources available only after the incubation program.

Freelancers who had joined the co-working community and offered services such as accounting or tax services were found to be very valuable to entrepreneurs once they had completed the program. Referrals from other entrepreneurs and the ability to ask questions and advice informally over a tea station helped entrepreneurs decide whether to procure services from freelancers in the broader community.

Events

A regular series of open events to the general public were scheduled as part of the pilot program. These included pitch nights to a panel of local investors, founder forums for informal question and answers with more experienced entrepreneurs and learning lunches that covered a practical topic that was relevant to the cohort. The aim was to help build a community of entrepreneurs and engage the broader ecosystem beyond the start-ups in the pilot program.

The pilot identified a few important lessons for developing events that add value:

- Events must align to the specific needs of an incubators' target group, otherwise they add very little value. The calibre of speakers is critical and should be assessed in advance.

- Incubators should ensure their calendar of events complements what the broader ecosystem is offering and doesn't clash with other talks that might be scheduled for the same date.

- Demo days are useful to showcase start-ups to potential investors, clients and the broader community who can provide additional support such as coaching or advisory work.

Overall, events appeared to be enjoyed and were helpful to those who attended. However, some events or workshops were merely 'noise' for entrepreneurs and added little value. Some ventures emphasized that the quality of speakers was an important factor in whether they added value or not. The pilot showed that some topics, however interesting, were just not relevant to where a business was at. Later stage topics such as human resources and people management were just 'too out of reach' for founders.

The local entrepreneurship ecosystem calendar of events was also found to be very full, so 'Founder Forum' style events were stopped for the second program. There were already other opportunities in the broader ecosystem for entrepreneurs to listen to, and engage with, other founders. The pilot program also revealed the importance of connecting with key stakeholders in the local ecosystem to ensure the incubators' series of events complimented what was already on offer by other organizations. In mature entrepreneurship ecosystems where lots of organizations are scheduling different types of events, it becomes particularly important to ensure coherence across the ecosystem.

A demo day was also included in the pilot program, where entrepreneurs had to give a public presentation of the progress they had made in the program. The aim was to mark the culmination of the three-month program and provide an end point to assess start-ups' eligibility for post program support. While demo days have been largely criticized for adding little value to a start-up (where founders don't raise capital as expected), the pilot showed this to be a useful mechanism to ensure start-ups made progress – there is nothing like the pressure of having to stand up and present in front of a large audience. They also provided broad exposure to potential clients or individuals who were willing to make further introductions or offer pro bono advisory support.

Access to networks

Access to a leading business school's faculty, experts and alumni was a key differentiator for the incubation program. Networks facilitated advice from seasoned entrepreneurs or professionals with deep functional expertise and access to potential customers.

The pilot highlighted a few key lessons for developing networks that support start-ups:

- Industry expert days are a great way to engage busy professionals who might otherwise be concerned about the time commitment expected of them.

- An ecosystem connector or person responsible for fostering an engaged network was critical to ensure connections were made and key stakeholders were continually engaged.

The pilot found that exposing founders to a broader network of industry leaders was helpful to provide different perspectives on their business. This was best facilitated through a speed-dating format – where an entrepreneur pitches their business and the industry expert asks questions. This time-bound commitment helped attract busy professionals who might have been scared off from the expectation of further commitments. It also had the additional benefit of helping founders improve their communication skills, as they had to pitch their start-up multiple times to different people.

An ecosystem and industry connector were found to be critical to unlock value for the start-ups in the program. Having an individual responsible for ensuring that new ventures were able to access new networks helped deliver on this element. Incubators need someone working full-time to ensure that an incubator's ecosystem is vibrant, relevant and engaged. This connector facilitated both local and international connections and opportunities.

Challenges and other lessons

Many additional lessons, broadly applicable to other programs, were learnt during the pilot phase. Some examples are:

- Selection processes are critical to the success of an incubator. The process should be able to interrogate the dynamics of the team, overall commitment and coachability.

- Creating accountability from entrepreneurs was challenging, and teams of two or more seemed to have a greater degree of accountability and make better progress compared with individual entrepreneurs.

Selection of entrepreneurs is one of the most important elements of an incubation program. An online application can test how developed and well considered a business is. However, the pitch and interview helps to test whether a founder could clearly articulate their business, and provides an opportunity to further interrogate the team and the characteristics of the founders. The pilot selection method was limited and more creative ways were needed to test and understand applicants better. Much like the job interview, an interview and/or pitch does not definitively ascertain motivation, commitment, character and competence. The pilot found that the selection process was not robust enough, and for subsequent programs it was decided to include one additional step in the form of a 3-day design sprint to further stress-test both the business idea and the team.

Creating accountability from entrepreneurs was challenging. Regular check-in sessions were a helpful way of developing accountability amongst entrepreneurs. There was a significant shift in momentum when check-ins were no longer part of the weekly routine. The pilot also showed that when one-on-one check-ins with our EiR were scheduled, peer accountability/competition and engagement decreased significantly. Overall, the pilot also found that founders who were already in a team of more than two were able to benefit most from the program and take advantage of the resources and network available to them. There appeared to be stronger accountability between two or more co-founders than a single entrepreneur and our mentor or program team. Accountability was seen to be incredibly powerful as it helped ensure that founders were hitting key milestones through the three-month program.

Conclusion

Overall feedback received from entrepreneurs and key stakeholders was positive. One entrepreneur reflected, "This program literally saved us hundreds of thousands of rands we were about to spend on something that we didn't need." Another explained, "Not only did we grow as a company, but we also have found new confidence in what we are doing and the direction of the business."

The difference between incubation and acceleration became an unexpected focus for the pilot program team who were continually challenged on the difference between where the pilot incubation program fitted in the entrepreneurship ecosystem. Was this program actually an accelerator given the short time frame and other similarities?

In this context, entrepreneurs were often first-time founders, and therefore lacked the experience often seen in international accelerators. Incubators can play an important role in developing first-time founders and entrepreneurs to quickly test and validate their assumptions in a safe environment. Key insights from our conversations with ecosystem partners and other accelerators revealed the following needs for first-time founders that incubators are well positioned to meet:

- Development of the founder mindset and skillset

- Development of confidence to set stretch-targets and think bigger

- Understanding the value of networks and maximising opportunities presented

- The art of good communication and 'packaging'

- Understanding of basic start-up terminology

While three months is a short amount of time for start-ups at this early-stage, a core objective for the pilot program was to equip the start-up with the right mindset and skillset to tackle challenges they would face as they continued on their entrepreneurial journeys as well as connect founders to a supportive network of peers and the broader ecosystem. Ecosystem partners, such as other accelerators, co-working spaces and venture capitalists were seen as crucial to ensure that the pilot program did not graduate ventures into a valley of death. However, more time was needed to ensure the broader ecosystem was working together to support local entrepreneurs collectively.

Perhaps the most critical lesson learnt from the pilot program was revisiting the overall objectives of the incubator to determine whether graduating successful companies or reliable entrepreneurs from the program was the more important. These two goals were often at odds with each other. Not every business was going to be a success (particularly at this early stage where the risks are high), yet entrepreneurs with the right skillset and experience could go on to pursue other entrepreneurial opportunities, either by starting a new venture or joining other local or international start-ups.

Chapter 10

Educating a New Generation of Sustainable Leaders by Working with Social-Impact Founders in Africa

Prof. André Habisch

Business schools – still part of the problem or already part of the solution?

Business schools can play an important role in the mindset formation of a new generation of business leaders. In particular, they influence the self-concept and professional identity of their graduates:

- in the way they describe and portray the main entrepreneurial challenges in their courses;

- with the type of case studies, business games or lecture topics they suggest;

- through the guest speakers from BusinessLIVE they invite;

- with student engagement opportunities, internships or service-learning facilities they implement; and

- more generally, by the cultural flavor which their theories and concepts are enfolding both directly and indirectly.

In particular, these and other instruments of b-school curriculum frame what students perceive as truly 'professional' business practice.[1] Moreover, they help them to define their own personal role in the economic, cultural and social transformations of their regional and national society. However, it is particular here, that business schools – voluntarily or involuntarily – may also contribute to a profound cultural alienation of their students. As it has been discussed for years now, educational systems in general and business schools in particular do not always prepare students well for assuming their role as responsible leaders in society; nor do they support them in contributing effectively to the sustainable development in their community and/or country. For MBA programs, this shortcoming was already explicitly discussed before and after the financial crises (see, inter alia Pfeffer & Fong,[2] Ghoshal,[3] as well as Bachmann et

---

1   Khurana, 2007.
2   Pfeffer & Fong, 2002.
3   Ghoshal, 2005.

al.[4] for a summary). More precisely, the abstract scientific character and the lack of practical wisdom in their teachings have been criticized. Few publications expressed that criticism as drastically as the (posthumously published) article of LBS Professor Samantha Goshal entitled *Bad Management Theory is Destroying Good Management Practice*.[5] In particular, Goshal's argument is referring to economic theories of organization. For example, Jenssen & Meckling's influential *Principal-Agent-Theory*[6] is modelling employees as opportunistic 'agents' longing to exploit their corporate 'principal.' Consequently, a 'professional' employer is supposed to incentivize and/or control employees in order to channel their opportunism. Once a student's mind-set is affected by these kinds of mainstream business school instructions, however, managers as employers may treat real-world employees exactly as distrustfully as they were instructed to do during their b-school time.[7] This behavior may (probably) still make some sense in the anonymous atmosphere of a large company in the context of the US 'hire-and-fire' culture; it would rather destroy, however, the corporate culture of a family firm in a more collectively minded national culture in Africa, Asia or Latin America. This holds especially true in emerging economies, in which teaching materials, conceptual building blocks and mind-sets of the so-called 'developed' world dominate business school instruction – thereby depriving students of their own social and economic traditions.

Following this line of thought, like everywhere else in the World, also in Africa, Business Schools are not always well equipped to prepare their graduates for running a business in their own country. On the contrary, after finishing the b-school years, graduates may even find it harder to adapt to the necessities of clients, employees, business and the socio-cultural environment. Business is portrayed in text-book and journal literature mostly authored by Western authors, who are guiding their empirical studies and selecting their reference models mostly from their own culture. Moreover, and probably even more problematic: practitioners and external presenters introduced in courses and seminars often also reproduce the dominant Western business culture. As a result, business school students in the Southern Hemisphere are threatened by alienation from their cultural origins. More precisely, habits and action patterns may be reproduced, which may indeed negatively affect employment, business cultures and economic development in Africa. Ultimately, depending on their career path inside of the organization, young business leaders together with their families may even end up in the US, in the UK, in Germany or in another developed country. In order to counteract this latent but nevertheless strong tendency, *African business schools should create learning spaces, courses and programs, which help graduates*

---

4   Bachmann et al., 2017.
5   Ghoshal, 2005.
6   Jenssen & Meckling, date missing
7   Goshal, 2005.

to consider an alternative career as (Start-up) Entrepreneur in their own country. For
that purpose, case studies and business examples in teaching and research are
required, which help them to keep in touch with their own countries' norms, values
and 'wisdom-traditions' as well as their most relevant SDG problems and challenges.[8]

Entrepreneurial ecosystems: working with Social-Impact Start-ups

It is precisely here that action learning formats with local start-up companies come
into play. An increasing number of Social or Social-Impact Entrepreneurs are popping-
up across Africa; these are young local entrepreneurs, who figured out business
solutions not modelled after the necessities of Western developed economies
but rather addressing the needs and business situations of their own African
contemporaries. In particular, they are often substituting (or helping to cope with) a
lack of public infrastructure – for example, bringing together suppliers and clients on
digital platforms, providing remote health care solutions, improving the productivity
of traditional food-gathering methods, addressing the needs of clients who find
themselves excluded from financial or insurance markets, etc. In that context, those
entrepreneurs mostly develop management, marketing, recruiting or stakeholder
communication methods, which are particularly adapted to their own cultural and
economic position. In other words, low-budget social-impact founders often draw
on the social or cultural capital of their socio-cultural environment – thereby making
use of their knowledge as citizens. Consequently, in order to overcome the above-
mentioned challenges of cultural alienation and to orientate a future generation of
business leaders towards the business chances waiting for them in their own country,
postgraduate educational (MA, MBA or EMBA) classes should consider working
with and for social-impact entrepreneurs across Africa. The latter may indeed also
profit from this kind of learning partnerships. What precisely would they learn from
business students, however?

Many social-impact founders indeed possess a professional background as technician,
natural scientist etc. Consequently, they spend a lot of time and energy on caring for
their product. What is then mostly lacking, however, is applied business knowledge,
for example, familiarity with marketing or scaling strategies, basic financial skills etc. It
is here, that (advanced) business students could make a large difference; connecting
groups of students with a start-up founder does indeed help both sides. Students
are motivated when, despite seeing their essays ending up in the dustbin after class,
they are enabled to support a real-world entrepreneurial person. For example, they
may challenge the business model, develop a market-entry concept, lay the ground
for a 'make-or-buy' decision, design marketing or social media contents etc. Action-
Learning theory tells us that active problem-solving is the most effective instrument

---

8   Habisch & Schmidpeter, 2017.

for acquiring knowledge and reflection; therefore, working with social-impact start-up entrepreneurs, who are struggling in real-world business situations, is delivering exactly that! Complementarily, founders may serve as an anchor person for the students – nudging them to also consider a similar career themselves! Moreover, quick feedback from the founder may channel the students' search for innovation – helping them to avoid losing time for unnecessary mistakes. Moreover, another tangible advantage is generated if these partnerships take place in an international context. For example, if an eMBA or MBA class in a South-African graduate school of business collaborates with a start-up from Ghana, Ethiopia or Kenya, students, beyond doing general business consulting, may also support founders with their insider knowledge concerning particular health or food markets institutions in their country. Herewith, confronted with an instruction to 'bring this product to your country' students may – based on their own local knowledge – develop sophisticated strategies. These may include, for example, a recommendation, as to which organization would have to be addressed first, which (explicit or implicit) rule has to be followed when dealing with them, which location would fit best etc. As a result, based on the quality of these proposals and contributions, founders may even decide to accept a student or student-team as local franchise taker, who would implement their plans to introduce the respective product or service into that country. Thus, a learning partnership could also luckily result in long-term business cooperation.

Even if mutual gains therefore seem possible from these kinds of partnerships, they nevertheless also face substantial challenges. One of the most salient ones results from the very different contexts and realities partners are living in. More precisely, the social-impact founders find themselves confronted with the – more or less urgent – necessity to deliver profit in order to refinance their organization. On the one hand, this may pique their interest in getting support and advice from the student groups. On the other hand, however, their ability to patiently support students in their learning process remains naturally limited. In contrast, students live in the somewhere imaginative world of a more or less isolated learning environment. They usually take it for granted to tread staff and clinical professors as (empowering) 'learning environment', which is dedicated to support them in their apprehension process. Consequently, they tend to ignore the high opportunity costs founders face when explaining them details of their business model. The missing synchronicity of the partners often results in substantial challenges for the cooperation process – with students' shortcomings of serious engagement and Entrepreneur's unwillingness or lack of time to instruct them accordingly.

Which are the guidelines organizers of these programs should therefore follow?

1. Priority should be given to the careful selection of Start-up-partners, whose products or services are technically ripe and elaborated enough to profit from serious business knowledge. If students perceive their engagement to make a real difference, they are stronger motivated; complementarily, founders confronted with innovative and challenging ideas are more curious and dedicate more of their precious time and energy to the academic contact.

2. Moreover, the interaction and exchange between both parties should be carefully prepared and administered by program managers; on the one hand, they have to prevent that students 'overuse' the scare resource of founder's willingness to answer questions or comment on proposals. On the other hand, nothing frustrates students more than not getting any feedback from 'their' founder after weeks and months of work. Therefore, organizers should make sure that with joining the program, founders also accept the duty to spend at least 90 minutes for an initial exchange with their student group and subsequently at least 20-30 minutes every 2-3 weeks in order to answer questions or feedback on proposals. On the contrary, students should not contact founders outside of designated communication slots.

3. Finally, it can make good sense to embed the cooperation between founders and students within an overall support landscape. In our case, the Social Innovation course series executed by Catholic University's Entrepreneurship MA specialization corresponds with a dedicate program of BAYER Cares foundation, Leverkusen, which aims at identifying and effectively supporting Social Impact Start-up founders. Hence, social-impact start-up (SIST) entrepreneurs financially are supported financially by Bayer Cares Foundations' "Grants4Impact" program and are additionally provided with assistance from Master students for working on their specific challenges and problems. This could happen either in a classroom setting or in the context of a thesis topic executed by a MA student in an action-learning format during 6 months. Most of the SISTs are either native Africans or are active in the continent. The Bayer Cares Foundation usually provides financial assistance for a duration of 24 months to support SISTs in the development of their business ideas. This architecture supports the continuous mutual engagement of founders – recipients of foundation money.

4. Of a similar importance is also the sound implementation of the cooperation courses in the teaching programs of the b-school. For KUEI MA students in the specialization of 'Entrepreneurship of Social Innovation', for example, the course series represents an obligatory module, which in addition is taught by the coordinator of the program. Such a deep implementation into the curriculum proved to be advantageous in many respects. It increases the visibility and attractiveness compared with a mere selective course or a cooperation organized

and run as an additional, extracurricular activity only, which rank much lower in the internal priority list of postgraduate students.

5. According to the United Nations Principles of Responsible Management Education (UN-PRME), the orientation of b-school teaching and research towards the UN Sustainable development goals represents an important goal. Implementing Partnerships with Social Impact start-ups into the curriculum may indeed help to redirect the orientation of African innovators and industry leaders towards Sustainable development.

Conceptual perspective: the role of entrepreneurial initiative for social innovation in Africa

As shown above, enriching entrepreneurial ecosystems in universities (and especially in postgraduate courses) by implementing partnerships of students working for Social impact Start-ups may ultimately boost Social Innovation for Sustainable development in Africa.

This is precisely where the latest work of Harvard Professor *Clayton Christensen* together with his co-authors *Efosa Ojomo* from Nigeria and *Karen Dillon* comes in. In their actual book entitled The *Prosperity Paradox. How Innovation can Lift Nations Out of Poverty,*[9] these authors further elaborated the Innovation concept presented already in Christensen's earlier work *on* the *Innovation Dilemma* published in 1997. Although he had therein coined the influential concept of 'disruptive innovation', the coauthors of the actual book did no longer use it but instead coin the term 'Market creating Innovations'. Hence, they focus more on the macroeconomic dimension of Innovation and spell out its consequences for the context of development in transition economies. The authors emphasize the (potential) role of start-up entrepreneurs to 'convert non-consumers into consumers', thereby driving socio-economic change in their countries.

In line with this argument, Christensen, Ojomo and Dillon also deplore the predominance of institutional economics in developing country research. Their argument here is not, that institutions would not play an important role for the sustainable development of a country. Rather they oppose an exclusive focus of donor organizations on reforming institutions (for example by anti-corruption laws, implementing democratic decision making etc.) to the expense of supporting 'market-creating' entrepreneurs. Christensen, Ojomo and Dillon illustrate this argument with a sideways glance at the economic history of the US, here. During the 1890s, the country could definitely be characterized as a corruption and crime-ridden economy; however, at the same time

---

9   Christensen, Efosa & Dillon, 2019.

these years also marked one of the most vibrant economic growth periods in human history. US Americans witnessed spectacular market creating innovations like the Ford company's famous T-model that boosted car usage; or the introduction of the light bulb by Thomas A. Edison. Moreover, when the US economy prospered later on, citizens and voters have successfully 'pulled in' compliance and legal structures curbing corruption. It seems therefore, that even today's successful Western countries had never really solved their compliance and crime problems before starting their impressive growth trajectory. Rather complementarily, successful 'market-creating innovations' brought about new jobs and infrastructure; the latter then enabled them to grow a political and societal momentum, which 'civilized' their business transactions and created institutional and social capital. Therefore, as Christensen and his co-authors make impressively clear, market creating innovation may substantially foster social and economic development in Africa. Essentially, this is because it implies the perception of poor people as 'non-consumers' who could be turned into consumers if products and services address their specific living conditions and are therefore successful on the market.

Not all the aspects and implications of the complex book of Christensen, Ojomo and Dillon can be reproduced, here. However, even what has been mentioned so far already retains important implications for business education – especially in Africa, where large parts of the continent are still impoverished and nevertheless many young people with Entrepreneurial ambitions strive for the realization of their projects. Therefore, if we follow the authors and perceive market creating innovators as an important driver of economic development: then *Business schools could play an important role for supporting these people*. For example, most Social-Impact Start-ups the Bayer Cares Foundation (BCF) works with, are either native Africans or are active on the continent. However, in the context of their home countries, these founders often have no access to any kind of assistance, logistical or financial support. For sure, donor institutions like Foundations can play an important role, here. Beyond capital, however, what founders really need is strategic or organizational support, as advanced business students can already provide it: the following example may provide some evidence about that.

One of BCF's 'Grants for impact' winners is the Ghanaian software developer Raindolf Owusu, who established the "BISA" App in his home country. More precisely, this app enables people from remote rural areas to make a first contact via mobile phone with doctors, who volunteer for that purpose. The basic idea is already expressed by the organization's title - as "BISA" is the Ghanaian word for "questions". Statistics estimate that in Ghana, there is just one doctor for approx. 8,500 people; in addition, many people from the countryside live in regions that are more than a day's walk away from the nearest doctor or hospital. Consequently, rural dwellers not only suffer from poor access to fundamental health and medical services, but rather also have to learn and decide which doctor to turn to before they set out. "Ghana has a very young population and smartphones are widely spread and also used in everyday life, for example for making payments. This means that you can reach a large number of people via an app", explains the Master student Marco Miglietta. In the context of the 'Social Innovation I' seminar, Raindolf Owusu entrusted him and other fellow students with the task of finding a way to also include Foreign doctors as initial contacts for BISA users in order to reduce their waiting times. In their subsequent research, the students found out that especially retired doctors and medical students form a suitable target group for BISA - as they might be more likely to participate in the initiative. On that background, the students recorded a video in which they provided a brief overview on BISA and its background in order to support the operator of the app in approaching prospective volunteers. "We are always looking for doctors who would like to support us. The work carried out by the students, which we incorporate in our concept, is a valuable contribution when it comes to finding and recruiting additional practitioners", emphasizes BISA founder Raindolf Owusu. For the support video recorded by our Master students for their SIST partner.[10] One result of that communication tool is a contact with a Dutch hospital group, which – according to Owusu – brought him in contact with several new doctor-volunteers.

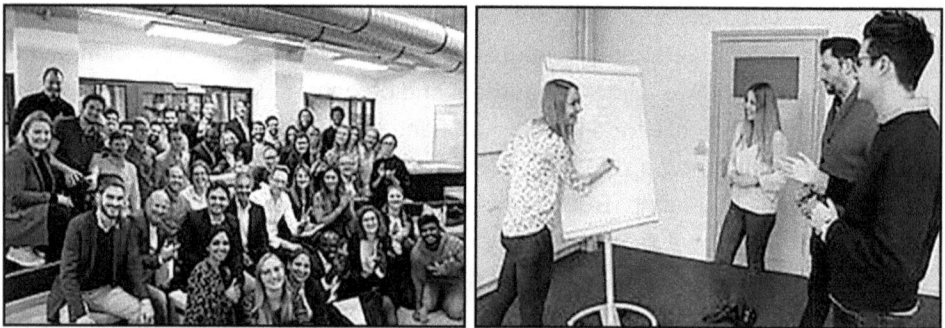

Picture 1: Student groups used the kick-off event in Berlin for intense discussions with the social entrepreneurs supported by the Bayer Cares Foundation.

Another student group has established a collaboration with the Berlin-based Start-up company "COOLAR", which developed an innovative cooling system for use in African countries – mainly to adequately store drugs and vaccines. Conventional refrigerators depend on a reliable, stable power supply and make use of compressors, which wear out quickly in harsh conditions. On the contrary, the COOLAR devices do require neither electrical energy nor movable parts. Instead, the inventors of the system make use of the cooling produced during evaporation and use a special gel in

---

10   see https://www.youtube.com/watch?v=sivnOH3y77s&feature=youtu.be

order to keep the cooling circuit up and running. Catholic University Master student Sarah Kühne and her team have supported the project by analyzing whether the production should be entirely taken over by the developers themselves or whether parts of the production process can be outsourced to African production sides. For that purpose, they extensively consulted with experts from the industry nationally and internationally. Ultimately, they recommended COOLAR to having the cooling device assembled in the African country of destination, which allows them to also create jobs in the local production chain. In addition, they calculated the most cost-efficient way of production and set up a purchasing strategy. "In particular, aid organizations and governments are potential buyers of this cooling system" Sarah Kühne and her team found out during talks with the Deutsche Gesellschaft für Internationale Zusammenarbeit (GIZ), an organization of the German government. Finally, COOLAR co-foun-der Christoph Göller summarized: "My team and I were really impressed by the students' work. They make it a lot easier for us to find a production strategy and make a well-founded pre-selection of potential business partners and contractual models". What are important course guidelines in order to support students bringing about these results?

1. One important element here are weekly meetings during the whole semesters, in which the team's progress as well as potential challenges or communication problems during the search process are critically discussed. In that context, course organizers do not dictate any ideas nor do they up-front refuse any proposals of the team – even if those are surprising or go against intuitive reasoning; however, critical questions are raised concerning the realism of certain ideas as well as the willingness of important stakeholder groups to (really) cooperate.

2. If students for example propose a certain cooperation with external stakeholders, they are invited to verify by direct communication, whether this idea is really accepted by the proposed organization or group. If their inquiries do not bring about robust results, however, teams are invited to also consider alternative ideas. The most important goal – which also determines the course's final assessment for the team – is to help the Social-Impact start-up realizing his or her goals. On the contrary, mere ideas, which are not grounded in an exact analysis of the facts, are not accepted and would result in low grading: the realism of proposals remains a crucial quality indicator of a proposal.

3. If students face objective difficulties in pursuing their inquiry process, course organizers are also willing to help. This implies to open-up doors of consultants or field experts for them, to invite professionals to answer certain questions or simply to gain the support of a company the students had repeatedly contacted in vain. Creating opportunities for student teams, however, never implies that course organizers would take over doing their job. Whether or not they make

use of the opportunities opened to them rather represents another important element of the final group assessment.

Picture 2: Students communicate with Christian from Ethiopia, 21 year-old-founder of GEBEYA, a platform to connect rural vegetable producers and urban farmers in Ethiopia. Supported by the local IT consultant 80:20, they help him to insure more transportation facilities for his venture.

4. Albeit students are supposed to effectively support Start-ups in their struggle, they nevertheless do not understand themselves as mere service-providers. Rather, based on theoretical concepts and practical tools, they are also critically analyzing and challenging their business models. This specification is important as – empowered by business knowledge – students may often perceive shortcomings or hurdles, which the founder himself is not (yet) aware off. Obliging the students to work only on the instructions of the founder might then result in demotivation, if they consider the assigned task as useless as long as the bigger issues are not solved.

SISTAC: Social Impact Start-up Academy

By working with Social Impact Start-ups, the young researchers were also able to define aims and objectives for their own future careers: "This exchange showed me, that it is indeed pos- sible to do good and earn money with it. And I was able to apply my knowledge in a practical context. I could imagine working in a start-up company myself" says Kühne. For the subsequent course "Social Innovation II" consultant teams work with students on issues like business canvas, design thinking, and ethical campaigning on Social Media.

Based on the positive experiences, a similar course was offered at the Social Leadership MBE at Ben-Gurion University, Beer Sheva (Israel) in February 2019. Here, the same Social Impact Start-up Entrepreneurs were presented – with the explicit task for student groups to bring these products to Israel's poorer regions (like the Berber settlement in the Negev very close to the BGU). For that purpose MBE student groups made use of their 'special knowledge' about the Health care system in their country, about social support structures in the Negev region, their insider knowledge about living conditions of poor fishermen in the Gaza strip etc. Finally, they came up with proposing very creative and well adapted solutions, which offered additional perspectives to the SIST founders. Which guidelines of course organizations proved to be particularly useful, here?

1. Also in this alternative format, which no longer aims primarily at generic advice but rather stimulates to transfer the product/service from one county to another, students remain in full control of their ultimate results. Even if the course facilitator him- or herself stems from the country or region as well, it has to be their ideas or proposals to guide their inquiries.

2. However, additional instruments to unleash the creativity and imagination of students might be added in order to help them avoiding a mere mechanical transmission or copy. Given the complex economic, social, legal or physical conditions of a business model, a careful adaptation is quasi always required and provides ample opportunities to bring in own proposals or ideas.

Based on the above-mentioned experiences, a *Social Impact Start-up Academy* was recently founded as a non-for-profit association. The goal is to scale the existing experiences by creating a global network of business schools running action-learning courses with business schools from all parts of Africa. Therefore, albeit started in Germany, the SISTAC nevertheless especially addresses Southern Hemisphere business schools – because it is precisely here, that 'market creating' innovators can make the biggest difference. For that purpose, specially designed 'SISTAC courses' are supposed to effectively coordinate the activities of founders and MBA/ MA students in different countries. Beyond the effects characterized above, another goal of the initiative is to link consumer markets with comparable living conditions around the Southern Hemisphere globally. For example, exporting her products and services to South Africa, Brazil or Indonesia may then help a Social Impact Start-up Entrepreneur from Ghana in West Africa to scale-up her company more quickly and stabilize her profits. For that purpose, she may ultimately even decide to collaborate with a student from the South African, Brazilian or Indonesian business school, who came up with a convincing proposal and is willing to spread her business model as a franchise taker. Networks of former SISTAC Entrepreneurs will be formed around business schools all over the African continent in order to mutually support each other, allow for benchmarking and collective learning as well as involve themselves in teaching and research of their local Business schools. Complementarily, after the period of active collaboration with the business school students, mentors from business may accompany the founders helping them to implement the recommended measures thereby consolidating the business. In order to complement the action learning process, SISTAC will provide its business school partners access to online teaching materials for Start-up Entrepreneurs (for example design thinking, business model canvas, Social Media communication etc.). Moreover, bi- or tri-annual conferences will be organized within the SISTAC global network in order to foster the continuous improvement of action learning courses. Finally, SISTAC will also channel impact-investments as well as venture capital for promising start-ups. Sponsors from the private sector as well as public funds are welcome to help SISTAC to play this developmental role.

Summary

As such, emphasizing the crucial role of (local) Entrepreneurs for socio-economic development in Africa is no longer very innovative. In that respect, the above-mentioned publication of Clayton Christensen, Efosa Ojomo and Karen Dillon only provided an additional (however rather concise) expression. Rather multiple initiatives have been started in recent years and they already managed to gain considerable support. Down that road, African Business schools can play an important and even here, a lot of networking activity has recently taken place. For example, the African Association of Business School (AAB) represents an important network in that respect. In order to transform the still rather salient alienations and cultural estrangement of mainstream b-school teaching practice, however, innovative forms of teaching and learning have also to be stimulated. For that purpose, structures like the Social Impact start-up Academy (SISTAC.world) and others want to support Business schools to increasingly serve market creating innovators in Africa – thereby ultimately playing an increasing role in fostering their home country's socio-economic development.

Chapter 11

Toward a Fearless Social Enterprise: Using Psychological Safety to Create Social Value

Assoc. Prof. Hamieda Parker

For as long as Toyota Production Systems has upheld the principle of *respect for people* in manufacturing firms, there has been intentional consideration within the field of operations management for the psychological wellbeing of the people who carry out operations. Typically filed under the auspices of human resource management (HRM) in our contemporary discourse about business operations, however, these considerations tend to be overshadowed by those of control systems, tools, and performance metrics.

Contrast this with the discourse about social enterprises, where the imperative to create social value regularly elevates the discussion of employee wellbeing above other operational controls. This comes as part of social enterprise's explicit commitment to sustainability, which includes the wellbeing of all stakeholders. Yet, even as some firms – whether they identify as a social enterprise, a social business, or a for-profit business – might equate their espoused commitment to stakeholders with the creation of social value, these intentions have little bearing on the actual relationship between the firm's operations and the actual social value created for their most important internal stakeholders, employees.

Perhaps the most important social value any organization can create for its employees is that which is most within its control: facilitating a positive experience of the work and the organization. Historically, HRM has drawn on a number of constructs to assess this value. In its moments of greatest empowerment and respect for humans, the metrics of job satisfaction, employee engagement, and extrinsic motivation feature prominently. At its lower points, KPIs and turnover rates serve as proxies. But over the past two decades, a different construct that bridges employee experience and performance has emerged in management research as a critical asset within operations-intensive organizations.

According to Amy Edmondson's extensive study of healthcare and manufacturing organizations, *psychological safety* within working teams is the engine of positive working team behaviors, including learning, adaptation, efficacy, and creativity. It captures a shared positive experience among team members that they are included,

153

listened to, and safe to express themselves. They are "fearless". On its face, the prioritization of employee wellbeing embedded in the construct is symmetric with the principle of social value creation. And yet, the unique organizational dynamics of the social enterprise, even one in a traditional industry such as manufacturing, present similarly unique challenges for creating psychological safety.

This chapter examines the application of psychological safety within traditional operations-intensive organizations in parallel with the operations management challenges of social enterprises in order to determine how social enterprises can unlock greater social value for their employees through psychological safety.

Social entrepreneurship and models of social enterprise

Social missions that elevate environmental and community concerns, although once the provenance of humanitarian organizations, have become increasingly common in other sectors. The justification for the very existence of social enterprises within fields such as manufacturing or healthcare, resides in a growing expanse of unmet social needs. As more and more social needs get pushed outside the territories of business, government, and the third sector into a "no-man's land" of sorts, social entrepreneurship has emerged as an alternative approach to meeting these needs. Borrowing from different forms of organization and process, social entrepreneurs endeavour to create hybrid models that transcend organizational and institutional boundaries to affect systemic change.

The social enterprise is just one incarnation of this hybrid approach: a cross between a purely non-profit organization and purely for-profit business, packaged in any number of configurations. As proponents of social enterprise would attest, it is this fluidity of form that gives these kinds of organizations their impact,[2] as they can design solutions to fit a specific social need using the best principles from both worlds. As one might expect of any new model for which few or no best practices exist, social enterprises face unique, often unforeseen, challenges once they become operational. Ultimately, they are all subject to a difficult balancing act as their organizational strategy becomes constrained by conflicting objectives, and their commercial and social missions compete for resources.

Of particular interest here is how this challenge is experienced by social enterprises that, from one angle, give the appearance of a traditional for-profit business, adopting a fee-for-service operational model. Their strategy of social value creation involves producing a market solution for their target population, the sales of which fund

---

1   Edmondson, 2019.
2   Nicholls, 2006.

their core activities. This is considered an embedded model of social enterprise: the business is the social value generator.[3] Those enterprises that endeavour to achieve full cost recovery and profit from the operation can also be considered a social business.[4] In many respects, organizations like this have all the trappings of a typical business. Their products and services are bought and sold like any other; the means of production require facilities and infrastructure that resemble those in traditional industries; and they are supported by a multidisciplinary team of skilled employees.

Social enterprises distinguish themselves from businesses that offer products or services of social value – an apt description for any business – in at least one key respect: their commitment to social value creation in both processes and outcomes. Their social mission is manifest in their activities, including supplier selection, hiring policies, decision-making processes, and ways of working. Where commercial entrepreneurs might sacrifice social imperatives in these processes for economic efficiencies, social entrepreneurs consider the need to embed the social mission throughout the value chain non-negotiable.[5]

But what is the *value* of the process-oriented social value? Particularly in the case of the social business that holds many of the same obligations as a for-profit business, it can be unclear what advantages such a model confers upon the organization, employees, and the target consumer, over a traditional business in the same field. However, the examples of operations-intensive social businesses operating in emerging markets illustrate the unique contributions these organizations can make to the market, the economy, and society at large.

The case for the social business

Beyond the intangible value of moral leadership that can be attributed to social business's ethos, social business can create tangible economic and social value for different stakeholders in at least three key dimensions. Beginning with their core market mission, social businesses can develop affordable and accessible market solutions for vulnerable populations whose problems might go unnoticed, or be considered too niche, by traditional business. Silulo Ulutho Technologies, a South African information communications technology (ICT) services, is one such case of social enterprise serving marginalized markets with a full-picture customized solution. The firm was started in 2004 by school teacher Luvuyo Rani who initially saw an opportunity to increase the availability of computers and technology within South African townships – the informal communities created under apartheid-era

---

3   Alter, 2006.
4   Yunus, 2006.
5   Nicholls, 2006.

segregation laws. In these areas where infrastructure is under-developed, schools are under-resourced, and unemployment is high, opportunities to interact with computers or technology are limited. As the apprehension of Silulo's customers with devices became clear, Rani recognized that the technology gap was not just a market failure but an inhibitor of community development. Students, teachers, professionals, and business owners were not able to take full advantage of the tools that could enhance performance, simplify processes, and improve their lives. Silulo therefore began shaping itself to the broader scope of the community needs with a portfolio of customized, locally available services offered: internet access, ICT training, business solutions, and employment services.

Silulo's approach of offering a range of ICT solutions that equip the target population with a more complete set of skills and information would likely have been considered too prohibitively inefficient, and the market too narrow, for an ordinary entrepreneur to justify the endeavour. It was, however, Rani's own experience with the knowledge gap he saw in the school system as computers were being integrated into classrooms that led him to see the scale of the issue. In this sense, social businesses like Silulo develop a product-service offering that is not only inclusive of the direct, short-term needs of a market overlooked by mainstream providers, but of the longer-term systemic needs that can be unlocked within the community.

Separate from, and sometimes in addition to, their outputs, the second dimension where social businesses can create value is through their internal processes. At their core, social businesses recognize their internal stakeholders as primary beneficiaries of their operations, sometimes placing the prosperity of the team at the forefront of their social mission. Such is the case for the office furniture manufacturer Ergoform. The company's commercial mission of designing and producing premium furniture for high-profile corporate clients directly feeds their social mission to create high-quality, meaningful jobs for a lower-skilled, marginalized workforce. Since its founding in 1994, the company has incrementally evolved its corporate and operational strategy to create rewarding career opportunities for the broad cross-section of South Africans who are most affected by the country's staggeringly high unemployment rates and have limited access to education and other upskilling opportunities. After cultivating a culture of learning and open communication, Ergoform has created an environment where committed but inexperienced employees, who might otherwise be boxed in and undervalued as an "unskilled labour" resource in similar manufacturing firms, are valued team members and well-compensated beneficiaries of their operation. Two hallmarks of Ergoform's process, their lean and agile operations within the factory and distributed decision-making practices throughout the company, elevate and level the contributions of all members of the organization to create ever more opportunities for career and personal growth, particularly for those employees who enter the company with few to no skills.[6] More recently, this value has translated into equity as the company became a majority employee-owned company in 2018.

By choosing to shape their culture and operational practices to the needs of their workforce, which are themselves largely shaped by systemic forces far beyond the scope of any organization, Ergoform has achieved the dual success of being a market leader in a traditional manufacturing field and of creating a healthy, well-nourished workforce. This achievement is impossible to divorce from the social value-laden processes that Ergoform has intentionally undertaken as part of their core mission. And while many of the lean methodologies and communication practices that Ergoform employs are rooted in the traditional industry, it is their social mission of investing in employees' lifelong development that has driven them to the unique operational model that services both customers and employees equally.

Looking to the future, Ergoform's leaders are confident that it is this model which will liberate them to innovate for greater stakeholder value in all directions, including product innovation and expanding employee benefits.[7] This relates to the third dimension of value that social businesses are uniquely positioned to create: systemic innovation. Because social businesses like Ergoform choose to engage with the full context of their operating environment, they can develop solutions that more appropriately address the social need in question, and employ strategies that involve multiple stakeholders in delivering the solution better than a market solution built unilaterally in a vacuum. The trajectory of Vitalite, a provider of solar household power systems in Zambia, demonstrates how the immersion of social entrepreneurs in a complex system prompts them to address societal needs at different steps in the value chain, which in turn assures more effective delivery. Founders John Fay and Sam Bell created the company in 2015 after ten years of working in Zambia on rural development and habitat conservation projects led them to the conclusion that a renewable energy solution would be the key to many of the country's environmental degradation issues and a major driver of human development.

Over the next three years, Vitalite refined a range of solar power products and distribution models for the 96% of rural, low-income households living without power across the country. Working closely with the communities they wanted to convert from coal power to solar, Vitalite became familiar with the practical challenges of creating a unified network for a culturally diverse and geographically diffuse population, as well as the opportunities associated with the agriculture-based economy prevalent in the regions. One of the major operational innovations to come from Vitalite's immersion was their partnership with regional agricultural dealers that

---

6   Boyd, 2017.
7   Ibid.

served smallholder farmers, to form a distribution network to more rural regions.[8] After increasing their reach, Vitalite developed an integrated product-service solution for farmers that addressed common issues they faced with the timely delivery of inputs, managing payments within their business cycle, and inadequate service delivery from government programs. Partnering "Agri Solutions" offered farmers a solar pump and inputs supply under a flexible payment model that matched their business cycle.[9]

By building on the expertise and resources of other organizations already thriving in the region, Vitalite positioned itself to create more value for its target population, gearing the household solutions they provided in the region with the extended small business solutions. Their own expertise with understanding the systemic nature of environmental issues – its connection to larger economic and social issues – moved them to place social value creation at the forefront of their mission and to follow that mission even as it took them into different sectors and products. They were thus liberated to use their own expertise to create products and services that were not previously available, by involving disparate actors to a tackle major economic development issue.

Of course, the stories laid out here represent the cream of organizations like Ergoform and Vitalite: the very best of what social business can be and do at a given point in time, when their social ethos liberates them to think beyond the norms of business as usual. In the time between snapshots, however, the same ethos that liberates the organization in some ways, can constrict it in other ways.

Operational challenges and the pressure to professionalize

There are multiple points of organizational development at which the hybrid nature of social businesses creates conflict between its dual missions. As in the case of Vitalite and Silulo, where their products and services are the vehicle of social value creation for end-users, product access and affordability are two crucial qualifiers for their consumers who face significant economic and geographic barriers to mobility and energy resources, respectively. These social businesses opt to keep their prices low and often create unique payment models to maximize their reach within the target populations. Consequently, they can easily slip into cash-scarce, hand-to-mouth cycles that leave no reserves for re-investment in critical areas like staff development or factory maintenance. In such situations, it is not just the core commercial mission that is strained but the team members who must fulfil their tasks with limited resources.

---

8   Verumdal, 2016.
9   Munthali, 2017.

Other times, social businesses find themselves facing textbook operations management issues: quality control, supply chain management, and cost management. And as in traditional businesses, these are also often symptoms of organizational growth cycle – the growing pains that indicate the unstructured startup is transitioning to a more mature business and requires the appropriate structures and processes. However, for leaders and decision makers in these firms, their view of the situation can be clouded by their social value imperatives. The solutions that would be obvious in a typical business carry additional risk for social entrepreneurs who are unwilling to sacrifice social value for added professionalism. What they may not realize, however, is that they may already be sacrificing a degree of social value in the form of their team's emotional wellbeing.

In some respects, the disorder caused by operations issues is not an inherent failure. In the context of social entrepreneurship, it could even be considered a strength. For an organization tasked with delivering customized solutions or being extremely agile, messiness of process could be intuitively conceived as a tradeoff for flexibility and "getting it done". The social entrepreneur may even say the costs of quality issues, late deliveries, or mistakes are justified as the costs of doing social business – irreducible given the high standard of variability and service they are trying to achieve in tandem.

By a similar logic, a lack of internal structure can also be argued away as a tradeoff for a culture that puts people first. An organization that values its relationships with team members and wants to create a positive experience for them might also create an environment free of corporate controls and performance management tools that induce stress. These logics all speak to intention: the plans and expectations of decision-makers within the organization. But when the reality of the organizational experience – either in the operational performance or the wellbeing of employees – suggests that these tradeoffs are not being realized, the social ethos of the organization is in jeopardy.

There is a reason social enterprises can find themselves caught in this "worst of both worlds" scenario. The pressure to professionalize and adopt tried and true management methodologies may seem benign in the face of spiralling operations. But for some social entrepreneurs, there is a fear that the adoption of certain practices and ideologies is tantamount to a capitulation to a purely commercial mission. This fear of conforming in structure and practice is founded. The path to what DiMaggio and Powell[10] called "institutional isomorphism" is well trodden by other organizations, such as certain not-for-profits, who have seen their identities eroded by pressures to conform, adopt best practices, or adhere to regulations.[11]

---

10   DiMaggio & Powell, 1983.
11   Nicholls & Cho, 2006.

From here, the risk of "mission drift" toward service provision and away from serving a vulnerable target population is a real phenomenon in social value-oriented organizations.[12] There is ample evidence that when social value-oriented firms adopt more managerial approaches and become increasingly focused on processes and efficiencies, they compromise the ways they create change and the extent of that change.[13] Once social enterprises start measuring things to manage, they can easily begin measuring value in units that no longer serve their social purpose.

Importantly, this view of strategy in social enterprises puts a disproportionate emphasis on the decision-making power of the executive leaders as singular social entrepreneurs. However, for proponents of social entrepreneurship, there is increasing interest in understanding "systems change that addresses complex social problems without recourse to unusually heroic and talented actors".[14] An authentic application of this ethos within the organization requires members to see all organizational members as social entrepreneurs and focus on facilitating healthy team environments in which they can thrive.

Teams, psychological safety and learning behavior

As the challenges of social businesses illustrate, the balancing act between social and commercial value creation requires them to be extremely adaptable. They have to be able to adjust their strategies or business models in creative ways when slim profit margins provide little cushion for the kind of necessary internal changes or external economic pressures that strain all small enterprises. Muhummed Yunus's Grameen Danone – a joint venture social enterprise designed to make nutrient-enriched yogurt available, accessible, and affordable for malnourished children in rural Bangladesh – is often held up as an early case study of this dynamic.[15] After launching in 2007 as one of the first social businesses of its kind, the firm faced a steep learning curve when soaring input costs forced them to raise prices, which sent sales plummeting, and their rural sales network collapsed. Grameen Danone had to overhaul the model to mitigate their external risks and subsidize products for their target population. By 2010, the model was operational, and the firm continues to pursue innovations that can increase the economic, social, and environmental sustainability of the business.[16] The specifics of Grameen Danone's journey are its own, and certainly Yunus's own track record in the field of social entrepreneurship confers a unique level of attention and resources on the case. Outside the narrow space of high-profile social enterprises, such adaptability is more commonly associated with operation-intensive

---

12 Maier, Meyer & Steinbereithner, 2016.
13 Hvenmark, 2016.
14 Dorado & Ventresca, 2013: 80.
15 Kuratko, Hornsby & McMullen, 2011.
16 Storchi, 2018.

organizations on the extreme commercial end of the spectrum where exponential changes in technology and global economic tides are the forces for swift movement and organizational change.

When examining the learning behavior exhibited by high-performing, adaptive organizations, researchers often look at teams as the drivers of organizational change. As the people carrying out the core operations, teams are the ones performing new routines, learning new tools, or responding to new conditions on the front lines. The body of research on optimizing team performance is wide and entrenched in management literature, with the roles of the obvious variables like team composition and team leader behavior well established. Narrowing the view to team learning behavior, Edmondson's research on the construct of psychological safety on teams in operation-intensive organizations highlights a social value component to team learning and performance.

Psychological safety describes the shared experience within an environment that people are safe to be themselves and express their ideas. The concept was first introduced by Schein and Bennis as a mechanism for reducing employee anxiety around change, later expanded on as a lever of employee engagement by Kahn, and eventually applied to the organizational team experience by Edmondson.[17] Following from Edmondson's contributions, this construct directly relates to employees' experience of their work: how respected and accepted they feel as they perform their tasks.

Her study of teams in a manufacturing organization found that psychological safety is a positive mediator of team learning behavior.[18] The act of learning in an organization is risky behavior that requires tolerance for error at the team level. In addition to a qualitative study of the teams' learning behavior, Edmondson also administered a survey she developed to assess psychological safety across seven defining team experiences. Her findings showed that when members of a team felt psychologically safe, they were more willing to experiment and learn from possible mistakes to unlock higher performance. By contrast, in teams that had lower psychological safety, members were less likely to learn by asking for help or questioning their objectives.

In another study of cardiac surgery units, where routines and tasks are highly controlled and standardized across hospitals and carried out multiple times a day, again psychological safety emerged as the underpinning mechanism that enabled teams to be adaptive.[19] When tasked with integrating a new technology into their surgery routines, teams that were able to communicate more openly about the new

---

17 Edmondson, 2019.
18 Edmondson, 1999.
19 Edmondson, Bohmer & Pisano, 2001.

processes, practice and experiment with the technology, and reflect on the trials as a group, were more successful in adopting new routines because their collective learning was enabled by a higher degree of psychological safety within the team.

The link between team psychological safety and team performance is therefore clear: when teams learn effectively because they feel safe, they are able to adopt and perform the new routines that unlock higher levels of organizational performance. In the studies above, this meant higher levels of customer satisfaction and improved processes for the manufacturing teams, and more streamlined, successful surgeries for the cardiac teams. But performance gains are not the only positive outcomes of psychological safety.

In her book on "fearless organizations," Edmondson discusses the rewards of human development that come from processes that promote employee well-being.[20] She uses the example of an American machine manufacturer whose mission includes measuring "success by the way we touch the lives of people".[21] On the surface, this large for-profit, which has been making equipment for the brewing industry since the mid-1880s, is worlds away from mid-sized social businesses of interest here. Yet their commitment to a social mission in "caring for team members" – which some would say qualifies them as a social enterprise – is evident in all aspects of the company, from the treatment of employees to the development "listening sessions" where all employees can speak their minds. Because of the psychological safety the company has cultivated with this approach, not only do employees feel respected and benefit from that value, they are empowered to design and implement changes.

One of the most important findings of Edmondson's research of psychological safety is that it is not innate to certain personalities or the "chemistry" of the group, but a feature that can be created within groups and can vary within an organization from one group to another.[22] Across her research she found "what was clear was that leaders in some groups had been able to effectively create the conditions for psychological safety while other leaders had not. This is true whether you're looking across floors in a hospital, teams in a factory, branches in a retail bank, or restaurants in a chain".[23]

Creating fearless social entrepreneurs

For social businesses, the barrier to high operational performance remains the fear that the integrity of internal processes will be degraded. This fear presumes that the social mission of the firm is intrinsically imbued in these processes, to the benefit

---

20 Edmondson, 2019.
21 Ibid, 120.
22 Ibid.
23 Ibid, 13.

of all stakeholders. When this is not the case, when organizations fail to create the value for their employees that they want to create for their target population, or when their pursuit of a particular value inhibits the overall social value creation for employees, professionalization offers a pathway to social value-laden processes. The success of different professionalization approaches is varied across different types of hybrid organizations in different sectors and geographies, and there is evidence that these approaches can still be people-centred and mission-focused.[24] Indeed, certain managerial practices can be positively associated with employee satisfaction in social value-driven organizations, when the mission and identity of the organization are also preserved.[25]

Irrespective of form, professionalization provides the structure and guidelines that can create psychological safety for employees as they work together to fulfil core tasks, learn new skills, and grow the organization. In social businesses, the relationship between leaders or decision makers, and operational team members, remains strategically important to achieving this. Kuratko, Hornsby, and McMullen[26] have proposed a model for sustainably applying principles of corporate entrepreneurship in social businesses in order to become more strategically adaptive in the long term. They find that the antecedents of corporate entrepreneurship are innovative, social entrepreneurial behavior from individuals within the organization, and the communication of its positive effects to senior leaders. Employees on the factory floor need to be encouraged to be entrepreneurial in ways that support the social mission, and to feel that this behavior is rewarded – with respect, trust, monetary compensation, or positive work experiences. Leaders need to be able to see how this strategy translates to performance – as measured by employee satisfaction, customer satisfaction, productivity, or an alternative metric that reflects the social mission.

Any number of operations management methodologies could be employed to achieve this manner of coordination between leaders and team members in social enterprises. What is not prescribed in most of these frameworks, however, are steps to creating psychological safety. Incidentally, social businesses may be some of the organizations best disposed to achieving it. In the same way that social businesses like Silulo, Ergoform, and Vitaliate, endeavour to create processes, products, and services that satisfy the needs of their stakeholders, so does psychological safety require organizations and leaders to listen to team members for expressions of learning, experimentation, questioning, and risk-taking. Of course, it also means organizations must remain open to expressions of fear and have a willingness to change in response.

---

24 Maier, Meyer & Steinbereithner, 2016.
25 Melnik, Petrella & Richez-Battestia, 2013.
26 Kuratko, Hornsby & McMullen, 2011.

Edmondson reminds that creating psychological safety in organizations, much like achieving sustainability, is not done in a singular action, but continuously as part of "a constant process of smaller and larger corrections that add up to forward progress"[27] Only when team members feel fearless enough to be social entrepreneurs in their own right will they be able to exhibit the creativity, communication, and responsiveness necessary to enact real change for themselves, their organization, and their society.

---

27 Edmondson, 2019: 209.

Chapter 12

The Impact of Business Accelerators in Disadvantaged Areas: The Case of Solution Space Philippi Village

Assoc. Prof. Mikael Samuelsson, Shiela Yabo and Ndileka Zantsi

Introduction

Small and medium enterprises (SMEs) are the main contributors to economic growth.[1] They facilitate local development[2] as well as communities or regions in a country.[3] In addition, SMEs contribute to employment as well as higher economic growth rates for emerging economies as compared to developed countries.[4] This is attenuated in disadvantaged areas where the failure rates of new firms range between 50 and 90% within three years.[5] In spite of their critical role in economic growth, SMEs are faced with a number of challenges which negatively affect the extent to which they can meaningfully contribute to economic development.[6] As a result, governments across the globe have developed policies and programs to promote the growth and profitability of SMEs.[7] These have translated into an array of institutional frameworks for business development for creation of entrepreneurial and business skills.[8] Such institutional frameworks are deemed to be effective in facilitating entrepreneurship.[9]

However, Boter and Lundstrom[10] suggest that the extent to which such frameworks could influence the propensity to start new businesses and develop existing ones varies across the different types of environments and types of frameworks. In this study we seek to develop a better understanding of how to develop a business accelerator in a disadvantaged area in South Africa. We look at the development of the Solution Space Philippi Village and its high-impact program.

---

1   Allahar & Brathwaite, 2016; dos Santos, 2015; Katua, 2014; Mahemba & Lundström, 2005; OECD, 2017.
2   Oh, 2014.
3   OECD, 2017; Salem, 2014.
4   dos Santos, 2015.
5   Bushe, 2019.
6   Sharmilee & Muhammad, 2016.
7   OECD, 2017.
8   Gnyawali & Fogel, 1994.
9   Smallbone, Welter, Voytovich & Egorov, 2010.
10 Boter & Lundstrom, 2005.

The Solution Space Philippi was developed in 2016 as part of the Graduate School of Business, UCT, out of this vision, as an innovation hub that has developed strong community networks, resources and local insights. Based in Philippi, a low-income community on the Cape Flats in Cape Town, the project was initiated with the vision of creating economic opportunity through the active inclusion of those who are excluded from the mainstream of development. The Solution Space Philippi finds its relevance in the existence and dire need for solutions to the social challenges that most constrain Africa's social and economic prosperity. Within this context, the traditional mission of universities (teaching and research) is broadening to incorporate a more contemporary ideal of a collaborative, embedded institution. In emerging economies like South Africa, universities play an integral social responsiveness role in developing knowledge and ways of learning that attempt to understand and address societal challenges. This requires engagement with the lived experiences of fellow South Africans and understanding of the national socio-political landscape. These social challenges also represent opportunities for African talent to develop innovative solutions, from the bottom-up, appropriate to the context and culture. In order to achieve this, however, an innovation hub and a supportive ecosystem of key partners is required to overcome existing barriers to innovation.

The question we set out to answer is whether it is possible to establish an environment in a township to develop and grow high-impact businesses with a social impact and an economic impact. Evidently, there are challenges in answering the impact questions, which arise from inadequate peer reviewed studies that could provide empirical evidence on the impact of business incubation/accelerators.[11] The lack of clarity among scholars on both the conceptual meaning of a business incubator/ business accelerator and its potential impact has complicated the problem further.[12] The situation is further exacerbated by lack of a specific theory that could be used to study business incubation/accelerators. This has resulted in adaptation of several management theories.[13] It has led to the scarcity of knowledge, both empirical and theoretical, that could explain the characteristics and drivers of business accelerator models.[14]

In addition, our understanding of 'incubator effect' is marginalized by the fact that earlier research in this area has concentrated on developed countries, i.e., US and Europe.[15] As such, it becomes even more challenging to explain the concept of 'business accelerators' from a developing country perspective, where there is a

---

11 Al-Mubaraki & Busler, 2010; Amezcua, 2010; Ratinho, 2010.
12 Meru & Struwig, 2015.
13 Charry, Perez, & Barahona, 2014.
14 Bhatli, Borella, Jelassi, & Saillant, 2015; Pauwels, Clarysse, Wright, & Hove, 2016.
15 Allahar & Brathwaite, 2016.

growing concern about the level of innovation.[16] This study therefore approaches the subject of the effect of business incubators/accelerators environments by associating the impact with the behaviors of those targeted to benefit from such environments.

The remaining sections of this paper are organized as follows: Section two reviews business incubators and accelerators to set the scene for the study. Section three explains the theories and develops the hypotheses. We then present the methodology, results and discussions in sections four, five and six respectively. Our conclusions and suggestions for future research are presented in section seven.

Business incubators and accelerators

Lately, many countries have resorted to business acceleration and incubation to stimulate entrepreneurial development.[17] Since both business incubators and business accelerators purpose to facilitate growth of new ventures, they are commonly referred to in literature as start-up assistance organizations[18] or business incubation environments.[19] However, there are notable differences between business incubation environments i.e. accelerators and business incubators and other start-up support organizations.[20] In this paper we focus on business acceleration as one of the business incubation environments.

Nascent literature points to business accelerators as a new form of business incubation environments.[21] The term 'business accelerator' refers to a type of business incubator that seeks to facilitate speedy development, and commercialisation and exit of start-ups.[22] It is a new generation of business incubators that provides clients with knowledge-intensive and intangible support services such as mentorship, networking opportunities and access to funding over and above the standard business incubator services.[23] In addition, business incubators/accelerators select start-ups that have high growth potential as evidenced by a compelling business model and a strong founding team.[24]

Whilst the study on which this paper is based uses the terms 'business incubators' and 'business accelerators' interchangeably, the researchers note the inherent differences

16 Denanyoh, Adjei, & Nyemekye, 2015; Kropp, Lindsay & Shoman, 2018.
17 Centre for Digital Entrepreneurship & Economic Performence, 2015; Acs & Stough, 2008.
18 Centre for Digital Entrepreneurship & Economic Performence, 2015; Dempwolf, Auer, & D'Ippolito, 2014.
19 Ganamotse, Samuelsson, Abankwah, Tibaingana, & Mphela, 2017; Mozzarol, 2015.
20 Ganamotse, et al., 2017; Bliemel & Flores, 2015; Dempwolf et al., 2014; Ganamotse, 2013.
21 Alberto-Morant & Oghazi, 2016; Bliemel et al., 2016; Pauwels et al., 2016; Schiopu, Vaseli, & Tuclea, 2015.
22 Bhatli et al., 2015; Pauwels et al., 2016.
23 Pauwels et al., 2016.
24 Regmi, Ahmed, & Quinn, 2015.

between the two concepts. The main differences between business incubators and business accelerators are that business accelerators use a shorter period of up to one year; the accelerator takes equity; they at times provide funding; they use intensive coaching practices; and encourage network practices in order to get a fast response to the questions as to whether the start-up is viable or not.[25]

Theory

Entrepreneurship in developing nations has been seen as a way of creating employment opportunities, spearheading innovation, enhancing economic growth, reducing poverty, fighting hunger, minimizing rural-urban migration, and fostering competition.[26] In developing countries, the entrepreneurship concept presents an opportunity through which governments can deal with economic and social challenges which are ubiquitous and on the rise.[27] It is a vehicle for structural transformation as entrepreneurs strive to fill gaps that have resulted from underdeveloped markets.[28]

Hence, many developing countries' governments are looking for ways in which young people can be encouraged to take part in start-up ventures in a bid to reduce high employment levels. The International Labor Office[29] has indicated that rising unemployment levels are a major problem facing many developing countries. This observation creates the need to look at the factors that affect their penchant to taking up entrepreneurial initiatives.

Particularly, Henderson and Robertson[30] suggest that studies on entrepreneurship should focus on people within the age range of 25-44 years and should identify factors which influence their intention to start a business. Such factors include personality characteristics as well as cultural, social, economic, political, demographic, political and technological factors.[31] From an African perspective, Mitchel[32] concluded that entrepreneurs are motivated to start new ventures by "security for self and family", the need for continuous learning, the desire to grow a successful company, the desire to make money as well as freedom of implementing own approaches to work.

From the developing nations' context, studies have suggested that entrepreneurial intentions could be associated with demographic variables such as age[33] and

---

25 Ganamotse, Samuelsson, Abankwah, Tibaingana, & Mphela, 2017; Bliemel & Flores, 2015.
26 Holmgren & From, 2005; Mwatsika, 2015.
27 Briggs, 2016; Ozaralli & Rivenburgh, 2016.
28 Acs & Virgil, 2009.
29 The International Labor Office, 2015.
30 Henderson & Robertson, 2000.
31 Denanyoh et al., 2015.
32 Mitchel, 2004.
33 Jekwu, 2016; Ozaralli & Rivenburgh, 2016.

gender.[34] For instance, Jekwu[35] indicated that Nigerian male graduates had higher entrepreneurial intentions as compared to their women counterparts. Ozaralli and Rivenburgh[36] also found that Turkish female students had lesser intentions of starting a business as compared to their male counterparts who were likely to become entreprenuers. Consistent with Acs, Arenius, Hay and Minitti[37] the above authors found that almost twice as many men as women develop into entrepreneurs.

Not only that, the effect of gender on entrepreneurial intentions seems to be experienced by many countries across the globe. For instance, Langowitz and Minitti[38] found that women's propensity to enterprise was explained by gender in seventeen (17) countries. Furthermore, research on business students in the United States, India, and Turkey established that both male and female respondents associated entrepreneurs with masculine traits as a benchmark (Gupta et al., 2009). This has been attributed to societal norms, which marginalize women and therefore tend to thwart women's entrepreneurial intentions, that are still strongly rooted in patriarchal beliefs of some societies.[39]

Furthermore, human capital has previously been associated with a propensity to engage in entrepreneurial behavior whereby, human capital pertains to the knowledge possessed by individuals that could be attained through experience, education and vocational training.[40] The educational background and experience are categorized in literature as general and specific human capital respectively by scholars who seek to differentiate between the two types of human capital.[41]

General human capital is not transferable and therefore it is tacit; that is, the knowledge, skills and abilities that individuals employ to execute tasks.[42] Tacit knowledge forms part of the entrepreneurial capital alongside attitudes which have been known to influence intentions to start an enterprise.[43] However, studies on the impact of human capital on entrepreneurial activities have yielded somewhat inconclusive results.

Previous studies have negated the effect of educational background (general human capital) on entrepreneurial activities in general[44] and specifically on individuals'

---

34 Gupta, Turban, Wasti , & Sikdar, 2009; Jekwu, 2016; Langowitz & Minniti, 2007; Ozaralli & Rivenburgh, 2016.
35 Jekwu, 2016.
36 Ozaralli & Rivenburgh, 2016.
37 Acs, Arenius, Hay & Minitti, 2005.
38 Langowitz & Minitti, 2007.
39 Acs et al., 2005; Langowitz & Minniti, 2007.
40 Popescu & Diaconu, 2008.
41 Aliaga-Isla, 2014; Becker, 1993; Estrin, Mickiewicz, & Stephan, 2016; Matanda, nd.
42 Baron, 2007; Colombo & Grilli, 2010; McGuirk, Lenihan, & Hart, 2015; C.C. Popescu & Diaconu, 2008.
43 Dauglus & Shepherd, 1999.
44 Colombo & Grilli, 2010; Douglus & Shepherd, 1999; Estrin et al., 2016.

propensity to enterprise.[45] Notwithstanding that, using Global Entrepreneurship Monitor data, Estrin, Mickiewicz and Stephan[46] suggest that the importance of general human capital tends to be significant for social entrepreneurship and less so for commercial entrepreneurship.

The importance of education is premised on that fact that education is one of the tools for developing human capital.[47] In addition, education is one of the factors that has been associated with entrepreneurial intentions.[48]

However, there are studies that associate experience (specific human capital) with entrepreneurial activities[49] and intentions.[50] Experience, as defined by one's occupational status, is deemed to have a positive effect on propensity to enterprise,[51] albeit with an inclination towards necessity-driven enterprises.[52] However, Estrin, Mickiewicz and Stephan[53] suggest that specific human capital is more important for commercial entrepreneurship compared to general human capital (Education).

In view of the above we ask ourselves: Is it possible to build an accelerator environment in a disadvantaged area that can enhance societal impact and economic development by a combination of structure, human capital development and impact?

In the next part of this section we examine the theory of planned behavior in order to develop hypotheses that could help us to explain business accelerator impact on students' intentions to start up and grow companies.

Business accelerators are highly selective in scouting for business ideas that have high growth potential. They do not only increase the intention to start business but also motivate entrepreneurs to come up with innovative products and services. This is due to the fact that structured higher education experiences contribute towards cultivating an innovative potential and spirit among college students.[54] Moreover, once admitted into the accelerator, start-ups are provided with innovation acceleration services.[55] As such, the presence of business incubators and accelerators in universities is expected to influence students' intention to start their own business ventures by giving them a chance to try out their ideas.

---

45 Aliaga-Isla, 2014; Davidsson & Benson, 2003.
46 Estrin, Mickiewicz & Stephan, 2016.
47 Passaro, Quinto, & Thomas, 2018; Popescu, Bostan, Robu, Maxim, & Diaconu (Maxim), 2016.
48 Douglus & Shepherd, 1999; Uddin & Bose, 2012.
49 Davidsson & Benson, 2003.
50 Saraf, 2015.
51 Rachamania, Rakhamaniar, & Setyaningsih, 2012; Saraf, 2015.
52 Saraf, 2015.
53 Estrin, Mickiewicz & Stephan, 2016.
54 Mayhew et al., 2016.
55 Dempwolf, Auer, D'Ippolito 2014.

According to Namatovu et al.,[56] four factors could stimulate and support innovation as well as encouraging successful entrepreneurial activity. Firstly, is the availability of financial resources; equity, debt, grants and subsidies for new businesses. Secondly, Research and Development (R & D) conducted at universities that could lead to new commercial opportunities are available for new businesses.

Thirdly, the presence of commercial and professional services as well as institutions which promote the emergence of newly established businesses. Mueller[57] suggests that supporting entrepreneurial networks and support structures can increase the perceived behavioral control, thus raising the individuals' perceptions, which results in higher entrepreneurial intention, whilst, Yousafazai, De-Soriano and Muffatto[58] argue that support organizations play a crucial role in the formation of students' entrepreneurial intention.

Fourthly, business training and entrepreneurial education, i.e. training which contributes to the creation and management of new, small or growing business entities, that is incorporated within the education and training system. Autio et al.[59] suggest that courses in entrepreneurship and the image of business founders that act as role models within the university encourage graduates to become self-employed. They concluded in a study of technology students from four different countries that career preferences and entrepreneurial convictions are influenced by the support received from the university environment.

Evidence from both developed and developing countries attests to the importance of universities in general, and university incubators in particular, in the development of students' entrepreneurial intentions. For instance, Yousafazai, De-Soriano and Muffatto[60] posit that the university environments and faculty facilitate students' entrepreneurial intention. In addition, from an African perspective, previous studies have highlighted the business incubators' role in the promotion of entrepreneurship among university graduates as a means to create entrepreneurial intention.[61] In summary, the theory regarding business incubators/accelerators suggests a lack of consistency between the concepts of how training and human capital development interventions might lead to opportunity-based entrepreneurial intentions instead of just entrepreneurial intentions.

---

56 Namatovu et al., 2012.
57 Mueller, 2011.
58 Yousafazai, De-Soriano & Muffatto, 2014.
59 Autio et al., 2001.
60 Yousafazai, De-Soriano & Muffatto, 2014.
61 Adegbite, 2001.

Methodology

Previous business incubation research[62] has focused on tenant firms and others' collected data from incubator managers. In order to answer our research question, we use a qualitative approach where we follow the process from idea and over the first cohort of start-ups coming out of the Solution Space process and its impact. We were able to get primary data from the selection process, the acceleration process and subsequent. The study is exploratory and mainly descriptive, and focuses on the learnings from our first cohort.

Empirical Setting

Philippi Village background

Philippi is a low-income settlement on the Cape Flats in Cape Town, which presents both potential and a range of challenges. It is strategically located in close proximity to transport nodes and economic opportunities such as the Cape Town International Airport, the Philippi Industrial Area and the Philippi Horticultural Area. Philippi Village is a 12-hectare social real estate development joint venture between an NGO, the Business Activator, with a 14-year history on site and well-established networks in Philippi and the Bertha Foundation. The overall development was initiated with the vision of creating economic opportunity, skills development and employability development, through the provision of infrastructure and attracting a relevant mix of tenants to the 6 000m2 business hub near the intersection of Klipfontein and Govan Mbeki Drive. Solution Space Philippi are tenants within this overall development and have actively worked over the past two years with other local tenants such as the Philippi Economic Development Initiative (PEDI), Business Activator, Harambee, Desmond Tutu HIV Foundation, Silulo, and Columba Leadership.

Community background

With population growth the number of both formal and informal settlements has rapidly increased, which in turn has placed increasing pressure on city administrations to provide basic services. Within the residential area of Nyanga/Crossroads/Philippi, the apartheid legacy of a lack of social and physical infrastructure has placed great strain on the community. Efforts to build the economy of Philippi through development of businesses and light industry in Philippi East have faced obstacles such as lack of adequate access to and from the area, extreme poverty and resulting social breakdown, and a workforce with a low skills base.

---

62 Mas-Verdu et al., 2015.

Team background

The team is a multidisciplinary team with unique access to the community and access to the whole UCT research output in the form of students, research, specialists, funding and a long experience creating innovation. The Director has over 20 years of global experience from developing and running business incubators, business labs and science parks both in developed and in emerging markets. He is also a core faculty member of UCT and associate professor which allow him unique access to researchers and faculty. The program manager at the Philippi hub and the team have unique access to community involvement and our space in Philippi is designed to cater for the living lab process. The program manager has over 10 years of experience from innovative processes and community work. The liaison and marketing manager has over two years of contextual competence experience from working with high-performing teams in underserved areas.

Objectives

Our programs are designed to provide a supportive ecosystem to help early-stage innovation-driven entrepreneurs who want to test and validate their business model. Startups have access to a range of resources including co-working space, practical learning clinics, mentors, weekly check-ins and staff advisors, and a community of peers who learn and grow together. Our overarching core objectives are to:

- Help founders build viable and scalable impact innovation-driven startups by providing a supportive ecosystem.

- Be the leading Research & Development (R&D) platform for organizations in Africa and value creator for our partners.

Our approach is informed by the continual cycle of designing, developing, testing and evaluating different support mechanisms for entrepreneurs. The broad heading "social impact through economic development" provides an umbrella for our goals:

- Access to critical resources

- Information and advice provision

- Skills development

- Access to networking and opportunities

- Psycho-social support

- Ensure more robust and focused social enterprise concepts

- New venture support and creation

Target audience

Our Impact Venture Incubation Program targeted entrepreneurs as defined below:

An early-stage enterprise whose purpose is to bring innovative products or services to market. These enterprises aim to develop viable businesses by delivering products or services that meet a marketplace need that relates to social impact.

Criteria:

1. Must have an impact in a local community;

2. Must have a prototype or first version of the product currently in the market;

3. Founder or majority shareholder must be the lead participant;

4. The idea must have progressed beyond concept and should demonstrate evidence of early market testing, customers, revenues, patents or intellectual property filings.

We focused on local entrepreneurs and youth (from surrounding communities such as Nyanga, Crossroads, Philippi, Gugulethu, Mitchell's Plain, Khayelitsha, Langa). We place importance on the calibre of the team (with the right mix of skills/ability to build, test and deliver). At an early stage the right team is the most crucial element of a start-up and therefore our target audience must have the required ability, passion, drive and commitment. Other important criteria with regards to our target audience include strategic fit with our Partner's priorities and attractiveness of the opportunity.

Results

We ran two cohorts under 2018. The first in spring IVIPSS and the second in the winter VIPSW. Below we have summarized the results from both cohorts. The first started with a marketing campaign in February and March in 2018. We used the following campaign Elements: Press Release, Social Media Elements, Flyer, Emailer and the following campaign channels: Word of Mouth, Local Radio, Local Newspaper, Local Libraries, Social Media Partner Pages, Direct Emails

How did you hear about IVIPSS?

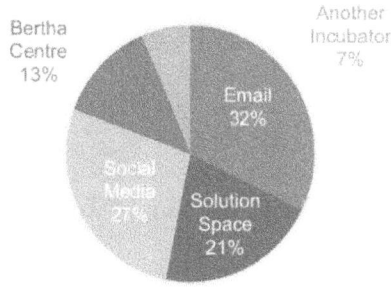

Ivipss18 demographics

NATIONALITY: APPLICATION

NATIONALITY: SELECTED

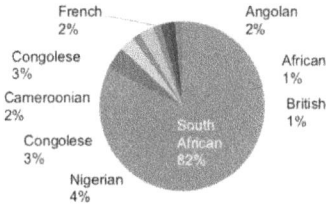

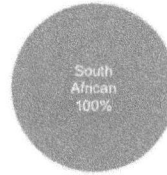

GENDER: APPLICATION

GENDER: SELECTED

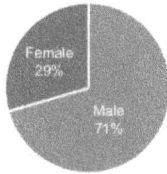

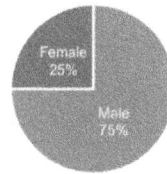

RACE: APPLICATION

RACE: SELECTED

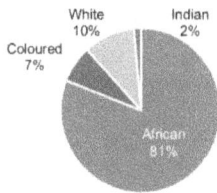

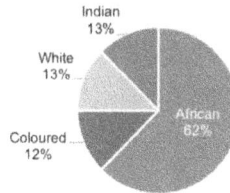

AGE: APPLICATION

AGE: SELECTED

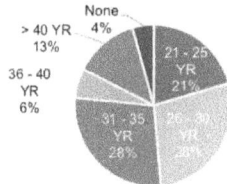

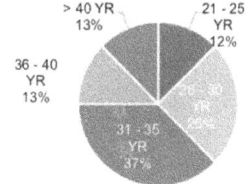

Ivipss18 start-up focus

IMPACT AREA: APPLICATION

- Financial Services 3%
- Recreation & Leisure 6%
- Health & Wellbeing 10%
- Cities & Infrastructure 3%
- Agriculture & Environment 26%
- Employment & Enterprise 16%
- Mobility & Communication 9%
- Education & Skills… 26%

IMPACT AREA: SELECTED

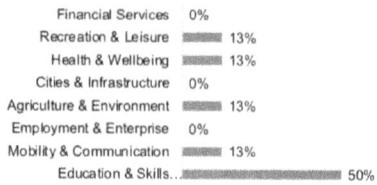

- Financial Services 0%
- Recreation & Leisure 13%
- Health & Wellbeing 13%
- Cities & Infrastructure 0%
- Agriculture & Environment 13%
- Employment & Enterprise 0%
- Mobility & Communication 13%
- Education & Skills… 50%

CUSTOMERS: APPLICATION

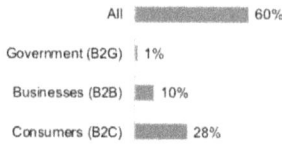

- All 60%
- Government (B2G) 1%
- Businesses (B2B) 10%
- Consumers (B2C) 28%

CUSTOMERS: SELECTED

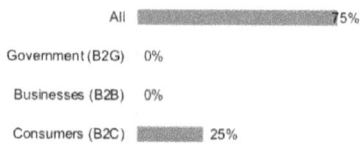

- All 75%
- Government (B2G) 0%
- Businesses (B2B) 0%
- Consumers (B2C) 25%

IP REGISTRATION: APPLICATION

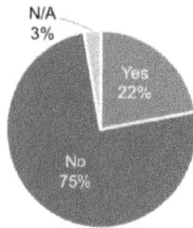

N/A 3%, Yes 22%, No 75%

IP REGISTRATION: SELECTED

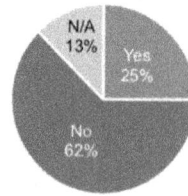

N/A 13%, Yes 25%, No 62%

Ivipss18 start-up stage

COMPANY FORMED YR: APPLICATION

2018 10%, 2017 25%, 2016 24%, 2015 15%, 2014 7%, 2013 6%, <2013 13%

COMPANY FORMED YR: SELECTED

2018 13%, 2017 13%, 2016 38%, 2015 13%, 2014 13%, 2013 0%, <2013 13%

COMPANY REGISTERED: APPLICATION

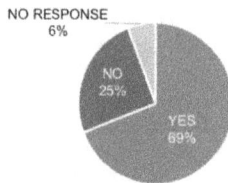

NO RESPONSE 6%, NO 25%, YES 69%

COMPANY REGISTERED: SELECTED

NO 13%, YES 87%

Company registered: selected

STAGE: APPLICATION

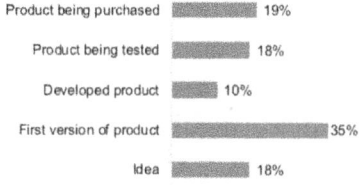

Product being purchased	19%
Product being tested	18%
Developed product	10%
First version of product	35%
Idea	18%

STAGE: SELECTED

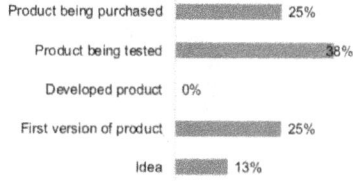

Product being purchased	25%
Product being tested	38%
Developed product	0%
First version of product	25%
Idea	13%

FOUNDER AGREEMENTS: APPLICATION

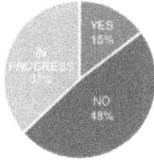

YES 18%
IN PROGRESS 37%
NO 48%

FOUNDER AGREEMENTS: SELECTED

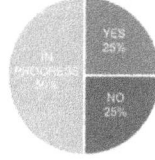

YES 25%
IN PROGRESS 50%
NO 25%

 # CUSTOMERS: APPLICATION

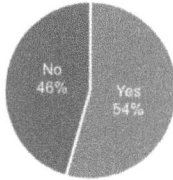

No 46%
Yes 54%

 # CUSTOMERS: SELECTED

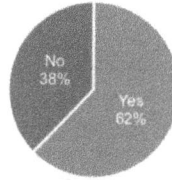

No 38%
Yes 62%

 # EMPLOYEES: APPLICATION

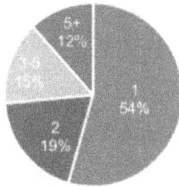

5+ 12%
3-5 15%
2 19%
1 54%

 # EMPLOYEES: SELECTED

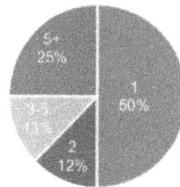

5+ 25%
3-5 13%
2 12%
1 50%

Ivipss18 start-up traction

CUSTOMERS: APPLICATION

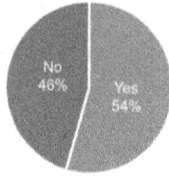

No 46%
Yes 54%

CUSTOMERS: SELECTED

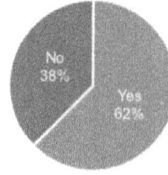

No 38%
Yes 62%

EMPLOYEES: APPLICATION

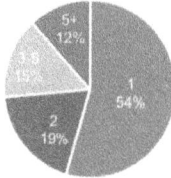

5+ 12%
3-5 15%
1 54%
2 19%

EMPLOYEES: SELECTED

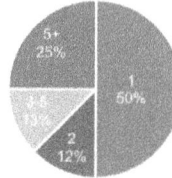

5+ 25%
3-5 13%
1 50%
2 12%

MONTHLY REVENUE: APPLICATION

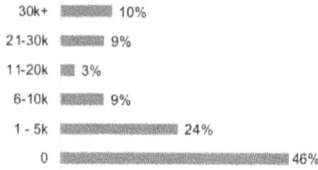

- 30k+ 10%
- 21-30k 9%
- 11-20k 3%
- 6-10k 9%
- 1 - 5k 24%
- 0 46%

MONTHLY REVENUE: SELECTED

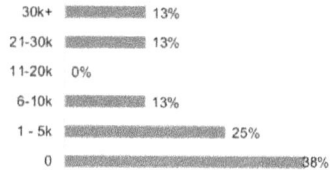

- 30k+ 13%
- 21-30k 13%
- 11-20k 0%
- 6-10k 13%
- 1 - 5k 25%
- 0 38%

Ivipss18 funding

FUNDING TYPE: APPLICATION

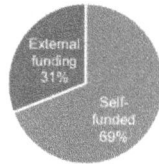

External funding 31%
Self-funded 69%

FUNDING TYPE: SELECTED

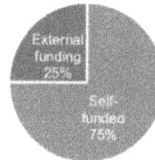

External funding 25%
Self-funded 75%

FUNDING SOURCE: APPLICATION

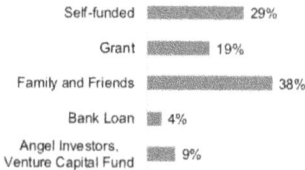

- Self-funded 29%
- Grant 19%
- Family and Friends 38%
- Bank Loan 4%
- Angel Investors, Venture Capital Fund 9%

FUNDING SOURCE: SELECTED

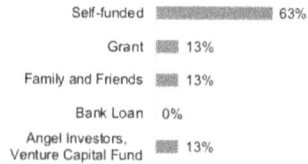

- Self-funded 63%
- Grant 13%
- Family and Friends 13%
- Bank Loan 0%
- Angel Investors, Venture Capital Fund 13%

FUNDING TYPE: APPLICATION

R1m+	3%
R500,000-R1m	1%
R250,000-R500,000	9%
R100,000-R250,000	9%
R0-R100,000	78%

FUNDING TYPE: SELECTED

R1m+	13%
R500,000-R1m	0%
R250,000-R500,000	13%
R100,000-R250,000	0%
R0-R100,000	75%

OTHER INCUBATORS: APPLICATION

YES 41%
NO 59%

OTHER INCUBATORS: SELECTED

YES 12%
NO 88%

EXAMPLES: APPLICATION

Raizcorp
Bandwidth Barn
NYDA
The Innovation Hub
Awethu
Shell Accelerate Her
Spark International
SEED

Fetola
Red Bull Amaphiko
Shanduka
YouthStart CoCT
Impact Hub
SAB Social Innovation /
Kickstart

EXAMPLES: SELECTED

NYDA

AREAS OF SUPPORT: APPLICATION

Mentorship	1%
Getting funding	25%
Financial skills	15%
Legal support	9%
Technical support	12%
Building a team	12%
Marketing support	13%
Getting customers	15%

AREAS OF SUPPORT: SELECTED

Mentorship	0%
Getting funding	24%
Financial skills	10%
Legal support	7%
Technical support	17%
Building a team	14%
Marketing support	14%
Getting customers	14%

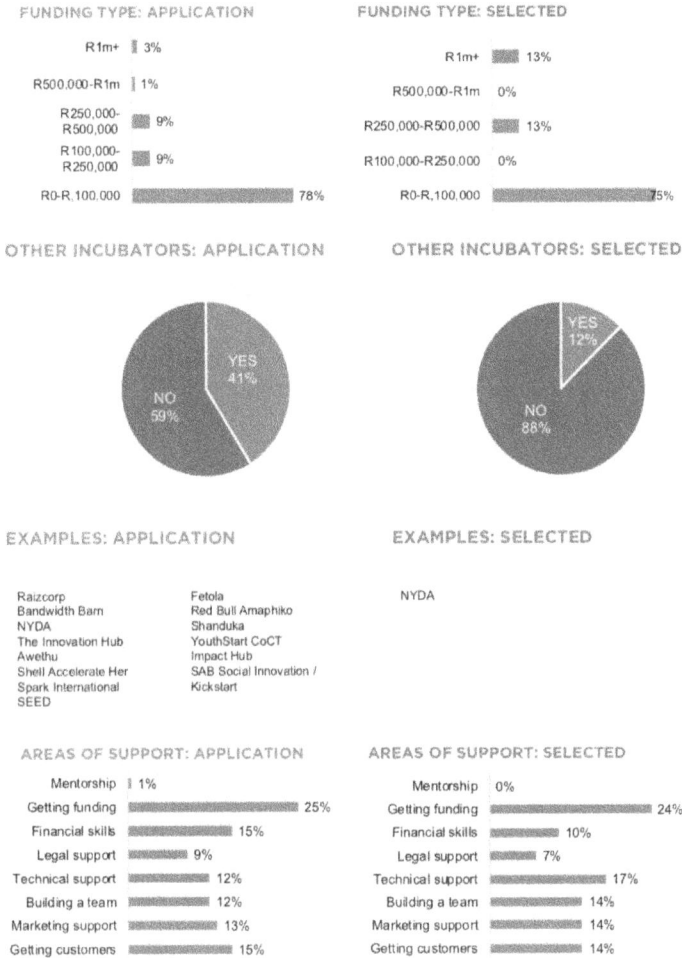

VIPSW 18 results

Ivipws18 campaign Dates: 9 July – 9 August 2018. The campaign elements were similar: Press Release, Social Media Elements, Flyer, Emailer and the campaign channels were similar: Word of Mouth, Local Radio, Local Newspaper, Local Libraries, Social Media Partner Pages, Direct Emails

How did you hear about VIPSW18?

How did you hear about IVIPWS18?

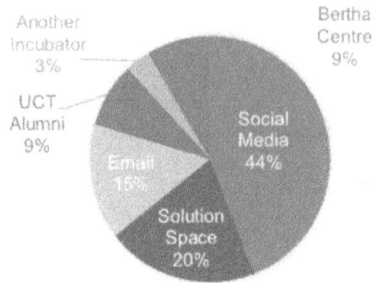

Another Incubator 3%

Bertha Centre 9%

UCT Alumni 9%

Social Media 44%

Email 15%

Solution Space 20%

Vipws18 demographics

NATIONALITY: APPLICATION

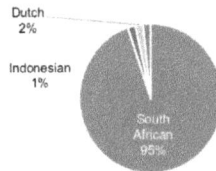

NATIONALITY: SELECTED

Dutch 2%

Cameroonian 2%

Indonesian 1%

South African 95%

South African 100%

GENDER: APPLICATION

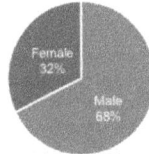

GENDER: SELECTED

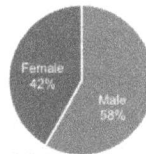

Female 32%

Male 68%

Female 42%

Male 58%

Vipws18 start-up focus

IP REGISTRATION: APPLICATION

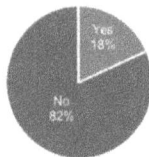

IP REGISTRATION: SELECTED

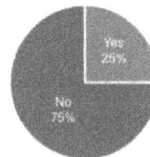

Yes 18%

No 82%

Yes 25%

No 75%

IMPACT AREA: APPLICATION

Financial Services	3%
Recreation & Leisure	3%
Health & Wellbeing	10%
Cities & Infrastructure	5%
Agriculture & Environment	10%
Employment & Enterprise	27%
Mobility & Communication	8%
Education & Skills...	32%

IMPACT AREA: SELECTED

Financial Services	0%
Recreation & Leisure	0%
Health & Wellbeing	25%
Cities & Infrastructure	0%
Agriculture & Environment	0%
Employment & Enterprise	17%
Mobility & Communication	8%
Education & Skills...	50%

CUSTOMERS: APPLICATION

All	75%
Government (B2G)	2%
Businesses (B2B)	7%
Consumers (B2C)	17%

CUSTOMERS: SELECTED

All	67%
Government (B2G)	0%
Businesses (B2B)	17%
Consumers (B2C)	17%

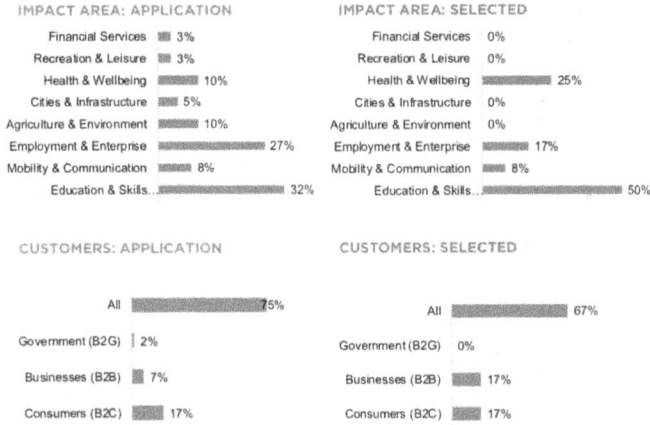

Vipws18 start-up stage

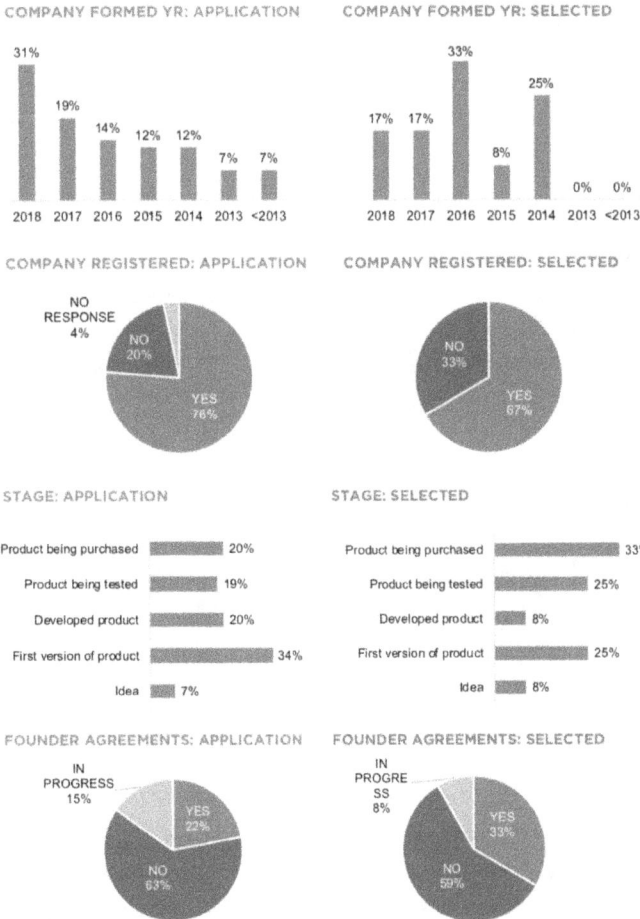

COMPANY FORMED YR: APPLICATION

2018	2017	2016	2015	2014	2013	<2013
31%	19%	14%	12%	12%	7%	7%

COMPANY FORMED YR: SELECTED

2018	2017	2016	2015	2014	2013	<2013
17%	17%	33%	8%	25%	0%	0%

COMPANY REGISTERED: APPLICATION

NO RESPONSE 4%
NO 20%
YES 76%

COMPANY REGISTERED: SELECTED

NO 33%
YES 67%

STAGE: APPLICATION

Product being purchased	20%
Product being tested	19%
Developed product	20%
First version of product	34%
Idea	7%

STAGE: SELECTED

Product being purchased	33%
Product being tested	25%
Developed product	8%
First version of product	25%
Idea	8%

FOUNDER AGREEMENTS: APPLICATION

IN PROGRESS 15%
YES 22%
NO 63%

FOUNDER AGREEMENTS: SELECTED

IN PROGRESS 8%
YES 33%
NO 59%

Vipws18 start-up traction

CUSTOMERS: APPLICATION

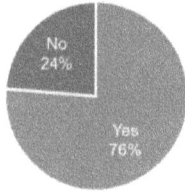

No 24%
Yes 76%

CUSTOMERS: SELECTED

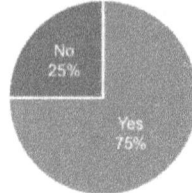

No 25%
Yes 75%

EMPLOYEES: APPLICATION

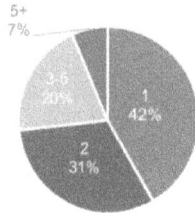

5+ 7%
3-5 20%
1 42%
2 31%

EMPLOYEES: SELECTED

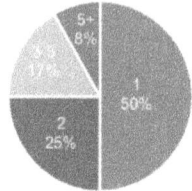

5+ 8%
3-5 17%
1 50%
2 25%

MONTHLY REVENUE: APPLICATION

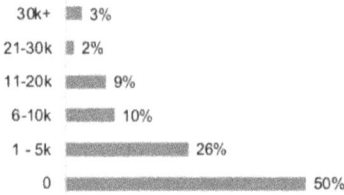

30k+	3%
21-30k	2%
11-20k	9%
6-10k	10%
1 - 5k	26%
0	50%

MONTHLY REVENUE: SELECTED

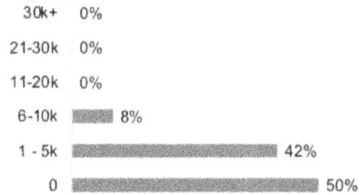

30k+	0%
21-30k	0%
11-20k	0%
6-10k	8%
1 - 5k	42%
0	50%

Vipws18 funding

FUNDING TYPE: APPLICATION

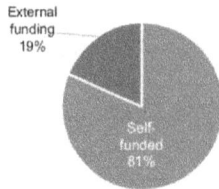

External funding 19%
Self-funded 81%

FUNDING TYPE: SELECTED

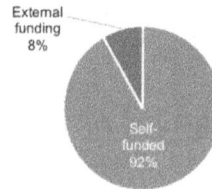

External funding 8%
Self-funded 92%

FUNDING SOURCE: APPLICATION

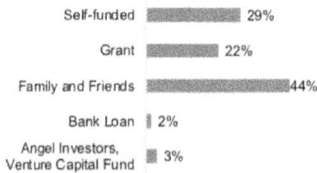

Self-funded	29%
Grant	22%
Family and Friends	44%
Bank Loan	2%
Angel Investors, Venture Capital Fund	3%

FUNDING SOURCE: SELECTED

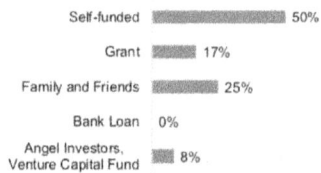

Self-funded	50%
Grant	17%
Family and Friends	25%
Bank Loan	0%
Angel Investors, Venture Capital Fund	8%

FUNDING TYPE: APPLICATION

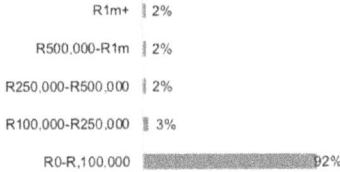

R1m+	2%
R500,000-R1m	2%
R250,000-R500,000	2%
R100,000-R250,000	3%
R0-R,100,000	92%

FUNDING TYPE: SELECTED

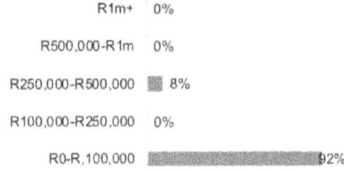

R1m+	0%
R500,000-R1m	0%
R250,000-R500,000	8%
R100,000-R250,000	0%
R0-R,100,000	92%

Vipws18 start-up support

OTHER INCUBATORS: APPLICATION

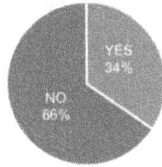

YES 34%
NO 66%

OTHER INCUBATORS: SELECTED

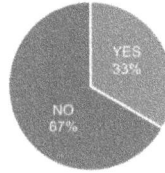

YES 33%
NO 67%

EXAMPLES: APPLICATION

NYDA
The Innovation Hub
SEDA
False Bay
YouthStart CoCT

RAA
PnP Boost Your Biz
Telkom Future Makers
RLabs

EXAMPLES: SELECTED

NYDA
PnP Boost Your Biz
Telkom Future Makers

AREAS OF SUPPORT: APPLICATION

Mentorship	0%
Getting funding	31%
Financial skills	11%
Legal support	7%
Technical support	10%
Building a team	9%
Marketing support	17%
Getting customers	14%

AREAS OF SUPPORT: SELECTED

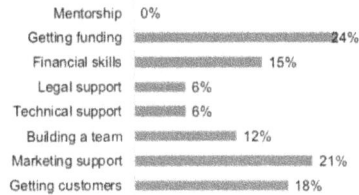

Mentorship	0%
Getting funding	24%
Financial skills	15%
Legal support	6%
Technical support	6%
Building a team	12%
Marketing support	21%
Getting customers	18%

Discussion

During our first phase (2016-2018) the GSB made a strategic decision to focus on two key themes: Local Enterprise and Youth Development. Following a process of appreciative inquiry with local organizations, mapping community assets, and piloting a handful of interventions – several key gaps and challenges were identified in the local innovation ecosystem. These gaps were specifically:

- Lack of sustained mentorship

- Access to advisory services and support for local enterprise

- Language barriers limiting efficacy of skills development

- Limited exposure for entrepreneurs and youth to new networks and associated opportunities

- Need for increased psycho-social support for entrepreneurs

- Limited co-creative approaches in the ideation and concept stage of venture creation

- Better coordination across initiatives to create sustainable pathways for youth and entrepreneurs to grow and develop.

While engagement at the grass-roots level is limited in wide-scale impact, the local innovation ecosystem of Philippi represents some of the key challenges facing other marginalized communities and provides an opportunity to test a variety of interventions on a small scale to learn what works for eventual scale and greater impact.

The review of data for applicants and selected start-ups to the 2018 Impact Venture Incubation Programs helped to further understand the profile of entrepreneur and identify key priorities for subsequent programs. The methodology involved compiling data from applicants to the program (via an online form) and contrasting this with selected startups. The Solution Space has collated these results as described above. Further evaluation and analysis revealed a number of insights and recommendations which are summarized below:

- Major interest from 21 – 35 years old

- Low level of female entrepreneurs (assess needs analysis and prioritise)

- Impact areas focused on Education & Skills, Health & Wellbeing, Employment & Enterprise and interventions that impact Youth within local communities (these businesses are not capital-intensive to start and sustain)

- Majority had registered a company but not finalized shareholder agreements

- Majority self-funded and generating revenues below R5k per month (particular challenge for social enterprises in the early phase is supporting beneficiaries with a sustainable business model).

The Solution Space also sends out a monthly feedback form to entrepreneurs who participate in the program to complete (in order to continually assess the various program elements), and at the end of the three-month program a 1-2-1 interview is conducted with each entrepreneur to discuss plans for the next six months, their priorities, support needs and feedback on most valuable aspects of the program. The interviews revealed the following insights:

- Facilitating peer support critical to the success of the program where entrepreneurs feel part of a community

- Facilitators who teach from practical experience most beneficial

- Translator essential to ensure jargon explained, ensured different levels accommodated to (this could be further enhanced through online resources)

- Credibility of program unlocked further resources and opportunities

- Support package (light snacks and travel stipend) critical to ensure continued participation from vulnerable resource-constrained entrepreneurs

- Mentorship model required further development (geographical distance impacted on participation)

This study set out to investigate the role of acceleration programs on entrepreneurs in disadvantaged areas in South Africa..We aimed at providing answers to the burgeoning acceleration centres and business start-ups particularly in challenging areas with a connection to a university. Our study found a significant contribution in the field of entrepreneurship by our descriptive results. Firstly, they bring new understanding about business accelerator effect in disadvantaged areas. It gives a better understand on how to reach potential entrepreneurs and how to facilitate a high-impact business acceleration process. Secondly our results contribute to an understanding of how business accelerators influence the process across time and with what consequences. If we, for example, compare the survival rates with our cohorts with the 10-30% survival rate, Solution Space start-up survival rates are above 70%. Also, from a diversity perspective it is interesting that we are able to attract a mixed group of entrepreneurs both in terms of gender and race especially in the second cohort where we have 42% women. Almost unheard-of levels in an international comparison.

The findings make a contribution in the field of entrepreneurship. Firstly, they bring new understanding about business accelerator effect in disadvantaged areas and its consequences from a social and economic point of view. Secondly, it contributes to our understanding on how business accelerators influence the intention to start innovative new firms. In line with the preliminary findings in the literature,[63] the study finds strong support for the accelerator impact line of thinking, at least for survival and impact. The researchers submit that there are three key implications from the results: Firstly, business accelerators have a halo effect on individuals who want to start a firm. Not only on the intentions to start a firm, but also that is positively related to the intention to start opportunity-based firms. The latter is important for economic development in general but the major problem in many developing countries is the

---

63 Namatovu et al, 2012; Yousafazai, De-Soriano, & Muffatto, 2014.

lack of opportunity-based ventures. This study shows that the business accelerator process has a positive impact on survival and impact; thus compelling both entrepreneurs and policy makers to invest their time and resources in business accelerators in order to move from necessity-based entrepreneurship to potentially more innovative entrepreneurship. Thirdly, although not hypothesized, there are more men in general with intentions to start firms which suggests that measures should be taken by policy makers and managers of business accelerators to strengthen women's intention to start businesses and in particular innovative- and opportunity-based firms. This is also an area for further research.

Part III

Micro-Level Foundations of Entrepreneurial Activities

Chapter 13

An Entrepreneurship Propensity Index as a Measure of New Venture Creation Potential

Gary Kurt Smith

Introduction

The entrepreneurial phenomenon has been studied through many academic disciplines, from social anthropology to organizational theory, mathematical economics, and business sciences.[1] However, there is considerably less of a consensus in the literature about what constitutes entrepreneurship.[2] There is ambiguity as to what external conditions encourage or restrict entrepreneurial activity. Entrepreneurship has been conceptualized in very different ways by scholars over time; and few studies have looked at entrepreneurship from a genuinely systemic and interdisciplinary perspective.[3] There remains a need for internationally comparable measures of the level of entrepreneurial activity in a country, the determinants of these levels and the impact that these levels have on an economy.[4] Furthermore, it is essential to identify the kind of entrepreneurship that contributes meaningfully toward economic development.[5]

Although several studies have addressed entrepreneurship determinants of an individual, they have done so in isolation of the ecosystem within which the individual operates. According to Buys and Havenga,[6] by excluding the environment in the quantification of human functioning, the information becomes non-effective. Without a comprehensive tool to measure individual and ecosystem determinants, economists will continue to forecast based on insufficient data, and governments will continue to allocate valuable resources to ineffective initiatives in an attempt to address poverty and unemployment in countries such as South Africa.

This research aims to provide a solution through the development of an index that can be used to measure entrepreneurship propensity. The index is based on an individual's entrepreneurial profile (intrinsic factors) and the status of the

---

1. Naudé, 2011.
2. Chowdhury, Terjesen & Audretsch, 2015.
3. Alvedalen & Boschma, 2017.
4. Ahmad & Hoffman, 2007.
5. Van Vuuren & Alemayehu, 2018.
6. Buys & Havenga, 2006.

entrepreneurship ecosystem (extrinsic factors). From an intrinsic perspective, the psychological aspects associated with the entrepreneurship personality profile are measured, such as locus of control, need for achievement, and entrepreneurial mindset. Whereas from an extrinsic perspective, the study measures keys aspects related to the entrepreneurship ecosystem, such as the nature of entrepreneurship policy, financial and non-financial support and other factors including entrepreneurial culture and access to markets.

This research aims to narrow the gap in theory related to entrepreneurship propensity and entrepreneurship ecosystem studies, more specifically concerning youth entrepreneurship. The key objectives are to identify and define the main intrinsic and extrinsic characteristics and primary constructs underlying youth entrepreneurship propensity and new venture creation potential. The objective is to develop an entrepreneurship propensity index for South Africa, using primary data collected on an individual's entrepreneurial profile and the status of the entrepreneurship ecosystem.

Entrepreneurship and economic development

The entrepreneurship literature utilizes a plethora of approaches and definitions, which operationalize entrepreneurship in a variety of ways, such as self-employment, new business registrations and nascent (emerging) entrepreneurial activity.[7] The Organization for Economic Cooperation and Development[8] distinguishes between aspects of entrepreneurship as follows: entrepreneurs (those who seek to identify and exploit new opportunities, products, or markets); entrepreneurial activity (the enterprising human action in pursuit of the creation of value, through economic activity) and entrepreneurship (the phenomenon associated with entrepreneurial activity). Entrepreneurship is further described as the act of initiating, creating and building an enterprise for long-term gain.[9]

The entrepreneurial process involves all the functions, activities, and actions associated with perceiving opportunities and creating businesses to pursue them. Entrepreneurship begins at the ideation stage, as the pre-start-up phase, where the entrepreneur conceptualizes a business idea that needs to be tested and prototyped. A triggering event is required to enable the transformation of an idea, developed through the ideation stage, into a new venture.[10]

---

7   Chowdhury et al., 2015.
8   Organization for Economic Cooperation & Development, 2017.
9   Van Aardt, Van Aardt, Bezuidenhout & Mumba, 2008.
10   Bygrave, 2009.

Based on the potential impact that entrepreneurship has on economic development, there is a growing need for youth entrepreneurship-related initiatives to identify, inspire, and nurture entrepreneurship from a young age. The National Youth Development Agency (NYDA) was established by an Act of Parliament (Act no 54 of 2008). The acts aim to initiate, facilitate, implement, coordinate, and monitor youth development. However, youth unemployment levels continue to rise in South Africa.

The South African National Youth Policy defines 'youth' as any person between the ages of 14 and 35 years. This is a broad definition of the youth age group with varied categories of youth, where high school students are generally between the ages of 13-19 years old. Entrepreneurship education in formal schooling is suggested as one of the most effective ways to encourage youth entrepreneurship. However, little has been done to promote awareness of entrepreneurship as a viable career option which may result in income-generating new venture creation.[11]

A developmental–contextual model of entrepreneurship was tested by Schoon and Duckworth[12] in a nationally representative sample, following the lives of 6,116 young people from birth, through a longitudinal study. The results showed that entrepreneurship in mid-adulthood is predicted by the intergenerational transmission of socio-economic resources, values and behaviors, all of which can be influenced by an education system.

International entrepreneurship research

The measurement of entrepreneurial activity across international contexts is a relatively new and under-represented area of research.[13] The following studies have many similarities in terms of their definition of entrepreneurship, the unit of analysis, country coverage, and phases of the entrepreneurship lifecycle. Yet, there are many gaps in terms of the key focus areas and availability of comparable data.

The Global Entrepreneurship Monitor (GEM) adopts the underlying assumption that national economic growth is the result of the personal capabilities of individuals to identify and seize opportunities.[14] By measuring individual activity, rather than firm-level or registered businesses, it captures both informal and formal activity. Important differentiations are made between opportunity- and necessity-driven entrepreneurs, and between entrepreneurs at different stages of their business. A lifecycle of nascent and new businesses, established businesses, and discontinuation is used. The central indicator of the GEM report is the Total Early-stage Entrepreneurial Activity

---

11   Cleveland & Cleveland, 2006.
12   Schoon & Duckworth, 2012.
13   Marcotte, 2013.
14   Herrington & Kew, 2016.

(TEA) rate. TEA measures the percentage of the adult population (18 to 64 years) who are in the process of starting or who have just started a business. However, GEM does not take into account the youth population age groups of high school students. Furthermore, the GEM does not consider personality profile related factors of the individual to determine the likelihood of becoming a successful entrepreneur.

The World Bank Global Entrepreneurship Survey, which covers 112 countries around the world, focuses on entrepreneurship specifically in the formal sector without paying attention to informal businesses, or youth entrepreneurship. Their definition emphasizes the start-up event and does not consider pre-start-up or pre-nascent entrepreneurship. OECD-Eurostat Entrepreneurship Indicators Programme (EIP) presents the collection of core indicators of entrepreneurial performance, as well as a selection of indicators of entrepreneurial determinants. However, their data is from an external source, and the focus on entrepreneurship is selective in terms of corporate companies. The central unit of analysis is the firm and not the individual, and their definition of entrepreneurship implies a focus on post-start-up.

The Kauffman Index of Start-up Activity report provides a broad index measure of business start-up activity, although limited to the United States. It is an equally weighted index of three normalized measures of start-up activity. The rate of new entrepreneurs in the economy (calculated as the percentage of adults becoming entrepreneurs in a given month). The opportunity share of new entrepreneurs (calculated as the percentage of new entrepreneurs driven primarily by "opportunity" vs. "necessity."). The start-up density of a region (measured as the number of new employer businesses normalized by total business population).[15] There is, however, a lack of comparable data from other countries around the globe and within various stages of economic development. Furthermore, the study places a focus on adults and does not include youth in its sample.

The Eurobarometer focuses on European Union countries (Croatia, Turkey, the US, Japan, South Korea, and China). This study considers both informal and formal business in its definition of entrepreneurship, and it measures entrepreneurial attitudes, motivations, and obstacles. The study contains information on the entrepreneurial activity of respondents who have set up businesses. It considers those who have taken the necessary steps to start a business and those who have started a business in the last three years as well as established companies in terms of those who have started a business more than three years ago, and which were still active at the time of the survey.[16]

---

15 Kauffman Index, 2016.
16 Eurostat, 2012.

Intrinsic entrepreneurship determinants

The sociological and psychological theories of an individuals' beliefs about entrepreneurship are essential in their entrepreneurial journey. A study aimed at measuring the psychological determinants of entrepreneurial success was conducted by Przepiorka,[17] and focused on the various stages of the entrepreneurial process. The study aimed to examine the relationship between action orientation, hope, goal commitment, entrepreneurial success, and life satisfaction; to determine the role of these psychological characteristics in the entrepreneurial process. Goal commitment was seen as a mediator in the relationship between these psychological characteristics and success. The relationship between personality and entrepreneurial status was examined by Zhao and Seibert.[18] The study relied on personality variables from previous studies, which are categorized according to the five-factor model of personality. Results indicated significant differences between entrepreneurs and managers on four of the personality dimensions. The findings showed that entrepreneurs score higher on conscientiousness and openness to experience, while entrepreneurs scored lower on neuroticism and agreeableness.

According to a study conducted by Kirch and Tuisk,[19] entrepreneurs have much higher overall self-evaluation, tolerance, individualism, and innovativeness. Those who are less entrepreneurial tend to reveal collectivistic values. Identity Structure Analysis (ISA), is often used to examine individuals' construals of themselves and others, based on, and anchored in, their value belief systems. ISA enables the analysis of identity formulation and reformulation in the case of aspiring and existing business owners, as they adopt, adapt, consolidate, and redefine their entrepreneurial identity over time.[20] According to Lin, Carsrud, Jagoda, and Shen,[21] scholars often recognize that beliefs are a cognitive component of the Theory of Planned Behaviour (TPB). The econometric results by Kautonen, van Gelderen, and Fink[22] support the predictions outlined in the TPB. Attitude perceived behavioral control, and subjective norms are significant predictors of entrepreneurial intention.

The literature suggests that entrepreneurial drive is rooted in some universal human needs, such as the need for achievement. The concept of achievement relates to individuals who are drawn to tasks that require much effort and skill in order to succeed. According to Need for Achievement theory, such individuals have a high need for achievement (nAch) and are often more prone to taking risks in pursuit

---

17 Przepiorka, 2016.
18 Zhao & Seibert, 2006.
19 Kirch & Tuisk, 2015.
20 Ibid.
21 Lin, Carsrud, Jagoda, & Shen, 2013.
22 Kautonen, van Gelderen & Fink, 2015.

of goals and developmental activities. Entrepreneurship, though an integral part of society, usually requires apparent effort and attracts substantial risk in return for potential profit. Entrepreneurship begins with an idea, followed by enormous effort and skill to transform it into a successful business. According to Zhao and Seibert[23] everyone has ideas by virtue of being human, and many of these ideas would have great potential for income. Though, according to Stewart and Roth,[24] not all human beings are entrepreneurs. In their study, they found that the desire to become an entrepreneur was limited to a few individuals. Carsrud and Brannback[25] suggest that this desire is often limited in strength and resilience to the few who are not easily discouraged by failures and who are persistent in their pursuit of long-term goals. High nAch individuals are prone to seek out challenges and continue to take more significant risks than the last, thereby becoming dominant in entrepreneurship and thus allowing them to explore their creativity and take risks without having to deal with unnecessary boundaries.[26]

Schjoedt and Shaver[27] suggest that individuals are motivated by two forms of locus (perspective), either external or internal. The external locus relies on the external environment to guide success. Such individuals are drawn to little risk because they feel they have little, if any, form of control of their destiny. In addition, such individuals tend to make poor business decisions because they often blame external factors for their failure. They are therefore not motivated to improve on their decisions, abilities, and skills since they have little control over factors affecting them. According to Kroeck, and Reynolds,[28] external factors are often malleable and consistently changing over time. They can't be substantiated and relied upon. It is therefore essential to find an alternative avenue for motivation, one that remains practical and sustainable over extended periods to achieve success as an entrepreneur.

There are those individuals who are motivated by an internal locus of control. They believe that they have a certain level of control over their destiny. Fayolle[29] found that internal locus is an essential trait for entrepreneurs when facing setbacks. In his study, he found that the majority of small enterprises take a minimum of three years to break even, after which profits are far from guaranteed. It often requires the entrepreneur to raise funding and accrue debt in pursuit of "elusive" success. There are many external factors that tend to negate the possibility of income and return on investment, often forcing businesses to operate at a loss. It is not just the case for new

---

23 Zhao & Seibert, 2006.
24 Stewart & Roth, 2007.
25 Carsrud & Brannback, 2011.
26 Rauch & Frese 2007.
27 Schjoedt & Shaver, 2012.
28 Kroeck & Reynolds, 2010.
29 Fayolle, 2005.

business start-ups; even well-established businesses often face many hurdles in the pursuit of growth and sustainability. Stevenson and Jarillo[30] indicate that the market is transient, forcing firms to change frequently to cope with the needs of customers and to maintain a competitive advantage. The amount of effort that is required to keep a business running requires far more than external motivation. Without internal locus of control, entrepreneurs cannot endure and navigate their way to success. They would most likely encounter helplessness and high levels of stress, forcing them to quit the venture and resort back to employment. External factors influencing success, growth, and income are more stable and predictable.

Developing countries typically have very different socio-cultural and politico-institutional environments from those in developed countries. These environments relate differently to an individual's internal or external locus, entrepreneurial attitudes, motivations, resources and both the constraints and opportunities, for starting and running a business.[31]

Extrinsic entrepreneurship determinants

From an extrinsic perspective, the entrepreneurship ecosystem is a system in which there are several mutually reinforcing aspects interacting in a highly complex and idiosyncratic way. The entrepreneurship ecosystem has a direct impact on creating an enabling or inhibiting environment for entrepreneurship, which ultimately influences one's propensity to pursue an entrepreneurial venture.

According to Isenberg,[32] an effective entrepreneurship ecosystem requires enabling policies, sound leadership, availability of and access to appropriate finance, a supportive culture, a variety of institutional and infrastructural support, quality human capital and venture-friendly markets. Central to the ecosystem is the entrepreneur and their entrepreneurial profile. Each element of an entrepreneurship ecosystem is just as important as the next in creating and encouraging entrepreneurial activity in an economy. These elements are usually a function of the social, economic, political, geographic conditions, and contextual events which are integrated to create holistic ecosystems that drive venture creation and growth. Isenberg[33] suggests that "an entrepreneurship ecosystem strategy represents a unique and cost-effective approach to encouraging economic success". An ecosystem could be seen as a pre-condition to cluster strategies, innovation systems, knowledge-based economies, and national competitiveness policies.

---

30 Stevenson & Jarillo, 2007.
31 Karimi, Biemans, Mahdei, Lans, Chizari & Mulder, 2017.
32 Isenberg, 2011.
33 Ibid.

Bruns et al.[34] propose that an entrepreneurship ecosystem cannot be directly measured based on the nature of the multidimensionality. However, the Kauffman Foundation suggests that there are four indicators. Density – in terms of new and young firms, the share of employment in new and young firms, and high-tech (or other target sectors). Fluidity – population fluctuation, labor market reallocation, and the number of high-growth firms. Connectivity – in terms of program connectivity, spinoff rates, and dealmaker networks; Diversity – economic diversification, immigration, and income mobility. Other considerations should include necessary inputs like the educational attainment of a region's population and the quality of entrepreneurship programs at schools, colleges, and universities.[35]

In terms of the South African entrepreneurship ecosystem, before the advent of democracy in South Africa in 1994, the promotion of a vibrant SMME economy was neglected and to some extent actively discouraged through repressive laws.[36] At a national level, the first post-apartheid strategies on enterprise development articulated in the "White Paper on National Strategy for the Development and Promotion of Small Business in South Africa".[37] This strategy is linked to objectives deriving from perceptions of three critical roles for SMMEs, namely employment promotion, redistribution, and improvement in global competitiveness.

A ten-year review of government SMME programs found several areas of underperformance, with plans that were found to have conflicting objectives.[38] The white paper on strategy was revised as the "Integrated Strategy on the promotion of entrepreneurship and small enterprises".[39] This new strategy tried to incorporate the lessons learned from the first ten years of democracy, as well as worldwide shifts taking place in enterprise development. Organizations such as the Small Enterprise Finance Agency (SEFA) were mandated to foster the establishment, survival, and growth of SMMEs and contribute towards poverty alleviation and job creation. The creation of a new ministry, the Department of Small Business Development (DSBD) in 2014, provides further indication of government's commitment to SMME development. The department aims to promote SMMEs through a focus on the economic and legislative drivers that stimulate entrepreneurship to contribute to radical economic transformation.[40]

---

34 Bruns et al., 2017.
35 Kauffman Index, 2016.
36 Rogerson, 1999.
37 DTI, 1995.
38 Masutha & Rogerson, 2014.
39 DTI, 2005.
40 SEDA, 2017.

Oosthuiszen[41] undertook a study of the South African entrepreneurial ecosystem to determine the status of each of the key elements and to determine the interaction, alignment, and integration between them. While this study was limited to 100 respondents, whom he identifies as users of the ecosystem, his findings show similarities to other related research. Oosthuiszen[42] determined that collectively, the South African entrepreneurial ecosystem appears not to be ideally favorable to optimally stimulate entrepreneurial activity. Although the domains of an entrepreneurial ecosystem exist, there are low levels of entrepreneurial activity and success in comparison with other developing countries. This could be from a deficit in some domains as well as insufficient integration between the elements.

Considering the extent of both intrinsic and extrinsic entrepreneurship determinants, it is of vital importance to empower researchers, policymakers, and practitioners with an instrument through which to measure entrepreneurship propensity and new venture creation potential of an economy.

Strategy and methodology

The research relies on a survey strategy, using interviews and questionnaire methods to enable data collection of both a qualitative and quantitative nature. The survey strategy offers more control over the research process through the use of sampling, and it tends to generate findings that are representative of the whole population. The research follows a mixed-methods approach to improve confidence and ensure the quality and depth of results. The approach combines qualitative and quantitative aspects through triangulation to address the shortfalls of using a single method. Both methods complement each other and assist in improving the reliability and validity of the findings. According to Leedy and Ormrod[43] and Saunders, Lewis and Thornhill,[44] triangulation is used as a strategy to increase the probability of the results observed. Observations are done through two or more independent sources of data or data collection methods to substantiate research findings within a study. According to Maree,[45] the mixed methods approach allows for contextual interpretations and flexibility in choosing the best strategies to address the research questions. Triangulation is suited to provide generalizable answers to the research questions through empirical investigation.

The mixed-method approach enables the researcher to quantitize qualitative data by converting it into numerical codes so that it can be analyzed statistically. It also

---

41 Oosthuiszen, 2015.
42 Ibid.
43 Leedy & Ormrod, 2015.
44 Saunders, Lewis & Thornhill, 2012.
45 Maree, 2011.

enables the researcher to qualitize quantitative data by converting it into a narrative that can be analyzed qualitatively.[46] This method enables the researcher to investigate both intrinsic and extrinsic aspects related to the phenomenon.

The qualitative aspects of the study make use of Interactive Qualitative Analysis (IQA)[47] through a constituency of successful entrepreneurs and entrepreneurship support practitioners, regarded as authorities on the entrepreneurship phenomenon. IQA is used as an innovative systematic qualitative technique which provides a structured approach to conducting qualitative research.[48] The study further relies on the collection of quantitative data to investigate social phenomena by using statistical, mathematical, and other computational techniques to analyze the data.[49] A Structural Equation Model (SEM) is developed based on latent constructs, with multiple indicator measures and observed variables, considering the correlation and reciprocal causation between constructs. A cross-level model is then developed to describe the relationship among variables at different levels of analysis.

The research makes use of various scales and items. The locus of control construct is measured using items from a unidimensional locus of control scale. According to Schjoedt and Shaver,[50] the scale is considered reliable, valid, unidimensional, and appropriate for the entrepreneurship domain. The entrepreneurial mindset is measured using items from the Entrepreneurial Mindset Profile (EMP).[51] The EMP distinguishes between personality scales and skills scales. Entrepreneurial behavior is measured using items from Kautonen, van Gelderen, and Tornikoski,[52] to predict new venture creation intentions. Action orientation, hope, and goal commitment are measured using items from Przepiorka.[53] These psychological determinants assist in the measurements of potential entrepreneurial success. Creativeness is measured using an imaginativeness scale used in new venture ideation, which was developed by McMullen and Kier.[54] Entrepreneurial intentions are measured using scales from Bacq, Ofstein, Kickul, and Gundry,[55] to examine the factors that influence entrepreneurial intentions, through the interaction between cognitive factors and perceived environmental factors. Entrepreneurial Orientation (EO) is measured using The Hughes and Morgan EO Scale. According to Covin and Wales,[56] the dimensions of EO may vary independently of each other in a given context. The scale incorporates

---

46 Sandelowski, Voils & Knafl, 2009.
47 Northcutt & McCoy, 2004.
48 Bargate, 2014.
49 Saunders et al., 2012.
50 Schjoedt & Shaver, 2012.
51 Davis, Hall & Mayer, 2014.
52 Kautonen, van Gelderen & Tornikoski, 2013.
53 Przepiorka, 2016.
54 McMullen & Kier, 2017.
55 Bacq, Ofstein, Kickul & Gundry, 2017.
56 Covin & Wales, 2012.

separate first-order reflective scales pertaining to the EO subdimensions. The subdimensions include risk-taking, innovativeness, proactiveness, competitive-aggressiveness, and autonomy. Further data is gathered based on the respondent's perceptions of the entrepreneurship ecosystem as well as other key business and entrepreneur indicators.

Conclusion

The need for the study is emphasized through the identification of seminal research, where previous studies do not allow for the collection of internationally comparable data related to youth entrepreneurship propensity. There is little evidence of studies that measure an individual's propensity and that of an economy in relation to new venture creation potential. The significant contribution of the study is towards improved economic forecasting through the measurement of entrepreneurship propensity in determining new venture creation potential. The index accounts for intensity structures that may exist among attributes. It places potential entrepreneurs and the entrepreneurship ecosystem on a continuum, which guides the development and implementation of specific strategic interventions. The index is applied through a cross-sectional study to determine the entrepreneurship propensity and new venture creation potential of high school students in Gauteng. A multi-step process is followed in the development of the index as a systematic and structured multivariate approach. Several base variables are combined into a single measure, namely that of an index variable. This is done through classification rules based on characteristics that can be observed or elicited by asking a series of specific questions. The index enables an individual entrepreneur and the entrepreneurship ecosystem, to be grouped by propensity segment.

The outcome of the study is a robust entrepreneurship propensity measurement tool that provides a comprehensive approach, through the form of an equation, considering intrinsic and extrinsic aspects that impact entrepreneurship propensity. The index provides a method to calculate index scores to incorporate in decision-making criteria related to entrepreneurship and economic development policies and programs.

Chapter 14

Locus of Control and The Happy Entrepreneur

Dr. Babar Dharani and Prof. Kurt April

Abstract

Does entrepreneurship or employment allow for happier personnel in business organizations? Research conducted in South Africa indicates a statistically significant correlation – that earlier stages of an organizational life cycle are associated with happier personnel in the organization. Additionally, in respect of locus of control, scholars have largely concluded that internality is strongly associated with successful entrepreneurship and externality with lower levels of well-being. So, does this entail that traits borne by internals are the key to successful entrepreneurship and happiness at work? While scholars have largely agreed with the hypothesis, research conducted in South Africa revealed no relationship between earlier stages of an organizational life cycle and locus of control expectancy. Examining the nuances, small firms which incorporate innovative strategies in stable industries are ideally suited for internals when the following are present: (a) space for pro-activity, (b) opportunities to follow a high-risk strategy, and (3) when internals can have personal, direct control, whereas their external counterparts tend to prefer low-cost strategies in dynamic industries due to their ability to manoeuvre well in chance-dependent scenarios. Hence, rather than an overall preference of internality to entrepreneurship and happiness at work, research is now indicating that there is a best-fit of locus of control expectancy with the environment, strategy and industry.

Introduction

Entrepreneurship is frequently viewed as an economic solution to the slow growth and high unemployment rates faced by many African economies. However, are entrepreneurs happy? While happiness at work is a subjective concept, research is fast approaching an objective means to calculate levels of happiness at work using a variety of constructs, such as: job satisfaction, affective organizational commitment, and work engagement.[1] As a quantitative measure, questions regarding happiness at work are better asked in relation to a benchmark, or as a comparative. While it may be fairly obvious that self-employment presents a better option than unemployment, a more ambiguous question to ask is whether entrepreneurs are happier at work than employees.

---

1   Fisher, 2010.

Founders of businesses can face difficulties that employees can avoid. Firstly, the fear of possibly losing equity invested in the start-up presents entrepreneurs with a risk that employees do not face. The risk is exacerbated when funding is scarce, as is the case for many African entrepreneurs. Additionally, entrepreneurs often take on an overwhelming burden of responsibilities of running their business which impacts their stress levels; hence, their well-being. Despite tight community ties which are characteristic of most African cultures, entrepreneurs may feel alone in their struggles in managing their businesses. There are also scenarios where the entrepreneur may feel unfulfilled despite achieving success in the business. For example, even if the business may provide for the entrepreneur and their family, in African cultures, there is frequently an expectation by the community to uplift the extended family and others in their ethnic sub-group or community. This transforms the objective of the business from merely achieving personal success to contributing to the community, placing increased pressure on business owners in the African context.

On the contrary, businesses usually start with the birth of lots of ideas; where visions are conceived and fantasies are born. This requires creativity and deep optimistic thoughts for the future.[2] The process of starting a business is one that is embedded in high levels of mental and even physical absorption at work, which is a vital ingredient for experiencing 'flow' at work.[3] Subsequent to the generation of ideas, a high level of commitment to the business that is seeded is needed to develop a sense of mission for the entrepreneur.[4] It requires high levels of energy and vigor, and complete dedication to the business, requiring an emotional attachment, and a resultant affective commitment to the business idea and the organization are created. Long hours are spent to innovate using an informal communication and structure system within the organization to launch the business and undertake the risk of setting up an organization, tapping into an identified niche, and marshalling of resources. There tends to be little planning and coordination; however, entrepreneurial activities thrive as resources are collected, and a niche market is targeted which supports development of a commitment towards the business idea.[5] All the above characteristics of a business start-up are a recipe for happiness at work. Nonetheless, what are the chances that an entrepreneur's creation becomes overwhelming, operates in an environment not suited to their personality, and is not their preferred nature of work, making them unhappy, or even thus, making it a better option to be employed instead?

---

2   Shane & Venketaraman, 2000.
3   Csikszentmihalyi, 1990.
4   Meyer & Allen, 2016.
5   Quinn & Cameron, 1983.

Entrepreneurship and happiness at work

Researched for decades, there is consensus that organizational development typically follows a set path of development, from the birth of the business untill its death, known as the organizational life cycle.[6] Entrepreneurs are placed in the early part of the organizational life cycle. Research has concluded that entrepreneurs have a significantly lower incidence of physical and mental illnesses, visit the hospital less often, and report higher levels of life satisfaction than employees.[7] Not only for the founder, but it was found in research conducted in 35 departments in an accounting firm across 12 office locations in South Africa that happiness levels at work for the employees were higher in organizations in the early stages of the development life cycle than in well-established organizations, or compared to those in decline.[8] The results of the research are shown in Table 14.1. The negative correlation coefficients for Spearman Rank -order tests indicate happier personnel in earlier stages of the life cycle than in the latter ones.

Table 14.1: Business life cycle and happiness at work constructs correlation

Stage of development	Affective organizational commitment	Work engagement	Job satisfaction
Correlation Coefficient (ρ)	-.125*	-.167***	-.122*
Sig. (2-tailed)	0.023	0.002	0.026
N	334	334	334
Stage of development of the department and affective organizational commitment and job satisfaction of employee correlation is significant at 0.05 level.			
Stage of development of the department and work engagement of employee correlation is significant at 0.01 level.			

Additionally, a study out of Baylor University and Louisiana State University combined data from the Center for Disease Control and the US Census to conclude that as the number of small businesses increased, the health of not just the entrepreneur and their employees, but also of the surrounding community improved. For example, Summit County in Colorado (where there is an incredibly high number of small businesses) census reported a mortality rate, obesity rate, and diabetes rate that were less than half of the national average.[9]

---

6   Adizes, 1979.
7   Stillman, 2017.
8   Dharani, 2019.
9   Stillman, 2017.

Locus of control and happiness

Major dispositional contributors to personal levels of happiness, at work or otherwise, are: a genetic predisposition[10] and psychological trait of the individual in question.[11] Meta-analyses, including individual empirical studies13, have concluded a significant correlation between constructs of happiness at work and the core self-evaluation traits of: self-esteem, generalized self-efficacy, locus of control, and emotional stability (low neuroticism),[12] as have.[13]

Control perspectives in psychology are the fundamentals of the psychological trait known as locus of control.[14] It is a core self-evaluation personality trait that reflects one's belief or perception about who controls life and the environment. Perceived control in psychology is a "person's belief that he or she is capable of obtaining desired outcomes, avoiding undesired outcomes, and achieving goals".[15] This belief can exist at varying levels, reflecting the degree to which one perceives personal control in life.

Locus of control has been described as a dimension with two opposing differentiates. The dimensions reflect the extent to which individuals believe that what happens to them is within their control (internal locus of control expectancy or internality) or beyond it (external locus of control expectancy or externality). This presents a continuum of an internal-external belief system that is measured using Rotter's[16] Internal-External (I-E) Scale. All theories of personality are built on assumptions, and the linearity of human nature is one of the basic assumptions to build a theory where two polar dimensions identified by the theorists are assumed to have a linear continuum from one pole to the other.[17] Similar is true of the Rotter's Internal-External (I-E) Scale (Rotter, 1966), where the two poles are defined as internal expectancy (internality) and external expectancy (externality), and a linear scale is said to join the two. In addition to an internal and external locus of control expectancy, the concept of dual control, or shared responsibility, is described as a balance of externality and internality. Individuals who believe that both internal and external forces control their lives and the environments are labelled as bi-locals[18] or as having a balanced locus of control expectancy.[19]

---

10 Diener, 2013; Weiss, Bates, & Luciano, 2008.
11 Judge, Heller, & Mount, 2002.
12 Judge, Thoresen, Bono, & Patton, 2001.
13 Näswall et al. 2005; Rahim & Psenicka 1996; Chen & Silverthorne 2008a; Kirkcaldy & Furnham 1993.
14 Rotter, 1966.
15 Landau, Kay, & Whitson 2015: 695.
16 Rotter, 1966.
17 Hjelle & Ziegler 1976.
18 Torun & April 2006.
19 April, Dharani, & Peters, 2012.

In reference to locus of control and happiness, externality, a belief in a lack of a link between personal actions to consequences in one's life and the environment, is proven to be associated with many mental health problems. Externals' believe that a relationship does not exist between action and consequences, or that consequences are random to personal action, makes externals dependent on aspects in their environment, such as powerful others, luck or fate, making them prone to feelings of helplessness,[20] learnt helplessness[21] extending to hopelessness[22] and were found to be more dependent on the organizational environment than other expectancies. There is also an increasing argument and empirical evidence that optimal subjective well-being[23] is associated with a balanced locus of control expectancy.[24]

Locus of control and entrepreneurship

So, based on the above, research has confirmed that there is a statistically significant relationship between entrepreneurship and happiness at work, and also that there is a statistically significant relationship between locus of control and happiness; therefore, we can hypothesize that there is a possible relationship between entrepreneurship and locus of control, where internality is associated with happier entrepreneurs and externality with less happy employees in entrepreneurship scenarios.

Locus of control has been extensively examined in entrepreneurship research, and many scholars have concluded that internality, a belief that what happens to oneself and the environment around one is the result of one own actions, is strongly associated with entrepreneurship. This is explained by the fact that the traits of internals, who have a propensity to take control of organizations and consciously steer their actions to ensure success, are effective leaders in organizations and as entrepreneurs.[25] Their counterparts, who depend on external forces for consequences, were mostly viewed as lacking traits that are essential for entrepreneurship. Their belief that outcomes are randomly administered does not promote risk-taking, which is an integral part of entrepreneurship. Nor does their belief that external forces, God or powerful others, are responsible for outcomes, lead to pro-activity to take control, also seen as an essential ingredient for entrepreneurship. Research conducted in the big six accounting firms[26] examined the influence of systematic differences in levels of structure in the firms on auditors' performance.[27] Their research concluded that internals tend to perform more efficiently in environments that allow them more control over their actions than

---

20 Seligman, 1972, 1975.
21 Peterson, Maier, & Seligman, 1993.
22 Lefcourt, 1976.
23 Diener, Emmons, Larsen, & Griffin, 1985.
24 April et al., 2012.
25 Lefcourt, 1984.
26 The closure of Arthur Andersen due to the Enron scandal, & merger of Price Waterhouse with Coopers & Lybrand caused the decrease from big six to the current the big four accounting firms.
27 Hyatt & Prawitt 2001; Prawitt 1995.

in less structured firms. It remains to be tested if this entails that externals performed better when more control is imposed upon them.[28] Spector[29] suggested that locus of control might be a useful selection variable based on the argument that internals are better suited to positions that require independence, whereas externals may have superior person-organization fit when the position requires little independent action, or requires strict obedience to rules or commands. However, Coleman, Irving and Cooper[30] claim this as premature, deeming that further research is necessary for establishing the relationships – hence supporting the research which was subsequently conducted.

The trait was tested in a South African context[31] with the expectation of internals being abundantly present in earlier parts of the organizational life cycle than in later ones. Due to their proactive nature, it was expected that internals would not continue to work in organizations that do not make them happy, and do not allow them control. The findings of the research are shown in Table 14.2. The relationship was tested using Spearman Rank -order correlations and concluded a lack of statistical significance between the two constructs of position on the organizational life cycle and locus of control expectancy of the personnel. This entails that, while most scholars agree with the hypothesized relationship, it did not stand true in South Africa when tested using the organizational life cycle survey.[32]

Table 14.2: Business life cycle and locus of control correlation

Stage of Development	Locus of Control 0-11
Correlation Coefficient (ρ)	0.072
Sig. (2-tailed)	0.201
N	316
Stage of development of the department and locus of control of employee correlation is insignificant.	

This finding, being different from the generalized preference of internality in academic literature, was investigated further to develop an understanding of the acceptance of the null hypothesis in the research. Examining the nuances within the relationship, it is said that in small firms which incorporate innovation, pro-activity, risk-taking, and personal direct control, all aspects which are traits of internals, have been found to be useful characteristics for successful enterprise seeding.[33] While overall the statistics may have proved internals to be more successful at business seeding, these

---

28 Rotter, 1966; Spector, 1982.
29 Spector, 1982.
30 Coleman, Irving, & Cooper, 1999.
31 Dharani, 2019.
32 Lester, Parnell, & Carraher, 2003.
33 Lefcourt, 1976; Miller, Kets de Vries, & Toulouse, 1982.

entrepreneurs with an internal locus of control personality trait were said to follow a typical style of entrepreneurship, while externals were said to follow an alternative style, which has the capacity for success, even more so than those seeded by internals, subject to the organizational strategy, and industry environment. Spector[34] discovered the trend for internals to undertake innovative strategies, whereas their external counterparts tended to prefer low-cost strategies. Similarly, a stable industry environment was seen as appropriate for internals due to their scrupulous planning propensity, while a dynamic industry was seen as more suitable for externals due to their ability to manoeuvre well in chance-dependent scenarios.[35] Hence, research is now indicating that, based on an entrepreneur's locus of control expectancy, there is the best-fit of their respective expectancy with the commercial environment, strategy and industry that the business is started in. Since the African context generally represents a more unstable political, economic, and business environment than the West, it is unsurprising that the findings do not replicate the findings of the research conducted in developed countries.

Conclusion

The core self-evaluation personality trait of locus of control can allow for an insight into which strategies, industry environments, and risk profile based on level of predictability, are best suited for those with an internal or external locus of control expectancy. Overall, internals are generalized to be more successful at entrepreneurship, but new research is revealing many nuances to this generalization. Optimism and risk perspectives vary at the two ends of the I-E spectrum. As such, those with an internal locus of control are found to be better psychologically equipped to undertake innovative strategies whereas their external counterparts tend to prefer low-cost strategies; hence, matching their respective risk appetites. Similarly, a stable industry environment was seen to be more appropriate for internals due to their scrupulous planning propensity, while a dynamic industry was seen as more suitable for externals due to their ability to manoeuvre well in chance-dependent scenarios.[36] As such, the locus of control of the entrepreneur can assist in anticipating a best environment fit for optimizing entrepreneurs' happiness at work and success. Vital questions regarding bi-locals, or those with a balanced locus of control, and environments best suited for them that leverage both ends of the I-E spectrum remain largely unanswered in research. However, research conducted in one of the big ten accounting firms in South Africa shows that such an expectancy is most resilient to the environment, meaning that individuals with a balanced locus of control expectancy have the capacity to be happy at work and deliver success irrespective of the environment in which they operate.[37]

---

34 Spector, 1982.
35 Wijbenga & Witteloostuijn 2007.
36 Ibid.
37 Dharani, 2019.

Chapter 15

Self-empathy as it Relates to Entrepreneurship

Dr. Katherine Train and Dr. Lidewij Niezink

Abstract

The entrepreneur's heavy reliance on self for resources and self-employment is often associated with high levels of risk taking, uncertainty, work effort, decision autonomy, and responsibility, which yield considerable negative emotions and mental strain. A recent move to a more human-centred approach to business has introduced a focus on empathy in business. However, the attempt to empathize with others without adequate care and attention to self may challenge the entrepreneur's resilience and blur the boundaries between self and other in the work context. In this chapter we discuss the role of self-empathy as a coping tool which may be applied to ensure the entrepreneur is able to maintain empathy with customers and employees while keeping him or herself in the picture. We also illustrate the inter-related nature of the dispositional factors of empathy, self-care, boundary setting and agency through self-empathy as a method and practice for self-awareness and self-regulation.

Introduction

The entrepreneur's heavy reliance on self for resources and self-employment is often associated with high levels of risk taking, income and job uncertainty, required work effort, decision autonomy, and responsibility, which yield considerable negative emotions such as fear, anxiety, loneliness, and mental strain.[1] What is more, the demand to establish and maintain an innovative business that is relevant to customers and employees requires that an entrepreneur understand and consider the needs of others. A current move to a more human-centred approach to business[2] has introduced a focus on empathy in business. As the entrepreneur strives to be relevant in a competitive landscape, so the necessity to be innovative and relevant to both customers and employees becomes more pressing, and with it comes the responsibility to be aware of – and sensitive to – their needs. When most people think of empathy, they think of empathizing with someone else. No wonder, considering the many circumstances, in both personal and work life, where one finds oneself

---

1   Patzelt & Shepherd, 2011.
2   Amann et al., 2011; Kyrö, 2015; Terzaroli, 2018.

caught between people or groups of people, expecting one to 'understand.' These circumstances require an entrepreneur to manage, mediate or facilitate amongst different individuals as well as maintain some form of personal connection with each of them. If not maintained with care and attention, interpersonal relations may become sources of stress and can get in the way of doing what needs to be done. Constant vigilance to the requirements of others may challenge the entrepreneur's resilience and blur the boundaries between self and other, and also between the work self and the personal or private self. At the same time, the autonomy that comes with entrepreneurship provides individuals with various opportunities to use coping tools effectively in order to regulate negative emotions.[3] In this chapter we discuss the role of one such coping tool, namely self-empathy, in ensuring that the entrepreneur is able to maintain empathy with customers and employees while keeping him or herself in the picture. The concurrent consideration of self and other enables one to build and maintain a relevant and sustainable business model while maintaining one's own wellbeing. We also illustrate the inter-related nature of the dispositional factors of empathy, self-care, boundary setting and agency through self-empathy as a method and practice for self-awareness and self-regulation.

Self-empathy in Empathic Interpersonal Engagement

At work, an entrepreneur may experience pressure both from the task needing to be accomplished, as well as from interpersonal dynamics. Task-related pressures can vary from the need to provide direction to employees, to completing budget plans, having to reach a sales target or having to solve a design problem. The interpersonal difficulties are something else, often more complex and less clear. Despite the fact that they seem invisible, they can have a powerful effect on the entrepreneur's well-being and ability to function.

Engaging with empathy will help the entrepreneur to understand the people he is working with and to know more about their thoughts, feelings and actions. It is considered essential to a humanistic and human-centred approach to business[4] and it enables an experience and understanding of the deeper motivations behind thoughts, feelings and actions.

When a person is feeling challenged himself, empathizing with someone else is difficult. If the entrepreneur is not aware of his own inner experiential, emotional and mental state, he cannot be sure that that which is perceived to be part of the other, is not rather a projection of his own self. That is why the first step towards empathizing with someone else is to empathize with oneself.[5]

---

3 Patzelt & Shepherd, 2011.
4 Terzaroli, 2018.
5 Barrett-Lennard, 1997.

Self-empathy Observes and Integrates Experiences

Self-empathy means that an aspect of self observes, in an empathic manner, the aspect of self that experiences. In other words, the observer self notices the experiencing self. This is done with an attitude of suspended judgment and openness towards self.[6] It simply requires one to notice and recognise what is happening in oneself. Attentive self-empathy provides both affective and cognitive empathic access to one's own lifeworld. It provides an opportunity for one to integrate aspects of one's current and past experiences, and doesn't necessarily require reinvention or radical conversion of those experiences.[7]

Although there is some literature on self-empathy and its supposed effects in psychoanalysis,[8] surprisingly little is written on the skill itself. How does one empathize with oneself? What blocks to self-empathy can prevent one from doing so? The next sections describe a facilitative approach to self-empathy drawing upon a coaching case study with an entrepreneur. In this context, self-empathy, and indeed empathy itself, is considered a complex skill set that can be encouraged through facilitation, coaching and training in individuals and groups or teams. The skill set consists of four distinct but interconnected capacities: noticing and becoming aware of sensations, emotions, thoughts and needs in the self; committing to create an environment of ethical responsibility towards self; suspending judgment towards self, and setting intentions and attending to the needs identified in self. These iterative four steps open up a presence in self that is conducive to empathic engagement with others.

Noticing with self-empathy

In essence, self-empathy is a deeply personal exploration of that which happens in the interior world: The self observing itself, experiencing itself, feeling itself. Through self-empathy, the self develops self-awareness.

> *Ten years ago, Dan was tired of working the corporate hamster wheel, being at the beck and call of directors and a demanding workload but not seeing adequate personal rewards. He identified a need for a specific service amongst his corporate clients and knew that he had the skills to make a difference. He started out with no capital, but as he described, a lot of stamina. These days, Dan has an established company and is employing people, yet he still finds himself at the mercy of a very demanding workload. The external directors have been replaced by his own internal voice of command, customers who want bigger and*

---

6   Jordan, 1984.
7   Sherman, 2014.
8   Jordan, 1984; Jordan, 1992; Sherman, 2014.

better service and employees who need constant support from him. He works most nights until past midnight and the lack of personal time is taking a toll on his personal relationships. He has an escalating silent conflict with his financial manager and a concurrent escalating discontent with his performance.

Dan finds himself getting caught up in interactions with the manager that cause irritation for him. He avoids scheduling meetings with the manager who "talks too much and wastes my time. He is like an old woman". Dan finds himself taking on more of the financial roles in the business.

At this point in the escalating relationship, Dan recognised tension in himself. The tension can be marked by a lack of concentration, feeling distracted and insecure, or angry and powerless. Recognising tension when it occurs is good news, because it does not necessarily happen automatically. Sometimes, one might recognise the tension but not understand its causes, and yet end up with a breakdown in communication with colleagues. There might also be a non-specific experience of frustration, anger or withdrawal, without being aware of the causes. In all these examples the observer self is unable to notice the experiencing self.

In self-empathy one doesn't change the other person as much as one transforms oneself in response to the other person. The creation of a presence with one's own inner life requires that one focuses on oneself rather than on the person one is working with, in order to find an appropriate response. When working to complete a budget or fulfil a sales target, the entrepreneur is likely to need to motivate and lead others in order to get the task done. He or she needs to find within themselves the inner resources that speak directly to the other person's needs. Empathy and the willingness to transform oneself lies at the heart of being helpful to, or managing, others and to resolving both inner as well as outer conflict. To solve tensions, one must be willing to change oneself and become responsive to both one's own as well as other people's needs.

Becoming aware of sensations, emotions, thoughts and needs

Noticing oneself, and becoming aware of one's inner state, is achieved through getting in touch with the inner sensations, emotions, thoughts and needs, by feeling into the body and observing the mind. We notice how our mind becomes distracted and how we start mind-wandering into memories or plans ahead. After a little wandering while, we pay attention to the distraction without condemning it. This is how the mind works; it focuses and then gets distracted for a while until we bring it back to focus. We learn to be aware of where our mind is and how our body feels moment to moment. In other words, we develop a mindful meta-cognition.[9] And importantly, although we work to regulate our thoughts and our attention, we also accept ourselves as we are in that momentary state of being. There is no right or wrong, there is merely experience and observation.

During an early coaching session, Dan was facilitated to notice with self-empathy the sensations, emotions, thoughts and needs associated with his escalating irritation and discontent. The sensations he experienced were reminiscent of building a wall of protection around himself. The exercise helped him to name his experience as withdrawal and avoidance of his employee. Further prompting guided him to acknowledge his own feelings of being unsupported. He acknowledged that, had he been aware of his own inner experience and how it was contributing to automatic responses, it could have helped him to take a moment before responding impatiently to his financial manager. It could also have given him the opportunity to attempt to understand why the manager was speaking excessively.

Self-empathy With Ethical Responsibility and Centredness

Ethical exploration and agreement

Working with others to provide an encouraging, innovative and supporting presence requires creating an environment conducive for them to draw their attention towards their interior world. This helps to get in touch with themselves and how they think, feel and do things. Equally, transforming oneself in response to the person one is working with requires creating a space conducive to self-exploration. This too, is self-empathy. It encourages being in touch with one's experiences including thoughts, feelings and actions in the work context.

In order to notice these experiences, it is important to explore ethical responsibility in the sense of a commitment to be true to any insights about the thoughts, feelings and actions brought to awareness. This commitment brings clarity and space to the inner experienced world. It is a form of respectful inner listening, with a readiness to take seriously whatever signals arise internally. It opens one up, and enables self-regulation: the ability to alter or modify one's thoughts, feelings, or behaviours,[10] so that one is not swept away by the experience itself, nor overtaken by the emotion. One does not look for ways to change what is experienced in any direction, only to observe and sense what really takes place.

---

9   Jankowski & Holas, 2014.
10   Baumeister & DeWall, 2005.

When Dan felt impatience and discontent towards the financial manager the experience was overwhelming and he was swept along by it. Yet, he was not consciously aware of this experience in himself. His attention remained on the manager. Dan's perception was that the manager was not fulfilling his tasks adequately, that he was wasting Dan's time by reporting on unnecessary details. He wasn't aware of his own thoughts, feelings or indeed actions in response to the manager.

Centring and active sensation practice

To begin the process of finding the inner resources to be adequately available to another person, requires a quiet inner space with which to land, with an introspective and reflective mind. This can be done by taking ownership with the mind of the whole of the space inhabited by the body. One possible way is to close the eyes, and scan with awareness through each area of the body, an exercise called the 'body scan' in mindfulness practices.[11] When one turns inward into current bodily presence, one notices that the bodily experiences have a story to tell. Every mental state has a bodily expression.[12]

The mind and the body interact with each other, just as a hand fits into a glove, and the glove holds the image of the hand. By being more aware of the shape or gesture of the body, one is more aware of one's state of mind, and at the same time creates space within the body for more awareness with the mind. Following centring practice, one may notice an area of the body where there is intense sensation. Focusing on this sensation, giving it a shape or gesture represented with the hands and intensifying the shape with the hands or the body until it matches the sensation brings awareness of the mind in the body. The awareness enables one to make sense of the sensation and correspondingly to give a meaningful name to it with a few descriptive words. It enables one to bring conscious awareness to the experience which, until such time, is in a pre-reflective bodily consciousness.[13] By doing this, the entrepreneur can hold a space for himself and his experiences and sensations and yet not be enslaved to what these sensations demand. It creates the space to open up to a world beyond one's own consciousness.

Suspending judgment in self-empathy

Judgment is a function of the belief system. The life context elicits thoughts and emotions which are experienced internally and then given meaning to. The meaning is linked to the existing belief system. In other words, emotions and cognitions shape

---

11 Dreeben, Mamberg, & Salmon, 2013.
12 Niedenthal, 2007; Oosterwijk et al., 2012.
13 Legrand, 2006.

beliefs. Beliefs also filter the perspective one has on any situation. The belief in right and wrong determines that events or behaviours are judged to be either right or wrong. In this way, judgment prevents us from being open to the range of possibilities with which we can experience life. This is why there is an emphasis on suspending judgment in (self-)empathy. Suspending judgment means that for the time being, one lays aside one's own views and values in order to enter the inner and outer world without prejudice.

When Dan felt impatience and discontent towards the manager, he didn't pay attention to the fact that it was his interpretation and judgment of the manager's actions that created his tension in the first place. When he encountered the situation with self-empathy, he observed the manager's behaviour as well as his own response to it and thus noticed his own evaluation of the situation. The resulting mental distance to what happened at that moment opened him up to notice the manager and to consider his perspective.

Suspending judgment practice

But how does one suspend judgment while practising self-empathy? Evolution determined that evaluation of what is seen and felt occurs practically on a continuous basis. To take decisions, often in split seconds, on whether a given situation is 'safe' or not requires a constant evaluation of the surroundings. Evaluations often take place unconsciously, allowing for a reflexive response.[14] Suspending judgment then means to recognize the evaluation when it takes place, name it as judgment and pause it to reflect on it or divert from it. While noticing with self-empathy, one will need to look for the emergence of an experience of judgment, which can manifest itself as evaluation, doubt, fear, or any other experience for that matter. It is also important to be aware that not all judgment experiences are difficult or challenging. Pleasing experiences such as satisfaction when in agreement with a colleague's idea, or joy at what is perceived to be a job well done are also judgments.

One wants to be able to notice the evaluation pass through without feeling any compulsion to change it. This aspect of self-empathy allows for the observation and integration of experiences as they occur. Suspending judgment is a first step to being able to open the mind to possibilities and perspectives beyond personal reflexes and has a calming function on the emotional life.[15]

Emotions, thoughts, distractions, obsessions, come and go, if they are given time to do so. If not, one is enslaved to instinctive reactions, constantly responding to both

---

14   Bargh & Morsella, 2008.
15   Beddoe & Murphy, 2004.

inner and outer circumstances without consciously choosing how one would like to respond. Suspending Judgment Practice, the act of noticing, recognizing and naming the evaluation and allowing the experience of it to pass through, brings a certain level of control over one's behaviour and allows the possibility to choose how to act and respond in the world.

Setting personal intentions and attending to self in self-empathy

Empathy, and similarly self-empathy, becomes useful when applied as a means to an end. Attentive empathy based upon attentive self-empathy helps one to understand the thoughts, feelings and actions of others in order to interact with them in an efficient and effective manner. The outcome of the empathic and self-empathic interaction is better served if it is guided by a skilfully articulated intention.

Intentions act as a road-map guiding actions with a particular focus.[16] Self-empathy, as a practice, lays the foundation for specific outcomes through intention setting. One notices one's inner life of thoughts and feelings, and any evaluations and judgments that emerge. Once thoughts and feelings have been noticed and one is aware of – and able to – suspend judgments, insights into aspects of how one behaves in the world and how one presents oneself to the world appear. One gains a perspective on oneself as if observing another person. From this perspective, an 'outsider view' on the self appears. This might come with the realization that both self and others would be better served if one were different in the world. This insight can then lead into a personal intention.

Personal intention setting practice

The bodily sensation experienced during the active sensation exercise, the meaningful name given to it and the corresponding evaluations noticed, recognized and named, are made sense of. In asking the question: "What am I needing?" or "What is being asked of me?" one prepares to create an intention. Choosing to create a personal intention leads to the identification of inner resources needed in order to be present to the other person.

Dan initially interpreted the financial manager's feedback as irritating and long-winded. With the practice of self-empathy he noticed the strong sensation and described it as building a protective wall. He named it withdrawal. In reflecting on this mode of interaction, he recognized that he was not expressing his requirements adequately. The withdrawal also meant that opportunities to express his requirements were further diminished. Dan made the personal intention to speak more clearly of his needs.

---

16   Ajzen, 1985.

Attending to self

Attending to self requires that the intention is followed through. There are many ways to attend to the self, that follow from the specific compromise identified in the previous phases of self-empathy. There may be a need for self-care. Equally there may be a need to be more communicative, more assertive, or less assertive. A frequent compromise observed in interpersonal interactions is the nature and proximity of boundaries, both with other people and also between different aspects of one's work and personal life. Attending to self may require the refinement and renegotiation of roles and tasks and corresponding changes in the nature and proximity of boundaries. Awareness of the aspect of self contributing to the compromised situation will determine the path to resolve the compromise.

The first step for Dan in attending to self required that he identify and speak his needs to himself. He noticed that he had a tendency to put other people's needs before his own. He set aside some time to determine where he was compromising his own needs and resolved to put habits in place that would help him to transform the habit of putting his needs aside in the face of other more strongly expressed needs.

Self-empathy as a Tool for Empathy With Others

Choosing to practice self-empathy, as a deeply personal exploration, one observes and integrates one's own experiences. One brings awareness to the inner experiential, emotional- and mental state. One creates an openness by suspending judgments one may have about the self.[17] The result is an inner space that is open, expansive and receptive. When the inner life is noisy with random fragments of thought and feeling, the practice of self-empathy orders these fragments. Paradoxically, by bringing the mind into the inner world of experiences of thought and feeling, a receptive space to the experiences of others is created. The entrepreneur becomes ready to practice empathy with others.

Dan's facilitated self-empathy process culminates in him considering the perspective of his financial manager in this interaction. He considers that the financial manager is not aware of Dan's reaction of withdrawal and may feel excluded from important business actions. The potential feeling of exclusion may mean that the manager is needing more and more validation which is leading him to over-explain in meetings. From this perspective, Dan is more able to understand the response of the financial manager.

---

17   Jordan, 1992.

Empathy with others is as important as, and dependent on, empathy with self. The entrepreneur needs to deal with tensions, needs to get the job done, and is hardly ever independent of the people around him- or herself. Although one might be willing and inclined to empathize with others, success is determined by the level of awareness of one's own influence on the situation as it evolves. Coming back to one's own inner experiences and understanding that they are intrinsically personal to work with, will help one to create space for the experience and behaviours of others. Empathizing with others helps to build an authentic understanding of the prospective customer's experience. It can also reduce intrapersonal conflict while increasing creativity and feelings of group cohesion.[18]

Is empathizing with others different from empathizing with self? Yes and no. Yes, because empathizing with others is empathizing with the inherently unknowable experiences of other people. Their experiences, thoughts and feelings are theirs, and not meant to be experienced by the empathic actor. Empathizing with others does not mean experiencing what others are going through. It is meant to attentively tune into their expressions of those experiences. To open up to their perspectives on a given situation, to broaden one's own views on it, and to hold a space for others to be as they are, while at the same time, finding a common space in which both can move forward and co-create.

Empathizing with others is also similar to empathizing with self. Although the practices are different, they require a similar reflective presence: noticing, taking ethical responsibility, suspending judgment, setting intentions and attending to others. Self-empathy helps to develop agency, the awareness of self as being the initiator of actions, desires, thoughts and feelings.[19] With self-empathy the entrepreneur becomes aware of his or her own experiential state in the moment, which enables differentiation of personal emotional experiences from the experience of someone else. In other words, self-empathy prepares the entrepreneur to face the professional and interpersonal challenges ahead.

Conclusion

This chapter presents self-empathy as a theory and practice-informed process illustrated with excerpts from a coaching case study with an entrepreneur. It serves to illustrate the relevance of self-empathy as a coping skill enabling the entrepreneur to identify and access resources in self for improved wellbeing and interpersonal engagement. It places this in the context of a move towards a more human-centred approach and an increased focus on empathy in business. In the case study, self-

18   Ayoko, Callan, & Härtel, 2008.
19   Decety & Grèzes, 2006.

empathy was applied as a facilitated coaching process through multiple sessions. The entrepreneur was guided to observe and integrate his own experience in interaction with a colleague through multiple interrelated and iterative phases by noticing, becoming aware of and attending to his inner state. It was achieved through getting in touch with the inner sensations, emotions, thoughts and needs; creating an environment conducive to attentive awareness of the interior world through ethical exploration and agreement, and centring and active sensation practice. The suspension of judgment practice served to bring awareness and acceptance to all experience, thus encouraging a deeper awareness of experience. Personal intention setting and attending to self enables the entrepreneur to identify and access new coping resources.

Recommendations for Research

This chapter has described a process for self-empathy as it can be applied to individuals and groups in organizations: as a facilitated process in coaching practice and as a trained self-practice in organizational settings. To date, data has been captured through qualitative interviews which indicate to these researchers the potential for further studies to determine its effects on well-being, self-care, boundary setting and agency in entrepreneurs. The method has been applied in facilitated peer-to-peer support and learning groups in non-entrepreneurial settings where self-empathy has helped participants with relaxation, letting go of limitations, re-evaluating personal needs in the context of work and to set and maintain intentions. The method is also described to facilitate participants to re-evaluate and maintain healthy work-life boundaries and more assertive communication in the work setting.

Patzelt and Shepherd[20] provide a more general theory of entrepreneurial coping behaviours suggesting that problem-focused and emotions-focused coping may help the self-employed to balance negative emotions associated with self-employment (e.g., stress, loneliness, fear of failure) while their business is ongoing.

An interesting avenue for future research would be to evaluate the applicability and efficacy of the methods within the specific context and challenges of entrepreneurship as a problem- and emotions-focused coping strategy. It is also recommended that research be conducted to determine the relevance, applicability and efficacy of the methods in individual- and group-facilitated processes such as in coaching, for personal development as a personal practice and as a peer-to-peer support and learning context.

---

20 Patzelt & Shepherd, 2011.

Chapter 16

Executive Coaching as an Entrepreneurial Venture

Dr. Nicky Terblanche, Rajesh Jock and Prof. Marius Ungerer

Abstract

People from a variety of backgrounds become executive coaches, lured by the promise of flexible work hours, a more balanced lifestyle, and a reprieve from corporate politics. While anecdotal evidence suggests that it is not easy to make a living purely as an executive coach, research on the topic – which would be more conclusive – is sparse. The empirical study reported on in this chapter investigated the nature of starting and running an executive coaching practice as an entrepreneurial venture in South Africa. A standard business model template was used to analyse four dimensions of an executive coaching business: value network, value architecture, value proposition and value finance. Two focus groups (with a total of eight participants) and four semi-structured interviews with past and present executive coaches were analysed using deductive content analysis. Findings revealed that factors contributing to a successful executive coaching practice include forming alliances, leveraging previous experience, employing multiple income streams, and evolving as a business owner. Challenges include the lack of a business strategy, difficulties in finding clients, and underestimating earnings potential. The findings fill a gap in empirical research on factors that contribute to a successful executive coaching business.

Introduction

Coaching in the business context, or executive coaching (used interchangeably with the term 'coaching' in this article) can be defined as a confidential, individually-tailored engagement designed to meet the needs both of the executive being coached and the organization paying for the service.[1] It is a fast-growing industry with more than 53 000 coaches worldwide[2] and at least 1 300 in South Africa.[3]

---

1   Coutu & Kauffman, 2009.
2   Forbes.com, 2017.
3   Myburgh, 2018.

Executive coaching has been used widely during the past 20 years and has been shown to assist in various aspects of individual and organizational improvement, including management performance, the grasp of business complexity, accelerated leadership development, improved team performance and improved self-awareness.[4]

People are drawn to the executive coaching profession by the promise of increased freedom, a balanced lifestyle, self-control, and a reprieve from corporate politics, bureaucracy and pressure.[5] Unfortunately, this foray into a coaching business often ends in disappointment from a financial perspective. Data for South Africa are not available to the authors' knowledge, but a United Kingdom study found that, out of 400 business coaches surveyed, 25 per cent earned less than £5 000 per annum in 2009.[6]

To try and understand the dynamics of starting and running a coaching practice, it may be informative to view such a practice as an entrepreneurial small business. One approach to understanding the dynamics of a business is to study its functioning in terms of a business model (BM) template.[7] A firm's business model is the layer between a business strategy and business processes used to implement the strategy,[8] or the "rationale of how an organization creates, delivers, and captures value".[9] A BM template has the potential to provide an understanding of the aspects that contribute to an organization's short-term profitability and long-term sustainability. In the present study, we applied a BM lens to investigate the factors that play a role in the success and failure of executive coaching practices in South Africa.

Literature Review

Coaching as a small and medium-sized enterprise

Small and medium-sized enterprises (SMEs) in South Africa employ 60 per cent of the labour force and contribute roughly 34 per cent of gross domestic product (GDP).[10] The SME landscape in South Africa is challenging owing to competitive pressure fuelled by globalisation, legislation, relaxing trade barriers, an increase in market expansion resulting from emerging technologies and innovation, fluctuating exchange rates, high interest rates and inflation.[11] Coaching businesses share certain challenges with other small enterprises, such as such as lack of finance and difficulties

---

4   Coutu & Kauffman, 2009; Freedman, 2011; Kombarakaran, Yang, Baker & Fernandes, 2008.
5   Fairley & Stout, 2004; Passmore, 2015.
6   Cavett, 2015.
7   Zott & Amit, 2013.
8   Casadesus-Masanell & Ricart, 2010; Teece, 2010.
9   Osterwalder, Pigneur, Clark & Smith, 2010: 14.
10   Banking Association South Africa, 2016.
11   African Development Bank Group, 2014; Smith & Watkins, 2012.

in obtaining credit; inaccessibility of markets; constraints to developing relationships with customers; tardy recognition by large companies; and obstacles presented by corporate bureaucracy.[12]

Small businesses often fail because of inability to anticipate obstacles and more broadly as a result of (i) inattention to strategic issues; (ii) general management problems; and (iii) poor financial or accounting practices.[13] Individual characteristics of owners also play a significant role in the success of the business, as does the owners' previous experience.[14] Furthermore, strategic planning is typically lacking or is, at best, of a short-term nature with a focus on financial aspects only.[15]

Starting a coaching business presents additional challenges to the ones already mentioned. Entry barriers are low since coaching is a non-regulated industry. In fact, according to the International Coach Federation (ICF), trained coaches see "untrained people who call themselves coaches" as the biggest threat to the coaching industry.[16] Furthermore, coaches often compete with consultants and companies with large marketing budgets. Delays in corporate decision-making lead to protracted sales cycles, which in turn affect cash flow.[17] Coaching is often seen as a non-essential spending item by corporates and is discontinued or reduced during an economic downturn.[18] From this brief overview, it appears that people setting up a coaching practice face additional challenges compared to those setting up other SMEs – leading to an operating environment more challenging than initially imagined.

Using a business model template to analyse an SME

Osterwalder et al.[19] define a business model (BM) as being the "rationale of how an organization creates, delivers, and captures value". A BM offers a systematic perspective on how to do business, encompassing organizational activities and providing a view on the process of value creation and value capture. Zott and Amit[20] thus define a BM as "a system of interdependent activities that are performed by the firm and by its partners and the mechanisms that link these activities to each other" and "a template that depicts the way the firm conducts its business".[21]

---

12   Banking Association South Africa, 2016.
13   Timmons & Spinelli, 2007.
14   Naqvi, 2011.
15   Thompson, Bounds & Goldman, 2012.
16   ICF, 2012.
17   Fairley & Stout, 2004.
18   Ibid.
19   Osterwalder et al., 2010:14.
20   Zott & Amit, 2010: 1.
21   Zott & Amit, 2013: 404.

The BM methodology allows for making start-up decision-makers more perceptive to further related opportunities or place them in a better position to cope with delays from the environment.[22]

For the purpose of this study, the four generic business model components,[23] as originally proposed by Al-Debei and Avison[24] in their unified framework of the BM concept, were used as a lens to examine the experiences of running a coaching business from the perspective of owner-coaches. The core value chain components of the business model[25] are:

(a) Value proposition (VP) – Factors related to the offer of services, products and activities that create value for users

(b) Value architecture (VA) – Factors related to how resources (tangible and intangible) are constructed in order to create value for users (e.g. technological configurations and organizational structure)

(c) Value network (VN) – Factors related to decision-makers (internal and external) and their roles in transactions and collaboration

(d) Value finance (VF) – Factors related to finance, ownership and costs

In summary, from the preceding review of literature it seems that the BM value chain of Al-Debei and Avison,[26] when applied as an analysis template, may be able to provide insight into the dynamics of an executive coaching practice. These insights may contribute to the understanding of the factors that play a role in starting and maintaining a successful coaching business in South Africa.

Research design

The research followed a qualitative research methodology of an explanatory and descriptive nature, as described by Babbie and Mouton.[27] Purposeful, non-probability convenience sampling was used to recruit two focus groups and one set of interview participants via social media and from the researcher's personal network. One focus group consisted of currently practising executive coaches (five participants, referred to as 'FG1'), while the second focus group represented former executive coaches who were not practising any more (three participants, referred to as 'FG2'). Four participants from the focus groups were selected for interviews (referred to as 'I'). By

---

22 Maurya, 2012.
23 Ranerup, Zinner, Henriksen & Hedman, 2016.
24 Al-Debei & Avison, 2010.
25 Ibid, 362.
26 Ibid.
27 Babbie & Mouton, 2014.

separating the participants into two focus groups, the researcher was able to acquire a wider range of perspectives.

Data were gathered during the focus-group discussions and individual interviews, using open-ended questions eliciting insights into participants' motivations for starting a coaching business; challenges faced; and strategies employed to overcome these challenges. Data for the focus-group discussions as well as the interviews included audio recordings, field notes, and photographed sticky notes.

The five-step qualitative analysis process of Taylor-Powell and Renner[28] was used to analyse the data collected. These steps are: (i) knowing the data; (ii) focusing the analysis; (iii) categorizing information; (iv) identifying patterns and connections; and then (v) interpreting. Directed content analysis was used to group the themes that emerged from the focus-group discussion and in-depth interviews in terms of the four BM template dimensions.[29] The ATLAS.ti computer software program was used to assist with data analysis.

Findings and discussion

The results of the deductive content analysis of the focus group and individual interviews are summarised in Figure 16.1. The themes identified were classified according to the four BM dimensions and the predominant sentiment of each theme (as judged by the researcher) is indicated as follows: significant positive factors ("+"); significant negative factors ("-"); and providing valuable information ("i").

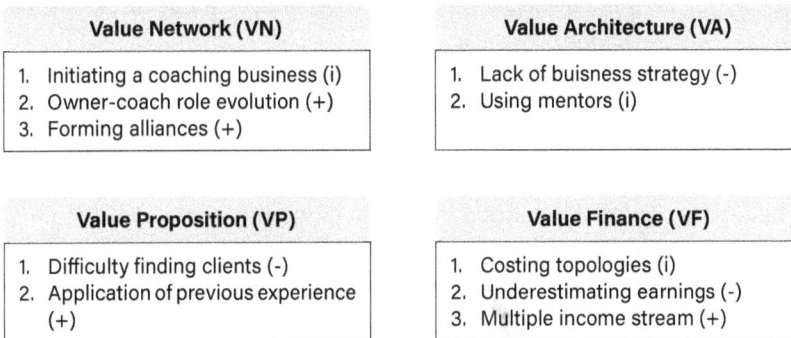

Value Network (VN)	**Value Architecture (VA)**
1. Initiating a coaching business (i) 2. Owner-coach role evolution (+) 3. Forming alliances (+)	1. Lack of buisness strategy (-) 2. Using mentors (i)

Value Proposition (VP)	**Value Finance (VF)**
1. Difficulty finding clients (-) 2. Application of previous experience (+)	1. Costing topologies (i) 2. Underestimating earnings (-) 3. Multiple income stream (+)

Figure 16.1: Themes classified according to the four BM dimensions

28 Taylor-Powell & Renner, 2003.
29 Hsieh & Shannon, 2005.

Value network (VN)

Value network refers to decision-making, the organization's relative value chain position, relationships with stakeholders, roles and actors.[30]

Theme 1: Initiating a coaching business

Participants distinguished between 'push' (being repelled by unpleasant situations) and 'pull' (being drawn towards enticing situations) factors[31] that led them to start a coaching business. Push factors included redundancy, burnout, and frustration at being overlooked for promotion, especially among women and previously disadvantaged individuals:

> 'Time spent at work has a detrimental effect on my social and family life and working in a corporate business consumed my whole life.' [FG2-2, Female, Previous owner-coach]

Pull factors included seeking more independence, keeping the rewards of own efforts, and a perceived greater earning potential, in line with Fairley and Stout's[32] assertion that autonomy is a key consideration for coaches to start their own practices.

Part of a successful initiation strategy included relying on past experience and connections to exploit opportunities:

> 'We have positioned ourselves to work primarily in the public management space and in the development sectors. We have a background there.' [I-2, Female, Owner-coach].

Theme 2 – Owner-coach role evolution

As their coaching businesses evolved, the owner-coaches' roles evolved. The initial focus of doing the coaching changed into managing others and spending more time on business development, in line with the findings of Gibb and Scott.[33] From the start, however, it was important to build a strong network and be in a circle of other experienced coaches and this aspect of the business received significant attention as the business matured. This is aligned with Martinez and Aldrich's[34] conclusion that strong, diverse ties associated with networking reduce uncertainty and contribute to the knowledge of small business owners.

---

30 Zott & Amit, 2013.
31 Ram & Jones, 2008.
32 Fairley & Stout, 2004.
33 Gibb & Scott, 1985
34 Martinez & Aldrich, 2011.

Theme 3 – Forming alliances

Linked to the previous theme, participants felt strongly that forming alliances through networking was crucial for the survival and growth of their coaching business. Alliances led to collaboration on projects in cases where the owner-coach did not have the capacity to fulfil a client's needs. This reaffirms the finding of Van Eeden, Viviers and Venter[35] that, in order to survive, a firm must interact with its network.

Some alliances led to risk-taking, for example, one participant advanced a sizeable capital investment into a multiparty project. This is in line with Kumar, Scheer and Kotler[36] who argue that risk-taking is part of an entrepreneurial mind-set.

Value architecture (VA)

This aspect of the BM template relates to the application of resources for the purpose of creating value.[37]

Theme 1 – Lack of business strategy

Many participants had a vision, mission and values statement for their coaching business and advertised these through their website and social media profile. While this is aligned with what Keeney[38] refers to as a proactive approach to value-focused thinking, it was superficial in terms of a business model approach:

> 'What gets me fired up is the art and craft of coaching. The act of designing transformational learning experiences. The business part is so far outside my area of knowing.' [FG1-2, Female, Owner-coach]

Thompson et al.[39] note that a sound business strategy is important for business success. The lack of a business strategy among the participants is therefore a concern – in particular since important aspects such as external and systemic effects on their businesses were not considered.

Theme 2 – Using mentors

Participants actively sought the help of mentors in their new businesses. They described the ideal mentor as someone familiar with their world of running a coaching business, but they also described the personal qualities of their ideal mentor as being

---

35 Van Eeden, Viviers & Venter, 2003.
36 Kumar, Scheer & Kotler, 2000.
37 Zott & Amit, 2013.
38 Keeney, 1992.
39 Thompson et al., 2012.

empathic and having the ability to listen, among others. This supports the findings of Matabooe, Venter and Rootman[40] that a mentor must understand the actual needs of the business owner and that proper diagnosis of business owners' problems is essential.

Value proposition (VP)

This aspect of the BM template relates to the offering of services, products and activities that create value for users.[41]

Theme 1 – Difficulty finding clients

One of the most difficult aspects of running a coaching business was finding clients:

> 'In the beginning I really struggled to get clients, which was surprising because my background was sales and marketing. I thought I used to sell a multimillion-rand software system so I figured that selling coaching for a few thousand rands would be a piece of cake. I was wrong.' [FG2-3, Female, Previous owner-coach]

The solution, according to some participants, was to aim for a reasonable market share within a niche market, an approach corroborated by Fairley and Stout.[42] To identify a niche market, some participants initially cast their nets wide; then, using the experience gathered, they honed in on a niche in which they felt their coaching business could be competitive. Other participants started with a niche and gradually expanded:

> 'The main journey I've been on to get this to be a successful practice is really defining my niche. I've known from the beginning that I've wanted to work with women, but that is not a niche, that's still 50% of the population. I had to narrow it down.' [FG1-4, Male, Owner-coach]

In both cases, they used their networks extensively.

Theme 2 – Application of previous experience

Participants leveraged their existing skill-sets obtained prior to becoming coaches in new coaching businesses. This phenomenon was also observed by Naqvi,[43] who emphasized the role of the owner's previous experience in business success. Participants who had experience in areas such as finance, strategic planning,

---

40 Matabooe, Venter & Rootman, 2016.
41 Zott & Amit, 2013.
42 Fairley & Stout, 2004.
43 Naqvi, 2011.

marketing (particularly sales), and especially operations management found their existing knowledge useful. Those who did not possess these skills felt at a disadvantage:

> 'I'm very under-skilled at things like selling, marketing and negotiations. I realise I have to get much more skilful at them.' [FG1-2, Female, Owner-coach]

VF – Value finance

This aspect of the BM template relates to the underlying economic logic of the enterprise.[44]

Theme 1 – Costing typologies

Participants employed a number of costing typologies. The first was charging a set fee for time. This approach had limited scalability and participants felt that there were "too few clients in a day and too few hours available". Even if there were sufficient client numbers, the act of coaching was psychologically taxing for the coach. Coaching for more than five hours every day would affect what Hall and Duval[45] refer to as the coach's need to have good levels of awareness, concentration, being present to the client, and matching and pacing the client. Some participants employing this approach concentrated on high-paying clients to maximize their income per hour.

The second costing typology involved a package-based offering consisting of more than coaching. This offering included diagnostic analysis, training, workshops and consulting. The third typology was to work within the prescribed consultancy rates of the hiring company; for example, those owner-coaches doing business with the government had to use the published scales for professional and specialized services. The final typology was to offer free and low-cost coaching. This typology was applied by new coaches trying to establish themselves, but participants felt that this could not be sustained for long and, in fact, was one of the reasons why so many coaches have exited the profession.

Theme 2 – Underestimating earnings

Many participants were aware beforehand that the move to a coaching business implied reduced income and they were initially willing to make the sacrifice in exchange for the anticipated lifestyle improvement. For some participants the reality proved unsustainable. Coaches who had exited the coaching profession provided emotional testimonies of financial hardship in trying to succeed on their own. This

---

44 Zott & Amit, 2013.
45 Hall & Duval, 2004.

hardship took many forms, such as the excessive withdrawal of funds from the new business that profit could not offset, the rising level of business debt, and reduced cash flow. Participants who had exited the coaching business reported unrealistic expectations about sustainability after start-up; for example, overestimating the rate of growth and the profit margins.

Some tried to work their way out of this situation, but suffered additional detrimental effects:

> 'I entered the coaching profession thinking that my success would be directly proportional to how good a coach I was. But it didn't work that way. Very few people hired me. I was getting exhausted and overwhelmed.' [FG2-1, Female, Previous Owner-coach]

Theme 3 – Multiple income streams

Many participants explained that coaching services formed part of a portfolio of services, characterized by a high degree of interaction between the coach and clients. Participants explained that it is essential to adapt coaching service offerings to specific client needs, and that the outcome of the full service provision may sometimes only be apparent a while after the assignment has been completed. Owner-coaches experimented and ultimately expanded their portfolios as per these examples:

> 'Okay, executive coaching is definitely the area that is my money generator. In addition to that, I do a lot of coaching with educators. I've launched some programs for parents. Also linking with my daughter who's now also come through coaching, we've launched some programs for teens. Together with another coach, we also launched a mother-daughter retreat.' [FG1-1, Female, Owner-coach]

> 'First it started off with the coaching, then the coaching led me into the health and wellness business. Trying to get more clients into coaching, I had to have something more. I've added massage, yoga, good eating, there's walks on the beach and then there's coaching. So we have actually brought the two together.' [FG1-4, Male, Owner-coach]

Practical implications

Aspiring coaches should take note of the findings presented here to help them create a realistic view of their prospective coaching businesses. They could also employ some of the strategies mentioned that worked for other coaches. Established coaches could adapt their approach by incorporating the findings from this research to their strategy and operations. Coaching training providers are encouraged to expose coaching students to the findings of this research as part of preparing them not only as coaches, but as SME owners.

Conclusion

By using a standard business model template, this study sheds light on the experiences of both successful and less successful coaching businesses as experienced by their owners. Factors that contribute to a successful coaching business include forming alliances, leveraging previous business experience, employing multiple income streams and evolving as a business owner along with the business. Factors that hamper coaching business success include the lack of a clear business strategy, the difficulty of finding coaching clients, and underestimating the earnings potential of a coaching business. It is hoped that the findings presented here will be of practical value to the coaching industry and will lay the foundation for future research.

Chapter 17

Micro-Entrepreneurs and Their Start-Up Teams: Impact of Emotions and Trust

Dr. Christina Swart-Opperman and Dr. Badri Zolfaghari

Introduction

This chapter aims to provide value for grand challenges aimed at tackling massive inequality, unemployment and persistent poverty[1] – even though these are not particular to developing countries. We are also cognisant of the role that the fourth industrial revolution, governance structures, institutional support structures or lack thereof, and market structures play in the development of venture creation in these settings. Currently, South Africa experiences one of the highest unemployment rates since its democratic elections in 1994 and a particular concern is the youth (between the ages of 15 and 34) unemployment at 38.6% and 58%.[2] This trend occurred despite the increase in skilled labour, with the young labourer being on average more educated than their parents, particularly among those previously disadvantaged. In an attempt to address this challenge, South Africa has become home to an increasing number of (social) entrepreneurs and innovators who have made advances in the creation of new ventures that will ultimately lead to mid- to long-term job opportunities. In fact, several scholars have tied job creation, economic growth, regional development and entrepreneurship.[3]

However, while the entrepreneurial ecosystem to this consists of government funds, corporate initiatives and sponsorships, incubators, labour markets, culture, shared working spaces and university curricula, the failure rate among entrepreneurial ventures and their respective teams/networks remains its weakest link. Whilst acknowledging that part of this failure can be attributed to the lack of gained entrepreneurship knowledge and skills, this research seeks to explore whether an underlying portion of it pertains to entrepreneurs' emotional outlook and team-level dynamics, given the culturally, educationally, and vocationally diverse nature of the start-up team in South Africa. It is also acknowledged that micro-entrepreneurs could act solo and that team dynamics could be virtual.

1   Eisenhardt, Graebner & Sonenshein, 2016.
2   Statistics SA's Quarterly Labour Force Survey, 2017.
3   Friar & Meyer, 2003; Ruef, Aldrich & Carter, 2003.

In addition, a further aim of this chapter is to provide a conceptual framework for further empirical investigations to boosting the success rates of micro-entrepreneurial start-ups and their networks/teams in socio-economically complex settings. Micro-enterprises are considered being businesses with independent ownership, employing less than 25 people whilst focusing on creating income for the owner.[4] In so doing, it seeks to follow two streams of processes. The first stream pertains to the entrepreneur, and individual-level factors influencing the entrepreneurial behavioural repertoire during the start-up stage. The second stream pertains to the relationship between the entrepreneur and his/her start-up network/team, and team-level dynamics that influence the start-up stage. This contributes to theory and practice by exposing the micro-level antecedents of innovative projects that aim to tackle the mentioned grand challenges. It further provides insight for entrepreneurs regarding their self-understanding, their ability to build necessary networks and sustainable start-up teams.

Stream 1: The micro-entrepreneur and individual-level factors

This stream is approached from *The Person-in-Situation Perspective* that proposes that individual-level factors (personality and any other individual characteristics) must be considered within the context and environment that the individual finds him/herself in.[5] This then, implies that "personal characteristics that dispose people to act in certain ways should not be equated with actually acting in that way".[6]

A thorough examination of the literature reveals that factors pertaining to individual-level determinants influencing the entrepreneur are mindset[7] emotions,[8] personality traits[9] that are considered as identity attributes[10] and behaviours deriving from their personality.[11] The reason is that personality "predicts several entrepreneurial outcomes, thereby demonstrating personality's influence on entrepreneurial success"[12] whilst Morris and Webb define the entrepreneurial mindset as "a person's overall attitudes, assumptions, inclinations, disposition, and outlook".[13]

Arguments on the role of personality is convincing as a meta-analytical study of 23 papers by Zhao and Serbert[14] demonstrate that the link between the Big Five

---

4   Friar & Meyer, 2001.
5   van Knippenberg & Hirst, 2015.
6   Ibid, 229.
7   Morris & Webb, 2015.
8   Bron, 2008.
9   van Knippenberg & Hirst, 2015.
10 Morris & Webb, 2015.
11 Obschonka, Schmitt-Rodermund, Silberreisen, Gosling & Potter, 2013.
12 Leutner, et al., 2014: 61.
13 Morris & Webb, 2015: 467.
14 Zhao & Serbert, 2006.

Personality Factors Model (referred to as the 'Big Five' – collectively presenting personality universally) is a predictor of entrepreneurial roles and outcome. These personality traits are listed as extraversion versus introversion; agreeableness versus antagonism; conscientiousness versus lack of direction and openness versus closeness to experience as well as emotional stability versus neuroticism.[15]

The applicability of this model for predicting entrepreneurial start-up success in developing countries was illustrated by Baluku, et al.[16] In their assessment of 384 micro-entrepreneurs in Kampala City, Uganda, they determined that agreeableness ($p<.001$) and extraversion ($p<.01$) were the significant predictors for entrepreneurial success. Trustworthiness was also highlighted. Similarly, Abraham and Tupamahu[17] consider the big-five factor personality model as a useful indication of a successful entrepreneur's personality. Their assessment of 136 SMEs in Ambon City (Indonesia) confirm that interpersonal competence and personality characteristics impact the entrepreneur's market orientation and performance directly. They proposed a link between interpersonal competence and networking capabilities during the start-up phase of the business. Also, their findings suggest that emotional intelligence plays an important role in determining the quality of networking. FakhrEldin surveyed 378 entrepreneurs in ten governorates in Egypt and links emotional intelligence to the success of "necessity driven entrepreneurs".[18] The emotional competencies that relate to such a new venture success were interpersonal skills, internal motivation and self-awareness. The age of older emotionally intelligent entrepreneurs was reported as a moderating effect. It can thus be postulated that affect impacts all aspects of entrepreneurial behaviour. For example, in their study of 394 interdisciplinary students from the Universities of Spain and Columbia, emotional regulation and the effective utilisation of emotions have been linked significantly to entrepreneurial self-efficacy ($p<.001$).[19] Although the sample consisted of university students, these findings support our idea that entrepreneurs' emotive outlook could contribute towards their success. Therefore, despite several researchers (for example Kramer, Cesinger, Shuarzinger & Gelléri[20] supporting the notion that personality predicts entrepreneurial behaviour, not everyone agrees with this. Preisendörfer et al.[21] as well as Leutner et al.[22] notes that inconsistent empirical findings have been reported in personality trait studies, even though they recognized the importance of personality traits. This notion is supported by Martin and Webb[23] who highlight that "no standard

---

15   Holt, Bremmer, Sutherland, Vliek, Passer & Smith, 2012: 582.
16   Baluku, et al., 2016.
17   Abraham & Tupamahu, 2016.
18   FakhrEldin, 2017: 99.
19   Moran, Ripoll, Carvalho & Bernal, 2014.
20   Kramer, Cesinger, Shuarzinger & Gelléri, 2011.
21   Preisendörfer et al., 2012.
22   Leutner et al., 2014.
23   Martin & Webb, 2015.

prototype of the entrepreneur has emerged" as "becoming an entrepreneur is an emergent phenomenon"[24] whilst FakhrEldin mentions that "there is no one agreed upon model of the entrepreneurial individual"[25] In addition to the five factors of personality, Mathieu and St-Jean[26] propose that narcissism (feelings of dominance and exaggerated self-importance) is a confounding factor for the different personality traits.

We therefore concur with Zhao and Serbert[27] that entrepreneurship is culturally and contextually embedded. For example, the importance of socio-demographics such as family background and tradition has been acknowledged by Abtahi, Karamipour and Abbasi[28] as influential on the success of the entrepreneur. They adjusted their personality assessment for a sample of 350 students in Iran, empirically testing a need to succeed, idea fluency and pragmatism. They report that all three constructs are positively correlated with entrepreneurship. Similarly, Preisendörfer, Britz and Bezuidenhout[29] explored possible reasons for the lack of black entrepreneurs in South Africa. Based on 24 expert interviews, collectivism was predicted as a specific challenge for black entrepreneurs.

Furthermore, entrepreneurial intention has also been linked to personality traits by Karabulut[30] who assessed 480 graduate students from the Institute of Social Sciences in Istanbul Turkey. They coupled the personality dimensions of an internal locus of control, a need for achievement, risk tolerance and entrepreneurial alertness with entrepreneurial intention. Entrepreneurial intention is defined as the intentional choice by the prospective entrepreneur that, in turn, "initiates entrepreneurial actions". [31]

Sesen[32] investigated the impact of certain personality traits (need for achievement, locus of control and self-efficacy) as well as pre-identified environmental factors (access to capital, business information, social networks and a university education) on entrepreneurial intention. Assessing 356 students (sciences and business administration and health) from two universities in Ankara, Turkey, self-efficacy showed the strongest relation ($r=0.55$, $p<0.01$) with entrepreneurial intention. Interestingly, access to capital correlated negatively ($r=0.22$, $p<0.01$) with entrepreneurial intention. Other environmental factors, such as social networks and the university environment, had no significant impact.

---

24 Martin & Webb, 2015: 465.
25 FakhrEldin, 2017: 99.
26 Mathieu & St-Jean, 2013.
27 Zhao & Serbert, 2006.
28 Abtahi, Karamipour & Abbasi, 2013.
29 Preisendörfer, Britz & Bezuidenhout, 2012.
30 Karabulut, 2016.
31 Karabulut, 2016: 16.
32 Sesen, 2013.

Another study by Ruangkrit and Techatakerng[33] acknowledges the role of the entrepreneurs' personality in entrepreneurial success clustering characteristics of successful entrepreneurs into achievement, planning and power. The power cluster lists "Persuasion and Networking" as well as "Self-Confidence" and as reported strengths persuasion and networking (13.58%), followed by self-confidence (15.72%) and a demand for efficiency and quality (15.88%).

Kosubiková, et al.[34] link personality characteristics to perception and the management of risk in a study of 449 SME owners in Slovakia, Czech Republic. They divided entrepreneurs into artist-entrepreneur and entrepreneur-labourers based on their attitude. Although 79.55% of entrepreneurs-artists and 81.48% of entrepreneurs-labourers considered market risk as key, their assessment of business risk was not dependent on personality characteristics.

Entrepreneurial networks are important for entrepreneurial success, especially for the provision of information and mentors. In a meta-analysis of 70 papers on the role of networks in an entrepreneurial context, Hoang and Antoncic[35] refer to three components of an entrepreneurial network. It is useful to consider "the content of the relationships; the governance of the relationships and the structure of pattern that emerges from the crosscutting ties".[36] The governance aspect relates to trust and the enhancing aspect thereof on information and flow.

Viewing entrepreneurship from a positive psychology perspective, Juhdi and Juhdi assert that a re-conceptualisation of entrepreneurial success is eminent. They argue that entrepreneurial success is mostly measured from a financial perspective. In addition, personality traits are considered "as means in assessing entrepreneurial success".[37] Although such views have been useful, the implication is that insufficient attention has been paid to the well-being and optimal functioning of the entrepreneur. Therefore, they propose "entrepreneurial work engagement," a mental state reflective of "experience of high satisfaction, a feeling of gratitude and entrepreneurial preparedness (to venture further) while maintaining high enthusiasm".[38] We found it useful that they proposed psychological capital (refer to Luthans, et al.[39]) as important for entrepreneurial success. From their assessments of 83 SMEs (identified from the SMI/SME Business Directory Malaysia 2000) psychological success (engagement and psychological capital) contribute toward entrepreneurial success.

---

33 Ruangkrit & Techatakerng, 2015.
34 Kosubiková et al., 2015.
35 Hoang & Antoncic, 2003.
36 Ibid, 166.
37 Juhdi & Juhdi, 2013: 286.
38 Ibid, 287
39 Luthans, et al., 2004.

Last, as motioned by Fatoki, "micro enterprise activity (especially in retail trade) is the most pervasive entrepreneurial activity".[40] In this study, they focused on identifying contributing factors that prevent start-up micro-entrepreneurs who formed their businesses in the past 3.5 years in Polokwane, Limpopo Province, South Africa, from succeeding. Based on 22 in-depth interviews of these start-up micro-entrepreneurs in the retail and services sectors, insufficient owners' capital, lack of start-up skills and difficulties in obtaining a sufficient customer base were identified as major stumbling blocks. We concur with the recommendation that, for example, commercial banks must intensify awareness creation of their loan options to micro-entrepreneurs.

Stream 2: Entrepreneurial network/team

The important role of 'informal networks' in the early stages of venture creation has recently received a great deal of attention.[41] Social networks of entrepreneurs have a particular impact on woman entrepreneurs, entrepreneurs in hostile environments as well as minorities. Our context for this research project inhabits all three of the mentioned criteria. Within this network, however, there are various team-level dynamics that contribute to, or inhibit the successful transition of the venture from a start-up stage to an established business. This research, however, intends to shed light on the dynamics at play during the early stages of venture creation given its foundational role.[42]

In the context of start-up teams, trust is of paramount importance due to high levels of risk and uncertainty that is associated with the early stages of venture creation which requires identity formation.[43] This is due to the fact that trust, as a cognitive state, increases our tolerance for uncertainty and ambiguity, and thus will allow for higher levels of cooperation among members when the success of the collaborative outcome is unclear. In this regard, trust is considered as a governance mechanism that promotes knowledge sharing, particularly in fragile environments with institutional voids. In such an environment, interpersonal trust, and team-level trust can be considered as a substitute for regulatory and legal frameworks that, if present, would protect the entrepreneurs and their start-up team.

The presence of institutional voids and the absence of legal frameworks result that the entrepreneur initially forms ties with members that (s)he 'trusts' but not necessarily those that acquire the relevant skills or knowledge for the venture creation, in other words, those members that (s)he 'needs', therefore reducing the chances of a successful venture. To this end, being able to facilitate and enhance

---

40 Fatoki, 2014: 34.
41 Welter, 2011.
42 Larson & Starr, 1993.
43 Powell & Baker, 2017; Welter, 2012.

trust development in the early stages of venture creation between the start-up team members is considered to be vital to its success rate.

The examination of the construct and development of trust among start-up teams has recently received a great deal of attention in organizational research settings.[44] Trust, which is defined as a *"psychological state comprising the intention to accept vulnerability based upon positive expectations of the intentions or behaviour of another"*,[45] *has various main and moderating positive effects on team-level outcomes.*[46] Higher levels of trust among organizational members result in positive attitudes, increased levels of cooperation, acceptance of interdependence, information sharing, and communication.[47] Organizations that foster interpersonal trust among their members experience significantly higher levels of employee engagement,[48] reduced levels of conflict and cost of control.[49] Trust among team members results in increased effectiveness,[50] decreased levels of monitoring and control,[51] and is positively related to a team's performance.[52]

Interpersonal trust development is severely hampered by cultural diversity. This is due to the fact that culture, as a composite of values and multifaceted determinants of behaviour influences various dimensions of trust (i.e. disposition, assessment of trustworthiness and behavioural trust). Our disposition to trust, for instance, is guided by our 'faith in humanity' and our 'trusting stance'.[53] Higher levels of 'faith in humanity' allow us to deal with people 'as though' they are well-meaning and reliable.[54] Moreover, culture, as a fundamental driver of our value contents such as benevolence, security, conformity, and universalism,[55] and a filter of our beliefs regarding human nature,[56] directly informs our initial inclination to make ourselves vulnerable to the actions of the other party prior to obtaining knowledge about that party's trustworthiness.[57] Upon interaction with a trustee, the trustor's cultural schemas influence the meaning attached to observed behaviour such as those contributing to the trustee's trustworthiness, namely the trustee's ability, benevolence

---

44 Ashleigh & Warren, 2015; Li, 2013; Welter, 2012.
45 Rousseau, Sitkin, Burt, & Camerer, 1998: 395.
46 De Jong & Dirks, 2012.
47 Gillespie & Mann, 2004.
48 Zak, 2017.
49 Dirks & Ferrin, 2001.
50 Wildman et al., 2012.
51 De Jong & Dirks, 2012.
52 De Jong, Dirks, & Gillespie, 2016.
53 McKnight, Cummings, & Chervany, 1998.
54 Nikolova, Möllering, & Reihlen, 2014; Thomas et al., 2015.
55 Schwartz, 1992.
56 Triandis, 1997.
57 Dietz, 2011; Moellering, 2005; Rotter, 1971.

and their integrity.[58] Moreover, Ferrin and Gillespie[59] posit that the trustor's decision to trust based on contextual factors (i.e. trustworthiness) or dispositional ones can be altered by the trustor's national culture. Where individualists might place more emphasis on contextual factors, collectivists might fall back on their disposition to trust.[60] This makes it harder to predict whether the trustor will trust the trustee based on observable, trusting behaviour.

Finally, the trustor's trusting behaviour, which entails the *action* of making oneself vulnerable to the other party, is influenced by culture. Considering that trusting behaviour is related to the acceptance of influence, the sharing of knowledge and information, and reduction of control,[61] and that cultural norms and values guide what we consider as 'appropriate' behaviour[62] it becomes evident that culture and behavioural trust are more intertwined than accounted for.[63] For example, Gibson et al.,[64] providing an overview of *when* culture matters, show that culture determines certain behaviours central to trust such as conformity, acceptance of influence, degree of disclosure and the reduction of conflict in the workplace.[65]

Cultural diversity therefore, which results in the misalignment of cultural values and behavioural manifestations of culture between the trustor and trustee, has, on the one hand, direct negative effects on the development of trust. On the other hand, is known to be a source of problem solving, creativity and innovation.[66] Under conditions of psychological safety, team-level demographic diversity results in increased creativity, whereas racial heterogeneity has been suggested to result in informational heterogeneity.[67] Phillips further argues that team members will be more receptive towards new ideas, when they come from members who are dissimilar to them.[68]

This research stream argues that cultural diversity among the start-up teams would allow for the creation of innovative solutions to complex social-economic problems persistent in South Africa.[69] While acknowledging that cultural diversity would be a rather inherent aspect of team compositions, culture in this context should be contextualized as a system comprising of various facets such as Nationality, Ethnicity, Age, Vocation, Urban/Rural background, Religion, etc.[70] In order to harness

---

58 Fiske, 2002; Gibson, Maznevski, & Kirkman, 2004.
59 Ferrin & Gillespie, 2010.
60 Kramer, 1999; Sanchez-Burks & Lee, 2007.
61 Zand, 1972.
62 Doney, Cannon, & Mullen, 1998; Schein, 2004.
63 Johnson & Cullen, 2002.
64 Gibson et al., 2004.
65 Leung, Bhagat, Erez, & Gibson, 2005.
66 Stahl, Maznevski, Voigt, & Jonsen, 2010.
67 Phillips, 2008.
68 Ibid.
69 Zanello et al., 2016.
70 Chao & Moon, 2005; Zolfaghari, Möllering, Clark, & Dietz, 2016.

the benefits of diversity among start-up teams, this project aims to put forward a framework that encapsulates the configurations of multiple cultural facets at play in the early stages of team formation and venture creation, identifying the divergent and convergent patterns that enhance and hinder trust development. Examining the intricate relationship between multiple dimensions of trust and trust development and the members' multiple cultural identities should be done with the aim of allowing the team to overcome initial barriers to a successful venture creation, thus increasing its impact on job creation.

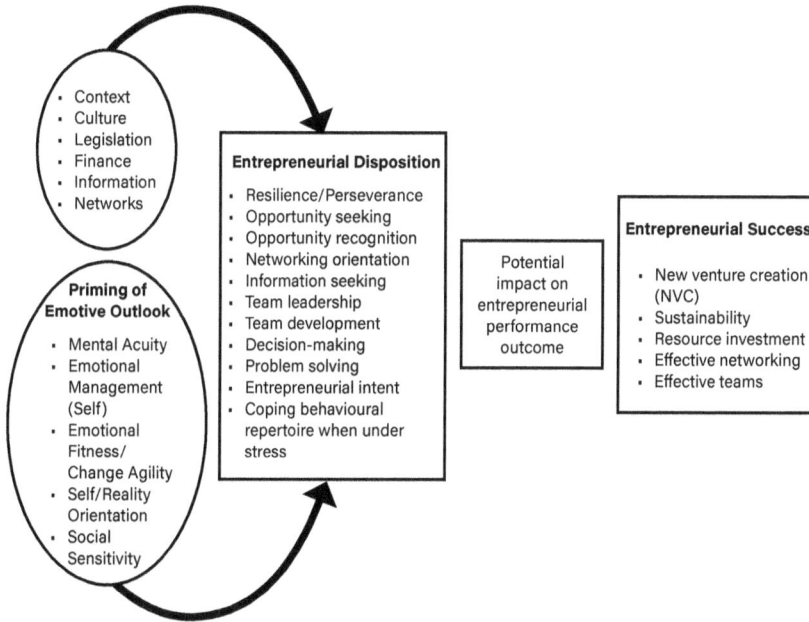

Figure 17.1: Theoretical Framework

Emotive outlook is defined as "a person's emotional disposition and subsequent behavioural manifestations, when faced with intra-psychological, interpersonal, team or organizational challenges"[71] Emotive outlook is proposed by them to consist of six categories: emotional management of self; mental acuity; self and reality orientation; emotional fitness and change agility; social sensitivity as well as social fitness

Directions for future research

Clearly emotional outlook and trust have a significant role in micro-entrepreneurs and their start-up teams. Social networks of entrepreneurs have a particular impact on woman entrepreneurs, entrepreneurs in hostile environments as well as minorities. It is recommended that future research inhabits all three of the mentioned criteria.

---

71 Swart-Opperman & April, 2018: 2.

Future research must shed light on the dynamics at play during the early stages of venture creation given its foundational role.[72]

Future research and theory development are needed to enhance our understanding of the role that the individual micro-entrepreneurs' emotive outlook and trusting behaviours play during the start-up phase of their ventures. It is recommended that individual-level constraints pertaining to the entrepreneur such as a locus of control, dispositional traits and emotive outlook be measured via previously developed and validated scales/surveys. Factors such as team-level dynamics, and the evolution of team dynamics should be explored utilising qualitative methods of inquiry such as one-to-one interviews.[73]

72 Larson & Starr, 1993.
73 Baker, Powell, & Fultz, 2011; Welter & Smallbone, 2006.

Chapter 18

Diversity and Entrepreneurship in South Africa: Intersections and Purposive Collaboration

Prof. Kurt April and Dr. Babar Dharani

Abstract

What is well established in the literature is that diversity and innovation are interlinked. There is also literature that argues that spatial concentration of diverse individuals increases personal interaction across economic sectors, which in turn generates new ideas, new products and new processes. However, in South Africa we often have people geographically displaced along ethnic/racial lines, as well as other intersectional markers. The spatial distribution makes collaboration both difficult and, when interaction does occur, such collaboration can be complex. So special effort needs to be made to bring people together in meaningful ways. Even when achieved, it is difficult when diverse people are eventually put together, because they do not naturally "hang out" with each other on a day-to-day basis, and so when confronted with 'others', their interactions are awkward, loaded with conscious and unconscious power differentials, defensive and reactionary. This is true across regions and provinces of South Africa where you have completely different ethnic/racial groups, and when ethnic/race groups in a region also have to engage with foreigners (where local South Africans are often more open to White Europeans and Americans, who tend to reside close to city centres or suburbs close to the CBD, and less open to other Black Africans and Asians, who often live further from such centres).

According to Statista Research Department,[1] as of 2018, South Africa's population was approximately 57.4 million inhabitants in total, of which the majority (roughly 46.5 million) were black Africans, roughly 5 million Camissa/Coloureds, roughly 4.5 million whites, and 1.4 million Indian/Asian. South Africa's mid-year population is estimated to have increased to 59,62 million in 2020, according to the report released by Statistics South Africa.[2] Gauteng province continues to record the largest share of South Africa's population, with approximately 15,5 million people (26,0%) living in this province. The second largest population, with approximately 11,5 million people has been recorded in KwaZulu-Natal province. The Northern Cape province maintained its status as the province with the lowest population in the country, estimated at

---

1 Statista Research Department, 2018.
2 Stats SA, 2020.

1,29 million people. The report indicates that approximately 51,1% (approximately 30,5 million) of the population is female. According to the report, about 28,6% of the population is aged younger than 15 years and approximately 9,1% (5,4 million) is 60 years or older. Of those younger than 15 years of age, the majority reside in KwaZulu-Natal province (21,8%) and Gauteng province (21,4%). Of the elderly (those aged 60 years and older), the highest percentage 24,1% (1,31 million) reside in Gauteng. The proportion of elderly persons aged 60 and older has grown from 7,6% in 2002 to 9,1% in 2020. The report further shows that for the period 2016–2020, Gauteng province and the Western Cape province are estimated to have experienced the largest inflow of migrants of approximately 1 553 162 and 468 568 respectively.

Stats SA in 2019[3] released the Multidimensional Inequality Trends Report, which highlighted that, while efforts to build a better South Africa have been consistent and have slowly led to positive change, the country on the whole remains deeply unequal, e.g., unemployment remains highest among African black South Africans (31%) and Camissa/Coloured South Africans (23%), whilst being significantly lower among Indians (11%) and white people (6%). As far as gender is concerned, women are paid less than men who have the same level of education as them. In terms of spending power and disposable income, white South Africans are still the biggest earners and spenders of any racial group, with Indians spending half as much, Camissa/Coloureds spending close to a quarter of whites do, and African blacks one tenth of what a white South African spends. Beyond race, the richest 10% in South Africa account for more than half of all household expenditure. Even in modern-day South Africa, a country with the highest GDP on the African continent, only 11% of people have access to the internet at home, 28% own a private vehicle, and 17% has access to medical insurance/aid. The majority of white and Indian South Africans use private healthcare facilities, while most African blacks and Camissa/Coloureds use the less-resourced public/government healthcare facilities (known for its inefficiencies and high volumes of patients).

According to the University of Cape Town's Transformation Report,[4] these examples of inequality highlight that, while the South African national and local governments, South African businesses and civil society organizations, as well as its citizens, have worked hard to build a nation, social relationships, and programs which challenge inequality, more work needs to be done. The report champions the critical diversity approach and claims that the approach acknowledges the role of power in constructing difference, and the unequal symbolic and material value of different locations – that the approach locates difference within a historical legacy as an outcome of social practice and an engagement with the transformation of these oppressive systems.

---

3   Stats SA, 2019.
4   UCT Transformation Report, 2019.

The traditional core focus areas of businesses are market share, scale, cost advantages, risk mitigation and efficiencies, among others – these are premised on staged, planned and predetermined milestones, which are adjusted bi-annually or annually – and seek to serve the shareholders of the businesses. Traditionally, in-company power networks tend to inform and support employees with similar social identities[5] and, in South Africa, that often refers to the economically dominant White minority population, who tend to hold the most senior positions in private businesses, and to the majority African Black population who hold the most senior positions in the public sector. The vast majority of the country's working population are trapped in low-paid and low-quality jobs with insecure wages and salaries – leaving their livelihoods and futures in states of precariousness, and the country with rising welfare costs. Even though creativity and innovation are spoken about, in practical reality they often occupy the bottom of the priority list in corporations and the public sector. Wealth and capital incomes are highly concentrated in South Africa and, if not addressed to ensure access by broader parts of society, greater deconcentration of such wealth and much wider ownership of the economic pie of the country, inequality will be further entrenched and exacerbated.

The case has been made for indigenous entrepreneurship in sub-Saharan Africa, as key to the sustainable development of that part of the continent.[6] Small and mid-sized enterprises, entrepreneurial ventures as well as social entrepreneurs, offer more opportunities to experiment, innovate and address societal gaps/challenges through improvised and context-relevant solutions, than most corporations and the government can. According to Bosman et al.,[7] The Global Enterprise Monitor estimates that sub-Saharan Africa has the highest proportion of social entrepreneurs in the world (outside of Australia and the USA). Diversity within entrepreneurial start-ups promises to promote such creativity and innovation on the back of full use of diverse engagement with people who are different on multiple levels, by allowing for the disruption of traditional ways/routines of working, by being mature enough to engage different thinking and holding multiple 'truths', by being open to new ways of doing things and depending very 'lightly' on established mental models and traditional problem-solving techniques, by removing structural, physical and psychological barriers to contributions of individuals from diverse backgrounds, and by encouraging life-work integration regulation of work and life in unprecedented ways. Essentially, when entrepreneurs purposefully step outside of their institutional and spatial settings, they can collaborate with professors, practising entrepreneurs, members of other race/ethnic groups, members of other socio-economic classes, funders and venture capitalists, and professionals and in disciplines other than their

---

5   Foldy, 2002.
6   Mirvis & Googins, 2018; AfDB, 2016; Hall et al., 2010.
7   Bosman et al., 2016.

own. Such collaborations, theoretically, can effectively draw on others' expertise, skills and networks to extend and deepen the entrepreneurs' learning and wisdom, and thereby better prepare them for the ever-changing, emerging realities of the South African landscape.

In South African economic hubs, where big corporates and large organizations almost naturally draw on multiple demographic identities of the communities in the various provinces, entrepreneurs find it harder to get together, mix, hang out and collaborate with members of groups other than their own race or ethnicity, as well as socio-economic class, because of the physical distances between where they live and where they work and run their entrepreneurial ventures. This is in addition to damaged and frayed social relationships as a result of the brutal apartheid past, and persistence of racially-based economic inclusion/exclusion and opportunities. We learn from researchers that entrepreneurial intersections are unknown territories, where past knowledge and experiences are poor guides for future success, and that such intersections require individuals to leave many of their preconceived notions behind.

Also, in the era of information, knowledge, technology-enablement and simultaneous integration and disintegration of communities in the modern era, the South African schooling system in the main has persisted with traditional forms of education that prepare school learners and college/university students for being employees in small and large organizations. Experts inform us that the necessary, future skills are: digital coding skills, leadership, care, craft and creativity, innovation, adaptability and flexibility, emotional maturity, tech savviness, data literacy, as well as critical thinking. Entrepreneurial organizations, these days, often ask that new graduates and students possess many of these skills with an entrepreneurial orientation, and corporates often, these days, ask that incumbent employees, as well as new employees and recruits, possess these skills with an intrapreneurial orientation. Neither the relevant local governments, educational departments, nor principals and teachers have thought it their responsibility to offer opportunities for learners and students to learn wider skill sets, more appropriate to the modern era, practically-based and particularly oriented to entrepreneurial ventures in communities and actual businesses. Corporate South Africa will never be able to take up all of the school and college/university leavers, and these learners and students will have to turn to starting their own businesses and ventures in order to survive and provide for their families and communities.

Currently around 40% of South Africa's youth is formally unemployed and not in training – an alarming statistic for the nation's democracy and economic sustainability (either because they are unskilled, wrongly skilled – studied courses, certificates, diplomas and degrees that have no real currency in modern South Africa – lack appropriate and adequate work experience, and because there are just not enough formal jobs to absorb the massive numbers of young people in the country). According to Stats SA,[8] "Of the 10,3 million persons aged 15-24 years in the first quarter of 2020, approximately 3,5 million or 34,1% were not in employment, education or training. Of the 20,4 million young people aged 15-34 years, about 8,5 million or 41,7% were not in employment, education or training". The Covid-19 pandemic has compounded racial disparities in learning and achievement, as well as skills development. For South Africa, policy attention has increasingly focused on the promotion of the country's SMME economy,[9] which supposedly can assist with the economic objectives by creating jobs, lowering unemployment and addressing this disproportioned distribution of wealth of the country. However, the lack of access to jobs, lack of dependable employment, inability of local governments and unwillingness of private businesses to tackle pressing socio-human needs and service delivery in South Africa, have left citizens disgruntled with the continuous waiting for solutions. They are therefore mobilizing individually and in groups across regional and suburban borders, and through informal capital networks. They do so in order to increase the transmission of ideas, to increase the permeability of traditional boundaries in the pursuit of solutions to social challenges, with the hope of bringing progress and easing of the lives of their communities and themselves.

Admirably, in November 2020, in its attempts to create a more inclusive Western Cape province, the City of Cape Town in collaboration with the national department of Women, Youth and People with Disability, the Western Cape Government's Department of Economic Development and various stakeholders, hosted a Disability Entrepreneurship Seminar with the theme: Promoting, Encouraging, Supporting Entrepreneurs with Disability – the intention being to grow entrepreneurship and small businesses among people with disabilities by critically evaluating government services that entrepreneurs with disabilities can access, and allowing for such entrepreneurs to communicate back about the challenges they experience when accessing these services.[10] The City of Cape Town expressed that their main focus areas have to do with working premises, accessibility (ramps, sign language interpretation, information in accessible formats), training, access to finance, and encouraging markets for the products and services of people with disabilities – the focus being on individuals and, even though needed, through the single, etic focus of disability.[11] However, no mention was made about the underlying issues to do with the double whammy of historical disadvantage, and that the treatment of all people with disability in the province equally is not equality nor inclusive (as a result of their lack

---

8   Stats SA, 2020: 9.
9   Rogerson, 2008.
10 DA Newsroom, 2020.
11 Tatli & Özbilgin, 2012.

of understanding of the additional intersectional disadvantages that different people face across the province).

In addition, no mention was made of the way in which innovation and ensuing entrepreneurship actually happens: collaborating and robust engagement of diverse individuals with vastly different skill sets, psychological orientations, thinking styles, racio-ethnic backgrounds; deeper understanding was not provided of the spaces where intersections of ideas from different fields, cultures and lived experiences happen and can ignite explosions of new ideas and solutions; there was no showing people with disabilities how to access and shift into those intersections; and, most importantly, there was no real unpacking of the challenges surrounding collaboration and what can be done about it, i.e., how to collaborate, who to collaborate with, what aids collaboration, where to collaborate, what to collaborate on, what each person's unique contribution to collaboration could be, how to overcome bias and systemic bias during collaborations, the necessary willingness to reach beyond one's selfish needs and wants through compromise when collaborating, how to lead collaborations, the resources required for and during collaborations, the direct and indirect costs of collaborating, and the personal and structural challenges surrounding collaboration. Some people thrive in collaborations but, for many, intersections are fear-inducing and disconcerting – as it is filled with many unknowns and requires leaning into untrusted partnerships, and generally with people who historically did not interact with each other. As a result, Wheeler[12] reminds us, "without awareness, skills, openness, and a real competence for maximizing opportunities, these intersections become culture clashes, breakdowns in communication, and missed understandings."

What, in South Africa, actually stops people from collaborating? Before the argument was raised by critical race theorists (as they did not exist as a recognized group then), Crenshaw[13] first coined the term 'intersectionality' to demarginalize the intersection of race and gender, in trying to understand the racial wealth gap in the USA. Holvino[14] also added the construct of class to her research. The current theories on intersectional analyses appear instructive in how we can understand the differentiated challenges of entrepreneurs in South Africa accessing the same economic region – the majority of theories focus on individual intersections such as race, or gender, or disability, or sexual orientation, or social class. However, the singular view of the category of race is particularly prevalent in South Africa, and remains the dominant lens through which people experience, and form their opinions of, each other. We know that to achieve the benefits promised by entrepreneurship, a minimum viable network of partners is required to participate in the ecosystem. Such 'luxury' is not

---

12 Wheeler, 2005: 53.
13 Crenshaw, 1989.
14 Holvino, 2010.

afforded most entrepreneurs, who often have to innovate while proceeding with their business – where short sprints are the order of the day, requiring high levels of collaboration and, in South Africa, often fast decision-making in loose governance and poorly implemented policy environments, continuous compromise through regular interaction with communities/customers, and collaborating with people with street savvy and not traditional skills/educational levels while serving a broader set of stakeholders and communities in which upholding the common good and what eases the lives and pain of society comes before any notions of traditional capitalism, are the order of the day.

In trying to uncover the hidden intersectional, entrepreneurial stories we, however, found that when discussing with entrepreneurs as to why something is a barrier to some people, so as to help unearth the root problems for low engagement around collaboration, the continuance of mistrust, and the unwillingness to reach out to the diverse 'other', the responses were a lot more nuanced and spoke to a number of additional intersectional challenges. Some of the more common, voiced examples of engagement- and inclusion-barriers that we have come across from all ethnic/race groups in South Africa, included:

> *"... other people are in different parts of the city"*
> *"... I have to be and act differently when I am with them"*
> *"... it is difficult for me to get to them"*
> *"... I spend over just half my monthly salary for transport to get to White neighbourhoods"*
> *"... I do not want to go to Black neighbourhoods, for fear of my safety and life"*
> *"... Black people are always late for meetings"*
> *"... Black people must stop making me feel guilty all of the time"*
> *"... I have to be entrepreneurial because there are no more jobs for White people"*
> *"... it is such long distances, and I am tired ... I have to leave very early to get there"*
> *"... my English is not very good, so I choose not to speak up"*
> *"... they are always judging me ... I feel it, I can see it in their eyes"*
> *"... my schooling never prepared me for starting my own business"*
> *"... there's no real incentive to do it, as they always get the main benefit from what we do"*
> *"... they need to stop being so defensive"*
> *"... the South African Police treats foreign entrepreneurs different to local ones ... it is like there are two different kinds of law"*
> *"... they have no idea what it takes for me to be here"*
> *"... I am just looking for a small break from others"*
> *"... they don't need to dedicate the same amount of energy to this"*
> *"... they had a good start in life"*
> *"... school took away our creativity ... we were taught how to fit into the traditions of how things always used to be"*
> *"... I am not welcome in their entrepreneurial ventures, but they are always looking to expand their market through mine"*
> *"... we don't hang out in those areas"*

"... we won't be welcome in their suburbs, because we look poor, we look dangerous"

"... I have got the networks in the informal sector ... they got no idea"

"... they have got book smarts but no street smarts"

"... my parents don't want me to partner with Black people in business"

"... my African-ness is not appreciated in the city ... the more Western I am, the more I act like a White person, the more acceptable I am to them"

"... they are scared of me, just because I am Black"

"... they want to double-check every one of my suggestions, because they don't have enough belief in the credibility of people like me"

"... it is very hard as a foreign entrepreneur ... I don't know who is out to get me"

"... they are known for being cheats ... you can't trust them"

"... White people never come hang out in our neighbourhoods ... why must we always go to them"

"... collaborating with them slows down our progress, because I have to explain everything"

"... they look down on us"

"... they just use us for the B-BBEE rating, so that they can keep operating"

"... I keep telling myself, in my mind, that I am not good enough to work with them"

"... I am a businesswoman, but I must also be a mother, wife, cleaner, cook, nurse, and negotiator in the house"

"... we are always caught in the middle – the Whites don't think we are good enough, and the Blacks think we have had similar privileges to the Whites ... which is not true. We also fought in the struggle for political and economic inclusion"

"... I always hold myself back, because I don't have their level of education"

"... the White feminists have no idea what it's like to be a Black woman, and then they want to talk for all women"

"... I have to work in the family business, even though I want to break out and meet other people to start other things"

"... they don't actually want to transform"

"... they don't understand what it really means to struggle ... they just want to opt out when things get tough"

"... there is no political will to make a difference for our people"

"... White people and Black African people have the power to decide who gets a stall or a space to set up shop around the city"

"... they always want us to change"

"... they have got no time management"

"... they do not have a nice way of asking for things ... like we were taught"

"... with no history of entrepreneurship in their family ... no generational understanding"

"... I trade to survive, they start businesses to make lots of money to pay for their holidays and expensive clothes"

"... they think that they understand all of me ... they do not!"

"... they are used to struggling ... this is new to me"

"... they are so aggressive in their discussions and debates"

"... they always think that we are hustling"

"... they don't understand our struggle"

"... they don't know of the dangers I face as a woman running my business"

"... they just want to exploit my networks and access"

> *"... even though we are a small business, we still have separate job functions ... I don't understand why. Certain groups get to hold certain roles ... not people like me"*
>
> *"... I must always act in a way that makes them comfortable ... make them feel at ease"*
>
> *"... we are so distant, that we don't really know each other"*
>
> *"... why don't they make an effort"*
>
> *"... they don't understand people like us".*

The responses above further highlight the work of Syed and Özbilgin, Tatli, Tatli and Özbilgin and Tatli, Ozturk and Woo[15] in which they make us aware of both the social-, relational- and agentic-level orientations and concerns commonly embedded in the practices, structures and infrastructures, processes and norms in various institutional contexts, such as family, society, school, employment, law, and politics. Many of the challenges around the cities of South Africa are related to the large geographic and spatial distances between White people and people of colour (African Black, Camissa/ Mixed Race/Coloured, Indian/Asian) – and there is little to no appreciation of, nor empathy for, the fact that people access space(s) differently, make choices around accessing and entering certain spaces, and of the collaborative penalties such spatial differences place on people of colour, particularly African Black people, who tend to live the furthest from the epicentre of the city CBD (spatial intersectionality).

In their research, Dennissen, Benschop and van den Brink[16] show how the single category structure of diversity networks marginalizes members with multiple disadvantaged identities and reveals how collaborations between diversity networks are hindered by processes of preserving privilege rather than interrogating it. This is particularly true in the more outwardly appearing liberal parts of South Africa's economic hubs, like in Cape Town in the Western Cape Province and Sandton in Gauteng, where the dominant liberal paradigm seeks to have us all operate as 'colour blind', eliminate notions of inequality and argue for competing on so-called "equal playing fields", and thus obscure the realities of differentiated access, collaborative challenges, and ultimately obscure the potential for higher levels of entrepreneurship across the multitude of multicultural communities that make up the major cities of the country. According to Kamasak, Özbilgin and Yavuz,[17] intersectional analyses which ignore the interaction of individual intersections and institutional intersections may fail to adequately represent the actual life courses of diverse people. According to Roberson,[18] beyond individual intersections, organizations also have intersections such as processes, structures, routines, ways of working, and functions that generate

---

15 Syed & Özbilgin, 2009; Tatli, 2011; Tatli & Özbilgin, 2012 & Tatli, Ozturk & Woo, 2017.
16 Dennissen, Benschop & van den Brink, 2020.
17 Kamasak, Özbilgin & Yavuz, 2020.
18 Roberson, 2013.

intersectional impact as they favour some individual intersections and discourage, or even penalize, others. Our respondents echo these by way of their comments:

"... they always expect us to bend over backwards for them, because they have always been in charge"

"... because he trained with the boss, he gets favours more than others"

"... we know who succeeds around here"

"... they both come from rich families, so her work gets looked on more favourably"

"... I won't do that again ... I know my place around here"

" ... because he speaks good English, as a black person who went to a Model C school [previously whites-only, well-resourced school], he gets into the inner circle"

"... only the clever ones ever get proper respect here"

"... she knows how to work the system"

"... I only learnt on the job, and can only do this work ... if the new processes come in, I won't know what to do and maybe even get fired"

"... this is how it has always been done around here"

"... they mustn't come here with their varsity ideas, I know how to run this place"

" ... I have made my own choices, in order to guarantee my success"

"... do they think I am stupid, just because I didn't do a project management course"

"... I go out of my way to get here on time, because it is important that we all start our processes at the same time every day"

"... it is hectic for me to get here at the start of the day ... I have to wake everyone up, make breakfast, dress everyone, take my daughters to school, and then try and get here on time, using multiple dysfunctional public transport systems"

"... they don't listen to people who come from my neighbourhood ... we are just considered the workers"

"... they don't know why I am late sometimes, or why I have to leave early"

" ... he can't just come here from that other department ... we have a way of doing things around here, and he must just fall in"

"... I just keep my head down ... White people have more opportunities if they have to leave this workplace, but I don't"

"... even though she broke away from corporate life, my boss, who is an entrepreneur now with her own business, still wants me to do things in traditional ways ... the way she has always done things"

"... why must they always bring up Apartheid ... they are always blaming the past for not being able to do their work properly"

"... only their kind gets promoted here ... even went and studied, and still they chose someone else before me"

"... Black people think that they are in charge now, but we have the experience and know-how ... and won't be sharing it"

"... I was told to stop challenging my bosses"

"... we don't take all of our leave ... because that looks bad, and the boss don't like it"

"... the owner wants things done just like that"

"... I've got no leeway to try new things".

We see from the above felt evaluations that there are differentiated outcomes for individuals with different backgrounds, and individual-organizational intersections – with a lot of blaming, victimhood and dehumanizing of others. Castro & Holvino[19] might go a long way in explaining some of these outcomes. Castro and Holvino[20] highlight the necessity of looking at the intersections of individuals and institutions to capture the complex reality, and define intersectionality as "a way of thinking that understands [individual] categories of social difference as interlocking and mutually constitutive at the micro level of individual experience and at the macro level of institutional and societal structures and cultural ideologies". Similarly, the study by Tatli and Özbilgin[21] argue for a more emic approach to intersectional approaches to diversity, with sensitivity to the emergence of new categories of difference ex post and embedded in specific time and place contexts. This is particularly relevant to the emerging economy and democracy of South Africa, in which people from different backgrounds are still finding each other as a result of a history of lack of contact, engagement and having forged their own micro contextual spaces. The statements above also highlight the power differentials and the perceptions thereof within modern day South African society, some of which are people of colour/white, foreigner/ indigenous, male/female/LGBTQIA++, well-resourced/under-resourced, university educated/other educated, formally skilled/formally unskilled, amongst others.

Self-esteem, rooted in historical assumptions, beliefs and experiences, fundamentally shapes the way in which self and others are conceived, engaged and feel accepted. Bortolan[22] suggests that self-esteem is best understood not just as an episodic emotion among others, but rather as a pervasive background sense of one's worth and of one's ability to deal with life's challenges and opportunities. The majority of South Africans of colour suffer serious deficits in self-esteem and self-trust, high doses of self-doubt, experience loss of hope, loss of agency and, unfortunately, think of themselves, their personal value and capacities in unfavourable terms, as a result of centuries of experiencing exclusion, dehumanization, oppression, and continuous threats as a reality – and not just threat possibilities as Heidegger[23] imagined. They have, however, found ways to coalesce and assist in each other's survival, aided by an orientation to Ubuntu, communalism, neighborliness, clan, family/extended family – through community. Some of our respondents who lived, and those who still live in townships shared the following:

---

19   Castro & Holvino, 2016.
20   Ibid, 329.
21   Tatli & Özbilgin, 2012.
22   Bortolan, 2018: 57.
23   Heidegger, 1927.

> *"... people go in and out of each other's homes. They give anything to you ..."*
> *"... everyone in my street is considered family. We look out for each other, each other's kids, each other's grandparents ..."*
> *" ... our traditions are rooted in our community ... we pass it on by telling stories around the communal fire ... with lekker [nice], braai'ed [barbequed] meat ..."*
> *"... the best ideas come from here ..."*
> *"... we have lots of neighbourhood gatherings ..."*
> *"... no-one is left out ... no one is left to suffer on their own. We will make a plan"*
> *"... right here in the township, this feels like real South Africa, our South Africa, our homeland".*
> *"... those gatherings, those people ... my people. I love the sharing ..."*
> *"... My family is everything to me. I have a responsibility to ensure that no-one in the family ... children, cousins, gogos [grandmothers] ... are all looked after, financially, with food, with shelter, with care."*
> *"... we share our stories of how to hustle [entrepreneurially] and make it. It's everyone's knowledge."*
> *" ... to understand our stories, you must understand our history as a people, our history of survival, our history together, our history overcoming ..."*
> *" ... it is where I feel my roots, where I am most alive, where I can create."*

The specific rhetoric above positively distinguishes group culture and marks symbolic boundaries and a redefined measure of social worth, and has the potential to legitimize a pride and dignity in their ethnic and racial groups not normally accorded them in the country in general. According to Vasquez and Wetzel,[24] the upside of speaking the language of 'us' allows group members to delineate dichotomous boundaries around issues such as roots (homeland, lineage, community), values (importance of extended family, fictive kin, and [lifestyles]), and cultural toolkit (language, food, traditions, beliefs)". The downside, they claim, is that the expectations that accompany symbolic boundaries and group membership can result in unanticipated and negative consequences, particularly the pressure to conform to an essentialized vision of the community. The personal confidence, though, to step out beyond necessity-driven and survivalist, in-community entrepreneurship and create businesses that employ others, to become established in other areas such as middle- to upper-class suburbs and in the cities, to take risks and debt on board in order to grow and serve larger societal needs, and to trust their intuitions and ideas, is sorely lacking. According to Prof. Jamil Zaki, Stanford University psychology professor and author of 'The War for Kindness', people with lower socioeconomic status or from under-represented backgrounds face disadvantages and vulnerabilities that make it obvious how much people need each other.[25] Andersen and Gaddefors[26] discussed how a renewed sense of belonging and a stronger sense of place meaning emerged in a previously depleted community through entrepreneurship, by realigning the meanings and

---

24 Vasquez & Wetzel, 2009: 1569.
25 Young, 2020.
26 Gaddefors, 2016.

attributes of place. This richer and broader view takes cognizance of the fact that entrepreneurship is a socialised phenomenon.

This linked strongly with Prof. Zaki's claim that people who are lower in status and power tend to practise or work on their ability to understand other people and get better at it[27] – this is particularly true in the many townships (lower socio-economic, informal areas) across South Africa, mainly because it is a way to survive and engage in the thriving informal economy. By contrast, Prof. Zaki claims that people with a lot of power are less inclined to focus on the plight of others because, in doing so, they realize that they are benefiting from the [privileged] systems that cause others harm – and damages their ability for greater levels of cognitive empathy and their ability to continue seeing themselves as good. It is when individuals, ventures and businesses feel cognitive empathy and have a willingness to be transformed by the lived experiences of others, and then chooses to act on their empathy to relieve some or all of the suffering and challenges of others (often less fortunate, marginalized, less resourced and less powerful), that we see cross-ethnic and inter-racial entrepreneurship really taking place. Often such entrepreneurial engagements seek to address the social challenges of the less powerful, and it is the people with a lot of privilege who can make the most difference, by empowering the less powerful to exert real influence over their external world and their communities – but, the downside is that when such compassion threatens the very identities and sense of who they are for the privileged, they might actually purposefully turn it down. There needs to be a courageous moving out, a letting go, admittance to the blind spots to the experiences of, and in relation to, others, an engaging and an embracing, an acceptance of the interdependence of all the country's citizens, and even a reparative stance and acts on the part of the privileged. There are many such examples in South Africa, at individual and institutional levels, but given the statistics presented at the start of this chapter, not nearly enough.

As more atypical (previously disadvantaged, disabled and other abled, female and those with fluid identities, minority religions) individuals step into entrepreneurial spaces that shift them away from traditional corporate jobs or mere survivalist ventures, diversity and intersectionality will gain further significance in producing more equality in the future entrepreneurial landscape of the country. Castro and Holvino,[28] in a Mexican context, explored individual intersections of gender, class, and racio-ethnicity and how they interacted with the institutional structures in specific sociocultural contexts – showing that when individual identity categories intersected with the institutional structures and cultural scripts of the sociocultural context, different types of inequalities, other than those created by merely individual

---

27 Young, 2020.
28 Castro & Holvino, 2016.

level constructs, were produced. Shifting away from the mainly racial analysis in South Africa to more multidimensional analyses, will yield differentiated outcomes of inequalities that are shaped by institutional/organizational intersections, as well as help practitioners and academics alike to better understand the competing, intersectional discourses in the unique socio-economic and racio-economic contexts of South Africa.

The prospect of being wealth creators, and problem-solvers of social and infrastructural community challenges in their localities/contexts, which governmental institutions and commercial organizations cannot solve in the near-term, is appealing to many emerging and established entrepreneurs in South Africa today. Entrepreneurship in South Africa can never merely be an economic phenomenon because it is intertwined in complex social and political ways in the daily interactions of individuals and communities in the country. By viewing entrepreneurs and their experiences merely through single etic lenses often leads to misinformed conclusions and misleading actions/non-actions in entrepreneurial motivations. Entrepreneurs do not exist in single-issue categories and are always intersectional by nature. Like entrepreneurs, we all crave respect, want to belong, and want to be heard and validated for who we are. Entrepreneurship requires a breaking down of barriers for honest engagement, bolstered by honest and candid dialogue about the real issues that get in the way of ordinary South Africans, and being honest about what hinders people from bringing their best selves to intersections and collaborative spaces.

Chapter 19

Challenging the Odds: A Critical Analysis of Refugee Entrepreneurial Resilience in South Africa

Henri Tshiamala

Abstract

This chapter seeks to add to the discourse on refugee entrepreneurship by exploring the resilience, efficacy and achievement of African refugee entrepreneurs in South Africa. The chapter examines theoretical literature on immigrant as well as refugee entrepreneurship. Refugee entrepreneurship literature's embeddedness in the immigrant entrepreneurship literature poses challenges in literature reviews but also opens opportunities for providing a unique contribution based on this study of the African refugee entrepreneurship phenomenon in South Africa. Local entrepreneurship in South Africa lacks much in the way of resilience, leadership and initiative. However, this contrasts with the success of many refugees in establishing and sustaining entrepreneurial activities. The question then arises as to what can South Africans learn from the refugee experience? Various theories are examined to explore this question. Furthermore, I relate my personal journey as a successful refugee entrepreneur on the understanding that role modelling is crucial in duplicating entrepreneurial success.

Background

The phenomenon of refugee entrepreneurship[1] has been extensively covered in various popular and academic studies around the world but South Africa presents a particular set of political and socio-economic circumstances regarding refugee and immigrant entrepreneurship. The literature on the success of African refugees when moving from one poor African country to become viable and successful entrepreneurs in another poor African country is still scanty. However, there is popular and scholarly empirical evidence that refugees as a resource, if dealt with proactively, can be beneficial for host countries.[2] Refugee entrepreneurship literature is embedded in the immigrant entrepreneurship literature.[3] This presents distinguishing as well as conflicting challenges. Nevertheless, some immigrant entrepreneurship realities can also be applied to refugee entrepreneurs.

---

1   Bizri, 2017.
2   Jacobsen, 2002.
3   Mehtap & Al-Saidi, 2018.

This chapter begins with an examination of the state of black entrepreneurship in South Africa and the socio-economic conditions surrounding that. It then looks at the challenges at a political and social level facing refugee entrepreneurs in the South African context. Various theories are examined to help review questions of resilience, efficacy and success among refugee entrepreneurs. I describe my journey as an African refugee entrepreneur as one among many examples of a positive outcome. Throughout the chapter I make recommendations regarding approaches and perspectives that could improve the outcome of entrepreneurship in South Africa.

The state of entrepreneurship in South Africa

One of the latest reports of the Global Entrepreneurship Monitor[4] states that South Africa's foremost socio-economic problems that have been critical contributory factors in its persistent inequality and poverty are: 1) its high unemployment levels; 2) under-employment; 3) high income inequality; 4) weak job-creating capacity.[5]

Unethical governance, corruption, political and social instabilities, wars, lack of business leadership and obscure business ethics are prominent among many other challenges that Africa has had to confront, claims Mills,[6] who has had hands-on personal experiences with Africa and its leadership. Some of these above-mentioned issues have been the cause of massive displacement of people in search of safety and economic opportunities away from their countries of origin into South Africa. Acemoglu et al.[7] argue that developed countries are economically strong because of the important role governments have played in setting, maintaining and supporting "inclusive economic institutions" i.e. institutions modelled on a mix of political influence combined with the principle of free market, hence creating incentives for private economic activities and entrepreneurial ventures to flourish.[8] This with the understanding that the state takes some responsibility to not only create but also drive the strengthening of infrastructures of development such as education, property rights as well as logistical infrastructures such as road, railways, airways and maritime networks. The lack of the aforementioned element of economic growth in the African context has created an environment of instability and chaos which has led to the massive displacement of population groups.

The South African government has established the Small Enterprise Development Agency (SEDA) and other incubating/coaching/mentoring agencies to assist in developing sustainable businesses at high cost to both the government and the private sector. The GEM reports suggest that only around 25 percent of the adult

---

4   GEM report, 2017.
5   Herrington, Kew, & Mwanga, 2017.
6   Mills, 2010.
7   Acemoglu et al., 2012.
8   Acemoglu & Robinson, 2012.

South African population are aware of the existence of SEDA, raising the question of the relevance, impact and efficiency of these government agencies that are running at high cost to the fiscus.[9] GEM reports and surveys from 14 years ago, and including the latest ones from 2014 to 2017, continue to confirm that the level of entrepreneurial activity in South Africa continues to be particularly low compared to GEM participating countries as well as other regions in Africa. Research has shown that entrepreneurial activities, when successful and sustainable, result in the socio-economic wellbeing of the societies within which they occur[10]; they stabilize or grow the middle class which results in growing the economies of these countries.

One of the latest GEM reports states:

> "South Africa's main social problems remain its extremely high income inequality and employment challenge. A weak job-creating capacity that has led to chronically high unemployment and – even more significantly – under-employment has been a critical contributory factor in the country's persistent poverty and inequality. Unemployment is at its highest level ever (27.6%), with an expanded rate of over 40% and youth unemployment at over 65%. It has never been more important or urgent for South Africa's policy makers to make a strong commitment to growing the economy. A key priority is to introduce reforms aimed at fostering a more enabling business environment, particularly for the small- and medium-sized enterprises which contribute so much to employment. In many developing economies, small businesses have been shown to contribute substantially to job creation, economic growth and more equal income distribution". (quoted in Herrington et al.[11])

Government reports as well as a GEM[12] report show that there is an increase in financing in an already meagre budget allocation to entrepreneurship, and that three quarters of the entrepreneurs are within the broad-based black community. The same report shows that there is a societal interest in entrepreneurship in South Africa with many people believing that there are opportunities in the country to start their own businesses. But this has not been translated into actual entrepreneurial activities and the rate of failure in entrepreneurial ventures is also high compared to regional levels. South African GDP growth stands at less than 1 percent and entrepreneurial intention has been found to be four times lower than the regional averages while the score for the efficiency-driven economies is more than double South Africa's.[13] Start-up business ventures and young businesses contribute up to 20 percent of gross (total)

9   Herrington et al., 2017.
10 Mitchell, Smith, Seawright, & Morse, 2000.
11 Herrington et al., 2017: 2.
12 GEM, 2017.
13 Herrington & Kew, 2016.

job creation in the United States of America (USA)[14] which has a considerable impact on the overall economy of the country.

There is a perceived tendency among some South Africans to expect the government alone to provide employment to the unemployed masses which is an unachievable prospect in any developing country. Hence the need to create or uncover more avenues, training models, and innovative ways that can facilitate and promote self-employment and entrepreneurial ventures in the underprivileged community. Training and financing are essential in this quest,[15] and so is the importance of understanding the phenomenon of refugee entrepreneurs' efficient business acumen as it has the potential to be an integral part of the solution to the unemployment problem South Africa is facing. The creation of SEDA and a few other public-private partnerships in supporting entrepreneurship in South Africa attest to the importance of getting black South Africans into a paradigm shift about entrepreneurship. Continuing the government's financing/incubating model in the underprivileged community in its current form is proving to be ineffective, counterproductive and problematic. An alternative or complementary model in entrepreneurial development needs to be proposed for a better outcome in addressing the unemployment issue facing South Africa.

The state of refugee-immigrant entrepreneurship in South Africa

The advent of democracy in the Republic of South Africa has seen an influx of migrants coming mostly from the African continent, Pakistan, Bangladesh, Afghanistan, India, China, from the American continents as well as from Europe.[16] Some of these immigrants have come to South Africa by choice or were driven by the prospect of better economic opportunities, bringing scarce skills from across the world to supplement the country's needs for economic growth.[17] The South African education and training system is not yet producing the required amount of critical skills needed to meet its economic demands in areas such as medical science, aeronautics, engineering, chemistry, informatics, agriculture, science and academia. It is well documented that immigrants – including refugees – carry a diverse set of skills that could be beneficial to the host countries.[18] Some of these skilled immigrants seem to be widely accepted and tolerated in South African society.

Another group of immigrants has come into South Africa as refugees – sometimes referred to as refugee-immigrants[19] – for various reasons, such as political instability,

---

14 Decker, Haltiwanger, Jarmin & Miranda, 2014.
15 Bruhn, Karlan, & Schoar, 2010; Herrington et al., 2017; Kerr, Lerner, & Schoar, 2010; Nieuwenhuizen & Kroon, 2002.
16 Jacobsen, 2002; Rogerson & Posel, as cited in Kalitanyi & Visser, 2010.
17 Bodvarsson & Van den Berg; Lazear, as cited in Bove & Elia, 2017.
18 Bove & Elia, 2017.
19 Bizri, 2017; Edin, Fredriksson, & Åslund, 2003.

wars, and socio-economic conditions in their countries of origin. They come from different geographical locations to settle in South Africa. This group has seen some of its members encountering enormous adversities such as societal and institutionalized xenophobia, exclusions from the labour market and banking infrastructure, socio-economic rejections and gross acts of xenophobic violence.[20] Despite these challenges, a considerable number of refugee entrepreneurs have shown resilience in entrepreneurship as an option to mitigate the consequences of economic exclusion. Some of the refugee entrepreneurs have become important economic players in both the informal as well as in the formal sectors of the South African economy, creating employment opportunities for themselves as well as for some local labour.[21] Non-scholarly empirical evidence suggests a strong environment of suspicion, resentment and social disharmonies based on the perception that refugees are taking jobs from previously disadvantaged South Africans and that refugee entrepreneurs are grabbing business opportunities that should have been taken by South Africans entrepreneurs.[22]

Many South Africans have historically been highly marginalized in their own country and have been subjected to discrimination, economic deprivation and mostly set for failure in more than one sector of the South African economy, including entrepreneurship. The recent xenophobic violence in the country and subsequent refugee demonstrations in Cape Town suggest the need for a more coherent, community-based program that will create rapprochement between the two communities. The facilitation and the understanding of refugee entrepreneurship in South Africa could also enrich entrepreneurial development in South Africa as well as potentially help to build bridges between refugee entrepreneurs and local previously disadvantaged entrepreneurs by exchanging critical information on entrepreneurship and its sustainability. This collaboration could range from sharing information on critical determining success factors of some refugee entrepreneurs to practical advice on pricing strategies, cost cutting and supply chain management.

A recent study by Griffin-El and Olabisi[23] found that African immigrant entrepreneurs operate across cultures and markets in a process called the *boundary-breaking intersective* business approach to entrepreneurship; not necessarily having allegiance to co-ethnic affiliations and markets but building entrepreneurial bridges across cultures and societies.[24] The *intersective* model does not restrict refugee-immigrant entrepreneurs to enclaves, giving them competitive advantage in their business operations and mitigating some socio-economic tension with locals, as there is some

---

20 Griffin-el & Olabisi, 2018; Kalitanyi & Visser, 2010.
21 Griffin-el & Olabisi, 2018.
22 Kalitanyi & Visser, 2010.
23 Griffin-El & Olabisi, 2018.
24 Ibid.

employment for locals in the process. One would hence submit that the dominating social network-related theories, even though they cover an important part of the discourse, do not reflect the path that refugees follow. Refugees are not homogenous ethnically and do not necessarily associate with kinfolk but can navigate across ethnicities to either work or seek business favours.[25]

Access to financial capital in nascent entrepreneurial ventures has been shown in the literature to be one of the many important drivers of entrepreneurial activities,[26] yet intriguingly, refugee entrepreneurs are generally excluded from formal financial infrastructure. They manage to support each other's business ventures within their co-ethnic enclave.[27] Finally, refugee entrepreneurial perceived "success" is found to be based on the strength of the refugee rather than on his shortcomings.[28]

Studies have suggested that both formal as well as informal entrepreneurship have the potential to alleviate desperation and societal anxieties as they can reduce economic inequalities and facilitate economic recovery.[29] Research has also shown that start-up business ventures and young businesses contribute up to 20 percent of job creation in the USA,[30] which has a considerable impact on the overall economy of the country.

Refugee entrepreneurship should also meet this criterion in the South African socio-economic environment. Research has proven that immigrant entrepreneurship is born from *bounded solidarity* caused by events that affect their community's stability and existence.[31] Even though immigration theory suggests that immigrant entrepreneurs operate and flourish within a *co-ethnic setup*,[32] most African refugee entrepreneurs in South Africa are operating in the informal sector across cultural boundaries creating an *intersective* business scenario.[33] Some amongst these African refugee entrepreneurs have moved on to grow sustainable and "successful" businesses in both the formal and the informal sectors of the economy, creating employment for locals and hence contributing to the overall South African economy.[34] Since entrepreneurship has been proven to be beneficial in stimulating the economic growth of nations[35] one is tempted to propose that refugee entrepreneurship in the South African context should be encouraged, or at least protected, rather than viewed with contempt.

---

25 Griffin-el & Olabisi, 2018.
26 Ibid.
27 McEvoy & Hafeez, 2008; Price & Chacko, 2009; Zhou, 2004.
28 Saleeby as cited in Fong, Busch, Armour, Heffron, & Chanmugam, 2008.
29 Aliaga-Isla & Rialp, 2013; Massey as cited in Kalitanyi & Visser, 2010; Mehtap & Al-Saidi, 2018; Peroni, Riillo, & Sarracino, 2016.
30 Decker et al., 2014.
31 Light & Bhachu, 1989; Portes, 1993.
32 Chaganti et al.; Levie as cited in Aliaga-Isla & Rialp, 2013; Bizri, 2017.
33 Griffin-el & Olabisi, 2018.
34 Ibid.
35 Fritsch & Wyrwich, 2017.

Financing or access to financial capital in the entrepreneurship sector, more importantly in nascent entrepreneurial ventures, has also been extensively covered in the literature as one of the many important drivers of entrepreneurial activities.[36] Refugees in South Africa do not have access to finance, scholarships or any other business incubation program, yet there is evidence of some progress in refugees' entrepreneurial activities looking at how many times their businesses have been looted and ransacked by local black communities around the country. The GEM reports indicate persistent low levels of entrepreneurial activity in South Africa relative to other participating countries in the region with a relatively acceptable level of government participation in financing and support.[37] However, the success rate and sustainability of these businesses is low. The report has found that three quarters of all-inclusive entrepreneurial activities is from black communities which perform below regional level.

Theoretical Grounding

Introduction

The theoretical grounding of this text is mainly drawn from the *refugee/ethnic (immigrant) entrepreneurship theories, social networks theories*, particularly that of the middleman minority theory, the ethnic economies theories, the enclave economies theory and the *economics of immigration theory*. In addition, for the purposes of defining the refugee entrepreneurship dynamics in South Africa, *entrepreneurial leadership theories* will also be touched upon. A review of the literature relating to these theories will also facilitate an understanding of the refugee entrepreneurs' business accomplishments in South Africa.

It is worth noting that refugee entrepreneurship literature in general, and on the African continent in particular, is scarce and mostly submerged in the broader immigrant entrepreneurship literature.[38] Refugees – sometimes referred to as *refugee-immigrants*[39] and asylum seekers – are an integral part of immigration, but they are distinct from other forms of immigration because of the underlying causes of the migration.[40] Nevertheless, some of the inferences on immigrant entrepreneurship could also be valid for refugee entrepreneurship.

---

36 Beck, 2012; Kerr et al., 2010.
37 Herrington et al., 2017.
38 Turcotte & Silka; Wauters & Lambrecht as cited in Bizri, 2017; Mehtap & Al-Saidi, 2018.
39 Bizri, 2017; Edin et al., 2003.
40 Borjas, 1989; Peri & Yasenov, 2019.

Middleman minority theory

The concept of middleman minorities was conceived by sociologist Blalock in the 1960s (quoted in Bonacich[41]) and further expanded by social scientist Edna Bonacich's article *"A Theory of Middleman Minorities"*.[42] This concept characterizes a group of marginalized minority tradesmen or entrepreneurs who deal, negotiate and navigate their way between two groups of people in a host society – the dominant and the subordinate groups; or play an intermediary economic role between the economically/socially strong group and the segregated weak groups; or distribute large corporations' merchandises to the minority customers. Middleman minority theory tends to suggest that societal trust, economical solidarities and reciprocal entrepreneurial favours are given and exchanged within a specific group of immigrants as a way of self-preservation as well as an economic emancipation strategy.[43]

Refugee entrepreneurs fit the profile of this concept as they are perceived to "tolerate" abuses in their quest to attain economic independence and succeed in entrepreneurial activities.[44] They become victims of violence, consumer boycotts, deportations, riots and murders such as in the cases of the Jews in Europe, the Chinese in South East Asia and South Koreans in the USA.[45] Tucker suggests that internal network ties which he calls "in-group ties" are one of the many reasons for refugees' (middleman minority) business ascendency.

> *"Due to their sojourner status and their strong in-group ties, middleman minorities develop a competitive business edge. In particular, these entrepreneurs minimize their labour costs through their reliance on family members and fellow ethnic workers willing to work long hours for little pay. These circumstances allow middleman minorities to establish positions of economic dominance..."*[46]

The competitive advantage of refugee entrepreneurs as a "middleman minority" includes strong ethnic attachment, access to co-ethnic cheap labour, access to internal and mostly organically-grown co-ethnic sources of finance, access to co-ethnic market networks, access to an internal business co-ethnic training which plays the role of an informal business incubator for the future 'home grown' entrepreneurs and strong frugality.[47] Social and economic solidarity and reciprocity play a big role

---

41 Bonacich, 1973: 583.
42 Ibid.
43 Bonacich, 1973; Light, Sabagh, Bozorgmehr, & Der-Martirosian, 1994; Min & Kolodny, 1994; Zhou, 2004.
44 Bonacich, 1973; Porter & Washington, 2019; Stewart et al., 2008.
45 Bonacich, 1973; Min & Kolodny, 1994.
46 Tucker, 2007: 147.
47 Bizri, 2017; Patricia Gene Greene & Butler, 1996; Light & Bhachu, 1989; Menzies, Brenner, & Filion, 2003.

in maintaining their business success. Labour costs within the middleman minorities' networks makes it difficult for mainstream entrepreneurs to compete, causing continuous conflict with the mainstream labour force as the latter see this as a threat to their ability to secure jobs or negotiate higher salaries and better working conditions.[48]

Ethnic enclave economy theory

The two concepts of *ethnic enclave economy and ethnic economy* – while overlapping – are not necessarily identical, for ethnic enclave economy concept emanates from the middleman minorities theories, whereas the concept of ethnic economy emanates from *labour segmentation literature*.[49] They theorize that the ethnic enclave economy is just a section within a wider concept of ethnic economy. Most researchers tend to agree that the existence of strong network interactions among immigrants, reciprocal businesses and labour favours within the ethnic economies and within the ethnic enclave economies, is one of the reasons for the economic strength of the immigrant groups, including refugees and other minorities.[50] The socio-economic savings that ethnic businesses achieve in the enclave, ranging from the employment of cheap co-ethnic labour, skills transfer from the most skilled members to the less skilled ones, as well as the opportunities and assurances of a self-contained employment market that less skilled immigrants get within these enclave economies, contributes to the ethnic immigrants becoming economically strong as groups but also as individuals within the group.[51]

Social network theories in the immigrant entrepreneurship literature

Refugee or immigrant networks are born out of affinities created through the ethnic identities of immigrants, acquaintance, culture or shared community origin, with a strong potential to integrate and develop strong enclave economic ties.[52] These immigrant networks are powerful. They are not only efficient tools used by immigrants in the creation of the immigrant economy in the host countries, but are also used to expand their economic opportunities while reducing the cost of labour both in the enclave economy as well as in the mainstream economy.[53]

The *refugee-immigrant entrepreneurship* theory is well situated within two *social network* theories: 1) the *middleman minority* theory, and 2) the *enclave economy*

---

48 Bonacich, 1973; Patricia G. Greene, 1997; Light & Bhachu, 1989.
49 Light et al., 1994.
50 Edin et al., 2003; Light et al., 1994; Portes & Manning, 2013.
51 Light & Bhachu, 1989; Sanders & Nee, 1992; Wilson & Portes, 1980.
52 Light & Bhachu, 1989; Massey, 1988; Serrie, 1998.
53 Edin et al., 2003.

theory[54]; it is referred to as entrepreneurial activities that are run and owned within refugee communities in a host country.[55] It is been proven in some instances that refugee entrepreneurship has a positive impact on host nations because they create employment and stabilize the refugee communities[56] as is the case of Korean immigrants in the California in the USA, Indians in East Africa, the Chinese in the Southeast Asia and the Jews in Europe.[57]

While refugee entrepreneurial ventures in host countries are widely recognized as valuable,[58] there are conflicting arguments contending that the *survivalist*[59] and *necessity-based* entrepreneurs cannot meaningfully benefit society or yield as much as *opportunity-based* entrepreneurship.[60] Although not all refugee entrepreneurs' ventures are successful in their host nations,[61] theory and empirical evidence seem to suggest that a considerable proportion of these ventures become sustainable and viable over time.[62]

Even though refugee entrepreneurs are included in the middleman minorities and the ethnic enclave theories profiles,[63] their entrepreneurial activities and merchandise supply chain are mostly dependent on local corporate suppliers and wholesalers that are not necessarily co-ethnic, in order to operate, while still maintaining a strong business network in their refugee communities.[64] Research has found that refugee-immigrant entrepreneurial successes are relative to or based on the context within which their business activities evolve.[65] Start-up financial support, correct information on supply chain etc... seem to be some of many challenges that refugee entrepreneurs encounter in their host countries.[66]

This tends to contradict the enclave theories that suggest that the enclave facilitates start-up funding.[67] Research suggests that immigrant entrepreneurs organically grow their businesses with ethnic enclave support and develop them without formal public or private financing and end up becoming important economic players in both the informal as well as the formal sectors of their host country.[68] While theory

54 Light & Bhachu, 1989; Serrie, 1998.
55 Vinogradov & Isaksen as cited in Bizri, 2017.
56 Griffin-el & Olabisi, 2018; Kalitanyi & Visser, 2010; Light & Bhachu, 1989.
57 Bonacich, 1973; Min & Kolodny, 1994; Yoo, 2000.
58 Kalitanyi & Visser, 2010; Mehtap & Al-Saidi, 2018.
59 Baycan-Levent & Nijkamp; Moyo as cited Griffin-el & Olabisi, 2018.
60 Marchand & Siegel, as cited in Bizri, 2017.
61 Edin et al., 2003.
62 Griffin-el & Olabisi, 2018; Yoo, 2000.
63 Bonacich, 1973; Edin et al., 2003; Portes & Manning, 2013.
64 Porter & Washington, 2019; Stewart et al., 2008; Zhou, 2004.
65 McKeever, Anderson, & Jack as cited in Bizri, 2017.
66 Dana & Morris as cited in Bizri, 2017; Mehtap & Al-Saidi, 2018.
67 Edin et al., 2003; Zhou, 2004.
68 Bonacich, 1973; Price & Chacko, 2009.

establishes that entrepreneurship and its resulting business ventures are critical for the development and well-being of societies as well as for the advancement of technology,[69] evidence of the inputs of refugee entrepreneurs to host nations is debatable and mostly inconclusive.[70]

Most researchers tend to agree that the existence of strong network interactions among immigrants, reciprocal businesses and labour favours within the ethnic economies and within the ethnic enclave economies is one of the reasons for the economic strength of the immigrant groups, including refugees and other minorities.[71] Some social scientists argue that socio-economic exclusion and discrimination could be beneficial, as this stimulates the need for self-reliance in entrepreneurial activities.[72] The stronger the economic exclusion of cultural minorities the more entrepreneurship is strengthened around cultural networks.[73]

The enclave economy theory, which asserts that immigrants benefit economically from their economic enclaves by providing employment, skills transfer etc., is criticized as being a "mobility trap".[74] This is found to have some validity in that assimilation policies yield more benefits than the segregation approach.[75] The enclave economy theory is problematized by the fact that there are conflicting definitions from different schools of thoughts. On the one hand, the enclave economy suggests being in one geographical location, whereas on the other hand, it is conceived as a group belonging to the same origin despite their geographical position. It is important to notice that refugee entrepreneurship may exist without necessarily fitting the profile defined by this theory as refugees can and do work within their enclaves or across different enclaves.

The middleman minority theory relates to the ethnic enclave economy theory. It also speaks to the benefits of the immigrants and the role they play in the host country in linking the rich community to the poor ones.[76] The problem with this theory is that refugees, even though they are immigrants, do not generally play the middleman minority role in most host countries. Most refugees face hostility much of the time, and they are directly targeted and victimized more than other immigrants.[77]

---

69   Fellnhofer & Puumalainen, 2017; Fritsch & Wyrwich, 2017; Mitchell et al., 2000.
70   Jacobsen, 2002.
71   Edin et al., 2003; Light et al., 1994; Portes & Manning, 2013.
72   Bonacich, 1973; Borjas, 1989, 2000; Edin et al., 2003; Light, 1979.
73   Light, 1979.
74   Portes & Jensen, 1992.
75   Sanders & Nee, 1992, 2016.
76   Bonacich, 1973; Zhou, 2004.
77   Bizri, 2017; Edin et al., 2003; Mehtap & Al-Saidi, 2018.

Entrepreneurial leadership and role modelling

The notion of entrepreneurial leadership emanates from the concept of *positive role modelling* in societies where leaders can influence, inspire and motivate people or followers.[78] Principles of theoretical and practical leadership such as transformational leadership and transactional leadership that underlie modelling are well covered in literature and found to be influential and important in community development and empowerment.[79]

Research studies – both popular and academic – emphasize the critical importance of role-modelling (inspiration/motivation) in various sectors of social life such as medical science, education, sport, music, science etc... including in the entrepreneurial sector.[80] Individual decisions to engage in a specific line of conduct, including within entrepreneurial ventures, can to some extent be influenced by the opinions and behaviour of others (as quoted in Bosma, Hessels, Schutjens, Praag, & Verheul).[81] However, the mechanism by which the strengthening of entrepreneurial intention is affected by role models is still to be properly understood.[82] The formation of entrepreneurial identity and intention, as well as entrepreneurial performance, is influenced by the presence of role models in the lives of aspiring entrepreneurs.[83] Gibson[84] theorizes that role modelling generally serves three interrelated functions in the lives of the observing people, which are: "to provide learning, to provide motivation and inspiration, and to help individuals define their self-concept".

My journey as a refugee entrepreneur in South Africa

My experience as a refugee entrepreneur who came to South Africa – running away from the persecution, violence and abuses of the dictatorship of the late President Mobutu in what was then known as Zaire – brings a personal perspective to this chapter.

I arrived in South Africa in 1991, into a society that was socially and politically dysfunctional and marred by political and social violence. I was rejected by the white community because I was a black man and I was also rejected by the black South African community because I was a foreigner. For the white man I was a "K-word" (an offensive designation legally banned in South Africa), and for the black man I was a "makwerekwere" (one of the many derogatory appellations that could mean "stupid

---

78 Steffens, Haslam, Ryan, Kessler, & Jena, 2013.
79 Alimo-Metcalfe, 1998; Bass, Avolio, & Atwater, 1996.
80 Fellnhofer & Puumalainen, 2017; Gibson, 2003; Nowiński & Haddoud, 2019; Tkachev & Kolvereid, 1999.
81 Bosma, Hessels, Schutjens, Praag, & Verheul, 2012, p. 410.
82 Nowiński & Haddoud, 2019.
83 Efrata & Maichal, 2018.
84 Gibson, 2003: 149.

stranger who speaks bizarre vernacular). Despite these challenges of insecurity, hatred and institutional and societal exclusions,[85] I had to cultivate and learn new street survival skills away from the local communities.

I had no role model in my community, no reference point for how to succeed in an environment that was very hostile towards black Africans from outside the Republic of South Africa. There were and still are no comfort zones for refugees in South Africa.[86] It is a "make it or die", "swim or sink" type of situation where one has no options but to navigate through life's waves. I did not have access to financial assistance for living, no scholarships for my studies, no permanent place to stay or any business incubation program to rely upon. Police harassments were frequent, keeping me on the run almost all the time because I was without immigration permits. I had to learn new street survival skills that could help me overcome a variety of challenges to secure both my safety as well as build my future. I had no financial support on the streets of Johannesburg and Cape Town, but I aspired to be "successful" just like some of the few Eastern and Western African businesses that seemed viable in South Africa. Street survival skills must have helped me to be resilient in entrepreneurship. Failure was not an option then, and is still not an option now, even though I have experienced sporadic xenophobic attacks resulting in the loss of a considerable amount of merchandise.

Through informal entrepreneurship as a refugee entrepreneur, I managed to complete my mostly self-funded studies in engineering at the Cape Peninsula University of Technology as well as my master's degree in business administration from the University of Cape Town. I initiated a successful small family retail and real estate enterprise without any financing from any government agencies or from the private sector, and I created employment for some locals. I am currently pursuing my PhD at the Graduate School of Business at the University of Cape Town and have found a way of paying back to the community through many years of pro bono entrepreneurship coaching, mentoring and lecturing at the Raymond Ackerman Academy of Entrepreneurship Development based at the Graduate School of Business of the University of Cape Town, at the TSIBA University and at many public engagements organized by community-based organizations, while my South African-born children are actively involved in tutoring in some disadvantaged schools around Cape Town.

I have realized in the process of my own development as a refugee entrepreneur that I have incidentally become a role model for other refugees who are inspired and motivated by what they have observed in my progress, many of whom went on to achieve more than I could ever imagine. They have read my story in the

---

85 Bonacich, 1973; Light, 1979; Zhou, 2004.
86 Kalitanyi & Visser, 2010.

Succeed magazine, in the Cape Argus newspaper, and in the now defunct University of Cape Town's Graduate School of Business's *Breakwater* magazine. Some of these refugees are working hard to achieve accomplishments in their studies and create their own business ventures as well. I assume that they think if one refugee can make it then nothing is impossible for all of them to achieve success. I was, and still am, invited to speak at motivational conferences and schools because some think that my career path and humble achievement is worth emulating.

My journey as a refugee is one among many other stories of resilience. Hence one needs to retrospectively explore the leading factors that led to the outcomes refugee entrepreneurs have produced.

Conclusion

Could it be that one of the many solutions to South Africa's perceived "lack" of entrepreneurial drive may reside in understanding the achievement of refugee entrepreneurship and duplicate the learnings for local underprivileged communities, rather than just allocating resources to people who have no hope, no business orientations/training and no entrepreneurial motivation? Could the refugee entrepreneurial journey and experiences be used as one of the few blueprints to solve the issue of unemployment in South Africa? I submit that great care needs to be put on the importance of understanding the determinants of this phenomenon in order to stimulate entrepreneurial growth and mastery in South Africa.

Refugee entrepreneurship is a world-wide phenomenon that is in many instances viewed with apprehension. However, well-managed refugee entrepreneurship can be beneficial to the host country.[87] It has been established that entrepreneurship – both "subsistence" as well as "transformational" entrepreneurship[88] and its resulting business ventures – are critical for the development and wellbeing of societies as well as for the advancement of technology.[89] South Africa needs strong entrepreneurial activities to strengthen its economy, reduce the debilitating effect of poverty and create much-needed sustainable employment. Cross-community interactions and joint business forums between the refugee entrepreneurs and local South African entrepreneurs are some of the ways that could foster a shared and more productive entrepreneurial culture for both the refugee entrepreneurs and for local entrepreneurs alike.

---

87 Balagopal, 2011; Bizri, 2017; Edin et al., 2003; Jacobsen, 2002; Kalitanyi & Visser, 2010; Mehtap & Al-Saidi, 2018.
88 Schoar, 2015.
89 Fellnhofer & Puumalainen, 2017; Mitchell et al., 2000.

Conclusion: Africaneurs of Sub-Saharan Africa

Prof. Kurt April and Dr. Badri Zolfaghari

Sub-Saharan Africa is challenged and blessed with a dynamic mix of formal and informal sectors, laced with effective and ineffective layers of individual and collective entrepreneurial behaviour and action. With Africa's population projected to grow to 2.4 billion by 2050, over 70% under the age of 30 years old, with 60% in cities and towns, there is an urgent need for more social enterprises and entrepreneurial businesses, operating across the continent to creatively deliver relevant solutions, often under resource constraints not experienced in more industrialized economies, to the multitude of needs of the people and sectors of the continent – some of which are in education, healthcare, employment, sanitation and water, security, food security, electricity, transportation, and housing. Many list the continent's numerous contextual factors as reasons for not fully understanding how to overcome the social challenges and the justification for inaction, i.e., poverty, unemployment, inequality, discrimination, legacies of colonialism, resource ownership by foreigners and foreign powers, lack of service delivery and institutional failures – local, regional and pan-African institutional failures.

Being entrepreneurial is not necessarily about creating entirely new business models only, but about understanding the context, the social needs, the environment, supply efficiency and security, the socio-economic layout, knowing the pain points for a community and society, and seeking to relieve some or all of that pain by stepping into the available gaps/opportunities. When discussing B Corps in the book, we explain why it is essential that the B Corps movement on the African continent be driven by an unwavering commitment to local communities by creating relationships of mutual trust between companies/entrepreneurial ventures and the local context. There are many diverse communities, as well as formal and informal economies, in Africa that work well. For example, there are various rotating savings and credit associations (ROSCAs), e.g., the well-known stokvels in South Africa, that support economic empowerment and community upliftment, and may help to support inclusive business practices.

The presented economic ecosystems perspectives, in our book, offer holistic, conceptual frameworks that can help bridge the formal-informal sector divide, help make sense of the continuous and necessary adaptations, and can shine a light on and engender multi-level economic activity that is required for the African continent. The informal sector and quasi-informal sectors, in particular, have not received the necessary attention in research and publications – odd, given the importance of these sectors for providing employment and survival, and the fact that a significant number of successful, and large-scale, businesses in African contexts began their operations either as family-run entrepreneurial businesses and/or began within the informal sector. According to Musara and Nieuwenhuizen[1]: "Informal sector entrepreneurship activities contribute 10-20% of the GDP in developed countries and up to 60% in developing economies. In South Africa, the informal sector accounts for 15-17% of total employment and about 5.2% of the country's GDP". Throughout the multiple chapters in the book, we recognize and discuss the importance of place and spatial boundaries/constraints, cross-cultural boundaries/constraints, values boundaries/constraints, ethno-racial boundaries/constraints, cognitive and knowledge boundaries/constraints, boundaries/constraints of intention, leader and managerial boundaries/constraints, as well as time boundaries/constraints – an understanding of which is quite important if one wants to appropriately address the entrepreneurial challenges of the continent.

A number of organizational and individual examples are presented to demonstrate what is possible, as well as what can be, and what has been, overcome. From the more formal side of entrepreneurship, in the manufacturing sector specifically, we are reminded that many of the prescribed frameworks in thinking about innovative and entrepreneurial processes do not focus on the human element – the psychological safety required by employees and individuals. Our book makes the claim that social businesses may be some of the best organizations for achieving it, through processes of continuous, small and large corrections. In addition to organizations creating processes, products, and services that satisfy the needs of their stakeholders, psychological safety requires organizations and their founders/leaders to listen to team members and employees for expressions of learning, experimentation and failure recovery, questioning and critiquing, risk-taking and risk mitigation, and listen out for their fear of change. When team members and employees have the freedom to speak up and act fearlessly as social entrepreneurs, in their own right, they will exhibit the necessary creativity, communication, and responsiveness to enact real change for themselves, their organizations, and their communities.

Entrepreneurial activity, though, is not without its shadow side. The formal sector is notorious for crushing dissent from employees, for killing off new ideas and innovations that challenge the status quo, for avoiding the necessary hard work to ensure inclusion of diverse staff and employees, and for engaging in corruption, bribery and withholding of all the necessary information from clients, suppliers and partners. Webb, Tihanyi, Ireland and Sirmon[2] defined informal sector entrepreneurship as a set of illegal, yet legitimate activities through which individuals recognize and exploit

---

1   Musara & Nieuwenhuizen, 2020: 194.
2   Webb, Tihanyi, Ireland & Sirmon, 2009.

business and societal opportunities and challenges. In other words, according to Webb et al., informal sector entrepreneurship exists at the intersection between legitimacy and legality. This is true for all forms of entrepreneurship, as well as in corporate endeavours, however, the lack of formal monitoring in the informal sector makes it more susceptible to unethical practices in the Western social construction of capitalism on the continent. Botha[3] lists some of the unethical activities: corruption, bribery, coercion, deception, theft and unfair discrimination. Operating outside of the formal boundaries of the economic system has been further encouraged by the hardships induced through the Covid-19 pandemic, during which millions of Africans have lost their jobs, lost the markets and customers to their informal businesses, and had the precariousness of their livelihoods exposed in very real ways.

The book has explored ways in which technological solutions, ascribed to the fourth industrial revolution, offer opportunities to drive innovation and to entrepreneurially assist underserved communities. Through the technological lens, we have suggested, and described the dynamic Artificial Mind Engine (AME), an example of a responsible ecosystem of distributed, collective minds and brains (agents) that emerge and are able to serve the common good through sophisticated hyperstructures that continually evolve through incremental learning from interactions between, and feedback loops from, partner networks, processes and people. We have described the challenges which entrepreneurs face when attempting to transform digital and knowledge economies to attain and sustain competitive advantage in emerging intelligence economies. One of the core challenges for entrepreneurs is an enabling environment, no matter which country or region they find themselves operating in – and this often requires local and/or national government enablement, through conducive policies, programs and legal processes to support budding and established entrepreneurs, as well as overcome barriers and bridge divides. These policies should not only be for indigenous entrepreneurs, but should equally target migrant and refugee entrepreneurs. The founding entrepreneurs themselves, as well as their teams, need to invest time, resources and effort in building strong, ethical, transparent and transformative organizations that have real impact on communities and propel their development. For instance, in the book we examined the link between path-dependent, framing strategies and the emergence of a shielded, renewable energy niche, i.e., a small-scale bio-based energy project, that led to nurturing and empowerment. The diagnostic frame helped identify problems and influenced the mobilization process of potential stakeholders in the nurturing and empowering process – we discussed enablers and stumbling blocks in attracting and mobilizing other relevant parties who would have been willing to experiment in the regional market for economic and societal benefit.

---

3   Botha, 2012.

In Africa, Western-styled capitalism is not considered to be the only economic model – many countries have turned to forms of socialism and social democracies in attempts to indigenize their economies and local knowledge systems. Pyke,[4] as well as April and Daya[5] and Millard,[6] refer to several anti-colonial writers, such as Biko, Fanon, Freire, and Memmi, to highlight the psychological and inferiority effects of the colonized mentality that seeks to compare with and emulate the previous socio-political and current-day economic colonizers, their knowledge and their solutions – erroneously holding them up as the examples and role models of what should be copied and emulated on the continent of Africa. Oelofsen[7] encourages a deeper understanding of the relationship between the decolonisation of the mind and the decolonisation of the intellectual landscape – the intellectual landscape referring to schooling (primary and secondary schooling), colleges, universities and other institutions of knowledge production. In the book, we shed light on the unacceptability of the continued dominance of Eurocentric and North American knowledge production in addressing Africa's very unique challenges, and the need to shift and demand decolonisation of such knowledge production.

We explore the need to enrich the graduate curricula of universities and Business Schools across the continent with African content, African leaders, and case studies that reflect the unique challenges of sub-Saharan Africa. Once again, technology and digitally-enabled platforms are enablers for such shifts. Promoting change through the education curriculum remains an effective means of reaching a very large number of people. However, transformation and epistemological redress cannot be achieved without a reformed educational curriculum. In the book, we discussed the role of companies like GetSmarter and 2U, and also the production of video cases and written cases of African, values-led leaders and organizations. We explore leadership trajectories and defining moments, unique to the specific contexts and lenses of Africa, that can then be closely connected to relevant emerging stories and narratives. When incorporated into the curriculum of a trusted university, video-led cases will further enhance trust, by combining the text-based authority of resources and sources of information with direct, visual communication with key figures within the curriculum's narrative – giving voice to African leaders and African organizational stories, both as complementary knowledge as well as alternative perspectives to the currently dominant institutional narratives of the global North corporate institutions and leaders. For Business Schools, the African Association of Business Schools (AABS) represents an important network in that respect. Schools, colleges and universities have the opportunity to have teachers and lecturers who can act as

---

4   Pyke, 2010: 551.
5   April & Daya, 2021.
6   Millard, 1984.
7   Oelofsen, 2015.

mentors to budding entrepreneurs or those wanting to gain experience in starting ventures outside of school or tertiary educational institutions – as core parts of their classes/courses or as extramural activities.

In the book, we shed understanding about business accelerator effects in disadvantaged areas and its consequences from a social and economic point of view, the halo effect of business accelerators on individuals who want to/have started ventures, and how it contributes to our understanding of how business accelerators influence the intention to start innovative, new ventures. There are more men, in general unfortunately, with intentions to start ventures – thus, business accelerators and local/national policymakers should engage, encourage and incentivize more women to start entrepreneurial start-ups and businesses. We also explore how innovative hubs, incubators and accelerators can be places of collaboration, as mentors are eager to collaborate with start-ups and established entrepreneurs, particularly if they share similar personal values and societal orientations to them. Mentors often share lessons gained from other entrepreneurial ventures, as they seldom mentor only one founder or organization, and they also role model a truly collective attitude, putting the good of the whole above their own monetary gain (since mentoring is rarely paid for) and often form long-term, confidence-inducing relationships with their mentees. In the book, we discuss the difference between incubation and acceleration in relation to a pilot program team who were continually challenged on the difference between where the pilot incubation program fitted in the entrepreneurship ecosystem.

We also saw that experience was an important criterion for entrepreneurs, and that incubators can play an important role in developing first-time founders and entrepreneurs to quickly test and validate their assumptions in a safe environment – highlighting, for first-time founders and entrepreneurs, the importance of incubators in: learning basic start-up terminology, developing the right mindset and skillset, using stretch targets and projects to expand their confidence, expanding the thinking skills and operations management skills of the founding entrepreneurs, guiding founders in how to identify and maximize opportunities, demonstrating the value of networks/collaborators and good relationships, educating them in how to establish support in the broader ecosystem, and emphasizing the importance of the art of good communication and listening.

In addition, we point out that structures like the Social Impact Start-Up Academy (SISTAC World) and others want to support Business Schools and educational institutions to increasingly serve market-creating innovators in Africa and other developing regions in the world – thereby, ultimately playing an increasing role in fostering their home country's socio-economic development, through providing value-adding, networked assistance for developing innovative ideas. A critical lesson for budding entrepreneurs is that not every business is going to be a success, especially in high-risk environments in the early stages of a start-up – however, successful entrepreneurs have demonstrated the importance of starting again and again after failing or when they were unable to realize their initial dreams.

We discuss the need for internationally comparable data related to youth entrepreneurship propensity. In the book, we explore improved economic forecasting through the measurement of entrepreneurship propensity in determining new venture creation potential. The proposed multivariate index accounts for intensity structures that may exist among attributes, and places potential entrepreneurs and the entrepreneurship ecosystem on a continuum – which guides the development and implementation of specific strategic interventions. The index provides a method to calculate index scores to incorporate in decision-making criteria related to entrepreneurship and economic development policies and programs. Additionally, in the book, we explore how the core self-evaluation personality trait of locus of control can allow for insight into which strategies, industry environments, and risk profiles are best suited for those with an internal (I) or external (E) locus of control psychological expectancy. Overall, we notice that internals are generalized to be more successful at entrepreneurship, but new research is revealing many nuances to this generalization. At the two extreme ends of the I-E continuum, optimism and risk perspectives vary. As such, those with an internal locus of control are found to be better psychologically equipped to undertake innovative strategies, whereas their external counterparts tend to prefer low-cost strategies; hence, matching their respective risk appetites. Similarly, a stable industry environment was seen as appropriate for internals due to their scrupulous planning propensity, while a dynamic industry was more suitable for externals due to their ability to manoeuvre well in chance-dependent scenarios.[8] Also, on the human-centred, personal front, we discuss self-empathy as a practice-informed process for entrepreneurs in the book – by way of a case study of an entrepreneur in a facilitated coaching engagement to help him integrate his own experiences through awareness, noticing, attendance and integration. We show that attentive awareness of one's interior world through ethical exploration and agreement, centring, active sensation practice (embodiment), suspension of judgment, and personal intention-setting enables entrepreneurs to identify and access new, personal coping resources – so necessary in the dynamic environments and contexts across sub-Saharan Africa.

We explore the notion of interpersonal trust in the book, and how its development is severely hampered by cultural diversity – as a result of values differences, disposition, assessment of trustworthiness, behavioural trust, perceived reliability of other people, trusting stance differences, and faith in humanity.[9] The social norms of operating and

---

8   Wijbenga & Witteloostuijn 2007.
9   Thomas et al., 2015; Nikolova, Möllering, & Reihlen, 2014; McKnight, Cummings & Chervany, 1998.

living, sometimes termed 'culture', directly informs individuals' initial inclination to reveal themselves to others, make themselves vulnerable to the actions of others, and determines the level at which and how individuals choose to engage others – particularly those who are different from themselves or who are not indigenous to their culture, region or country. Trusting behaviours are related to acceptance of others, and to the sharing of, and being open to, their lived experiences and knowledge – this is particularly pertinent in the face of xenophobia on the African continent with lots of cross-border travel, migrant labour, as well as refugee entrepreneurship. We notice that, if managed well, refugee entrepreneurship can be beneficial for the development and wellbeing of societies and to the host country.[10] We share a deeper look into understanding the achievement of refugee entrepreneurship and share the learnings for local, underprivileged individuals and communities who can learn and act from said lessons to start their own entrepreneurial ventures. It often is the lack of personal confidence to step out and create entrepreneurial ventures and businesses, the confidence in one's own abilities, and one's fear of taking risks and fear of taking on debt that are deterrents for many – this is perhaps what indigenous individuals and communities can learn from migrants and refugees in their respective countries. In this way, symbolic and cultural boundaries can be overcome, with the potential for a redefinition of individual and collective social worth, even in relation to those considered as 'other'. We explored the intersectional challenges that many, less powerful and less resourced face in their marginalized and, often precarious, livelihoods. In the book, we encourage a courageous moving out by the privileged and the well-resourced, a letting go on their part, an admittance of their blind spots to the experiences of others, and an encouragement for actioned interdependence of all the country's inhabitants, and call for even greater reparative stances and acts on the part of the privileged.

Sub-Saharan Africa needs strong formal and informal entrepreneurial activities to strengthen its economies, communities and well-being, to reduce the debilitating effects of poverty, and to create much-needed sustainable employment for its, generally, young population. Cross-community interactions and collaboration, both in-country and across regions, are some of the ways in which more productive entrepreneurial cultures can be encouraged – and this needs to be aided by entrepreneurially-oriented education, legislation, protection of individual and business rights, and favourable tax/financial incentives by local and national governments. Big businesses and corporates, together with banks and other financial sector players, can play roles too in partnering with and assisting in opportunity identification and sharing with entrepreneurial ventures in producing more engaged and equitable futures for all on the continent.

---

10 Mehtap & Al-Saidi, 2018; Bizri, 2017; Jacobsen, 2002; Mitchell et al., 2000.

References

Chapter 1

AfDB. (2011a). *Africa in 50 Years Time. The Road Towards Inclusive Growth*. Tunisia, Tunis: African Development Bank (AfDB).

AfDB. (2011b). *The middle of the pyramid: Dynamics of the middle class in Africa* [Market Brief]. African Development Bank.

Africa Progress Panel. (2012). *Africa Progress Report. Jobs, Justice and Equity. Seizing Opportunities in Times of Global Change*. Africa Progress Panel.

African Union. (2017). *2017 Africa Sustainable Development Report. Tracking progress on Agenda 2063 and the Sustainable Development Goals*. Addis Ababa, Ethiopia: African Union, Economic Commission for Africa; African Development Bank and United Nations Development Programme.

Auerswald, P. E., & Dani, L. M. (2018). Economic Ecosystems. *The New Oxford Handbook of Economic Geography*. https://doi.org/10.1093/oxfordhb/9780198755609.013.47

Chakrabarti, S. (2013). Interrogating inclusive growth: Formal-informal duality, complementarity, conflict. *Cambridge Journal of Economics, 37*(6), 1349–1379.

Chen, M. A. (2007). *Rethinking the Informal Economy: Linkages with the Formal Economy and the Formal Regulatory Environment* [Working Paper]. United Nations Department of Economic and Social Affairs (UN DESA).

Cilliers, Paul. (1998). *Complexity and Postmodernism: Understanding Complex Systems*. London and New York: Routledge.

Cirolia, L. R., & Scheba, S. (2019). Towards a multi-scalar reading of informality in Delft, South Africa: Weaving the 'everyday' with wider structural tracings. *Urban Studies, 56*(3), 594–611.

De Boeck, F., & Plissart, M.-F. (2005). *Kinshasa: Tales of an Invisible City*. Ghent: Ludion.

De Landa, M. (2006). *A New Philosophy of Society: Assemblage and Social Complexity*. Bloomsbury Academic: New York, NY, USA.

De Magalhães, L., & Santaeulàlia-Llopis, R. (2018). The consumption, income, and wealth of the poorest: An empirical analysis of economic inequality in rural and urban Sub-Saharan Africa for macroeconomists. *Journal of Development Economics, 134*, 350–371. https://doi.org/10.1016/j.jdeveco.2018.05.014

Feldman, M., & Zoller, T. D. (2011). Dealmakers in place: Social capital connections in regional entrepreneurial economies. *Regional Studies, 46*, 23–37.

Gastrow, C. (n.d.). Urban States: The Presidency and planning in Luanda, Angola. *International Journal of Urban and Regional Research.*, (In Press).

Gastrow, V., & Amit, R. (2015). *Lawless Regulation. Government and Civil Society Attempts at Regulating Somali Informal Trade in Cape Town* [African Centre for Migration Studies (ACMS) Report 2015].

Gunderson, L. H., & Holling, C. S. (2002). *Panarchy: Understanding Transformations in Human and Natural Systems*. Washington DC: Island Press.

Hidalgo, C. A., Klinger, B., Barabasi, A., & Hausman, R. (2007). The product space conditions the development of nations. *Science, 317*, 482–487.

Hodgson, G. M. (1993). *Economics and Evolution: Bringing Life Back Into Economics*. University Of Michigan Press & Polity Press.

Klaus Schwab. (2015, December 12). The Fourth Industrial Revolution: What It Means and How to Respond. *SNAPSHOT*.

Kojima, M., Zhou, X., Han, J. J., de Wit, J., Bacon, R., & Trimble, C. (2016). *Who Uses Electricity in Sub-Saharan Africa? Findings from Household Surveys*. https://doi.org/10.1596/1813-9450-7789

Lee, M., Ramus, T., & Vaccaro, A. (2018). From protest to product: Strategic frame brokerage in a commercial social movement organization. *Academy of Management 61*(6), 2130-2158.

Marshall, A. (1920). *Principles of Economics* (8th ed.). London: Macmillan.

Mazzucato, M. (2013). *The Entrepreneurial State. Debunking Public vs. Private Sector Myths.* New York: Anthem Press.

McKinsey. (2010). *Lions on the Move: The Progress and Potential of African Economies.* McKinsey Global Institute, McKinsey and Company.

MinHwa Lee, JinHyo Joseph Yun, Andreas Pyka, DongKyu Won, Fumio Kodama, Giovanni Schiuma, ... Xiaofei Zhao. (2018). How to Respond to the Fourth Industrial Revolution, or the Second Information Technology Revolution? Dynamic New Combinations between Technology, Market, and Society through Open Innovation. *Journal of Open Innovation: Technology, Markets and Complexity, 4*(21). Retrieved from www.mdpi.com/journal/joitmc

Mobile phones are replacing bank accounts in Africa | IOL Business Report. (2019, August 14). Retrieved August 16, 2019, from BusinessReport website: https://www.iol.co.za/business-report/international/mobile-phones-are-replacing-bank-accounts-in-africa-30731499

Muth, J. F. (1986). 'Search theory and the manufacturing production function.' *Management Science, 32,* 948–962.

Nadin, S., & Williams, C. C. (2012). Blurring the formal/informal economy divide: Beyond a dual economies approach. *Journal of Economy and Its Applications, 2*(1), 85–103.

Peter, C. (2018, December). How African cities can harness green technologies for growth and jobs. *The Conversation.* Retrieved from https://theconversation.com/drafts/107722/edit

Peter, C. (2019, October 4). Sustaining the African Middle Class: Leveraging Green Technologies and the Fourth Industrial Revolution. *World Financial Review,* (September/October 2019), 29–33.

Pieterse, E. (2010). *City Futures: Confronting the Crisis of Urban Development* (2nd ed.). Zed Books.

Schumpeter, J. A. (1911). *The Theory of Economic Development. An Inquiry Into Profits, Capital, Credit, Interest and the Business Cycle.* Cambridge, MA: Harvard University Press.

Schumpeter, J. A. (1939). *Business Cycles: A Theoretical, Historical and Statistical Analysis of the Capitalist Process.* New York: McGraw-Hill Book Company.

Simone, A. M. (2001). On the wording of African cities. *African Studies Review, 44*(2), 15–41.

Smit, S., Musango, J. K., & Brent, A. C. (2019). Understanding electricity legitimacy dynamics in an urban informal settlement in South Africa: A Community Based System Dynamics approach. *Energy for Sustainable Development, 49,* 39–52.

South Africa's cheapest bank accounts: Capitec vs the rest. (2019, February 19). Retrieved August 16, 2019, from BusinessTech website: https://businesstech.co.za/news/banking/300452/south-africas-cheapest-bank-accounts-capitec-vs-the-rest/

Stangler, D., & Bell-Masterson, J. (2015). *Measuring an Entrepreneurial Ecosystem.* Kansas City, MO.

Swilling, M. (2010). *Africa 2050: Growth, resource productivity and decoupling.* International Panel for Sustainable Resource Management of the United Nations Environment Programme.

United Nations. (2008). *The State of African Cities Report 2008. A Framework for Addressing Urban Challenges in Africa.* Nairobi: United Nations Human Settlements Programme, UN HABITAT.

United Nations. (2010). *The State of African Cities 2010. Governance, Inequality and Urban Land Markets.* Nairobi: United Nations Human Settlements Programme, UN HABITAT.

United Nations. (2014). *The State of African Cities 2014. Reimagining Sustainable Urban Transitions.* Nairobi: United Nations Human Settlements Programme, UN HABITAT.

United Nations. (2019). *Economic Report on Africa 2019: Fiscal Policy for Financing Sustainable Development in Africa.* https://doi.org/10.18356/5d8e4ec9-en

Van de Ven, A., Polley, D. E., & Venkataraman, S. (1999). Building an Infrastructure for the Innovation Journey. In A. Van de Ven, D. E. Polley, & S. Venkataraman (Eds.), *The Innovation Journey* (pp. 149–180). New York: Oxford University Press.

Water, Food and Energy | UN-Water. (n.d.). Retrieved August 16, 2019, from https://www.unwater.org/water-facts/water-food-and-energy/

WEF. (2017, November). *Harnessing the Fourth Industrial Revolution for Sustainable Emerging Cities*. Fourth Industrial Revolution for the Earth Series, World Economic Forum, In Collaboration with PwC and Stanford Woods Institute for the Environment.

Wright, S. (1932). The Roles of Mutation, Inbreeding, Crossbreeding, and Selection in Evolution. *Proceedings of the Sixth International Congress on Genetics, Vol. I*, 356– 366.

Chapter 2

Accenture & World Economic Forum (2018). *Digital Transformation Initiative in collaboration with Accenture: Unlocking $100 Trillion for Business and Society from Digital Transformation*. Retrieved from: https://www.accenture.com/_acnmedia/accenture/conversion-assets/wef/pdf/accenture-dti-executive-summary.pdf

April, K. (2002). Guidelines for developing a k-strategy. *Journal of Knowledge Management, 6*(5), 445-456.

Baas, N. A., & Emmeche, C. (1997). On emergence and explanation. *Intellectica*, 25, 67-83. Retrieved from: https://www.persee.fr/docAsPDF/intel_0769-4113_1997_num_25_2_1558.pdf

Brooks, R. A. (1991). *Intelligence without Reason [MIT AI Memo 1293]*. Retrieved from: https://people.csail.mit.edu/brooks/papers/AIM-1293.pdf

Gell-Mann, M. (1994). *The quark and the jaguar* (2nd ed.). London: Little, Brown and Company.

Heylighen, F. & Lenartowicz, M. (2017). The Global Brain as a model of the future information society: An introduction to the special issue. *Technological Forecasting and Social Change, 114*(C): 1-6.

Holland, J.H. (1995). *Hidden order: How adaptation builds complexity*. Massachusetts: Addison-Wesley.

Karbalayghareh, A., Qian, X., & Dougherty, E.R. (2018). Optimal Bayesian Transfer Learning. *IEEE Transactions on Signal Processing, 66*(14), 3724 – 3739.

Minsky, M. (1988). *The Society of Mind* (First Touchstone ed.). New York: Simon & Schuster.

Odell, J. (1998). Agents and beyond: A flock is not a bird. *Distributed Computing*, 52–54. Retrieved from: http://www.jamesodell.com/publications.html

Pearl, J. (2019). *The Book of Why. The New Science of Cause and Effect* (1st ed.). New York, USA: Basic Books.

Pico-Valencia, Pablo, Holgado-Terriza, Juan A., Herrera-Sánchez, Deiver, & Sampietro, José. (2018). *Towards the internet of agents: an analysis of the internet of things from the intelligence and autonomy perspective. Ingeniería e Investigación, 38*(1), 121-129. Retrieved from: https://dx.doi.org/10.15446/ing.investig.v38n1.65638

Potgieter, A. & Bishop, J. (2001). *Bayesian agencies on the Internet. Proceedings of the 2001 International Conference on Intelligent Agents, Web Technologies and Internet Commerce (IAWTIC '2001).*

Nkala, T. (2019). 4IR: The good, the bad and the inequality gap. Retrieved from: https://www.dailymaverick.co.za/article/2019-07-04-4ir-the-good-the-bad-and-the-inequality-gap/

United Nations (2015). Transforming our World: The 2030 Agenda for Sustainable Development. Retrieved from: https://sustainabledevelopment.un.org/post2015/transformingourworld/publication

Chapter 3

Plaizier, W. (2016). *2 Truths About Africa's Agriculture*. Retrieved from: https://www.weforum.org/agenda/2016/01/how-africa-can-feed-the-world/

Eberhard, A., Rosnes, O., Shkaratan, M. & Vennemo, H. (2011). *Africa's Power Infrastructure: Investment, Integration, Efficiency.* Retrieved from: http://documents1.worldbank.org/curated/en/545641468004456928/pdf/613090PUB0Afri158344B09780821384558.pdf

Nwuneli, N.O. (2016). *Social Innovation In Africa: A practical guide for scaling impact (Routledge Studies in African Development).* London: Routledge.

Chapter 4

African Union. (2012). *Report of the Global African Diaspora Summit.* Report of the summit held on 25 May, Sandton, South Africa.

Alvarez, S., & Barney, J. (2007). Discovery and creation: Alternative theories of entrepreneurial action. *Strategic Entrepreneurship Journal, 1,* 11–26.

Atkinson, W. (2016). *Beyond Bourdieu- From genetic structuralism to relational phenomenology.* Cambridge, UK: Polity Press.

Betts, A., & Omata, N. (2015). *Refugee economies.* RSC Research in Brief 2, Refugee Studies Centre.

Blaser, C., & Landau, L. (2014). The governance of multiple elsewheres: Evaluating municipalities' response to mobility. *Trialog,* pp. 33–38.

Block, J., & Sandner, P. (2009). *Necessity and opportunity entrepreneurs and their duration in self-employment: Evidence from German micro data. SOEP papers on Multidisciplinary Panel Data Research.* SOEP papers on Multidisciplinary Panel Data Research No. 191, German Socio-Economic Panel Study (SOEP).

Bourdieu, P. (1985). The social space and the genesis of groups. *Theory and Society, 14*(6), 723–744.

Bourdieu, P. (1988). *Homo Academicus.* Cambridge, UK: Polity Press.

Chrysostome, E. (2010). The success factors of necessity immigrant entrepreneurs: In search of a model. *Thunderbird International Business Review, 52*(2), 137–152.

Chunnett, W. (2018). A model for the utilisation of networks and leveraging of the economic benefits of migration capital in emerging markets (Unpublished doctoral dissertation). University of Cape Town, Cape Town.

Crush, J. (2009). The South African diaspora and the diaspora in South Africa. In *International Conference on Diaspora and Development.* Presentation at International Conference on Diaspora and Development, 13-14 July 2009.

Department_of_Home_Affairs. Immigration Act, 2002 (Act No.13 of 2002), Global Education Magazine 1–16 (2014).

Fielden, A. (2008). *Local integration: An under-reported solution to protracted refugee situations. Policy Development and Evaluation Service, UNHCR.* Research Paper No. 158, New Issues in Refugee Research, UNHCR.

Handmaker, J. (2001). No easy walk: Advancing refugee protection in South Africa. *Africa Today, 48*(3), 91–113.

Handmaker, J., de la Hunt, L. A., & Klaaren, J. (Eds.). (2011). *Advancing refugee protection in South Africa.* New York, NY: Berghahn Books.

Herrington, M., Kew, J., & Kew, P. (2014). *South Africa: The crossroads – a goldmine or a time bomb?* GEM South Africa Report, Global Enterpreneurship Monitor.

Homans, G. C. (1958). Social behavior as exchange. *American Journal of Sociology, 63*(6), 597–606.

Kavuro, C. (2015a). Refugees and asylum seekers: Barriers to accessing South Africa's labour market. *Law Democracy & Development, 19,* 232–260.

Kloosterman, R., & Rath, J. (2002). Working on the fringes: Immigrant businesses economic integration and informal practices. *Invandrares Foretagande,* 27–38.

Landau, L., & Amit, R. (2014). Wither policy? Southern African perspectives on understanding law, "refugee" policy and protection. *Journal of Refugee Studies, 27*(4), 534–552.

Lucas, R. E. B. (2004). *International migration regimes and economic development*. Third Coordination Meeting on International Migration, UN Department of Economic and Social Affairs, New York, 27-28 October.

Maystadt, J.-F., & Verwimp, P. (2014). Winners and losers among a refugee-hosting population. *Economic Development and Cultural Change, 62*(4), 769–802.

McMillan, J., & Woodruff, C. (2003). The central role of entrepeneurs in transition economies. In G. S. Fields & G. Pfeffermann (Eds.), *Pathways out of povery* (pp. 105–121). Netherlands: Springer.

Ministry: Finance Republic of South Africa. (2008). South African Women in Dialogue Forum (SAWID). Retrieved from: http://www.treasury.gov.za/comm_media/speeches/2008/2008092901.pdf

Nail , T. (2015). *The figure of the migrant*. Stanford, CA: Stanford University Press.

Orozco, M. (2008). Diasporas and development: Issues and impediments. In J. Brinkerhoff (Ed.), (pp. 207–230). Boulder, CO: Lynne Rienner.

Parker, L. (2013). *Upholding refugee rights: Cessation, transnationalism and law's limitations in the Rwandan case*. (SIHMA Wokring Paper) Scalabrini Institute for Human Mobility in Africa, Cape Town, South Africa.

Rwakaringi, M. (2017, January 27). Uganda gives refugees hope. *Mail & Guardian*, pp. 18–19.

SEDA. (2017). SEDA. Retrieved September 5, 2017, from www.seda.org.za

Silinda, G. (2008). The development of the Caravan Model of poverty eradication. In *South African Women in Dialogue*.

Smit, R., & Rugunanan, P. (2014). From precarious lives to precarious work: The dilemma facing refugees in Gauteng, South Africa. *South African Review of Sociology, 45*(2), 37–41.

UN High Commissioner for Refugees. (2015). *Universal Periodic Review: 3rd Cycle, 27th Session, Republic of South Africa*.

Verwimp, P., & Maystadt, J.-F. (2015). *Forced displacement and refugees in Sub-Saharan Africa: An economic inquiry. Policy Reserach Working Paper 7517*. (WPS7517) Policy Research Working Paper, World Bank.

Verwimp, P., & van Bavel, J. (2013). Schooling, gender and violent conflict in Burundi. *World Bank Economic Review, 28*(2), 384–411.

Waldinger, R., Aldrich, H., & Ward, R. (1990). *Ethnic entrepreneurs: Immigrant business in industrial societies. Sage Series on Race and Ethnic Relations*. London, UK: Sage.

Wellman, B., & Berkowitz, S. (1988). *Social structures: A network approach*. Cambridge, UK: Cambridge University Press.

Whitaker, B. E. (2002). Refugees in western Tanzania: The distribution of burdens and benefits among local hosts. *Journal of Refugee Studies, 15*(4), 339–358.

Zetter, R. (2012). Are refugees an economic burden or benefit? *Forced Migration, 41*, 50–52.

Chapter 5

Aernoudt, R. (1999). Business angels: should they fly on their own wings? *Venture Capital: An International Journal of Entrepreneurial Finance*, 1(2), 187-195.

Bastin, J. F., Finegold, Y., Garcia, C., Mollicone, D., Rezende, M., Routh, D., Zohner, C.M. & Crowther, T. W. (2019). The global tree restoration potential. *Science*, 365(6448), 76-79.

Benford, R. D., & Snow, D. A. 2000. Framing processes and social movements: An overview and assessment. *Annual Review of Sociology*, 611-639.

Czarniawska, B. (2004). On time, space, and action nets. *Organization*, 11(6), 773.

Geels, F., & Raven, R. 2006. Non-linearity and expectations in niche-development trajectories: ups and downs in Dutch biogas development (1973–2003). *Technology Analysis & Strategic Management, 18*(3-4), 375-392.

Goffman, E. (1974). *Frame analysis: An essay on the organization of experience*: Harvard University Press.

Harmaline, S. S., Sarasvathy, S. D., & Freeman, R. E. (2009). Related debates in ethics and entrepreneurship: Values, opportunities, and contingency. *Journal of Business Ethics, 84*(3), 341-365.

Hayton, J. C., George, G., & Zahra, S. A. (2002). National culture and entrepreneurship: A review of behavioral research. *Entrepreneurship theory and practice, 26*(4), 33-52.

Jacobsson, S., & Bergek, A. (2004). Transforming the energy sector: the evolution of technological systems in renewable energy technology. *Industrial and corporate change, 13*(5), 815-849.

Kemp, R., Rip, A., & Schot, J. (2001). Constructing transition paths through the management of niches. *Path dependence and creation*: 269-299.

Kemp, R., Rotmans, J., & Loorbach, D. (2007). Assessing the Dutch energy transition policy: how does it deal with dilemmas of managing transitions? *Journal of Environmental Policy & Planning, 9*(3-4), 315-331.

Kemp, R., Schot, J., & Hoogma, R. (1998). Regime shifts to sustainability through processes of niche formation: the approach of strategic niche management. *Technology Analysis & Strategic Management, 10*(2), 175-198.

King, B. G., & Pearce, N. A. (2010). The contentiousness of markets: politics, social movements, and institutional change in markets. *Annual Review of Sociology*, 36, 249-267.

Lounsbury, M., Ventresca, M., & Hirsch, P. M. (2003). Social movements, field frames and industry emergence: a cultural–political perspective on US recycling. *Socio-Economic Review, 1*(1), 71-104.

Negro, S. O., Hekkert, M. P., & Smits, R. E. (2007). Explaining the failure of the Dutch innovation system for biomass digestion—a functional analysis. *Energy Policy, 35*(2), 925-938.

Miles, M. B., & Huberman, A. M. (1994). *Qualitative data analysis. 2. Aufl.,* Thousand Oaks et al.

Rao, H. 2009. *Market rebels: How activists make or break radical innovations*: Princeton University Press

Raven, R. P. J. M., & Geels, F. W. (2010). Socio-cognitive evolution in niche development: Comparative analysis of biogas development in Denmark and the Netherlands (1973–2004). *Technovation, 30*(2), 87-99.

Rip, A., & Kemp, R. (1998). *Technological Change. In: Rayner S., Malone EL (editors)*: Battelle Press.

Schipper, M (2013) *Businessmodel voor Samen Stoken op Streekhout,* Bachelor Thesis
    University Twente.

Schot, J., & Geels, F. W. (2008). Strategic niche management and sustainable innovation journeys: theory, findings, research agenda, and policy. *Technology Analysis & Strategic Management, 20*(5), 537-554.

Scott, W. R., Ruef, M., Mendel, P., & Caronna, C. A. (2000). *Institutional change and organizations: Transformation of a healthcare field*. Chicago: University of Chicago.

Sengers, F., Raven, R., & Van Venrooij, A. (2010). From riches to rags: Biofuels, media discourses, and resistance to sustainable energy technologies. *Energy Policy, 38*(9), 5013-5027.

Sine, W. D., & Lee, B. H. (2009). Tilting at windmills? The environmental movement and the emergence of the US wind energy sector. *Administrative Science Quarterly, 54*(1), 123.

Smith, A., & Raven, R. (2012). What is protective space? Reconsidering niches in transitions to sustainability. *Research Policy, 41*(6), 1025-1036.

Snow, D. A., & Benford, R. D. (1988). Ideology, frame resonance, and participant mobilization. *International social movement research, 1*(1), 197-217.

Snow, D. A., Rochford Jr, E. B., Worden, S. K., & Benford, R. D. (1986). Frame alignment processes, micromobilization, and movement participation. *American Sociological Review*, 464-481.

Tarrow, S. G. (2011). *Power in movement: Social movements and contentious politics*. Cambridge University Press.

Unruh, G. C. (2000). Understanding carbon lock-in. *Energy policy, 28*(12), 817-830.

Van den Broek, T. A., Ehrenhard, M. L., Langley, D. J., & Groen, A. J. (2012). Dotcauses for sustainability: combining activism and entrepreneurship. *Journal of Public Affairs*, *12*(3), 214-223.

Van der Laak, W., Raven, R., & Verbong, G. (2007). Strategic niche management for biofuels: Analysing past experiments for developing new biofuel policies. *Energy Policy*, *35*(6), 3213-3225.

Vasileiadou, E., Huijben, J. C. C. M., & Raven, R. P. J. M. (2016). Three is a crowd? Exploring the potential of crowdfunding for renewable energy in the Netherlands. *Journal of Cleaner Production*, *128*, 142-155.

Verbong, G., & Geels, F. (2007). The ongoing energy transition: Lessons from a socio- technical, multi-level analysis of the Dutch electricity system (1960–2004). *Energy Policy*, *35*(2), 1025-1037.

Verhees, B., Raven, R., Kern, F., & Smith, A. (2015). The role of policy in shielding, nurturing and enabling offshore wind in The Netherlands (1973–2013). *Renewable and Sustainable Energy Reviews*, *47*, 816-829

Weber, K., Heinze, K. L., & DeSoucey, M. (2008). Forage for thought: Mobilizing codes in the movement for grass-fed meat and dairy products. *Administrative Science Quarterly*, *53*(3), 529.

Chapter 6

Africa World Press (2019). *About us*. Retrieved from: http://africaworldpressbooks.com/about-us/

Amnesty International (2017). *Investigate Shell for complicity in murder, rape and torture*. Retrieved from: https://www.amnesty.org/en/latest/news/2017/11/investigate-shell-for-complicity-in-murder-rape-and-torture/

AVERT. (2018a). *Prevention of mother-to-child transmission*. Retrieved from: https://www.avert.org/professionals/hiv-programming/prevention/prevention-mother-child

AVERT (2018b). *HIV and AIDS in South Africa*. Retrieved from: https://www.avert.org/professionals/hiv-around-world/sub-saharan-africa/south-africa

Bennis, W. G., & Nanus, B. (2007). *Leaders: The strategies for taking charge* (2nd ed.). New York, NY: Harper & Row.

Boseley, Sarah (2008). *Mbeki Aids denial 'caused 300,000 deaths'*. Guardian. Retrieved from: https://www.theguardian.com/world/2008/nov/26/aids-south-africa

Brighton Museums (2015). "Kalabari Masquerade". Retrieved from: https://brightonmuseums.org.uk/discover/2015/02/26/kalabari-masquerade/

Calderon, A. (2018). *The higher education landscape is changing fast*. University World News. Retrieved from: https://www.universityworldnews.com/post.php?story=2018062208555853

Chigwedere, P., Seage, G., Gruskin, S., Lee, T. & Essex, M. (2008). Estimating the Lost Benefits of Antiretroviral Drug Use in South Africa. *Journal of Acquired Immune Deficiency Syndromes*, *49*(4), 410-415. Retrieved from: https://journals.lww.com/jaids/Fulltext/2008/12010/Estimating_the_Lost_Benefits_of_Antiretroviral.10.aspx

Chugh, D. (2018). *The person you mean to be: confronting Bias to Build a Better Workplace and World*. New York: HarperCollins.

Cisco (2019). *Cisco Visual Networking Index: Forecast and Trends, 2017–2022*. White Paper. Retrieved from: https://www.cisco.com/c/en/us/solutions/collateral/service-provider/visual-networking-index-vni/white-paper-c11-741490.html

Communicare LLC. (2019). *What we do*. Retrieved from: https://www.aaccommunicare.com/what-we-do

Crayford, S. (1996). The Ogoni Uprising: oil, human rights and a democratic alternative in Nigeria. *Africa Today*, *3*(42), 183-197.

Cullinan, K. (2000). *Campaign for cheap drugs from Thailand*. Health E-News. Retrieved from: https://www.health-e.org.za/2000/07/14/campaign-for-cheap-drugs-from-thailand/

Diaspora Pavilion. (2017). *All the World Is Now Richer Meets the Woman Who Refused to Dance*. Retrieved from: https://www.seditionart.com/sokari-douglas-camp/all-the-world-is-now-richer-meets-the-woman-who-refused-to-dance

Dolan, S., Garcia, S., & Richley, B. (2006). *Managing by Values: A corporate guide to living, being alive and making a living in the 21ˢᵗ century.* New York: Palgrave Macmillan.

Meeker, M. (2018). *Internet trends, 2018.* Retrieved from: https://www.kleinerperkins.com/internet-trends

Heywood, M. (2009). South Africa's Treatment Action Campaign: Combining Law and Social Mobilization to Realize the Right to Health. *Journal of Human Rights Practice, 1*(1), 14-36.

Houghton, G. (2016). *Primavera: Sokari Douglas Camp C.B.E.* London, October Gallery. Retrieved from: http://www.octobergallery.co.uk/bookstore/sokari_catalogue_2016.pdf

Lewis, P. (1996). Blood and Oil: A Special Report. After Nigeria Represses, Shell Defends Its Record. *New York Times.* Retrieved from: https://www.nytimes.com/1996/02/13/world/blood-and-oil-a-special-report-after-nigeria-represses-shell-defends-its-record.html

Mbali, M. (2003). *HIV/AIDS policy-making in post-apartheid South Africa.* 318-320 in Daniel, J, Habib, A & Southall R, *State of the Nation: South Africa, 2003-2004.* Cape Town: Human Sciences Research Council Press.

Mbali, M. (2005*). The Treatment Action Campaign and the history of rights-based, patient-driven HIV/AIDS activism in South Africa.* Centre for Civil Society, University of KwaZulu-Natal, Research Report 29. Retrieved from: http://ccs.ukzn.ac.za/files/RReport_29.pdf

McNamara, C. (2012). *What are values, morals, and ethics?* Retrieved from: https://managementhelp.org/blogs/business-ethics/2012/01/02/what-are-values-morals-and-ethics/ .

Mignolo, W.D. (2011). *The Darker Side of Western Modernity: Global Futures, Decolonial Options.* Durham, Duke University Press.

McAfee, A., & Brynjolfson, E. (2017). *Machine, Platform Crowd: Harnessing our Digital Future.* New York, W.W. Norton.

MOSOP. (1991). *The Ogoni Bill of Rights.* Retrieved from: http://www.bebor.org/wp-content/uploads/2012/09/Ogoni-Bill-of-Rights.pdf

October Gallery. (2019). *Sokari Douglas Camp.* Retrieved from: http://www.octobergallery.co.uk/artists/sokari/index.shtml

Olin, M. (2012). *Touching Photographs.* Chicago: University of Chicago Press.

Northouse, P. (2019). *Leadership: Theory and Practice.* London, SAGE Publications.

PharmaLetter. (2000). *Pfizer plans to give fluconazole free to South African AIDS patients.* Retrieved from: https://www.thepharmaletter.com/article/pfizer-plans-to-give-fluconazole-free-to-south-african-aids-patients

Platform. (2018). *Update: The Bus, its seizure and our story.* Retrieved from: https://platformlondon.org/2018/05/14/update-the-bus-its-seizure-and-our-story/

Porter, M.E., & Kramer, M.R. (2011). Creating shared value. *Harvard Business Review, 89*(1-2), 62-77.

Rustin, S. (2015). *Ken Saro-Wiwa memorial art bus denied entry to Nigeria.* Guardian. Retrieved from: https://www.theguardian.com/environment/2015/nov/05/ken-saro-wiwa-memorial-art-bus-denied-entry-to-nigeria

Shell Nigeria. (2018). *Shell debunks Amnesty allegations on spills management in Niger Delta.* Retrieved from: https://www.shell.com.ng/media/2018-media-releases/shell-debunks-amnesty-allegations.html

Sokari Douglas Camp. (2019). *About Sokari.* Retrieved from: https://sokari.co.uk/about/

Sontag, S. (1977). *On Photography.* London: Penguin.

UNEP. (2011). *Environmental Assessment of Ogoniland.* United Nations Environment Programme, Nairobi. Retrieved from: https://wedocs.unep.org/bitstream/handle/20.500.11822/25282/ogoniland_chapter1_UNEP_OEA.pdf?sequence=1&isAllowed=y

Chapter 7

Akyeampong, E. (2018). African socialism; or, the search for an indigenous model of economic development? *Economic History of Developing Regions, 33*(1), 69-87. doi:10.1080/20780389.2018.1434411.

Armstrong, A. (forthcoming). Stokvels: A South African Innovation in Economic Justice for Women. In *Solidarity Banking & Invincible Women: Understanding the Worldwide Phenomenon of ROSCAs*, Caroline Shenaz Hossein (ed.).

B Corporation (2018a). *About B Corps.* Retrieved from: https://bcorporation.net/about-b-corps.

B Corporation (2018b) Certification Requirements, Retrieved July 4, 2019. Retrieved from: https://bcorporation.net/certification/meet-the-requirements.

B Corporation (2018c), ME to WE. Retrieved July 13, 2019. Retrieved from: https://bcorporation.net/directory/me-to-we.

B Corporation. (2018d). Oliberte Limited. Retrieved July 13, 2019. Retrieved from: https://bcorporation.net/directory/oliberte-limited.

Bogdanich, W., & Forsythe, M. (2018, June 26). *How McKinsey Lost Its Way in South Africa.* Retrieved July 13, 2019. Retrieved from: https://www.nytimes.com/2018/06/26/world/africa/mckinsey-south-africa-eskom.html.

Coen Gilbert, J. (2018). *Are B Corps An Elite Charade For Changing The World?* Retrieved July 13, 2019. Retrieved from: https://www.forbes.com/sites/jaycoengilbert/2018/08/30/are-b-corps-an-elite-charade-for-changing-the-world-part-1/.

Deribe, K., Kebede, B., Mengistu, B., Negussie, H., Sileshi, M., Tamiru, M., ... Fentaye, A. (2017). Podoconiosis in *Ethiopia: From Neglect to Priority Public Health Problem.* Retrieved July 13, 2019. Retrieved from: https://www.ncbi.nlm.nih.gov/pmc/articles/PMC5582632/.

Giridharadas, A. (2018). *Winners take all: The elite charade of changing the world* [Kobo]. New York: Alfred A. Knopf.

Oliberté (2019) *Goodbye Ethiopia.* Retrieved July 13, 2019. Retrieved from: https://www.oliberte.com/pages/goodbye-ethiopia/.

Honeyman, R. (2014). *B Corp Handbook:How to Use Business as a Force for Good* [Kindle]. S.l.: Berrett-Koehler. Retrieved July 13, 2019.

Kerr, J. (2018, October 15). *Craig Kielburger Founded WE to Fight Child Labour. Now the WE Brand Promotes Products Made By Children.* Retrieved July 13, 2019. Retrieved from: https://www.canadalandshow.com/craig-kielburger-founded-we-to-fight-child-labour-now-the-we-brand-promotes-products-made-by-children/.

Kerr, J. (n.d.). *Inside The "Cult"of Kielburger.* Retrieved July 13, 2019. Retrieved from: https://www.reddit.com/r/onguardforthee/comments/c59yi3/new_canadaland_investigation_inside_the_cult_of/.

Leke, A., Chironga, M., & Desvaux, G. (2018). *Africa's business revolution how to succeed in the world's next big growth market.* Boston, MA: Harvard Business Review Press.

Maritz, J. (2018). *How we made it in Africa: Learn from the stories of 25 entrepreneurs who've built thriving businesses* [Kindle]. Cape Town: Maritz Africa. Retrieved July 13, 2019.

Muiru, O. W. (2019). The B Movement in East Africa: A shift in the culture of business. *African Evaluation Journal, 7*(1). doi:10.4102/aej.v7i1.333.

Norton, L. (2018). *BlackRock's Larry Fink: The Conscience of Wall Street?* Barrons, June 23, Retrieved January 7 2019. Retrieved from: https://www.barrons.com/articles/in-defense-of-social-purpose-1529716548.

Oxford Reference. (2017). *Repressive tolerance.* Retrieved July 13, 2019. Retrieved from: https://www.oxfordreference.com/view/10.1093/oi/authority.20110803100414515.

Pisanello, L. (2018, October 15). *B-Corp businesses can be a force for good.* Sandton Chronicle, Retrieved July 13, 2019. Retrieved from: https://sandtonchronicle.co.za/212071/b-corp-businesses-can-be-a-force-for-good.

Schwabel, D. (2017). *Unilever's Paul Polman: Why Today's Leaders Need to Commit to Purpose*, Forbes, Retrieved January 7 2019. Retrieved from: https://www.forbes.com/sites/danschawbel/2017/11/21/paul-polman-why-todays-leaders-need-to-commit-to-a-purpose/#541c3dbf1276.

Silverthorne, S. (2011). *Rethinking the Purpose of Business: Why 'Maximizing Shareholder Value' hasn't Worked*, CBS News, June 7, Retrieved January 7 2019. Retrieved from: https://www.cbsnews.com/news/rethinking-the-purpose-of-business-why-maximize-shareholder-value-hasnt-worked/.

The B Economy (2019). *B Economy*, Retrieved July 1, 2019 from https://bcorporation.net/b-economy.

Tsele, L. (2017). *10 'Founderisms' From the Founders Of One Of Africa's Hottest Startups.* Retrieved July 13, 2019. Retrieved from: https://smesouthafrica.co.za/17410/Zoona-Startup-Quotes/

Zoona. (2018). *Zoona "ISMS".* Retrieved July 13, 2019. Retrieved from: https://issuu.com/zoonatransactionsafrica/docs/zoona_isms

Zoona. (2019a). *About Us.* Retrieved July 13, 2019. Retrieved from: https://ilovezoona.com/about-us/

Zoona. (2019b). *Business Timeline.* Retrieved July 13, 2019. Retrieved from: https://ilovezoona.com/

Zoona. (2019c). *Home.* Retrieved July 13, 2019. Retrieved from: https://ilovezoona.com/about-us/

Chapter 9

Blank, S. (2013) *The Four Steps to the Epiphany. 2nd edn.* California: K&S Ranch.

Hacket, S.M., & Dilts, D.M. (2004) A Systemic Review of Business Incubation Research. *'Journal of Technology Transfer.'* 29, 55-82. Retrieved from: at: https://link.springer.com/article/10.1023/B:JOTT.0000011181.11952.0f

Miller, P., & Stacey, J. (2014) *Good Incubation: The Craft of Supporting Early-stage Social Ventures.* London: Nesta.

Chapter 10

Bachmann, C., Habisch, A. & Dierksmeier, C. (2017). Practical wisdom: management's no longer forgotten virtue. *Journal of Business Ethics, 153*(1), 147-165.

Christensen, C. (2016). *The innovator's dilemma: when new technologies cause great firms to fail.* Boston: Harvard Business Review Press.

Christensen, C., Ojomo, E., & Dillon, K. (2019). *The Prosperity Paradox. How Innovation can Lift Nations Out of Poverty.* Cambridge: Cambridge University Press.

Christensen, C.M., Ojomo,E. & Dillon, K. (2019). *The prosperity paradox: How innovation can lift nations out of poverty.* New York: Harper Business.

Ghoshal, S. (2005). Bad Management Theories Are Destroying Good Management Practice. *Academy of Management Learning & Education, 4*(1) 75-91.

Ghoshal, S., 2005. Bad management theories are destroying good management practices. *Academy of Management Learning & Education, 4* (1), 101-103.

Habisch, A. & Schmidpeter, R. (2017). *Cultural Roots of sustainable management. Practical Wisdom and Corporate Social Responsibility.* Switzerland: Springer International Publishing.

Hirschman, A.O. (1958). *The Strategy of Economic Development.* New Haven: Yale University Press.

Jensen, M.C. & Meckling, W.H. (1976). Theory of the firm: managerial behavior, agency costs and ownership structure. *Journal of Financial Economics, 3*(4), 305-306.

Khurana, R. (2007). *From Higher Aims to Hired Hands: The Social Transformation of American Business Schools and the Unfulfilled Promise of Management as a Profession.* Princeton, NJ: Princeton University Press.

Pfeffer, J. & Fong, C. T. (2002). The end of business schools? Less success than meets the eye. *Academy of Management Learning & Education, 1*(1), 78-95.

Rakesh, K. (2007). *From Higher Aims to Hired Hands: The Social Transformation of American Business Schools and the Unfulfilled Promise of Management as a Profession.* Princeton, N.J.: Princeton University Press, 2007.

Schmitt-Lord, T.V., Beissel von Gymnich, J., & Habisch, A. (2017). *The Beauty of Impact Health.* Munich: Knesebeck.

Chapter 11

Alter, S.K. (2006). Social enterprise models and their mission and money relationships. In A. Nicholls (Ed.). *Social Entrepreneurship: New models of sustainable social change.* (205-232). New York: Oxford University Press.

Boyd, S. (2017). Examining the relationship between organization development and social change in traditional business organizations through the lens of positive institutional work: An exploratory case study of inclusive manufacturing operations at Ergoform (Master's dissertation, University of Cape Town Graduate School of Business, Cape Town, South Africa). Retrieved from http://gsblibrary.uct.ac.za/researchreports/2017/Boyd.pdf.

Dennehy, M. (2018). On purpose: leading job-shop manufacturing at Shonaquip social enterprise – a teaching case study (Master's dissertation, University of Cape Town Graduate School of Business, Cape Town, South Africa). Retrieved from http://gsblibrary.uct.ac.za/researchreports/2018/Dennehy.pdf.

DiMaggio, P., & Powell, W. (1983). The iron cage revisited: institutional isomorphism and collective rationality in organizational fields. *American Sociological Review, 48,* 147-160.

Dorado, S., Ventresca, M. (2013). Crescive entrepreneurship in complex social problems: Institutional conditions for entrepreneurial engagement. *Journal of Business Venturing, 28,* 69-82.

Edmondson, A. (1999). Psychological safety and learning behaviour in work teams. *Administrative Science Quarterly, 44*(2), 350-383.

Edmondson, A., Bohmer, R., & Pisano, G. (2001). Disrupted routines: Team learning and new technology implementation in hospitals. *Administrative Science Quarterly, 46.*

Edmondson, A. (2019). The fearless organization. Hoboken, NJ: John Wiley & Sons.

Hvenmark, J. (2016). Ideology, practice, and process: A review of the concept of managerialism in civil society studies. *Voluntas, 27,* 2833-2859.

Kuratko, D., Hornsby, J., & McMullen, J. (2011). Corporate entrepreneurship with a purpose: Exploring the antecedents to social business.

Maier, F., Meyer, M., & Steinbereithner, M. (2016). Nonprofit organizations becoming business-like: A systemic review. *Nonprofit and Voluntary Sector Quarterly, 45*(1), 64-86.

Melnik, E., Petrella, F., & Richez-Battestia, N. (2013). Does the professionalism of management practices in nonprofits and for-profits affect job satisfaction? *The International Journal of Human Resource Management, 24*(6), 1300-1321.

Munthali, P. (2017). Business model innovation for social enterprises in bottom-of-the-pyramid contexts: the case of Vitalite Zambia (Master's dissertation, University of Cape Town Graduate School of Business, Cape Town, South Africa). Retrieved from http://gsblibrary.uct.ac.za/researchreports/2017/Munthali.pdf.

Nicholls, A. (Ed.). (2006). *Social Entrepreneurship: New models of sustainable social change.* New York: Oxford University Press.

Nicholls, A., & Cho, A.H. (2006). Social entrepreneurship: The structuration of a field. In A., Nicholls (Ed.). *Social Entrepreneurship: New models of sustainable social change.* (99-118). New York: Oxford University Press.

Perumal, V. (2016). Vitalite Zambia Ltd.: The intersection of solar energy technology and mobile money in Zambia (Master's dissertation, University of Cape Town Graduate School of Business, Cape Town, South Africa). Retrieved from http://gsblibrary.uct.ac.za/researchreports/2016/Perumal.pdf.

Storchi, A. (2018). Critical analysis of Grameen Danone Food LTD case as a model of sustainable private-NGO joint venture. Thesis: University of Manchester.

Yunus, M. (2006). Social business entrepreneurs are the solution. In A., Nicholls (Ed.). *Social Entrepreneurship: New models of sustainable social change.* (39-44). New York: Oxford University Press.

Chapter 12

Acs, Z. J., & Stough, R. R. (2008). Introduction to Public Policy in an Entrepreneurial Society. In Z. J. Acs, & R. R. Stough, *Public Policy in an Entrepreneurial Economy: Creating Conditions for Business Growth.* New York: Springer Science and Busin.

Acs, Z., & Virgil, N. (2009, March). Entrepreneurship in Developing Countries. *Jena Economic Research Papers,* 1 - 73. Jena, Jena, Germany: Friedrich Schiller University and the Max Planck Institute of Economics. Retrieved March 14, 2018, from Econstor: https://www.econstor.eu/handle/10419/31789

Acs, Z., Arenius, P., Hay, M., & Minitti, M. (2005). *GEM Global Report.* Global Entrepreneurship Monitor.

Adegbite, O. (2001). Business Incubators and Small Enterprise Development: The Nigerian Experience. *Small Business Economics,* 157 - 166. Retrieved from https://link.springer.com/content/pdf/10.1023%2FA%3A1011801018398.pdf

Alberto-Morant, G., & Oghazi, P. (2016). How Useful are Incubators for New Entrepreneurs. *Journal of Business Research, 69*(2016), 2125 - 2129. doi:https://doi.org/10.1016/j.jbusres.2015.12.019

Aliaga-Isla, R. (2014). Immigrants' perception of business opportunities in Spain: the impact of general and specific human capital. *Revista Brasileira de Gestão de Negócios, 16*(52), 416-433. doi:10.7819/rbgn.v16i52.1615

Allahar, H., & Brathwaite, C. (2016). Business Incubation as an Istrument of Inovation: The Experience of South America and the Carabbean. *International Journal of Innovation,* 71 - 86. doi:http://dx.doi.org/10.5585/iji.v4i2.107

Al-Mubaraki, H., & Busler, M. (2010). Business incubators: Findings from worldwide survey, and guidance for the G.C.C states, Vol. 11(1), *Global Business Review, 11*(1).

Amezcua, A. S. (2010). Performance Analysis of Entrepreneurship Policy: Which Business Incubators Generate the Highest Levels of Economic Performance? *Frontiers of Entrepreneurship Research, 30*(18).

Baron, A. &. (2007). *Human Capital Management: Achieving Added Value Through People.* London: Kogan Page Limited.

Becker, G. (1993). *Human Capital .* Chicago/London: The University of Chicago Press.

Bhabra-Remedios, R.K., C. B. (2003). Cracks in the Egg: improving performance measures in business incubator. *16th Annual Conference of Small Enterprise Association of Australia and New Zealand, 28 September -1 October 2003.*

Bhatli, D., Borella, P., Jelassi, T., & Saillant, N. (2015). Startup Accelerators: Entrepreneurial Match Makers. In K. Kubacki (Ed.), *The Academy of Marketing Science.* Springer, Cham. doi:org/10.1007/978-3-319-10951-0_92

Bliemel, M., & Flores, R. (2015). Defining and differentiating accelerators: Insights from the Australian context. *UNSW Business School Research Paper* (pp. 1–23). Vancouver, BC: Academy of Management.

Bliemel, M., Flores, R., de Clerk, S., Miles, M., Costas, B., & Monteiro, P. (2016). The role and performance of accelerators in the Australian startup ecosystem. (pp. 1–65). *UNSW Business School Research Papers,* 1 - 65. Sydney, Australia: Department of Industry, Innovation and Science.

Boter, H., & Lundström, A. (2005). SME perspectives on business support services: The role of company size, industry and location. *Journal of Small Business and Enterprise Development, 12*(2).

Boudewyns, V. (2013). A Meta-Analystical Test of Perceived Behavioral Control Interactions in the Theory of Planned Behavior. *Dissertation submitted to the Faculty of the Graduate School of the University of Maryland*, 1 - 265. College Park, Maryland, USA: University of Maryland. Retrieved March 18, 2018, from https://drum.lib.umd.edu/bitstream/handle/1903/13973/Boudewyns_umd_0117E_13960.pdf;sequence=1

Briggs, K. A. (2016). *Travels of Business Incubators: Exploring Entrepreneurship Support from an Embeddedness Perspective in Uganda and Tanzania.* Gothenburg: Chalmers University of Technology. Retrieved 03 29, 2018, from http://publications.lib.chalmers.se/records/fulltext/237892/237892.pdf

Bushe, B. (2019, July 17). The causes of and impact of business failure in South Africa. *Africa's Public Service Delivery and Performance Review*, 1-26.

Centre for Digital Entrepreneurship and Economic Performence. (2015). *Evaluating Business Accelleration and Incubation in Canada: Policy, Practice and Impact.* Centre for Digital Entrepreneurship and Economic Performence. Waterloo, Ontario: DEEP Centre. Retrieved March 30, 2018, from http://deepcentre.com/wordpress/wp-content/uploads/2015/10/DEEP-Centre-BABI-1-Taxonomy-and-Performance-Measurement-September-20151.pdf

Centre for Digital Entrepreneurship and Economic Performence. (2015). *Evaluating Business Accelleration and Incubation in Canada: Policy, Practice and Impact.* Centre for Digital Entrepreneurship and Economic Performence. Waterloo, Ontario: DEEP Centre. Retrieved March 30, 2018, from http://deepcentre.com/wordpress/wp-content/uploads/2015/10/DEEP-Centre-BABI-1-Taxonomy-and-Performance-Measurement-September-20151.pdf

Centre for Strategy and Evaluation Services (CSES). (2002). *Benchmarking of business incubators: Final report.* Centre for Strategy and Evaluation Services. CSES.

Chandra, A., & Chao, C.-A. (2016). Country Context and University Affiliation: A Comparative Study of Business Incubation in the United States and Brazil. *Journal of Technology Management and Innovation, 11*(2), 33 - 45. Retrieved 03 2018, 2018, from https://scielo.conicyt.cl/pdf/jotmi/v11n2/art04.pdf

Charry, G. P., Perez, J. E., & Barahona, N. E. (2014). Business incubator research: A Review and Future Directions. *pensamiento y gestión*, 41-65. doi:http://dx.doi.org/10.14482/pege.37.7020

Colombo, M., & Grilli, L. (2010). On Growth Drivers of High-Tech Start-ups: Exploring the Role of Founders' Human Capital and Venture Capital. *Journal of Business Venturing., 25*(2010), 610 - 626. Retrieved from On Growth Drivers of High-Tech Start-ups: Exploring the Role of Founders' Human Capital and Venture Capital.

Davidsson, P., & Benson, H. (2003). The Role of Social and Human Capital Among Nascent Entrepreneurs. *Journal Of Business Venturing, 18*(3), 301 - 331. Retrieved April 02, 2018, from http://eprints.qut.edu.au/5832/1/5832.pdf

Dempwolf, S. C., Auer, J., & D'Ippolito, M. (2014). *Innovation Accelerators: Defining Characteristics Among Startup Assistance Organizations.* Small Business Administration - Office of Advisory.

Denanyoh, R., Adjei, K., & Nyemekye, G. E. (2015). Factors That Impact on Entrepreneurial Intention of Tertiary Students in Ghana. *International Journal of Business and Social Research, 5*(3), 19 - 29. Retrieved from https://thejournalofbusiness.org/index.php/site/article/view/693/506

Douglus, E. J., & Shepherd, D. A. (1999). Entrepreneurship as a Utility Maximising Response. *Journal of Business Venturing*, 231 - 251.

dos Santos, J. F. (2015, August 04). *Why SMEs are key to growth in Africa.* Retrieved July 03, 2017, from World Economic Forum: https://www.weforum.org/agenda/2015/08/why-smes-are-key-to-growth-in-africa/

Estrin, S., Mickiewicz, T., & Stephan, U. (2016, May 29). Human Capital in Social and Commercial Entrepreneuship. *Journal of Business Venturing, 31*(2016), 449 - 467. Retrieved April 02, 2018

Ganamotse, G. (2013). *An Examination of of the Relationship Between Incubator Management Team Competencies and Successful Business Incubation: A Thesis Submitted for the Degree of Doctor of Philosophy in Entrepreneurship.* Essex: University of Essex.

Ganamotse, G. N., Samuelsson, M., Abankwah, R. M., Tibaingana, A., & Mphela, T. (2017). The Emerging Properties of Business Accelerators:The Case of Botswana, Namibia and Uganda Global Business Labs. *Journal of Entrepreneurship and Innovation in Emerging Economies, 3* (1), 1 - 25. SAGE Publications India Private Limited. doi:10.1177/2393957516684469

Gärling, T., & Fujii, S. (1999). Structural equation modeling of determinants of implementation intentions. *Göteborg Psychological Reports, 29*(4). Retrieved 3 18, 2018, from https://www.gu.se/digitalAssets/1286/1286051_gpr99_nr4.pdf

Gnyawali, D. R., & Fogel, D. S. (1994). Environments for Entrepreneurship Development Key Dimensions and Research Implications. *Entrepreneurship Theory and Practice,* 43 - 62.

Gupta, V. K., Turban, D. B., Wasti , A. S., & Sikdar, A. (2009, March). The Role of Gender Stereotypes in Perceptions of Entrepreneurs and Intentions to Become an Entrepreneur. *Entrepreneurship Theory and Practice.*

Hackett, S. M., & Dilts, D. (2004). A Systematic Review of Business Incubation Research. *The Journal of Technology Transfer.* doi:10.1023/B:JOTT.0000011181.11952.0f

Hallen, B. L., Bingham, C., & Cohen, S. (2016, July 8). *Do Accelerators Accelerate? If So, How? The Impact of Intensive Learning from Others on New Venture Development (July 8, 2016).* Retrieved from SSRN: http://ssrn.com/abstract=2719810

Henderson, R., & Robertson, M. (2000). Who wants to be an entrepreneur? Young adult attitudes to entrepreneurship as a career. *Career Development International, 5*(6), 279–287. doi:https://doi.org/10.1108/13620430010373755

Holmgren, C., & From, J. (2005). Taylorism of the Mind - Entrepreneurship Education from a perspective of Educational Research. *European Educational Research Journal, 4*(4), 382 - 390. Retrieved from https://www.bvekennis.nl/Bibliotheek/05-0986_EERJ_entrepreneurship.pdf

International Labour Organisation. (2015). *World Unemployment Social Outlook: Trends 2015.* Geneva: International Labour Organisation. Retrieved 03 08, 2018, from http://www.ilo.org/wcmsp5/groups/public/---dgreports/---dcomm/---publ/documents/publication/wcms_337069.pdf

Jekwu, L. O. (2016). Psychosocial Predictors of Entrepreneurial Intention Among Nigerian Graduates. *International Journal of Psychology and Counselling, 8*(6), 73 - 80. Retrieved 03 08, 2018, from http://academicjournals.org/journal/IJPC/article-full-text-pdf/107459158922

Katua, N. T. (2014). The Role of SMEs in Employment Creation and Economic Growth in Selected Countries. *International Journal of Education and Research, 2*(12), 461 - 472. Retrieved from www.ijern.com

Kropp, F., Lindsay, N. J., & Shoman, A. (2018, March 7). Entrepreneurial Orientation and International Entrepreneurship Business Venture Start-up. *International Journal of Entrepreneurial Behaviour and Research, 14*(2), 102 - 117.

Lalkaka, R., & Abetti, Pier. (2002, December). Business Incubation and Enterprise Support Systems in Restructuring Countries. *Creativity and Innovation Management, 8*(3), 197 - 209. doi:10.1111/1467-8691.00137

Langowitz, N., & Minniti, M. (2007). The Entrepreneurial Propensity of Women. *Entrepreneurship Theory and Practice,* 341 - 364.

Lose, T., & Tengeh, R. K. (2016). An evaluation of the effectiveness of business incubation programs: a user satisfaction approach. *Investment Management and Financial Innovations, 13*(2-2), 370 - 378. doi:10.21511/imfi.13(2-2).2016.12

Mahemba, C. M., & Lundström, A. (2005). SMEs perspectives on business support perspectives on business support services: The role of company size, industry and location. *Journal of Small Business Enterprise Development,* 244 - 258.

Mas-Verdu, F., Ribeiro-Soriano, D., & Roig-Tierno, N. (2015). Firm survival: The role of incubators and business characteristics. *Journal of Business Research, 68*(4), 793 - 796. doi:org/10.1016/j.jbusres.2014.11.030

Matanda, M. (N.D.). *Semantic Scholar.* Retrieved April 02, 2018, from https://pdfs.semanticscholar.org/9a9a/282ce425d376ac3d8aa08996e0f33300bd5d.pdf

McGuirk , H., Lenihan, H., & Hart, M. (2015). Measuring the impact of innovative human capital on small firms' Propensity to Inovate. *Research Policy, 44*(4), 965 - 976. doi:https://doi.org/10.1016/j.respol.2014.11.008

Meru, A. K., & Struwig, M. (2015). Business-incubation Process and Business Development in Kenya: Challenges and Recommendations. *Journal of Entrepreneurship and Innovation in Emerging Economies, 1*(1), 1 - 17. doi:10.1177/2393957514554982

Mitchell, B. (2004). Motives of Entrepreneurs: A Case Study of South Africa. *The Journal of Entrepreneurship, 13*(2), 168 - 183. Retrieved from http://journals.sagepub.com/doi/pdf/10.1177/097135570401300203

Mozzarol, T. (2015, August 1). Business Incubators and Start-up Accelerators: Valuable Assets or Waste of Time and Money. *Enterprise Society: The Role of Entrepreneurship, Innovation and Small Buisness in Society.* Retrieved from http://theconversation.com/business-incubators-and-start-up-accelerators-valuable-assets-or-a-waste-of-time-and-money-45551

Mwatsika, C. (2015). Entrepreneurship development and entrepreneurial orientation in rural areas in Malawi. *African Journal of Buisness Management,* 425 - 436. doi:https://doi.org/10.5897/AJBM2014.7552

OECD. (2017). *Meeting of the OECD Council at Ministerial Level ENHANCING THE CONTRIBUTIONS OF SMEs IN A GLOBAL AND DIGITALISED ECONOMY.* OECD.

Oh, D.-S. (2014). Business Incubation Strategy of High-Tech Venture Firms in a Science Park. In D.-S. Oh, & F. Phillips, *Technopolis: Best Practices for Science and Technology Cities* (pp. 145 - 167). LONDON: Springer. Retrieved June 12, 2017

Ozaralli, N., & Rivenburgh, N. K. (2016). Entrepreneurial Intention: Antecedents to Entrepreneurial Behavior in the U.S.A. and Turkey. *Journal of Global Entrepreneurship Research, 6*(3), 1 - 32. doi:10.1186/s40497-016-0047-

Passaro, R., Quinto, I., & Thomas, A. (2018). The Impact of Higher Education on Entrepreneurial Intention and Human Capital. *Journal of Interlectual Capital, 19*(1), 135 - 156. doi:https://doi.org/10.1108/JIC-04-2017-0056

Pauwels, C., Clarysse, B., Wright, M., & Hove, J. V. (2016). Understanding a new generation incubation model: The accelerator. *Technovation,* 13 - 24. Retrieved 09 01, 2017, from https://ac.els-cdn.com/S0166497215000644/1-s2.0-S0166497215000644-main.pdf?_tid=006e8475-46f9-4c74-b7e7-cc1bf91de60b&acdnat=1520513283_a9f6e5a4ce7c16c9a743948b7153a8b5

Popescu, C. C., Bostan, I., Robu, I.-B., Maxim, A., & Diaconu (Maxim), L. (2016). An Aanalysis of the Determinants of Entrepreneurial Intentions among Students: A Romanian Case Study. (M. A. Rosen, Ed.) *Sustainability: Sustainable Education and Approaches, 8*(8). doi:10.3390/su8080771

Popescu, C., & Diaconu, L. (2008). *Human Capital and Innovation.* Retrieved from SSRN: https://papers.ssrn.com/sol3/papers.cfm?abstract_id=1099025

Rachamania, I. N., Rakhamaniar, M., & Setyaningsih, S. (2012). Influencing Factors of Entrepreneurial Development in Indonesia. *International Conference on Small and Medium Enterprises Development with a Theme. 4,* pp. 234 - 243. Bandung, Indonesia: Elsevier Ltd. doi:10.1016/S2212-5671(12)00338-3

Ratinho, T. H. (2010). Are Business Incubators Helping? The Role of BIs in Facilitating Tenants' Development. *Academy of Management Annual Meeting 2010 : Dare to Care: Passion and Compassion in Management Practice and Research,. 6-10 August 2010.* Montreal, Canada: University of Twente.

Regmi, K., Ahmed, S. A., & Quinn, M. (2015). Data Driven Analysis of Startup Accelerators. *Universal Journal of Industrial and Business Management, 3*(2), 54-57. doi:10.13189/ujibm.2015.030203

Salem, M. I. (2014). The role of business incubators in the economic development of Saudi Arabia. *International Business and Economics Research Journal, 13*(4), 853–860.

Saraf, N. (2015). What Determines Entrepreneurial Intention in India? *Journal of Entrepreneurship and Innovation in Emerging Economies, 1*(1), 39 - 55. Retrieved from http://journals.sagepub.com/doi/pdf/10.1177/2393957514555255

Schiopu, A. F., Vaseli, D. C., & Tuclea, C. E. (2015). Principles and Best Practices in Successful Tourism Business Incubators. *Amfiteatru Economic*, 474-487. Retrieved from http://www.amfiteatrueconomic.ro/temp/Article_2399.pdf

Sharmilee, S., & Muhammad, H. (2016). Factors affecting the performance of small and medium enterprises in KwaZulu-Natal, South Africa. *Problems and Perspectives in Management (open-access), 14*(2), 277 - 288. doi:http://dx.doi.org/10.21511/ppm.14(2-2).2016.03

Soderlund, M., & Ohman, N. (2005). Assessing Behaviour Before it Becomes Behaviour: An Examination of the Role of Intentions as a Link Between Satisfaction and Patronising Behaviour. *International Journal of Service Industry Management, 16*(2), 169 -185. doi:https://doi.org/10.1108/095642305

Stubberud, A. H. (2016). Business Incubators and Entrepreneurial Performance: The influence of Network Value and Absorptive Capacity. Lubbock. Retrieved from https://brage.bibsys.no/xmlui/bitstream/handle/11250/2412398/Stubberud_phdthesis_2016.pdf?sequence=1

Stubberud, A. H. (2016, February). *Business Incubators and Entrepreneurial Performance: The Influence of Network Value and Absorptive Capacity.* Lubbock. Retrieved from https://brage.bibsys.no/xmlui/bitstream/handle/11250/2412398/Stubberud_phdthesis_2016.pdf?sequence=1

Tornatzky, L., Sherman, H., & Adkins, D. (2003). *A National Benchmarking Analysis of Technology Business Incubator Performance and Practices: Report to the Technology Administration.* U.S. Department of Commerce, Technology Administration. Washington, D.C: National Business Incubation Association.

Tsaplin, E., & Pozdeeva, Y. (2017). International Strategies of Business Incubation: The USA, Germany and Russia. *International Journal of Innovation.* doi:http://dx.doi.org/10.5585/iji.v5i1.130

Tsordia, C., & Papadimitriou, D. (2015). The Role of Theory of Planned Behavior on Entrepreneurial Intention of Greek Business Students. *International Journal of Synergy and Research*, 23 - 37. doi:10.17951/ijsr.2015.4.1.23

Uddin, M. R., & Bose, T. K. (2012). Determinants of Entrepreneurial Intention of Business Students in Bangladesh. *International Journal of Business and Management; 7*(24), 128 - 137. doi:10.5539/ijbm.v7n24p128

Chapter 13

Ahmad, N., & Hoffman, A. (2007). *A Framework for Addressing and Measuring Entrepreneurship.* Paris: Entrepreneurship Indicators Steering Group.

Alvedalen, J., & Boschma, R. (2017). A critical review of entrepreneurial ecosystems research: towards a future research agenda. *European Planning Studies, 25*(6), 887-903.

Bacq, S., Ofstein, L.F., Kickul, J.R., & Gundry, L.K. (2017). Perceived entrepreneurial munificence and entrepreneurial intentions: A social cognitive perspective. *International Small Business Journal: Researching Entrepreneurship, 35*(5), 639-659.

Bargate, K. (2014). Interactive Qualitative Analysis – A Novel Methodology for Qualitative Research. *Mediterranean Journal of Social Sciences, 5*(20), 11-19.

Bruns, K., Bosma, N., Sanders, M., & Schramm, M. (2017). Searching for the existence of entrepreneurial ecosystems: a regional cross-section growth regression approach. *Small Business Economics, 49*(1), 31-54.

Buys, P., & Havenga, K. (2006). Entrepreneurial Functionality Of New Venture Creation Learners. *SA Journal of Human Resource Management, 4*(3), 36-43.

Bygrave, W.D. (2009). *The Entrepreneurial Process.* Retrieved from: http://media.wiley.com/product_data/excerpt/43/04712715/0471271543.pdf

Carraher, S.M., Buchanan, J.K., & Puia, G. (2010). Entrepreneurial need for achievement in China, Latvia, and the USA. *Baltic Journal of Management, 5*(3), 378-396.

Carsrud, A., & Brännback, M., (2011). Entrepreneurial motivations: what do we still need to know? *Journal of Small Business Management, 49*(1),9-26.

Chowdhury, F., Terjesen, S., & Audretsch, D. (2015). Varieties of entrepreneurship: institutional drivers across entrepreneurial activity and country. *European Journal of Law and Economics, 40*(1), 121-148.

Cleveland, J., & Cleveland, J. (2006). *Youth entrepreneurship: theory, practice, and development.* Battle Creek, Michigan Orient: W.K. Kellogg Foundation Youth and Education Unit.

Covin, J.G., & Wales, W.J. (2012). The Measurement of Entrepreneurial Orientation. *Entrepreneurship Theory and Practice, 36*(4),677-702.

Davis, M., Hall, J., & Mayer, P. (2014). *Measuring the Entrepreneurial Mindset: The Development of the Entrepreneurial Mindset Profile* (EMP). Leadership Development Institute: Eckerd College. Retrieved from: https://www.emindsetprofile.com/wp-content/uploads/2015/10/EMP-White-Paper-Measuring-the-Entrepreneurial-Mindset.pdf

DTi. (1995). *White paper on national strategy for the development and promotion of small business in South Africa.* Cape Town: Department of Trade and Industry.

Eurostat. (2012). *Entrepreneurship determinants: culture and capabilities.* Luxembourg: Publications Office of the European Union.

Fayolle, A. (2005). Evaluation of entrepreneurship education: behavior performing or intention increasing? *International Journal of Entrepreneurship and Small Business, 2*(1), 89-98.

Herrington, M., & Kew, P. (2016). *Global Entrepreneurship Monitor South Africa report 2015-2016: Is South Africa heading for an economic meltdown?* Cape Town: Development Unit for New Enterprise, University of Cape Town.

Isenberg, D. (2011). *The Entrepreneurship Ecosystem Strategy as New Paradigm for Economic Policy: Principles for Cultivating Entrepreneurship.* Babson Entrepreneurship Ecosystem Project, Babson College, Babson Park, MA.

Karimi, S., Biemans, H.J.A., Mahdei, K.N., Lans, T., Chizari, M., & Mulder, M. (2017). Testing the relationship between personality characteristics, contextual factors, and entrepreneurial intentions in a developing country. *International Journal of Psychology, 52*(3), 227-240.

Kauffman Index. (2016). Kauffman Index of Startup Activity.[online]. Retrieved from: http://www.kauffman.org/microsites/kauffman-index/reports/startup-activity

Kautonen, T, van Gelderen, M., & Fink, M. (2015). Robustness of the Theory of Planned Behavior in Predicting Entrepreneurial Intentions and Actions. *Entrepreneurship: Theory & Practice, 39*(3), 655-674.

Kautonen, T., van Gelderen, M., & Tornikoski, E. (2013). Predicting entrepreneurial behavior: a test of the theory of planned behavior. *Applied Economics, 45*(6), 697-707.

Kirch, A., & Tuisk, T. (2015). Complex Patterns in Construction of Entrepreneurial Identity Among Youth in Estonia. *European Integration Studies, 9,* 208-223.

Kroeck, K.G., Bullough, A.M., & Reynolds, P.D. (2010). Entrepreneurship and differences in locus of control. *Journal of Applied Management and Entrepreneurship, 15*(1), 21.

Leedy, P.D., & Ormrod, J E. (2015). *Practical Research: Planning and Design.* 11th Ed. Essex, England: Pearson Education Ltd.

Lin, X., Carsrud, A., Jagoda, K. & Shen, W. (2013). Determinants of Entrepreneurial Intentions: Applying Western Model to the Sri Lanka Context. *Journal of Enterprising Culture, 21*(2),153-174.

Marcotte, C. (2013). Measuring entrepreneurship at the country level: A review and research agenda. *Entrepreneurship & Regional Development, 25*(3-4), 174-194.

Maree, K. (ed.). (2011). *First Steps in research.* Pretoria: Van Schaik Publishers.

Masutha, M., & Rogerson, C.M. (2014). Small enterprise development in South Africa: The role of business incubators, Bulletin of Geography. *Socio-Economic Series, 26*(1), 141-155.

McMullen, J.S., & Kier, A.S. (2017). You don't have to be an entrepreneur to be entrepreneurial: The unique role of imaginativeness in new venture ideation. *Business Horizons, 60*(1), 455-462.

National Planning Commission. (2011). *National development plan: Vision for 2030*. Pretoria: National Planning Commission.

Naudé, W. (ed.). (2011). *Entrepreneurship and Economic Development*. Hampshire, UK: Palgrave Macmillan.

Northcutt, N., & McCoy, D. (2004). *Interactive qualitative analysis*. Thousand Oaks, CA: SAGE Publications, Inc.

Oosthuizen, C. (2014). *An Exploratory Review of the South African Macro Entrepreneurship Ecosystem*: 8th Annual Business Conference. Swakopmund, Namibia.

Oosthuizen, J.H. 2016. An exploratory review of the South African macro entrepreneurship ecosystem.

Organization for Economic Cooperation and Development. (2017). *Entrepreneurship at a Glance*. Retrieved from: http://dx.doi.org/10.1787/entrepreneur_aag-2017-en

Przepiorka, A.M. (2016). Psychological Determinants of Entrepreneurial Success and Life-Satisfaction. *Current Psychology, 36*(1), 304-315.

Rauch, A., & Frese, M. (2007). Let's put the person back into entrepreneurship research: A meta-analysis on the relationship between business owners' personality traits, business creation, and success. *European Journal of Work and Organizational Psychology, 16*(4), 353-385.

Rogerson, C.M. (1999). *Small enterprise development in post-apartheid South Africa: Gearing up for growth and poverty alleviation*. In King, K., & McGrath, S. (Eds) (pp 83-95). *Enterprise in Africa: Between poverty and growth*. London: Intermediate Technology Development Group Publishing.

Sandelowski, M., Voils, C.I., and Knafl, G. (2009). On Quantitizing. *Journal of Mixed Methods Research, 3*(3),208–222.

Saunders, M., Lewis, P., & Thornhill, A. (2012). *Research methods for business students*. 6th ed. Essex: Pearson Education Limited.

Schjoedt, L., & Shaver, K.G. (2012). Development and validation of a locus of control scale for the entrepreneurship domain. *Small Business Economics, 39*(1), 713–726.

Schoon, I., & Duckworth, K. (2012). Who Becomes an Entrepreneur? Early Life Experiences as Predictors of Entrepreneurship. *Developmental Psychology, 48*(6), 1719-1726.

Small Enterprise Development Agency (SEDA). (2017). *SMME Quarterly Update: 3rd Quarter 2017*. Retrieved from: http://www.seda.org.za/Publications/Publications/SMME%20Quarterly%202017-Q3.pdf [accessed 10 September 2018].

Stevenson H.H., & Jarillo J.C. (2007). *A Paradigm of Entrepreneurship: Entrepreneurial Management*. In: Cuervo Á., Ribeiro D., Roig S. (eds) *Entrepreneurship*. Springer, Berlin, Heidelberg.

Stewart, W.H., & Roth, P.L., (2007). A meta-analysis of achievement motivation differences between entrepreneurs and managers. *Journal of Small Business Management, 45*(4), 401-421.

Turton, N., & Herrington, M. (2012). *Global Entrepreneurship Monitor 2012 South Africa*. Cape Town: University of Cape Town Graduate School of Business.

Van Aardt, I., Van Aardt, C., Bezuidenhout, S., & Mumba, M. (2008). *Entrepreneurship & New Venture Management*. 3rd ed. Oxford: Oxford University: Southern Press.

Van Vuuren, J., & Alemayehu, B.Z. (2018). The role of entrepreneurship in transforming efficiency economies into innovation-based economies. *Southern African Journal of Entrepreneurship and Small Business Management,10*(1), a140.

Zhao, H., & Seibert, S.E. (2006). The Big Five Personality Dimensions and Entrepreneurial Status: A Meta-Analytical Review. *Journal of Applied Psychology, 91*(2), 259-271.

Chapter 14

Adizes, I. (1979). Organizational passages—Diagnosing and treating lifecycle problems of organizations. *Organizational Dynamics, 8*(1), 3–25. https://doi.org/10.1016/0090-2616(79)90001-9

April, K., Dharani, B., & Peters, K. (2012). Impact of locus of control expectancy on level of well-being. *Review of European Studies, 4*(2), 124–137. https://doi.org/10.5539/res.v4n2p124

Chen, J., & Silverthorne, C. (2008). The impact of locus of control on job stress, job performance and job satisfaction in Taiwan. *Leadership & Organization Development Journal, 29*(7), 572–582. https://doi.org/10.1108/01437730810906326

Coleman, D., Irving, G., & Cooper, C. L. (1999). Another look at the locus of control-organizational commitment relationship: It depends on the form of commitment. *Journal of Organizational Behavior, 20*(6), 995–1001. https://doi.org/10.2307/3100378

Csikszentmihalyi, M. (1990). *Flow: The Psychology of Optimal Experience.* https://doi.org/10.5465/amr.1991.4279513

Dharani, B. (2019). *Organizational Lifecycle and Happiness at Work: Investigating Best-fit for Employees based on their Locus of Control Expectancy.* University of Cape Town.

Diener, E. (2013). The remarkable changes in the science of subjective well-being. *Perspectives on Psychological Science, 8*(6), 663–666. https://doi.org/10.1177/1745691613507583

Diener, E., Emmons, R. A., Larsen, R. J., & Griffin, S. (1985). The satisfaction with life scale. *Journal of Personality Assessment, 49*(1), 71–75. https://doi.org/10.1207/s15327752jpa4901_13

Fisher, C. D. (2010). Happiness at work. *International Journal of Management Reviews, 12*(4), 384–412. https://doi.org/10.1111/j.1468-2370.2009.00270.x

Hjelle, L., & Ziegler, D. (1976). *Personality Theories: Basic Assumption, Research and Applications.* New York: McGraw-Hill.

Hyatt, T. A., & Prawitt, D. F. (2001). Does congruence between audit structure and auditors' locus of control affect job performance? *The Accounting Review, 76*(2), 263–274. https://doi.org/10.2308/accr.2001.76.2.263

Judge, T. A., Heller, D., & Mount, M. K. (2002). Five-factor model of personality and job satisfaction: A meta-analysis. *Journal of Applied Psychology, 87*(3), 530–541. https://doi.org/https://doi.org/10.1037/0021-9010.87.3.530

Judge, T. A., Thoresen, C. J., Bono, J. E., & Patton, G. K. (2001). The job satisfaction–job performance relationship: A qualitative and quantitative review. *Psychological Bulletin, 127*(3), 376–407. https://doi.org/10.1037/0033-2909.127.3.376

Kirkcaldy, B. D., & Furnham, A. (1993). Predictors of beliefs about money. *Psychological Reports, 73*(3_suppl), 1079–1082. https://doi.org/10.2466/pr0.1993.73.3f.1079

Landau, M. J., Kay, A. C., & Whitson, J. A. (2015). Compensatory control and the appeal of a structured world. *Psychological Bulletin, 141*(3), 694–722. https://doi.org/10.1037/a0038703

Lefcourt, H. M. (1976). Locus of control and the response to aversive events. *Canadian Psychological Review Psychologie Canadienne, 17*(3), 202–209. https://doi.org/http://dx.doi.org/10.1037/h0081839

Lefcourt, H. M. (1984). *Research with the Locus of Control Construct: Extensions and Limitations* (Second). New York: Academic Press.

Lester, D. L., Parnell, J. A., & Carraher, S. (2003). Organizational life cycle: A five-stage empirical scale. *The International Journal of Organizational Analysis, 11*(4), 339–354. https://doi.org/10.1108/eb028979

Meyer, J. P., & Allen, N. J. (2016). A three-component conceptualization of organizational commitment. *International Journal of Academic Research in Business and Social Sciences, 6*(12), 538–551. https://doi.org/10.6007/IJARBSS/v6-i12/2464

Miller, D., Kets de, M. F. R., & Toulouse, J.-M. (1982). Top executive locus of control and its relationship to strategy-making, structure, and environment. *Academy of Management Journal, 25*(2), 237–253. https://doi.org/10.2307/255988

Näswall, K., Sverke, M., & Hellgren, J. (2005). The moderating role of personality characteristics on the relationship between job insecurity and strain. *Work & Stress, 19*(1), 37–49. https://doi.org/10.1080/02678370500057850

Peterson, C., Maier, S. F., & Seligman, M. E. P. (1993). *Learned Helplessness: A Theory for the Age of Personal Control*. https://doi.org/10.1097/00008877-199204001-00099

Prawitt, D. F. (1995). Staffing assignments for judgment-oriented audit tasks: The effects of structured audit technology and environment. *The Accounting Review, 70*(3), 443–465. https://doi.org/10.2307/248533

Quinn, R. E., & Cameron, K. (1983). Organizational life cycles and shifting criteria of effectiveness: Some preliminary evidence. *Management Science, 29*(1), 33–51. https://doi.org/10.1287/mnsc.29.1.33

Rahim, M. A., & Psenicka, C. (1996). A structural equations model of stress, locus of control, social support, psychiatric symptoms, and propensity to leave a job. *The Journal of Social Psychology, 136*(1), 69–84. https://doi.org/10.1080/00224545.1996.9923030

Rotter, J. B. (1966). Generalized expectancies for internal versus external control of reinforcement. *Psychological Monographs: General and Applied, 80*(1), 1–30. https://doi.org/10.1017/CBO9781107415324.004

Seligman, M. E. P. (1972). Learned helplessness. *Annual Review of Medicine, 23*(1), 407–412. https://doi.org/10.1146/annurev.me.23.020172.002203

Seligman, M. E. P. (1975). Helplessness: On Depression, Development, and Death. In *A series of books in psychology*. San Francisco: Freeman.

Shane, S., & Venketaraman, S. (2000). The promise of entrepreneurship as a field of research. *Academy of Management Review, 25*(1), 217–226. https://doi.org/http://dx.doi.org/10.2307/259271

Spector, P. E. (1982). Behavior in organizations as a function of employee's locus of control. *Psychological Bulletin, 91*(3), 482–497. https://doi.org/10.1037/0033-2909.91.3.482

Stillman, J. (2017). Research: Entrepreneurs are happier and healthier than employees. Retrieved August 5, 2019, from Inc. website: https://www.inc.com/jessica-stillman/research-entrepreneurs-are-happier-and-healthier-than-employees.html

Torun, E., & April, K. (2006). Rethinking individual control: Implications for business managers. *Journal for Convergence, 7*(1), 16–19. https://doi.org/Available at: http://www.kurtapril.co.za/index.php?option=com_content&view=article&id=36&Itemid=27

Weiss, A., Bates, T. C., & Luciano, M. (2008). Happiness is a personal(ity) thing: The genetics of personality and well-being in a representative sample. *Psychological Science, 19*(3), 205–210. https://doi.org/10.1111/j.1467-9280.2008.02068.x

Wijbenga, F. H., & van Witteloostuijn, A. (2007). Entrepreneurial locus of control and competitive strategies – The moderating effect of environmental dynamism. *Journal of Economic Psychology, 28*(5), 566–589. https://doi.org/10.1016/j.joep.2007.04.003

Chapter 15

Ajzen, I. (1985). From intentions to actions: A theory of planned behavior. In J. Kuhl & J. Beckmann (Eds.), *Action Control. SSSP Springer Series in Social Psychology*. Berlin, Heidelberg: Springer.

Amann, W., Pirson, M., Spitzeck, H., Dierksmeier, C., von Kimakowitz, E., & Khan, S. (2011). Humanistic management education - Academic responsibility for the 21st century. In W. Amann, M. Pirson, C. Dierksmeier, E. Von Kimakowitz, & H. Spitzeck (Eds.), *Business Schools Under Fire: Humanistic Management Education as the Way Forward*. New York: Palgrave Macmillan.

Ayoko, O. B., Callan, V. J., & Härtel, C. E. J. (2008). The influence of team emotional intelligence climate on conflict and team members' reactions to conflict. *Small Group Research, 39*(2), 121–149.

Bargh, J. A., & Morsella, E. (2008). The unconscious mind. Perspectives on psychological science. *Journal of the Association for Psychological Science, 3*(1). https://doi.org/10.1111/j.1745-6916.2008.00064.x

Barrett-Lennard, G. T. (1997). The recovery of empathy: Toward others and self. In A. C. Bohart & L. S. Greenberg (Eds.), *Empathy Reconsidered: New Directions in Psychotherapy* (pp. 103–121). Washington DC, US: American Psychological Association.

Baumeister, R. F., & DeWall, C. N. (2005). The inner dimension of social exclusion: Intelligent thought and self-regulation among rejected persons. *The Social Outcast: Ostracism, Social Exclusion, Refection and Bullying*, 53–73.

Beddoe, A., & Murphy, S. (2004). Does mindfulness decrease stress and foster empathy among nursing students? *Journal of Nursing Education, 43*, 305–312. https://doi.org/10.3928/01484834-20040701-07

Decety, J., & Grèzes, J. (2006). The power of simulation: Imagining one's own and other's behavior. *Brain Research, 1079*(1), 4–14.

Dreeben, S. J., Mamberg, M. H., & Salmon, P. (2013). The MBSR body scan in clinical practice. *Mindfulness, 4*(394–401), 394.

Jankowski, T., & Holas, P. (2014). Metacognitive model of mindfulness. *Consciousness and Cognition, 28*, 64–80.

Jordan, J. V. (1984). *Empathy and self boundaries.* Wellesley, MA: Wellesley Centrers for Women.

Jordan, J. V. (1992). Through mutual empathy. *Growth (Lakeland)*, 343–351.

Kyrö, P. (2015). *Handbook of Entrepreneurship and Sustainable Development* (Vol. 17). Cheltenham: Edward Elgar. https://doi.org/10.4337/9781849808248

Legrand, D. (2006). The bodily self: The sensori-motor roots of pre-reflective self-consciousness. *Phenomenology and the Cognitive Sciences, 5*(1), 89–118.

Niedenthal, P. M. (2007). Embodying emotion. *Science, 316*(5827), 1002–1005. https://doi.org/10.1126/science.1136930

Oosterwijk, S., Kindquist, K. A., Anderson, E., Dautoff, R., Moriguchi, Y., & Barrett, L. (2012). States of mind: Emotions, body feelings and thoughts share distributed neural networks. *Neuroimage, 62*, 2110–2128. https://doi.org/10.1016/j.neuroimage.2012.05.079

Patzelt, H., & Shepherd, D. A. (2011). Negative emotions of an entrepreneurial career: Self-employment and regulatory coping behaviors. *Journal of Business Venturing, 26*(2), 226–238.

Sherman, N. (2014). Recovering lost goodness: Shame, guilt, and self-empathy. *Psychoanalytic Psychology, 31*(2), 217–235. https://doi.org/10.1037/a0036435

Terzaroli, C. (2018). *Developing entrepreneurship through design thinking: A new frontier for adult education.*

Wright, P., & McCarthy, J. (2005). The value of the novel in designing for experience. In A. Pirhonen, P. Saariluoma, H. Isomäki, & C. Roast (Eds.), *Future Interactive Design.* London: Springer.

Chapter 16

African Development Bank Group. (2014). *South Africa economic outlook.* [Online]. Available: http://www.afdb.org/en/countries/southern-africa/south-africa/south-africa-economic-outlook/ [2018, February 16].

Al-Debei, M.M., & Avison, D. (2010). Developing a unified framework of the business model concept. *European Journal of Information Systems, 19*,359–376.

Babbie, E., & Mouton, J. (2014). *The practice of social research.* 15th edition. Cape Town: Oxford University Press.

Banking Association South Africa. (2016). *SME enterprise.* [Online]. Available: http://www.banking.org.za/ [2018, March 8].

Casadesus-Masanell, R., & Ricart, J.E. (2010). From strategy to business models and onto tactics. *Long Range Planning, 43*,195–215.

Cavett, B.E. 2015. Book review. *International Journal of Evidence Based Coaching and Mentoring, 13*(1), 2013–2015.

Coutu, D., & Kauffman, C. (2009). What can coaches do for you? *Harvard Business Review, 87*(1),91–97.

Fairley, S.G., & Stout, C.E. (2004). *Getting started in personal and executive coaching: How to create a thriving coaching practice.* John Wiley & Sons.

Forbes.com. (2017). *The success and failure of the coaching industry.* [Online]. Available: https://www.forbes.com/sites/forbescoachescouncil/2017/10/05/the-success-and-failure-of-the-coaching-industry/#3239dbdb6765 [2018, May 9].

Freedman, A. (2011). Some implications of validation of the leadership pipeline concept: Guidelines for assisting managers-in-transition. *The Psychologist-Manager Journal, 14,* 140–159.

Gibb, A.A., & Scott, M. (1985). Strategic awareness, personal commitment and the process of planning in the small business. *Journal of Management Studies, 22*(6), 597–631.

Hall, L.M., & Duval, M. (2004). *Meta-coaching Volume 1: Coaching change.* Clifton CO: Neuro-Semantics Publications.

Hsieh, H.F., & Shannon, S. (2005). Three approaches to qualitative content analysis. *Qualitative Health Research, 15,*1277–1288.

ICF. (2012). *Global coaching study.* [Online]. Available: http://icf.files.cms-plus.com/includes/media/docs/2012ICFGlobalCoachingStudy-ExecutiveSummary.pdf [2018, May 4].

Keeney, R.L. (1992). *Value-focused thinking. A path to creative decision making.* Cambridge, MA: Harvard University Press.

Kombarakaran, F., Yang, J., Baker, M., & Fernandes, P. (2008). Executive coaching: It works! *Consulting Psychology Journal: Practice and Research, 60*(1), 78–90.

Kumar, N., Scheer, L., & Kotler, P. (2000). From market driven to market driving. *European Management Journal, 18*(2), 129–142.

Martinez, M.A., & Aldrich, H.E. (2011). Networking strategies for entrepreneurs: Balancing cohesion and diversity. *International Journal of Entrepreneurial Behaviour & Research, 17,* 7–38.

Matabooe, M.J., Venter, E., & Rootman, C. (2016). Understanding relational conditions necessary for effective mentoring of black-owned small businesses: A South African perspective. *Acta Commercii, 16,* 1–11.

Maurya, A. (2012). *Running lean: Iterate from plan A to a plan that works.* Sebastopol, CA: O'Reilly.

Myburgh, J. (2018). Research Chair, COMENSA. Cape Town: Personal communication, 10 April.

Naqvi, S.W.F. (2011). Critical success and failure factors of entrepreneurial organizations: Study of SMEs in Bahawalpur. *Journal of Public Administration and Governance, 1*(4), 96–100.

Osterwalder, A., Pigneur, Y., Clark, T., & Smith, A. (2010). *Business model generation: A handbook for visionaries, game changers, and challengers.* Self-published.

Passmore, J. (ed.). (2015). *Excellence in coaching: The industry guide.* Kogan Page Publishers.

Ram, M., & Jones, T. (2008). Ethnic-minority businesses in the UK: A review of research and policy developments. *Environment and Planning C: Government and Policy, 26,* 352–374.

Ranerup, A., Zinner Henriksen, H., & Hedman, J. (2016). An analysis of business models in public service platforms. *Government Information Quarterly, 33,* 6–14.

Smith, Y., & Watkins, J.A. (2012). A literature review of small and medium enterprises (SME) risk management practices in South Africa. *African Journal of Business Management, 6*(21), 6324–6330.

Taylor-Powell, E., & Renner, M. (2003). *Analyzing Qualitative Data.* [Online]. Available: http://learningstore.uwex.edu/assets/pdfs/g3658-12.pdf [2018, April 20].

Teece, D.J. (2010). Business models, business strategy and innovation. *Long Range Planning, 43,* 172–194.

Thompson, C., Bounds, M., & Goldman, G. (2012). The status of strategic planning in small and medium enterprises: Priority of afterthought? *The Southern African Journal of Entrepreneurship and Small Business Management, 5*(1).

Timmons, J.A., & Spinelli, S. (2007). *New venture creation: Entrepreneurship for the 21st century.* 7th edition. New York: McGraw Hill.

Van Eeden, S., Viviers, S., & Venter, D. (2003). A comparative study of selected problems encountered by small businesses in the Nelson Mandela, Cape Town and Egoli metropoles. *Management Dynamics: Journal of the Southern African Institute for Management Scientists, 12*, 13–23.

Zott, C., & Amit, R. (2010). Business model design: An activity system perspective. *Long Range Planning, 43*, 216–226.

Zott, C., & Amit, R. (2013). The business model: A theoretically anchored robust construct for strategic analysis. *Strategic Organization, 11*, 403–411.

Chapter 17

Abtahi, M.S., Karamipour, M., & Abbasi, K. (2013). Investigating the effects of personal entrepreneurial characteristics. *Management Science Letters, 4*, 417-420. DOI: 10.5267lj.msl.2014.1.031.

Abraham, F., Tupamahu, S. (2016). Interpersonal Competence, entrepreneurial characteristics as market orientation basis and micro and small enterprises in start-up business phase. *Journal of Applied Management (JAM), 14*(4), 609-618. DOI: http://dx.doi.org/10.18202/jam23026332.14.4.01.

Ashleigh, M., & Warren, L. (2015). Trust – the essential element of early stage entrepreneurship. In *Annual SEAANZ Conference Proceedings*, 1–16.

Baluku, M.M., Kikooma, J.F., & Kibanja, G.M. (2016). Does personality of owners of micro enterprises matter for the relationship between startup capital and entrepreneurial success? *African Journal of Business Management, 10*(1), 13-23. January. DOI: 10.5897/AJBM2015.7738.

Chao, G. T., & Moon, H. (2005). The cultural mosaic: a metatheory for understanding the complexity of culture. *The Journal of Applied Psychology, 90*(6), 1128–1140. https://doi.org/10.1037/0021-9010.90.6.1128

De Jong, B., & Dirks, K. T. (2012). Beyond shared perceptions of trust and monitoring in teams: Implications of asymmetry and dissensus. *Journal of Applied Psychology, 97*(2), 391–406.

De Jong, B., Dirks, K. T., & Gillespie, N. (2016). Trust and team performance: A meta-analysis of main effects, moderators, and covariates. *Journal of Applied Psychology, 101*(8).

Dietz, G. (2011). Going back to the source: Why do people trust each other? *Journal of Trust Research, 1*(2), 215–222.

Dirks, K., & Ferrin, D. (2001). The Role of Trust in Organizational Settings. *Organization Science, 12*, 450–467.

Doney, P. M., Cannon, J. P., & Mullen, M. R. (1998). Understanding the influence of national culture on the development of trust. *Academy of Management Review, 23*(3), 601–620.

Eisenhardt, K., Graebner, M.E., & Sonenshein, S. (2016). Grand Challenges and Inductive Methods: Rigor Without Rigor Mortis. *Academy of Management Journal, 59*(4), 1113–1123.

Fatoki, O., (2014). Micro Enterprises' Start-Up Constraints in South Africa. *Mediterranean Journal of Social Sciences, 5*(23), pp. 30-35. DOI: 10.5901/mjss.2014.5n23, p. 30.

Ferrin, D. L., & Gillespie, N. (2010). Trust differences across national-societal cultures: much to do or much ado about nothing? In R. J. Saunders, M. N. K., Skinner, D., Dietz, G., Gillespie, N. & Lewicki (Ed.), *Organizational Trust*. Cambridge: Cambridge University Press.

Fiske, A. P. (2002). Using individualism and collectivism to compare cultures--a critique of the validity and measurement of the constructs: comment on Oyserman et al. (2002). *Psychological Bulletin, 128*(1), 78–88. https://doi.org/10.1037/0033-2909.128.1.78

Friar, J.H., & Meyer, M.H. (2003). Entrepreneurship and Start-ups in the Boston Region: Factors differentiating High-Growth Ventures from Micro-Ventures. *Small Business Economics, 21*, 145-152.

Gibson, C. B., Maznevski, M. L., & Kirkman, B. L. (2004). When does culture matter? In R. S. Bhagat & R. M. Steers (Eds.), *Cambridge Handbook of Culture, Organizations, and Work* (pp. 46–68).

Gillespie, N., & Mann, L. (2004). Transformational leadership and shared values: the building blocks of trust. *Journal of Managerial Psychology, 19*(6), 588–607. https://doi.org/10.1108/02683940410551507

Hoang, H. & Antoncic, B. (2003). Network-based research in entrepreneurship: A critical review. *Journal of Business Venturing*, 18, pp. 165-187. DOI: 10.1016150883-9026(02) 00081-2.

Johnson, J., & Cullen, J. (2002). Trust in cross-cultural relationships. In M. J. Gannon & K. L. Newman (Eds.), *The Blackwell handbook of cross-cultural management* (Vol. 10, p. 509). Blackwell Publishing.

Judhi, N.H., Judhi, N. (2013). Entrepreneurial success from positive psychology view. In *4th International Conference on Business and Economic Research*, Bandung, March, 285-295.

Karabulut, A.T. (2016). Personality Traits on Entrepreneurial Intention. *Procedural, Social and Behavioural Sciences*, 229, pp. 12-21. DOI: 10.1016lj.sbspro.2016.07.109.

Kozubiková, L., Belás, J., Bilan, Y., Bartoš, P. (2015). Personal characteristics of entrepreneurs in the context of perception and management of business risk in the SME segment. *Economics and Sociology*, 8(1), 41-54. DOI: 10.14254/2071-789X.2015/8-1/4.

Kramer, R. M. (1999). Trust and distrust in organizations: emerging perspectives, enduring questions. *Annual Review of Psychology*, *50*, 569–598. https://doi.org/10.1146/annurev.psych.50.1.569

Larson, A., & Starr, J. A. (1993). A Network Model of Organization Formation. *Entrepreneurship Theory and Practice*, *17* (1990), 5–15. https://doi.org/10.1177/104225879301700201

Leung, K., Bhagat, R. S., Erez, M., & Gibson, C. B. (2005). Culture and international business: Recent advances and their implications for future research. *Journal of International Business Studies*, 36, 357–378.

Li, P. P. (2013). Entrepreneurship as a new context for trust research. *Journal of Trust Research*, 3(1), 1–10.

Mathieu, C., & St-Jean, É. (2013). Entrepreneurial personality: The role of narcissism. *Personality and Individual Differences*, pp. 55, 527-531. DOI: http://dx.doi.org/10.1016lj.paid.2013.04.026.

Mcknight, D., Cummings, L., & Chervany, N. (1998). Initial Trust Formation in New Organisational Relationship. *The Academy of Management Review*, *23*(3), 473–490.

Moellering, G. (2005). The Trust/Control Duality: An Integrative Perspective on Positive Expectations of Others. *International Sociology*, *20*(3), 283–305. https://doi.org/10.1177/0268580905055478

Morris, M.H., & Webb, J.W. (2015). Entrepreneurship as emergence in Shalley, C.E., Hitt, M.A., & Zhou, J., (Eds.). *The Oxford Handbook of Creativity, Innovation and Entrepreneurship*, Chapter 26, 457-475. New York, NY: Oxford University Press.

Nikolova, N., Möllering, G., & Reihlen, M. (2014). Trusting as a ' Leap of Faith ': Trust-building practices in client – consultant relationships. *Scandinavian Journal of Management*, 31(2), 232–245.

Phillips, K.W. (2008). *Diversity and Groups* (Vol. II). United Kingdom-North America-Japan-India-Malaysia-China: Emerald Group Publishing Limited.

Powell, E. E. & Baker, T. (2017). In the beginning: Identity processes and organizing in multi-founder nascent ventures. *Academy of Management Journal*, 60(6), 1–34. https://doi.org/10.5465/amj.2015.0175

Preisendörfer, P., Britz, A., & Bezuidenhout, F.J. (2012). In search of black entrepreneurship. Why is there a lack of entrepreneurial activity among the black population in South Africa? *Journal of Developmental Entrepreneurship*, 17(1), 1250006 (18 pages). DOI: 10.11425184946712500069.

Rauch, A., & Frese, M. (2000). Psychological approaches to entrepreneurial success. A general model and an overview of findings in Cooper, C.L., & Robertson, I.T., (Eds.). *International Review of Industrial and Organizational Psychology*, 101-142. Chichester: Wiley.

Rotter, J. B. (1971). Generalized expectations for interpersonal trust. *American Psychologist*, 26, 443–452.

Rousseau, D. M., Sitkin, S. B., Burt, R. S., & Camerer, C. (1998). Not so different after all: A cross-discipline view of trust. *Academy of Management Review*, 23(3), 393–404. https://doi.org/10.5465/AMR.1998.926617

Ruangkrit, S., & Thechatakerng, P. (2015). Characteristics of Community Entrepreneurs in Chiangmai, Thailand. *World Journal of Management*, 6(1), 58-74. Mark.

Sanchez-Burks, J., & Lee, F. (2007). Cultural Psychology of Workways. In S. Kitayama & D. Cohen (Eds.), *Handbook of Cultural Psychology*. New York: The Guilford Press.

Schein, E. H. (2004). *Organizational culture and leadership* (Third). San Francisco: Jossey-Bass.

Schwartz, S. H. (1992). Universals in the content and structure of values: Theory and empirical tests in 20 countries. In M. Zanna (Ed.). *Advances in Experimental Social Psychology, 25*, 1–65.

Sesen, H. (2013). Personality or environment? A comprehensive study on the entrepreneurial intentions of University Students. *Education & Training, 55*(7), 624-640. DOI: 10.1108/ET-05-2012-0059.

Stahl, G. K., Maznevski, M. L., Voigt, A., & Jonsen, K. (2010). Unravelling the effects of cultural diversity in teams: A meta-analysis of research on multicultural work groups. *Journal of International Business Studies, 41*(4), 690–709. https://doi.org/10.1057/jibs.2009.85

Thomas, D. C., Liao, Y., Aycan, Z., Cerdin, J.-L., Pekerti, A. a, Ravlin, E. C., ... van de Vijver, F. (2015). Cultural intelligence: A theory-based, short form measure. *Journal of International Business Studies*, 1–20. https://doi.org/10.1057/jibs.2014.67

Triandis, H. (1997). *Cultural complexity in organizations: inherent contrasts and contradictions.* Thousand Oaks, CA: SAGE.

Van Knippenberg, D., & Hirst, G. (2015). A cross-level perspective on creativity at work: Person-in Situation Interactions in Shalley, C.E., Hitt, M.A., & Zhou, J., (Eds.). *The Oxford Handbook of Creativity, Innovation and Entrepreneurship*, Chapter 13, 225-244. New York, NY: Oxford University Press.

Welter, F. (2011). Contextualizing Entrepreneurship—Conceptual Challenges and Ways Forward. *Entrepreneurship: Theory and Practice, 35*(1), 165–184. https://doi.org/10.1111/j.1540-6520.2010.00427.x

Welter, F. (2012). All you need is trust? A critical review of trust and entrepreneurship literature. *International Small Business Journal, 30*(3).

Wildman, J. L., Shuffler, M. L., Lazzara, E. H., Fiore, S. M., Burke, C. S., Salas, E., & Garven, S. (2012). Trust Development in Swift Starting Action Teams: A Multilevel Framework. *Group & Organization Management, 37*(2), 137–170.

Zak, P. J. (2017). The Neuroscience of Trust Management behaviors that foster employee engagement. *Harvard Business Review.* Retrieved from https://levelfiveexecutive.com/wp-content/uploads/2017/03/hbr-neuroscience-of-trust.pdf

Zand, D. E. (1972). Trust and Managerial Problem Solving. *Administrative Science Quarterly, 17*(2), 229–239.

Zhao, M., Serbert, S.E. (2006). The big five personality dimensions and entrepreneurial status: A meta-analytical review. *Journal of Applied Psychology, 91*(2), 251-271. DOI: 10.1037/0021-9010.91.2.259.

Zolfaghari, B., Möllering, G., Clark, T., & Dietz, G. (2016). How do we adopt multiple cultural identities? A multidimensional operationalization of the sources of culture. *European Management Journal, 34*(2), 102–113.

Chapter 18

AfDB. (2016). *African development report 2015 – Growth, poverty and inequality nexus: Overcoming barriers to sustainable development.* African Development Bank. Retrieved from https://www.afdb.org/en/documents/document/african-development-report-2015-growth-poverty-and-inequality-nexus-overcoming-barriers-to-sustainable-development-89715

Andersen, A., & Gaddefors, J. (2016). Entrepreneurship as a community phenomenon: Reconnecting meaning and place. *International Journal of Entrepreneurship and Small Business, 28*(4), 504-518.

Bortolan, A. (2018). Self-esteem and ethics: A phenomenological view. *Hypatia, 33*(1), 56-72.

Bosman, N, Schøtt, T., Terjesen, S., & Kew, P. (2016). *Global entrepreneurship monitor: Special topic report. Social entrepreneurship.* Global Entrepreneurship Monitor. Retrieved from https://www.gemconsortium.org/file/open?fileId=49542

Castro, M. R., & Holvino, E. (2016). Applying intersectionality in organizations: Inequality markers, cultural scripts and advancement practices in a professional service firm. *Gender, Work and Organization, 23*(3), 328–347.

Crenshaw, K. (1989). Demarginalizing the intersection of race and sex: A black feminist critique of antidiscrimination doctrine, feminist theory and antiracist politics. *University of Chicago Legal Forum, 1989*(1), 139–167.

DA Newsroom (2020). City aims to empower entrepreneurs with disabilities to grow their businesses. Retrieved from: https://www.da.org.za/government/undefined/2020/11/city-aims-to-empower-entrepreneurs-with-disabilities-to-grow-their-businesses

Dennissen, M., Benschop, Y., & van den Brink, M. (2020). Rethinking diversity management: An intersectional analysis of diversity networks. *Organization Studies, 41*(2), 219-240.

Foldy, E. (2002). Managing diversity: Power and identity in organizations. In A. Mills, & I. Aaltio (Eds.), *Gender, identity and the culture of organizations* (pp. 92–112). London: Routledge.

Hall, J. K., Daneke, G. A., & Lenox, M. J. (2010). Sustainable development and entrepreneurship: Past contributions and future contributions. *Journal of Business Venturing, 25*(5), 439-448.

Heidegger, M. (1927/1962). *Being and time*. Trans. John Macquarrie and Edward Robinson. Malden, MA: Basil Blackwell.

Holvino, E. (2010). Intersections: The simultaneity of race, gender and class in organization studies. *Gender Work and Organization, 17*(3), 248–277.

Kamasak, R., Özbilgin, M., & Yavuz, M. (2020). Understanding intersectional analyses. In E. King, Q. Roberson, & M. Hebl (Eds.), *Pushing our understanding of diversity in organizations* (pp. 93-115). Charlotte, North Carolina: Information Age Publishing.

Mirvus, P., & Googins, B. (2018). Catalyzing social entrepreneurship in Africa: Roles for Western Universities, NGOs and Corporations. *Africa Journal of Management, 4*(1), 57-83.

Rogerson, C. M. (2008). Tracking SMME development in South Africa: Issues of finance, training and the regulatory environment. *Urban Forum, 19*(1), 61–81.

Sesko, A. K., & Biernat, M. (2010). Prototypes of race and gender: The invisibility of Black women. *Journal of Experimental Social Psychology, 46*(2), 356–360.

Statista Research Department (2018). Total population of South Africa by ethnic groups. Retrieved from https://www.statista.com/statistics/1116076/total-population-of-south-africa-by-population-group/

Stats SA (2019). Inequality trends in South Africa: A multidimensional diagnostic of inequality. Report No. 03-10-19. Retrieved from: http://www.statssa.gov.za/publications/Report-03-10-19/Report-03-10-192017.pdf.

Stats SA (2020). 2020 Mid-year population estimates. 9th July 2020. Retrieved from http://www.statssa.gov.za/?p=13453&gclid=CjwKCAiAq8f-BRBtEiwAGr3Dgfd_33wMTNMErfVfxc6dPJkd9cU98EdqGSBK5qvb0gsUyWQ_3mP4mBoCrpoQAvD_BwE

Stats SA (2020). Quarterly labour force survey: 1st Quarter 2020. Report No. P0211. Retrieved from http://www.statssa.gov.za/publications/P0211/P02111stQuarter2020.pdf

Syed, J., & Özbilgin, M. F. (2009). A relational framework for international transfer of diversity management practices. *The International Journal of Human Resource Management, 20*(12), 2435-2453.

Tatli, A. (2011). A multi-layered exploration of the diversity management field: Diversity discourses, practices and practitioners in the UK, *British Journal of Management, 22*(2), 238-253.

Tatli, A., & Özbilgin, M. F. (2012). An emic approach to intersectional study of diversity at work: A Bourdieuan framing. *International Journal of Management Reviews, 14*(2), 180–200

Tatli, A., Ozturk, M. B., & Woo, H. S. (2017). Individualization and marketization of responsibility for gender equality: The case of female managers in China. *Human Resource Management, 56*(3), 407-430.

UCT Transformation Report (2019). Building transformation at UCT: People, spaces and actions. Retrieved from http://www.oic.uct.ac.za/sites/default/files/image_tool/images/470/Documents/home/2019_UCT-Transformation-Report.pdf

Vasquez, J. M., & Wetzel, C. (2009). Tradition and the invention of racial selves: Symbolic boundaries, collective authenticity, and contemporary struggles for racial equality. *Ethnic and Racial Studies, 32*(9), 1557-1575.

Wheeler, M. L. (2005). Diversity: The performance factor. *Harvard Business Review*, March, 51-57.

Young, R. (2020). How power erodes empathy, and the steps we can take to rebuild it. *WBUR*, Retrieved from https://www.wbur.org/hereandnow/2020/07/09/jamil-zaki-empathy-power.

Chapter 19

Acemoglu, D., & Robinson, J. A. (2012). *Why Nations Fail: The Origins of Power, Prosperity, and Poverty*. Crown Publishing Group.

Aliaga-Isla, R., & Rialp, A. (2013). Systematic review of immigrant entrepreneurship literature: Previous findings and ways forward. *Entrepreneurship and Regional Development*, 25(9–10), 819–844. https://doi.org/10.1080/08985626.2013.845694

Alimo-Metcalfe, B. (1998). 360 DEGREE FEEDBACK AND LEADERSHIP DEVELOPMENT. *International Journal of Selection and Assessment*, 6(1), 35–44. https://doi.org/10.1111/1468-2389.00070

Balagopal, V. (2011). A matching theory of entrepreneurs' tie formation intentions and initiation of economic exchange. *Academy of Management Journal*, 54(1), 137–158. https://doi.org/10.5465/AMJ.2011.59215084

Bass, B. M., Avolio, B. J., & Atwater, L. (1996). The Transformational and Transactional Leadership of Men and Women. *Applied Psychology*, 45(1), 5–34. Retrieved from http://dx.doi.org/10.1111/j.1464-0597.1996.tb00847.x

Beck, T. (2012). The Role of Finance in Economic Development: Benefits, Risks, and Politics. In *The Oxford Handbook of Capitalism*. https://doi.org/10.1093/oxfordhb/9780195391176.013.0007

Bizri, R. M. (2017). Refugee-entrepreneurship: a social capital perspective. *Entrepreneurship and Regional Development*, 29(9–10), 847–868. https://doi.org/10.1080/08985626.2017.1364787

Bonacich, E. (1973). A Theory of Middleman Minorities. *American Sociological Review*, 38(5), 583–594.

Borjas, G. J. (1989). Economic theory and international migration. *International Migration Review*, 23(3), 457–485. https://doi.org/10.2307/2546424

Borjas, G. J. (2000). Ethnic enclaves and assimilation. *Swedish Economic Policy Review*, 7, 89–122. https://doi.org/10.1093/esr/jcl002

Bosma, N., Hessels, J., Schutjens, V., Praag, M. Van, & Verheul, I. (2012). Entrepreneurship and role models. *Journal of Economic Psychology*, 33(2), 410–424. https://doi.org/10.1016/j.joep.2011.03.004

Bove, V., & Elia, L. (2017). Migration, Diversity, and Economic Growth. *World Development*, 89, 227–239. https://doi.org/10.1016/j.worlddev.2016.08.012

Bruhn, M., Karlan, D., & Schoar, A. (2010). What Capital is Missing in Developing Countries? *The American Economic Review*, 100(2), 629–633. https://doi.org/10.1257/aer.100.2.629

Decker, R., Haltiwanger, J., Jarmin, R., & Miranda, J. (2014). The Role of Entrepreneurship in US Job Creation and Economic Dynamism. *Journal of Economic Perspectives*, 28(3), 3–24. https://doi.org/10.1257/jep.28.3.3

Edin, P. A., Fredriksson, P., & Åslund, O. (2003). Ethnic enclaves and the economic success of immigrants — Evidence from a natural experiment. *Quarterly Journal of Economics*, 118(1), 329–357. https://doi.org/10.1162/00335530360535225

Efrata, T. C., & Maichal, M. (2018). Role Model and Entrepreneurial Performance: the Role of Entrepreneurial Identity and Self-Efficacy As Intervening Variable. *Jurnal Aplikasi Manajemen*, 16(1), 27–34. https://doi.org/10.21776/ub.jam.2018.016.01.04

Fellnhofer, K., & Puumalainen, K. (2017). Can role models boost entrepreneurial attitudes? *International Journal of Entrepreneurship and Innovation Management*, 1(1), 1. https://doi.org/10.1504/ijeim.2017.10003379

Fong, R., Busch, N. B., Armour, M., Heffron, L. C., & Chanmugam, A. (2008). Pathways to Self-Sufficiency: Successful Entrepreneurship for Refugees. *Journal of Ethnic & Cultural Diversity in Social Work*, 3204 (May 2014), 37–41. https://doi.org/10.1300/J051v16n01

Fritsch, M., & Wyrwich, M. (2017). The effect of entrepreneurship on economic development-an empirical analysis using regional entrepreneurship culture. *Journal of Economic Geography*, *17*(1), 157–189. https://doi.org/10.1093/jeg/lbv049

Gibson, D. E. (2003). Role models in career development: New directions for theory and research. *Journal of Vocational Behavior*, *65*(1), 134–156. https://doi.org/10.1016/S0001-8791(03)00051-4

Greene, Patricia G. (1997). A resource-based approach to ethnic business sponsorship: A consideration of Ismaili-Pakistani immigrants. *Journal of Small Business Management*, *35*(4), 58–71.

Greene, Patricia Gene, & Butler, J. S. (1996). The minority community as a natural business incubator. *Journal of Business Research*, *36*(1), 51–58. https://doi.org/10.1016/0148-2963(95)00162-X

Griffin-el, E. W., & Olabisi, J. (2018). Breaking Boundaries: Exploring the Process of Intersective Market Activity of Immigrant Entrepreneurship in the Context of High Economic Inequality. *Journal of Management Studies*, *55*(3), 457–485. https://doi.org/10.1111/joms.12327

Herrington, M., & Kew, P. (2016). GEM South Africa 2015-2016 Report. In *Global Entrepreneurship Monitor*.

Herrington, M., Kew, P., & Mwanga, A. (2017). CAN SMALL BUSINESSES SURVIVE IN SOUTH AFRICA? In *gem-south-africa 2016-2017-report-1494860333*.

Jacobsen, K. (2002). Can refugees benefit the state? Refugee resources and African statebuilding. *Journal of Modern African Studies*, *40*(4), 577–596. https://doi.org/10.1017/S0022278X02004081

Kalitanyi, V., & Visser, K. (2010). African Immigrants in South Africa: Job Takers or Job Creators ? *South African Journal of Economic and Management Sciences*, *13*(4), 376–390.

Kerr, W. R., Lerner, J., & Schoar, A. (2010). *THE CONSEQUENCES OF ENTREPRENEURIAL FINANCE: A REGRESSION DISCONTINUITY ANALYSIS The Consequences of Entrepreneurial Finance: A Regression Discontinuity Analysis*. Retrieved from http://www.nber.org/papers/w15831

Light, I. (1979). Disadvantaged Minorities in Self-Employment. *International Journal of Comparative Sociology*, *20*(1-2), 31–45. https://doi.org/10.1177/002071527902000103

Light, I., & Bhachu, P. (1989). MIGRATION NETWORKS AND IMMIGRANT ENTREPRENEURSHIP. *Immigration and Entrepreneurship: Culture, Capital, and Ethnic Networks*, *V*(April), 25–50. Retrieved from http://search.ebscohost.com/login.aspx?direct=true&db=ecn&AN=0395885&site=ehost-live

Light, I., Sabagh, G., Bozorgmehr, M., & Der-Martirosian, C. (1994). Beyond the Ethnic Enclave Economy. *Social Problems*, *41*(1), 65–80. https://doi.org/10.2307/3096842

Massey, D. S. (1988). Economic Development and International Migration in Comparative Perspective. *Population and Development Review*, *14*(3), 383–413.

McEvoy, D., & Hafeez, K. (2008). Ethnic enclaves or middleman minority? Regional patterns of ethnic minority entrepreneurship in Britain. *International Journal of Business and Globalisation*, *2*(3), 265–274. https://doi.org/10.1504/IJBG.2009.021634

Mehtap, S., & Al-Saidi, A. G. (2018). Informal Refugee Entrepreneurship: Narratives of Economic Empowerment. In *Informal Ethnic Entrepreneurship* (pp. 225–242). Springer Nature Switzerland.

Menzies, T. V., Brenner, G. A., & Filion, L. J. (2003). Social capital, networks and ethnic minority entrepreneurs: Transnational entrepreneurship and bootstrap capitalism. *Globalization and Entrepreneurship: Policy and Strategy Perspectives*, (September), 125–151. https://doi.org/10.4337/9781843767084.00016

Min, P., & Kolodny, A. (1994). The middleman minority characteristics of Korean immigrants in the United States. *Korea Journal of Population and Development*, *23*(2), 179–202.

Mitchell, R. K., Smith, J. B., Seawright, K. W., & Morse, E. A. (2000). Cross-Cultural Cognitions and the Venture Creation Decision. *Academy of Management Journal*, *43*(5), 974–993.

Nieuwenhuizen, C., & Kroon, J. (2002). Creating wealth by Financing Small and Medium Enterprises of owners who possess entrepreneurial skills. *Management Dynamics: Contemporary Research*, *11*(1), 21–28.

Nowiński, W., & Haddoud, M. Y. (2019). The role of inspiring role models in enhancing entrepreneurial intention. *Journal of Business Research*, 96(October 2018), 183–193. https://doi.org/10.1016/j.jbusres.2018.11.005

Peri, G., & Yasenov, V. (2019). The labor market effects of a refugee wave: Synthetic control method meets the Mariel Boatlift. *Journal of Human Resources*, 54(2), 267–309. https://doi.org/10.3368/jhr.54.2.0217.8561R1

Peroni, C., Riillo, C. A. F., & Sarracino, F. (2016). Entrepreneurship and immigration: evidence from GEM Luxembourg. *Small Business Economics*, 46(4), 639–656. https://doi.org/10.1007/s11187-016-9708-y

Porter, J. R., & Washington, R. E. (2019). Minority Identity and Self-Esteem. *Annual Review of Sociology*, 19(1993), 139–161.

Portes, A. (1993). Embeddedness and Immigration : Notes on the Social Determinants of Economic Action. *American Journal of Sociology*, 98(6), 1320–1350. Retrieved from http://www.jstor.org/stable/2781823

Portes, A., & Jensen, L. (1992). Disproving the enclave Hypothesis. *American Sociological Review*, 57(3), 418–421.

Portes, A., & Manning, R. D. (2013). The Immigrant Enclave: Theory and Empirical Examples. *Theory and Empirical Examples*, 47–68. Retrieved from papers3://publication/uuid/C20B4D4E-EB3E-4A91-97C2-A65876B9C6D9

Price, M., & Chacko, E. (2009). The mixed embeddedness of ethnic entrepreneurs in a new immigrant gateway. *Journal of Immigrant and Refugee Studies*, 7(3), 328–346. https://doi.org/10.1080/15562940903150105

Sanders, J. M., & Nee, V. (1992). Problems in Resolving the Enclave Economy Debate. *American Sociological Review*, 57(3), 415–418.

Sanders, J. M., & Nee, V. (2016). *Limits of Ethnic Solidarity in the Enclave Economy.* 52(6), 745–773.

Serrie, H. (1998). Immigrant entrepreneurs, ethnic networks, and family dynamics. *Reviews in Anthropology*, 27(2), 213–223. https://doi.org/10.1080/00988157.1998.9978199

Steffens, N. K., Haslam, S. A., Ryan, M. K., Kessler, T., & Jena, F. (2013). *Leader performance and prototypicality : Their inter-relationship and impact on leaders ' identity entrepreneurship.* 613(October), 606–613.

Stewart, M., Anderson, J., Beiser, M., Mwakarimba, E., Neufeld, A., Simich, L., & Spitzer, D. (2008). Multicultural meanings of social support among immigrants and refugees. *International Migration*, 46(3), 123–159. https://doi.org/10.1111/j.1468-2435.2008.00464.x

Tkachev, A., & Kolvereid, L. (1999). Self-employment intentions among Russian students. *Entrepreneurship and Regional Development*, 11(3), 269–280. https://doi.org/10.1080/089856299283209

Tucker, J. (2007). Middleman minorities. *International Encyclopedia of the Social Sciences*, 1(2), 147.

Wilson, K. L., & Portes, A. (1980). Immigrant Enclaves : An Analysis of the Labor Market Experiences of Cubans in Miami. *American Journal of Sociology*, 86(2), 295–319.

Yoo, J.-K. (2000). Utilization of Social Networks for Immigrant Entrepreneurship: A Case Study of Korean Immigrants in the Atlanta Area. *International Review of Sociology*, 10(3), 347–363. https://doi.org/10.1080/03906700020014422

Zhou, M. (2004). Revisiting ethnic entrepreneurship: Convergencies, controversies, and conceptual advancements. *International Migration Review*, 38(3), 1040–1074.

Conclusion

April, K., & Daya, P. (Eds.) (2021). *12 lenses into diversity in South Africa.* Pretoria: KR Publishing.

Botha, H. J. (2012). *Investigating the ethical considerations faced by small business entrepreneurs in the informal sector.* Johannesburg: Zandspruit Township.

Bizri, R. M. (2017). Refugee-entrepreneurship: A social capital perspective. *Entrepreneurship and Regional Development*, 29(9–10), 847–868.

Fanon, F. (1952). *Black skin, white masks*. Paris: Éditions du Seuil (translated from the French in Richard Philcox).

Jacobsen, K. (2002). Can refugees benefit the state? Refugee resources and African statebuilding. *Journal of Modern African Studies, 40*(4), 577–596.

Mcknight, D., Cummings, L., & Chervany, N. (1998). Initial trust formation in new organizational relationship. *The Academy of Management Review, 23*(3), 473–490.

Mehtap, S., & Al-Saidi, A. G. (2018). Informal refugee entrepreneurship: Narratives of economic empowerment. In V. Ramadani, L. P. Dana, V. Ratten, & A. Bexheti (Eds), *Informal Ethnic Entrepreneurship* (pp. 225–242). Cham, Zug: Springer.

Mitchell, R. K., Smith, J. B., Seawright, K. W., & Morse, E. A. (2000). Cross-cultural cognitions and the venture creation decision. *Academy of Management Journal, 43*(5), 974–993.

Millard, A. (Ed.). (1984). *The testimony of Steve Biko*. HarperCollins: New York.

Musara, M., & Nieuwenhuizen, C. (2020). Informal sector entrepreneurship, individual entrepreneurial orientation and the emergence of entrepreneurial leadership. *Africa Journal of Management, 6*(3), 194-213.

Nikolova, N., Möllering, G., & Reihlen, M. (2014). Trusting as a 'leap of faith': Trust-building practices in client–consultant relationships. *Scandinavian Journal of Management, 31*(2), 232–245.

Oelofsen, R. (2015). Decolonisation of the African mind and intellectual landscape. *Phronimon, 16*(2), 130-146.

Pyke, K. D. (2010). What is internalized racial oppression and why don't we study it? Acknowledging racism's hidden injuries. *Sociological Perspectives, 53*(4), 551-572.

Thomas, D. C., Liao, Y., Aycan, Z., Cerdin, J.-L., Pekerti, A. a, Ravlin, E. C., ... van de Vijver, F. (2015). Cultural intelligence: A theory-based, short form measure. *Journal of International Business Studies, 46*(9), 1-20.

Webb, J. W., Tihanyi, L., Ireland, R. D., & Sirmon, D. G. (2009). You say illegal, I say legitimate: Entrepreneurship in the informal economy. *Academy of Management Review, 34*(3), 492-510.

Wijbenga, F. H., & van Witteloostuijn, A. (2007). Entrepreneurial locus of control and competitive strategies: The moderating effect of environmental dynamism. *Journal of Economic Psychology, 28*(5), 566–589.

Index

www.ingramcontent.com/pod-product-compliance
Lightning Source LLC
Chambersburg PA
CBHW082139210326
41599CB00031B/6030